OXFORDSHIRE AND NORTH BERKSHIRE PROTESTATION RETURNS AND TAX ASSESSMENTS 1641-42

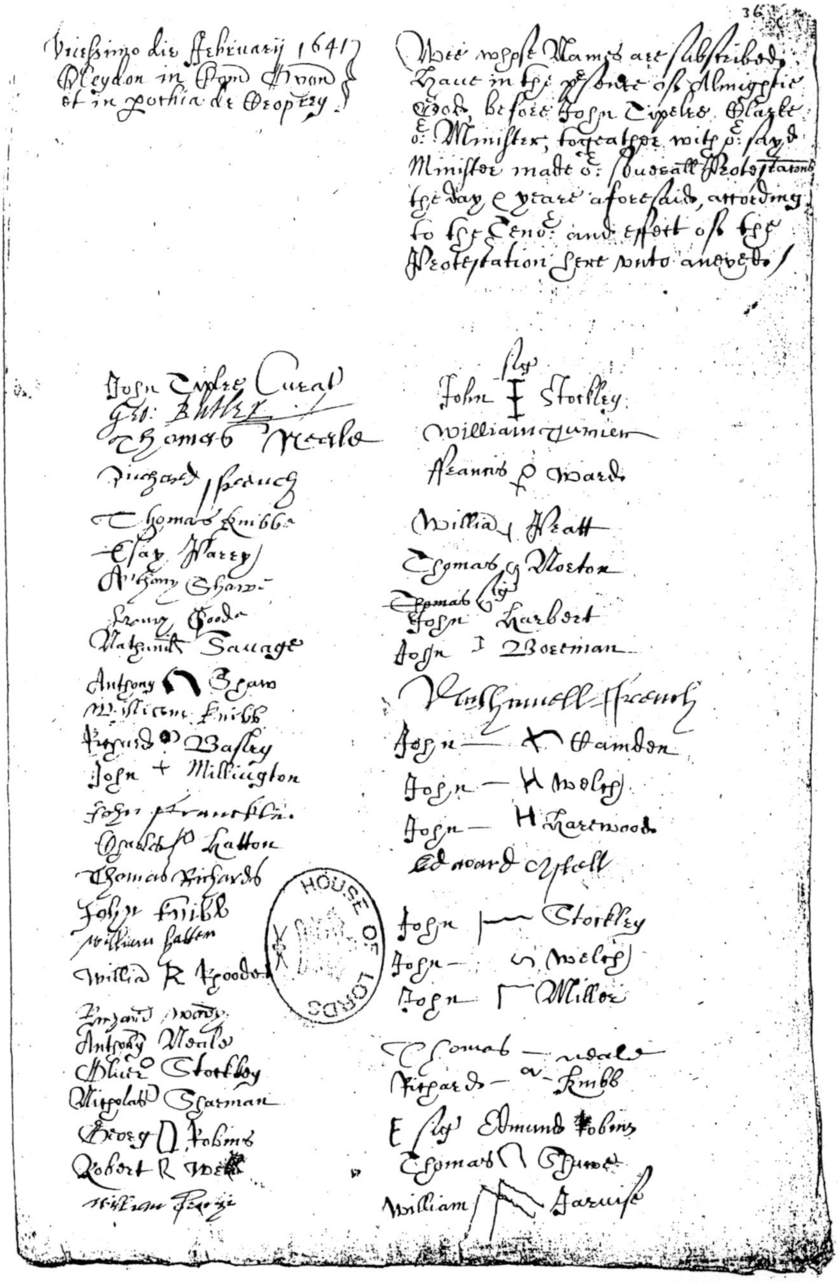

36

Vicesimo die Februarij 1641
Cleydon in Com Oxon
et in parochia de Cropredy.

Wee whose Names are subscribed,
haue in the presence of Almightie
God, before John Tipler Clarke
our Minister, togeather with our said
Minister made our seuerall Protestations
the day & yeare aforesaid, according
to the tenour and effect of the
Protestation sent unto us.

John Tipler Curat
Geo: Butler
Thomas Neale
Richard French
Thomas Kibble
Elias Harris
Anthony Shaw
Henry Goode
Nathaniell Sauage
Anthony Beare
William Kibble
Richard Basley
John + Millington
John Franklin
Charles Hatton
Thomas Richards
John Kibble
William Hatten
William R Goode
Richard Wardy
Anthony Neale
Oliuer Storkley
Nicholas Charman
George Robins
Robert R Wells
William Pearse

John I Storkley (his mark)
William Turner
Francis Ward
William Pratt
Thomas Norton
John Harbert (his mark)
John I Boreman
Nathaniell French
John Camden
John Wells
John Hartwood
Edward Ytell
John Storkley
John Wells
John Miller
Thomas Neale
Richard Kibble
Edmund Robins (his mark)
Thomas Turner
William Jarvise

Protestation Return for Claydon [Cleydon], a chapelry in the parish of Cropredy and hundred of Banbury (folio 36r, page 41); one of the rare returns with signatures and 'marks'.

The Oxfordshire Record Society

OXFORDSHIRE and NORTH BERKSHIRE PROTESTATION RETURNS and TAX ASSESSMENTS 1641-42

Edited by Jeremy Gibson

Oxfordshire Returns originally transcribed by
Christopher S.A. Dobson,
Assistant Librarian, House of Lords.
Tax Assessments and Berkshire Returns
transcribed by the Editor.

Index initially by Gwyn de Jong
and expanded by the Editor.

Originally issued as Volume 36
for the year 1955

Second Edition as

VOLUME 59

1994

Published by
The Oxfordshire Record Society,
c/o Bodleian Library, Oxford OX1 3BG,
in association with the Banbury Historical Society.

First edition, 1955.

Also published as Volume 24 in the Record Series of the Banbury Historical Society.

ISBN 0 902509 23 3

The cover illustration, a mural by Charles West Cope (1866) in the Palace of Westminster, "Speaker Lenthal asserting the privileges of the Commons against Charles I when the attempt was made to seize the five members" in January 1641/2, which gave impetus to the Protestation Oath (see page xiii), is reproduced from a Crown Copyright photograph by kind permission of the House of Lords. The frontispiece, a facsimile of a protestation return in the House of Lords Record Office, is reproduced by kind permission of the Clerk of the Records.

Illustrations of Barford St. John and Heythrop churches from Buckler drawings are reproduced by kind permission of the Bodleian Library, Oxford.

The maps on pages xx-xiii are based on those of Oxfordshire and Berkshire in Lewis' *Topographical Dictionary*, 1831.

Prepared on computer by Jeremy Gibson and
printed by
Parchment (Oxford) Limited.

CONTENTS

LIST OF RETURNS AND ASSESSMENTS

FOREWORD

Oxfordshire Protestation Returns, edited by Mr C.S.A. Dobson and published in 1955 as vol. 36 of the Oxfordshire Record Society series, is one of the most sought-after of the Society's volumes but has long been out of print. Several years ago Mr Jeremy Gibson offered to prepare what was then intended to be a straight reprint. However, it was realised that the volume would benefit from re-setting (if only to restore the correct order of names in individual lists, confused by the printers in the first edition). That gave the opportunity of adding other relevant records, subsequently discovered or transcribed, as described in Mr Gibson's introduction. Twenty years ago Oxfordshire was enlarged to include the Vale of the White Horse, formerly north-western Berkshire. The extant returns for that area, the Abingdon Division, have been added.

The near contemporary tax assessments for the northern hundreds of Banbury, Bloxham, and Ploughley had been transcribed some time ago by Mr Gibson. As General Editor of the Banbury Historical Society he had intended to include these lists in a volume to be published by that Society, and a generous grant had already been secured from the British Academy. The reissue of the Protestation Returns enables the tax assessments (with the addition of Bampton and Hormer Hundreds) to appear alongside rather than in a separate book: hence the collaboration and joint publication by the two societies.

Through lack of funds the earlier edition lacked any index. This was remedied as recently as 1993 in a separate publication by the Oxfordshire Family History Society. That index, prepared by Mrs Gwyn de Jong, is incorporated in this volume's index of personal names by kind permission of her and of that Society, but it has been greatly expanded. The process of compiling the indexes, and the publication of Dr D.M. Barratt's *Oxfordshire Probate Records 1516-1732* (British Record Society Index Library, 1984-5, vols. 94-5) have made it possible to identify many doubtful names whilst checking the manuscript returns. What has emerged is substantially a new, greatly enlarged edition.

The Oxfordshire Record Society is grateful to Mr Dobson for his warm encouragement. This new edition could not have been produced without Mr Gibson's familiar energy and tenacity, not just in checking the original manuscripts, transcribing fresh records, and almost doubling the size of the index, but also in preparing the entire volume on computer so that production costs were confined to printing and binding. In addition, in memory of his friend, and friend of many local historians, Mr Jim Brister, for many years on the staff of the Bodleian Library, he has generously met the considerable cost of including the indexes.

Oxford, December 1994

Christopher Day
General Editor, O.R.S.

INTRODUCTION

In February 1641/2 most adult males in England and Wales took the Protestation Oath as ordained by Parliament almost a year earlier. The background to this quasi-census is described below.

Just three months later a tax was raised as a fixed assessment, which had a much lower tax threshold, and consequently many more taxpayers, than the subsidies which had been the normal method of Stuart and Tudor taxation.

Geographical coverage is incomplete for both protestation returns and assessments. When both survive, this proximity in time means that many of the same names occur, albeit often under wildly differing spellings. The assessment also includes absent landowners or nobility whose oath would have been taken elsewhere. The occasional protestation return includes women. Tax collectors had no sex bias, and women (often, alas, without their Christian names) appear regularly in the assessment. Where one record is lost, the other can go some way to replacing it.

The tax assessments have only survived sporadically and infrequently (as indeed have the protestation returns). However, the advantages of parallel publication have already been perceived by T.L. Stoate, editor of *The Somerset Protestation Returns and Lay Subsidy Rolls 1641/2* (transcribed by A.J. Howard; Bristol, 1975).

As described in the Foreword, the Oxfordshire returns were first published by the Oxfordshire Record Society as volume 36, forty years ago. Since then, boundaries have been redrawn and Oxfordshire now includes much of what used to be northern Berkshire. For the purposes of the Protestation, Berkshire hundreds were arranged in Divisions, of which those for Abingdon, Newbury and Reading have extant returns. The hundreds comprising the Abingdon Division, Moreton, Ock, and Hormer, are now largely in Oxfordshire and, bordering the Thames, must always have had close links with the county. Also, the sole surviving Berkshire tax assessment is for Hormer Hundred.

The Protestation Returns of 1641/2

To the local historian and genealogist, the value of the Protestation Returns lies in the fact that they contain the names of persons living in the middle of the seventeenth century. Although the returns only survive for part of Oxfordshire, they still cover between a third and half of the adult male population of the county, to which is now added the Abingdon Division of north Berkshire.

The Protestation Returns owe their existence to the unrest which prevailed in Parliament during the passage of the Bill for the Attainder of the Earl of Strafford in 1641. The House of Commons had passed the Bill on 21st April and the House of Lords gave it a second reading on 27th April. The Upper House was known, however, to favour the continuation of the procedure by impeachment, and it was not certain whether it would finally pass the Bill. Moreover, the House of Commons learnt on 28th April that a plan had been made for rescuing Strafford, and rumours were current of various plots to persuade the King to use the army to overawe Parliament and thus release Strafford. An unsuccessful attempt made by the King to occupy the Tower of London caused rioting near the Houses of Parliament and his speech in the House of Lords on 1st May against the execution of Strafford also produced great alarm.

On 3rd May John Pym declared in the House of Commons that it was necessary to be careful that the King 'have good counsellors about him' and that the House of Commons ought to 'let him understand that he is bound to maintain the laws and that we take care for the maintaining of the Word of God.' After other speakers had spoken vaguely of the necessity for the organisation of some form of resistance, Henry Marten said: 'We are honest disjointed fellows. Let us unite ourselves for the pure worship of God, the defence of the King, and his subjects in all their legal rights.' George Peard reminded the House of the oath of association taken in Queen Elizabeth's reign, and Denzil Holles said that a similar protesation would show the world that they were united. Accordingly a committee of ten members was appointed to draw up a form of Protestation, and it was ordered that no members should stir out of the House without leave, nor speak to the messengers. The Protestation was agreed upon and all the members were ordered to sign it. On the following day, 4th May, the Protestation was agreed to by the House of Lords and all Protestant Peers signed it. It ran as follows:-

'I, A.B., do in the Presence of Almighty God, promise, vow, and protest to maintain to defend, as far as lawfully I may, with my Life, Power, and Estate, the true Reformed Protestant Religion, expressed in the doctrine of the Church of England, against all Popery and Popish Innovations, within this realm, contrary to the same Doctrine and according to the Duty of my Allegiance, His Majesty's Royal Person, Honour and Estate, as also the Power and Privileges of Parliaments, the lawful Rights and Liberties of the subjects, and every Person that maketh this Protestation, in whatsoever he shall do in the lawful pursuance of the same; and to my power, and as far as lawfully I may, I will oppose and by all good Ways and Means endeavour to bring to condign Punishment all such as shall, either by Force, Practice, Counsels, Plots, Conspiracies or otherwise, do any Thing to the contrary of any Thing in this present Protestation contained; and further that I shall, in all just and honourable ways, endeavour to preserve the Union and Peace betwixt the Three Kingdoms of England, Scotland and Ireland; and neither for Hope, Fear, nor other Respect, shall relinquish this Promise, Vow and Protestation.'

On 6th May a Bill was introduced in the House of Commons, imposing the obligation of signing the Protestation upon all Englishmen. It provided that those who refused to sign were to be held incapable of holding office, and that Peers who refused to sign were to be deprived of their seats in the House of Lords. It was doubtless this latter provision which led the Upper House to reject the Bill on 29th July. But on 30th July, the House of Commons passed a resolution that all who refused the Protestation were unfit to hold office in

Church or Commonwealth, and this was ordered to be printed. It was not, however, until the following January that the Protestation itself was printed. Copies were sent down to the sheriffs without further delay and accompanying them was a letter of instructions from the Speaker of the House of Commons:-

'Gentlemen,

It is now some months since the Protestation taken by the Lords and House of Commons was sent down into the country, with an Expectation, that it should be generally taken throughout the Kingdom, for a Testimony of their good Concurrence with the Parliament; but through the Remissness of some of those that had the Care of recommending it to others, very many there be that have not hitherto taken it; Now the House of Commons, having discovered many dangerous Designs plotted against the Parlaiment, and especially, that of the Fourth of this Instant January,* which, had it taken Effect, would have strucken not only at the Privileges, but at the very Being of Parliament (as will more appear by the Declaration herewith sent unto you, which the House desires you to publish throughout all Parts of the County) have thought fit once again to recommend the Taking of this Protestation; and have therefore commanded me, in their name, to desire you the High Sheriff and the Justices of the Peace of that County to meet together in one Place, as soon as possible you may, and there to take the Protestation yourselves; and then, dispersing yourselves into your several Divisions, that you will call together the Minister, the Constables, Churchwardens, and Overseers of the Poor of every Parish, and tender unto them Churchwardens, the Protestation, to be taken in your Presence, and to desire of them, that they will very speedily call together the Inhabitants of their several Parishes, both Householders and others, being of Eighteen Years of Age and upwards, into One or more Places, according to the Largeness of their Parishes, and to tender unto them the same Protestation, to be taken in their Presence; and to take their Names, both of those, that do take it, and do refuse to take the same Protestation; and to return them to yourselves, at such time as you shall appoint; which the House desires may be so speedily, from them, to the Knights and Burgesses serving for that County before the .... Day of ....; wherein the House desires your greatest care and Diligence, as a Matter very much importing the Good both of the King and Kingdom; which being all I have in Command, I rest,

Your very loving Friend.

London, January 19th 1641.'

The ministers, churchwardens, constables, and overseers of the poor took the Protestation before the justices of the peace at the local market town - for Bampton and Wootton Hundreds at Woodstock on 14th February (pages 1, 139); for Banbury and Bloxham Hundreds at Banbury (page 72); for the Abingdon Division on 28th February at Abingdon (page 173). Within the next few weeks the people in their various towns and villages had also taken it. The lists of names were collected together and sent to Westminster later in March.

* The attempt made by King Charles in person to arrest Sir Arthur Hesilrigge, Denzil Holles, John Pym, William Strode, and John Hampden in the House of Commons.

Unfortunately the returns have survived for only seven of the fourteen hundreds in Oxfordshire (see map, page xxiv): Langtree and Binfield in the south; Bampton, Banbury, Bloxham, Chadlington, and Wootton in the north and west. Even in these hundreds some parishes are missing: *Binfield:* Bix, Caversham (see below) and Shiplake; *Langtree:* Checkendon, Crowmarsh Gifford, Mapledurham and Whitchurch; *Wootton:* Bladon (including the borough of New Woodstock), Eynsham and Hanborough; *Chadlington:* Idbury, Little Rollright, Sarsden and Swerford; *Banbury:* Banbury (parish and borough) and the chapelry of Epwell (part of the parish of Swalcliffe, in Banbury Hundred, but itself part of Dorchester Hundred, which would account for its return being missing). Sibford Ferris and Sibford Gower, hamlets in Swalcliffe parish but in Bloxham Hundred, appear with Swalcliffe under Banbury Hundred. South Stoke (surrounded within the county by Binfield Hundred) was another outlying part of Dorchester Hundred which is consequently missing. Shenington, contiguous with Banbury and Bloxham Hundreds, and Widford, contiguous with Bampton and Chadlington Hundreds, were enclaves of Gloucestershire, so are not amongst the returns published here. Similarly, Langford and Shilton, enclaves of Berkshire in Bampton Hundred, do not appear, though Grafton and Radcot, Oxfordshire hamlets in Langford, are included. The hundreds that are entirely missing are Bullingdon, Dorchester, Ewelme, Lewknor, Pirton, Ploughley and Thame; and the city of Oxford (apart from the University). Caversfield, a Buckinghamshire enclave surrounded by Ploughley Hundred, was in Buckingham Hundred, for which there are protestation returns, and so that has been able to be included (page 109).

Of the places for which returns are extant, Ipsden and Yarnton give only the names of clergy, churchwardens and constables. Fortunately (since the first edition) the full return for Yarnton has been discovered misfiled under Shropshire and its alternative name of Eardington, so is included here. Lists for Caversham, missing from Binfield Hundred, were identified by the late Brigadier F.R.L. Goadby in the parish registers, and are also included here.

In former northern Berkshire the coverage is equally sparse, restricted to the three hundreds of Moreton, Ock and Hormer which comprised the Abingdon Division; nothing for the north-west Faringdon area or around Wantage. Places in the Newbury and Reading Divisions are listed in Appendix B (page 208). Avington, near Hungerford, was mistakenly identified as Abingdon, being listed as such and bound with the Abingdon Division places. It belongs in the Newbury Division, and is omitted here.

It is noticeable that in both counties borough returns - Abingdon, Banbury, Wallingford, and Woodstock - are missing, even when the hundreds in which they lay are extant; as well as Oxford itself. Why so many do not appear to exist is uncertain. There is one fact which suggests that the missing Returns were never sent to Westminster or were lost shortly after their despatch. Some person, either a County officer such as the Sheriff, or a Parliamentary officer at Westminster, compiled at the time a list of the recusants (see page 148) in the individual returns for Bampton, Banbury, Chadlington and Wootton hundreds (there being no recusants in Binfield, Bloxham or Langtree hundreds). There were certainly recusants in Ploughley Hundred (for which the Protestation is missing) as they were listed in the assessment (having been specially targetted for double taxation) and there must have been recusants in other hundreds and the city of Oxford too. It seems doubtful whether the compiler ever saw the returns for the rest of the county and whether in fact they ever reached Westminster. The fact that the list was made indicates that one of the principal objects of the Protestation was to discover the number of Roman Catholics in the country (as described below), and a committee was indeed appointed by the House of Commons on 16th April 1642 to consider what action should be taken towards the recusants. No further proceedings were, however, taken, probably owing to the outbreak of the Civil War.

The Protestation Returns are housed in the House of Lords Record Office in the Palace of Westminster. They are in general written throughout on paper, mostly in foolscap sheets watermarked with various kinds of devices, now guarded and bound in large volumes covering several counties each. They are arranged in approximate alphabetical order by hundreds or divisions, and that order is followed here, with the folio numbers of the original shown for each place. The order of names will be found to differ greatly from that in the first edition, as the printers of that effectively confused the original transcription by running on columns from one page to the next rather than completing each page in turn.

Usually the returns are in good condition and, as they were usually written in one hand only, probably the minister's, are reasonably legible. Occasional returns include signatures and 'marks'. In Oxfordshire there are just five: Alvescot (page 3); Claydon (frontispiece and page 41) and Mollington (pages 44-5), with the same curate; North Stoke (page 103); and Steeple and Middle Aston (page 119). However, Henley-on-Thames, whilst not showing marks, includes many signatures. In the Abingdon Division of Berkshire no less than ten places have signatures and marks. Difficult handwriting, unusual layouts and number of columns are shown with each place. Doubtful readings are indicated by '[?]'.

The Oxfordshire returns contain the names of approximately 11,800 men of the age of eighteen and over, with a further 1,375 in the Abingdon Division of Berkshire. The number in each place is shown in square brackets against the name or preamble, but these are not guaranteed as precisely accurate in all cases. In a few Oxfordshire instances the names of the women are included, either intermingled with the men (Asthall, Southleigh, Stanton Harcourt and Wilcote), or in separate lists (Combe, Minster Lovell and Steeple Barton). The most interesting are the adjacent parishes of Cokethorpe (with Hardwick and Yelford) and Ducklington, where the names are in family groups. Nicholas Shepard, vicar of Appleford and Sutton Courtenay in Berkshire, divided his lists into 'householders' and 'children and servants' (but no women!). Many uncommon names will be found, the most unusual being 'Earth & Ashes Gradnum' in the parish register list at Caversham (page 52).

Of particular interest on account of the special reservations and provisos is the Return from Oxford University. It is of some importance because it contains the names of over two thousand members of the University, some of whom have not been recorded elsewhere. This figure includes a small number of college servants. Unlike the parish lists there are almost no Christian names. More than a quarter of the entries are marked as *'ab'*[sent] or ill, leaving the impression that not everyone in the University was completely in favour of the Protestation. After Feilding's name (Balliol, page 162) was the word *'deliberabit'* and there were some independent souls who made up their own form of Protestation. Under each college or hall the names are to an extent grouped, with dashes separating them. Such grouping is here shown by breaks in the columns of names.

In the parishes there is a picture of wholehearted endorsement 'and none of all those persons did refuse but did all very willingly take it at the sayd time.' Even those absent would be vouched for: 'These parties ... are not in the towne nor have bine since this protestation was in agitation in our parish and wee doubt not but when they returne they will protest it and subscribe unto it.' In the riparian parishes of Rotherfield Greys (page 58) and Streatley (Berks., page 199) 'onely [those] upon necessary occasions were absent being Barge men & imployed in y'r vocations.' Even so, at Sunningwell (Berks., page 200) 'William Ariese have not taken it, he concealeth himselfe being in debt as they alledge.'

A major object of the exercise was to discover the number of people still faithful to the old Roman church. Some individuals like John Phippes of Charlbury 'simplye refuseth not but demurres upon it as pretending not to understand what is meant by the true reformed Protestant religion.' In Standlake three recusants were persuaded to sign all the same. In Steeple Barton Mr Ralph Sheldon 'assented to the protestation so far, as it concerned the defence of the King's Maiesties person and state, the priviledges of Parliament ... dissenting onely, from one clause of religion standing in opposition to what they professe, being the religion of the Church of Rome.' These names, for Oxfordshire, are summarised on page 148.

A list of the extant Protestation Returns for England and Wales will shortly appear in the series of Guides published by the Federation of Family History Societies, compiled by the editor of this volume.

The Tax Assessment of 1642

The king's need of money to pay for the Scottish wars forced him to abandon his lengthy period of personal rule and summon Parliament: first, in April 1640, the Short Parliament, which lasted only three weeks; and, after the disastrous Second Bishops' War, in November 1640, what became known as the Long Parliament.

Thus in 1641 and 1642 three methods of direct taxation were adopted: a Tudor type subsidy, a poll tax and a fixed assessment of a type which was later to become common during the Commonwealth period and in the reign of Charles II.

The Subsidy was passed in December 1640, and approved by the king in February 1640/1: an Act for the relief of His Majesty's army and the northern parts of the kingdom (16 Charles I c.2), granting four entire subsidies in two separate payments, the first by 27th February 1640/1 and the second by 15th April 1641. By a subsequent act (c.4) two more were granted to be paid by 20th November 1641. With subsidies, in general only the wealthier were taxed, half a dozen or so in villages, twenty to forty in towns. The records engendered by these subsidies are in the Public Record Office in class E.179. Those for Oxfordshire are referenced 164/477-508 and for Berkshire 75/352-362.

In July 1641 by an 'Act for the speedie provision of money for disbanding the Armies and settling the peace of the two Kingdoms of England and Scotland' (16 Charles I c.9) a Poll Tax was voted. No records of this appear to survive.

The preamble to legislation for the Assessment reads:

'An Act for the raising and leavying of moneys for the necessary defence and great affairs of the Kingdoms of England and Ireland and for the payment of Debts undertaken by Parliament ... and in order to suppress that most wicked and execrable rebellion in Ireland' (16 Charles I c.32).

The tax to some extent broke new ground. A fixed sum, £400,000, was to be raised from the whole country and this was broken down by counties in the Act, Oxfordshire's share being £6,418.4s.9d. (in comparison, Somerset had to raise £16,879). It was left to the commissioners to divide this first among the hundreds and then into parish totals. Assessors were appointed as in the subsidies to raise the parish amounts by assessments on individuals, but how this was done is not known. All Parliament did was to lay down the exemption limits, which were £1 in land, £3 in goods and £10 in wages, and then say that everyone who qualified was to pay his proportionate share. The wage limit was enough to exempt the ordinary labourer as the maximum rate of wages fixed by the (Somerset) county magistrates in 1685 was £4.10s. per annum for men servants *(Victoria County History, Somerset)*. Despite the fact that exemption limits were, apart from the wage clause, the same as those for the subsidy, the net was cast more widely, many more taxpayers were roped in and the assessments finely graded down as low as a few pence in a some cases; in some places fractions of a penny were taken into account.

Aliens and recusants had to pay double, and half of this was to be no part of the £400,000 but 'surplusage' (see pages 117 and 207) and disposed of for the purpose of the Act; if they did not contribute under this they paid a poll tax of 2s.8d. Payment was to be made in two equal amounts, the first to be taxed before 20th May 1642 and paid into the exchequer before 20th June and the second to be taxed before 20th November 1642 and paid before 20th December. The assessments published here all form part of the first collection.

An interesting and, for the local historian, a most useful feature of the tax was that unlike the subsidy 'every person to be rated and taxed shall be so in every county for the estate he hath and if he have an estate in severall places in one county then to be rated in the said severall places in each severall county'. As a result of this some individuals appear as taxpayers in more than one parish and it should be possible to obtain some idea of the extent of a man's property. For example, see Lord Saye and Sele's various holdings in north Oxfordshire or, at a humbler level, those of the Vivers family, Banbury tradesmen, in neighbouring villages. This rarely occurs in the subsidy and, when it does, in theory at any rate, it should be accompanied by the certificate of residence excusing him from payment in all but his home parish.

The great importance of this assessment, in comparison with other surviving taxation records of this time, is its low tax threshold. At Banbury (borough and parish) there were 47 subsidy taxpayers in May 1641 [P.R.O. E.179/164/481]. A year later 328 taxpayers were named in the assessment published here. This is doubly useful, as the protestation return for Banbury is missing. The same is the case for Ploughley Hundred.

As mentioned above, for those places where the assessment can 'duplicate' the protestation returns, the discrepancies in the spelling of names can be a salutary reminder of the need to check every possible variant. It has also made it possible, combined with a long experience of the surnames of north Oxfordshire, to correct a number of misreadings which occurred in the first edition. It must be emphasised how ambiguous the handwriting can make these names. A glance at the list of clergy and officials for Bampton Hundred (pages 1-3), where the names as they appear in the parish lists are shown in square brackets, will show how inaccurate even contemporaries could be. There are sure to be misreadings still, which those with a close knowledge of particular places may be able to correct.

Unfortunately, these valuable tax assessments survive only sporadically. Oxfordshire, with returns for four hundreds, is better off than most counties, whilst Berkshire has only Hormer Hundred (P.R.O. references are given on page 207). The nationwide coverage will be shown in the forthcoming guide to these mid-seventeenth century listings by the present editor.

Index

The first edition of the Oxfordshire Protestation Returns was unindexed. At the suggestion of the present editor, Mrs Gwyn de Jong compiled a full index to that, which was published by the Oxfordshire Family History Society in 1993. As this was a publication to be used separately from the actual book, it was necessary (as it had been for the earlier O.F.H.S. index to the 1665 Hearth Tax) to identify each reference by abbreviated placenames rather than the traditional page numbers. Such a system, although not as immediately easy to follow, offers many advantages. To this editor, at least, it has made it possible to add first the assessment entries and then the Berkshire section without laborious re-indexing. It also means that, once the system is understood (see page 296) the index in itself can convey plenty of information. At a glance one can see in which places names occur, decide whether they are near to each other or far distant, and if those referenced were assessment payers (indicated by the letter 'S', for Subsidy). Much effort has gone into grouping names with variant spellings, appropriately cross-referenced. Even so, users should be vigilant for other possible versions.

Acknowledgments

From Mr C.S.A. Dobson's first edition:

I wish to thank Sir Frank Lascelles, Clerk of the Parliaments, for giving permission for the Returns to be printed, and Mr Maurice Bond, Clerk of the Records, House of Lords, who kindly read my manuscript and identified some names which I had been unable to decipher. Finally I must express my grateful thanks to Mr Charles Clay, Librarian to the House of Lords, who also read much of my work and has constantly given me the kindly encouragement, gentle guidance, and sound advice needed by one who, at the beginning, was almost entirely unfamiliar with the characteristics of seventeenth century handwriting.

C.S.A. Dobson

For this edition:

As with the earlier edition I wish to thank the appropriate authorities at the Palace of Westminster for permission to publish the Oxfordshire returns once again, and this time to include the Abingdon Division of Berkshire. I would also like to thank Mr David Johnson, the present Clerk of the Records, for his friendly welcome and for personally checking various dubious readings; and his staff at the House of Lords Record Office for their courteous supervision and very prompt provision of photocopies.

The Oxfordshire and Berkshire taxation assessments are reproduced by permission of Her Majesty's Stationery Office and the Public Record Office. Staff there, too, have as usual been very helpful. In particular I would like to thank Mrs Susan Lumas, who allowed me to use her office when transcribing the Berkshire return, has checked dubious readings for me, and has provided constant support and friendship.

The Caversham protestation return is reproduced from the Caversham parish registers by permission of the Berkshire Record Office and the present incumbent.

Mr Christopher Dobson has kindly allowed the re-use of much of his introduction to the first edition. Dr T. L. Stoate has similarly allowed me to use, mainly verbatim, appropriate parts of his introduction to his pioneering edition of the Somerset protestation returns and contemporary tax listings.

Mrs Elizabeth Hampson retyped on to disc all the first edition. Mrs Gwyn de Jong has allowed her index to be the basis of that published here. Bob Boyd of the Oxfordshire Family History Society, who published that index, was able to provide the computer disc from which it was prepared. Kevin Tombs of my printers (and his colleagues) have converted discs. Jeff Long has all along been instrumental in enabling this computer-illiterate editor to prepare the entire text in camera-ready form, with a control over presentation denied to his predecessor. Chris Day, General Editor of the Oxfordshire Record Society, has been supportive throughout the many vicissitudes of this new edition. They all know me well enough to know already how much I owe and thank them.

Jeremy Gibson

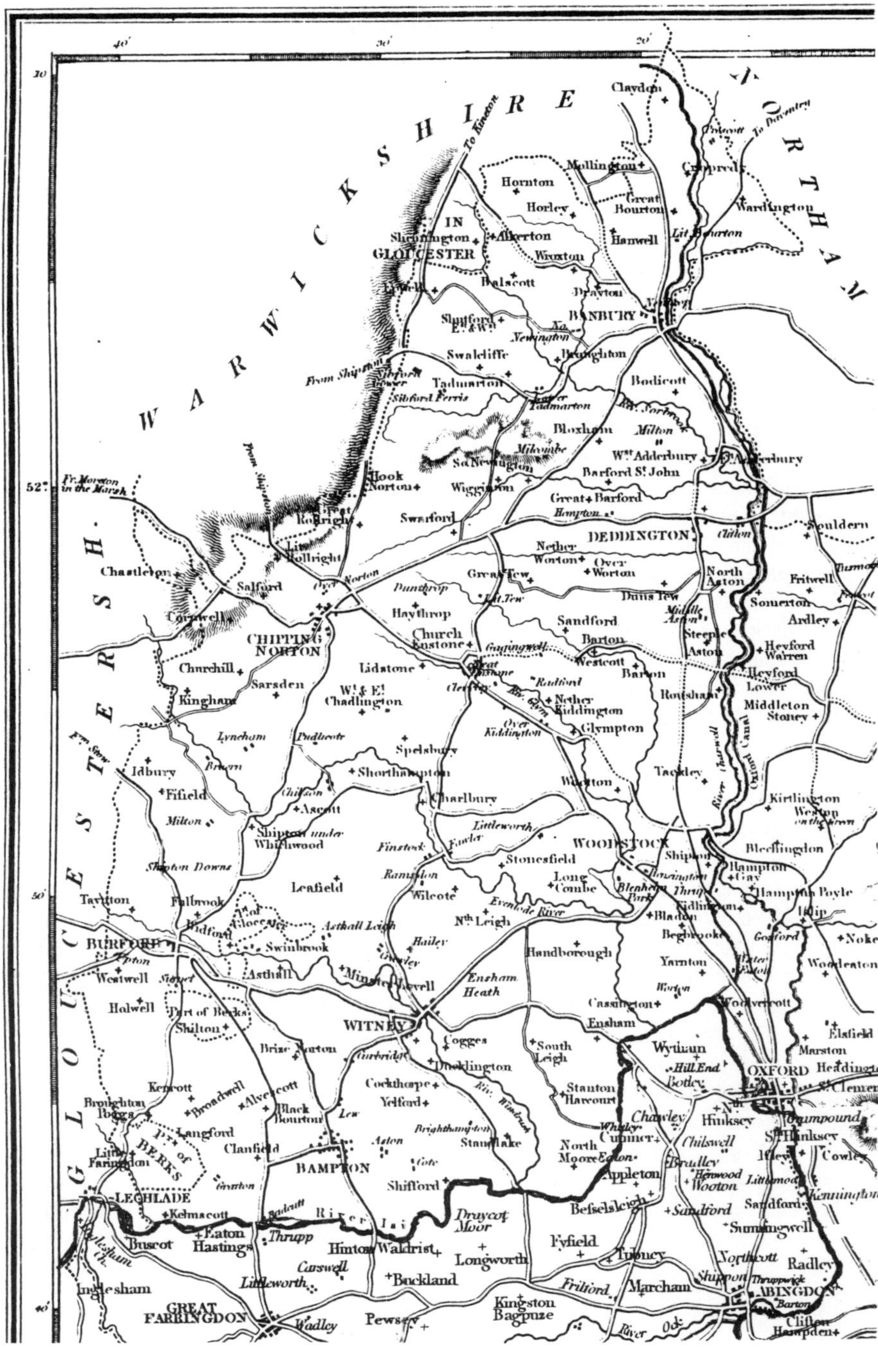
WARWICKSHIRE
NORTHAM
GLOUCESTERSH.
IN GLOUCESTER
Claydon
Mollington
Cropredy
Hornton
Horley
Great Bourton
Wardington
Shennington
Alkerton
Hanwell
Wroxton
Balscott
Drayton
BANBURY
Shutford E. & W.
Swalcliffe
Broughton
Tadmarton
Sibford Ferris
Bodicott
Bloxham
Milcombe
Milton
Wt. Adderbury
Barford St. John
Hook Norton
Wigginton
Swarford
Great Barford
Hempton
DEDDINGTON
Chastleton
Salford
Great Rollright
Lit. Rollright
Over Norton
Nether Worton
Over Worton
North Aston
Souldern
Great Tew
Duns Tew
Fritwell
Dunthrop
Heythrop
Somerton
Ardley
Cornwell
CHIPPING NORTON
Church Enstone
Sandford
Barton
Steeple Aston
Heyford Warren
Churchill
Sarsden
Lidstone
Westcott
Kingham
W. & E. Chadlington
Radford
Nether Kiddington
Rousham
Middleton Stoney
Over Kiddington
Glympton
Lyneham
Spelsbury
Idbury
Fifield
Shorthampton
Tackley
Chilson
Ascott
Charlbury
Kirtlington
Milton
Shipton under Whichwood
Finstock
Fawler
Stonesfield
WOODSTOCK
Shipton
Bletchingdon
Shipton Downs
Leafield
Long Combe
Blenheim Park
Hampton Gay
Hampton Poyle
Taynton
Fulbrook
Wilcote
Evenlode River
Bladon
Islip
Widford
Asthall Leigh
N. Leigh
Begbrooke
Noke
BURFORD
Swinbrook
Hailey
Handborough
Yarnton
Woodeaton
Westwell
Asthall
Minster Lovell
Ensham Heath
Holwell
Part of Berks
Cassington
Elsfield
Shilton
WITNEY
Ensham
Marston
Brize Norton
Curbridge
Cogges
South Leigh
Wytham
Ducklington
Hill End
OXFORD
Headington
Kencott
Broadwell
Alvescott
Cockthorpe
Botley
St. Clements
Broughton Poggs
Black Bourton
Yelford
Stanton Harcourt
Chawley
Hinksey
Langford
Clanfield
Aston
Standlake
Cumner
Chilswell
Cowley
Little Faringdon
Pt. of Berks
BAMPTON
Cote
North Moore
Eaton
Bradley
Wooton
Kennington
LECHLADE
Grafton
Shifford
Appleton
Sandford
Kelmscott
Radcott
Draycot Moor
Besselsleigh
Sunningwell
Buscot
Eaton Hastings
Thrupp
Hinton Waldrist
Fyfield
Tubney
Northcott
Radley
Carswell
Longworth
Inglesham
Littleworth
Buckland
Fritford
Marcham
ABINGDON
Barton
GREAT FARRINGDON
Wadley
Pewsey
Kingston Bagpuze
Clifton Hampden
River Isis
Oxford Canal
River Charwell

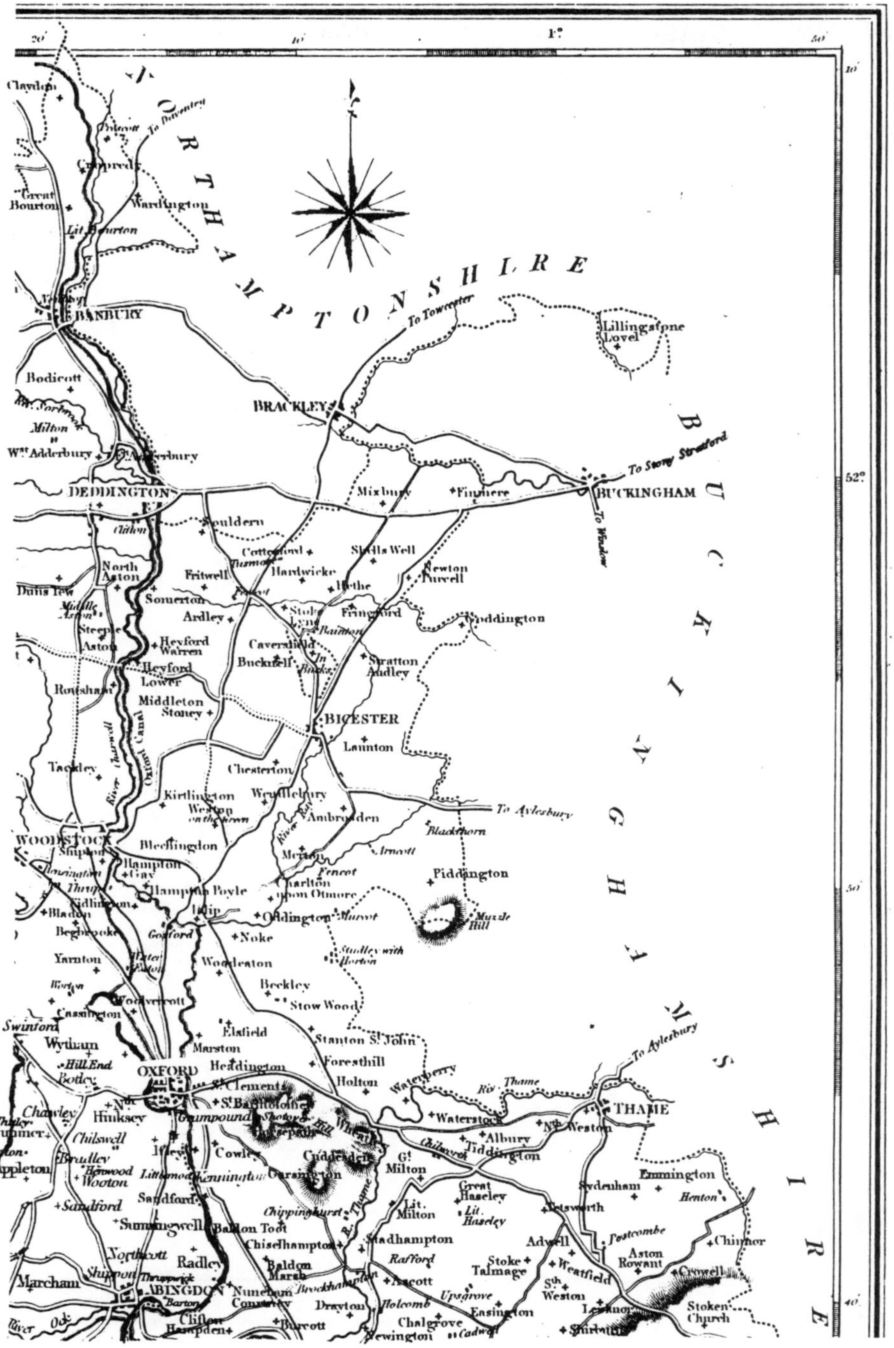

NORTHAMPTONSHIRE
BUCKINGHAMSHIRE
52°
Claydon
To Daventry
Cropredy
Great Bourton
Wardington
Lit. Bourton
BANBURY
To Towcester
Lillingstone Lovel
Bodicott
Milton
Wst Adderbury
BRACKLEY
To Stony Stratford
DEDDINGTON
Mixbury
Finmere
BUCKINGHAM
To Winslow
Clifton
Souldern
Cottesford
Shells Well
North Aston
Fritwell
Hardwicke
Newton Purcell
Duns Tew
Hethe
Middle Aston
Somerton
Ardley
Stoke Lyne
Fringford
Godington
Steeple Aston
Heyford Warren
Caversfield
Bainton
Heyford Lower
Bucknell
Stratton Audley
Rousham
Middleton Stoney
BICESTER
Launton
River Cherwell
Oxford Canal
Tackley
Chesterton
Kirtlington
Wendlebury
Weston on the Green
Ambrosden
To Aylesbury
WOODSTOCK
Bletchingdon
River Ray
Blackthorn
Shipton
Merton
Arncott
Hampton Gay
Fencot
Piddington
Thrup
Hampton Poyle
Charlton upon Otmore
Kidlington
Bladon
Islip
Oddington
Murcot
Muzzle Hill
Begbroke
Gosford
Noke
Studley with Horton
Yarnton
Water Eaton
Woodeaton
Beckley
Cassington
Wolvercott
Stow Wood
Swinford
Elsfield
Wytham
Marston
Stanton St. John
Hill End
Botley
OXFORD
Headington
Foresthill
To Aylesbury
St. Clements
Holton
Waterperry
Riv. Thame
THAME
Chawley
Nth. Hinksey
St. Bartholomew
Shotover
Waterstock
Cumner
Chilswell
Grampound
Albury
Nth. Weston
Iffley
Cowley
Tiddington
Appleton
Bradley
Cuddesdon
Gt. Milton
Emmington
Henwood
Wooton
Littlemore
Kennington
Garsington
Great Haseley
Sydenham
Henton
Sandford
Sandford
Chippinghurst
Lit. Milton
Lit. Haseley
Tetsworth
Sunningwell
Baldon Toot
Postcombe
Northcott
Chiselhampton
Stadhampton
Adwell
Chinnor
Radley
Baldon Marsh
Rafford
Stoke Talmage
Aston Rowant
Marcham
ABINGDON
Nuneham Courtney
Brookhampton
Ascott
Upsgrove
Wheatfield
Crowell
Barton
Sth. Weston
Drayton
Holcomb
Easington
Lewknor
Stoken Church
River Ock
Clifton Hampden
Burcott
Chalgrove
Newington
Cadwell
Shirburn

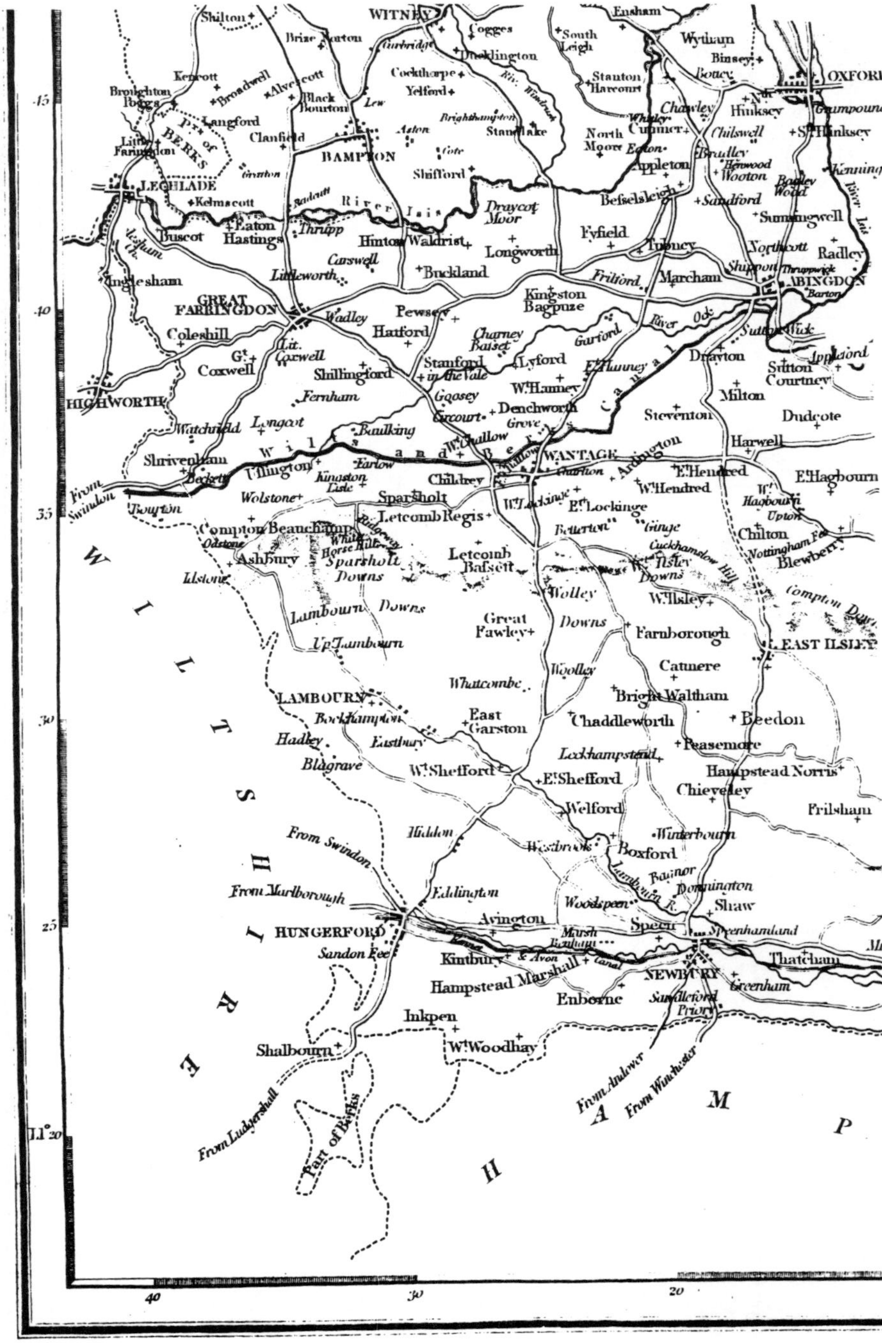
WITNEY
OXFORD
Shilton
Brize Norton
Cogges
Ducklington
Ensham
South Leigh
Wytham
Binsey
Stanton Harcourt
Kencott
Broadwell
Alvescott
Black Bourton
Cockthorpe
Yelford
Broughton Poggs
Langford
Clanfield
BAMPTON
Aston
Standlake
North Moore
Cumner
Hinksey
Chilswell
Kennington
Little Farringdon
LECHLADE
Kelmscott
Shifford
Appleton
Besselsleigh
Sandford
Bradley
Wooton
Eaton Hastings
Buscot
Thrupp
Hinton Waldrist
Draycot Moor
Fyfield
Tubney
Sunningwell
Radley
Northcott
Inglesham
Carswell
Littleworth
Buckland
Longworth
Fritford
Marcham
ABINGDON
Barton
GREAT FARRINGDON
Wadley
Pewsey
Kingston Bagpuze
Coleshill
Hatford
Charney Baiset
Garford
River Ock
Sutton Wick
Drayton
Gt. Coxwell
Lit. Coxwell
Shillingford
Stanford in the Vale
Lyford
Sutton Courtney
Appleford
HIGHWORTH
Fernham
Goosey
W. Hanney
Milton
Circourt
Denchworth
Steventon
Dudcote
Watchfield
Longcot
Baulking
Grove
Harwell
Shrivenham
WANTAGE
Uffington
Childrey
E. Hendred
W. Hendred
E. Hagbourn
Ardington
From Swindon
Bourton
Wolstone
Kingston Lisle
Sparsholt
W. Lockinge
E. Lockinge
Letcomb Regis
Compton Beauchamp
Betterton
Ginge
Chilton
Blewbery
Ashbury
Idstone
Letcomb Basset
Sparsholt Downs
W. Ilsley
Compton Downs
Lambourn Downs
Great Fawley
Downs
Farnborough
Up Lambourn
EAST ILSLEY
Catmere
Whatcombe
Bright Waltham
LAMBOURN
Bockhampton
East Garston
Chaddleworth
Beedon
Hadley
Eastbury
Peasemore
Blagrave
W. Shefford
E. Shefford
Leckhampstead
Hampstead Norris
Chieveley
Frilsham
Welford
Hiddon
Winterbourn
From Swindon
Westbrook
Boxford
From Marlborough
Eddington
Donnington
Woodspeen
Shaw
Avington
Speen
Speenhamland
HUNGERFORD
Sandon Fee
Kintbury
Thatcham
Hampstead Marshall
NEWBURY
Greenham
Enborne
Inkpen
W. Woodhay
Shalbourn
From Andover
From Winchester
From Ludgershall
Part of Berks
W I L T S H I R E
H A M P
40
30
20

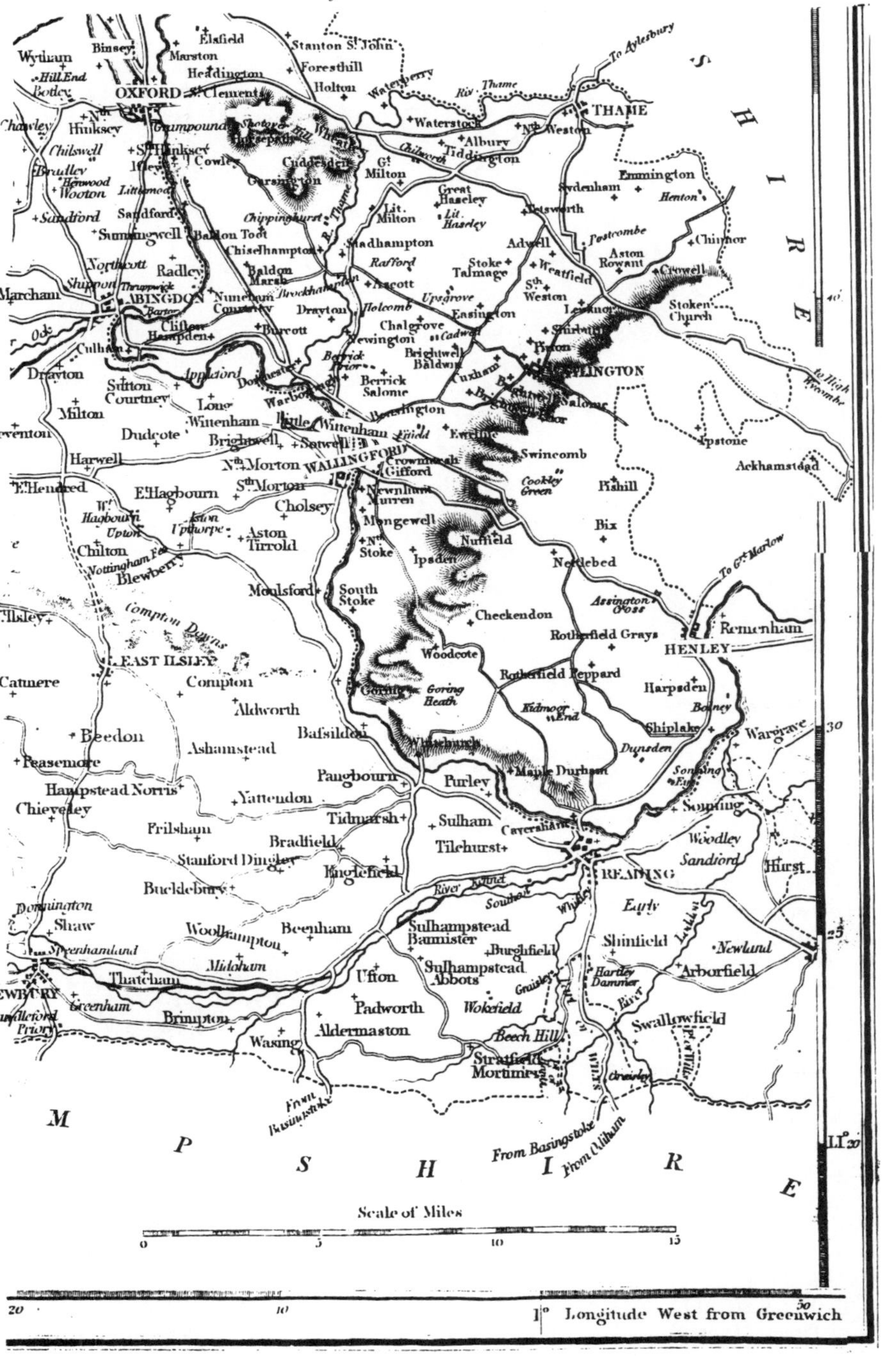
Wytham
Binsey
Elsfield
Marston
Headington
Stanton St. John
Forestshill
Holton
OXFORD
Hinksey
Cowley
Cuddesden
Garsington
Wheatley
Waterstock
Albury
Tiddington
Thame
THAME
Emmington
Sydenham
Chinnor
Aston Rowant
Crowell
Stoken Church
Lit. Milton
Great Haseley
Lit. Haseley
Tetsworth
Postcombe
Adwell
Stoke Talmage
Wheatfield
Sth. Weston
Lewknor
Chalgrove
Newington
Brightwell Baldwin
Berrick Salome
Benson
Ewelme
Swincomb
Pishill
Bix
Nettlebed
Nuffield
Ipsden
Checkendon
Rotherfield Grays
HENLEY
Remenham
Harpsden
Rotherfield Peppard
Woodcote
Goring
Goring Heath
Whitchurch
Shiplake
Wargrave
Dunsden
Sonning
Woodley
Sandford
Hurst
Caversham
READING
Earley
Shinfield
Arborfield
Newland
Swallowfield
Sandford
Sunningwell
Radley
Abingdon
ABINGDON
Marcham
Culham
Clifton Hampden
Drayton
Sutton Courtney
Milton
Steventon
Long Wittenham
Little Wittenham
Brightwell
Sotwell
Dorchester
Warborough
Dudcote
Harwell
Nth. Morton
Sth. Morton
WALLINGFORD
Crowmarsh Gifford
Newnham Murren
Mongewell
Nth. Stoke
South Stoke
E. Hendred
E. Hagbourn
Wt. Hagbourn
Upton
Chilton
Blewbery
Aston Upthorpe
Aston Tirrold
Cholsey
Moulsford
Compton Downs
EAST ILSLEY
Catmere
Compton
Aldworth
Basildon
Beedon
Ashamstead
Peasemore
Hampstead Norris
Chieveley
Yattendon
Pangbourn
Purley
Frilsham
Tidmarsh
Sulham
Tilehurst
Bradfield
Stanford Dingley
Englefield
Bucklebury
Donnington
Shaw
Speenhamland
Woolhampton
Beenham
Midgham
Thatcham
NEWBURY
Greenham
Sandleford Priory
Brimpton
Wasing
Ufton
Padworth
Aldermaston
Sulhampstead Bannister
Sulhampstead Abbots
Burghfield
Wokefield
Beech Hill
Stratfield Mortimer
From Basingstoke
From Odiham
SHIRE
HAMPSHIRE
Scale of Miles
0
5
10
15
20
10
1°
Longitude West from Greenwich
30
25
40

OXFORDSHIRE
and the Abingdon Division of Berkshire

Protestation Returns survive for the shaded areas of historic Oxfordshire (except for places mentioned in the Introduction), and for the Hundreds of Hormer, Moreton and Ock, comprising the Abingdon Division of Berkshire (not shaded).

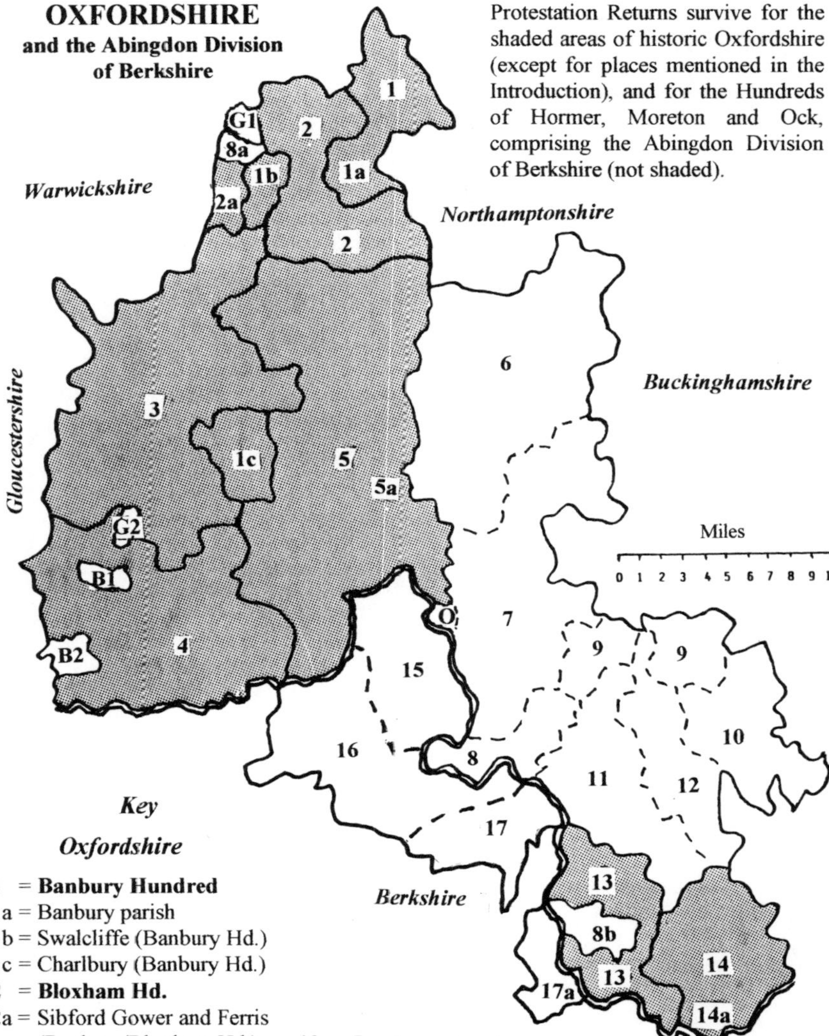

Key

Oxfordshire

1 = Banbury Hundred
1a = Banbury parish
1b = Swalcliffe (Banbury Hd.)
1c = Charlbury (Banbury Hd.)
2 = Bloxham Hd.
2a = Sibford Gower and Ferris (Banbury/Bloxham Hd.)
3 = Chadlington Hundred
4 = Bampton Hundred
5 = Wootton Hundred
5a = Woodstock borough
6 = Ploughley Hundred
7 = Bullingdon Hundred
8 = Dorchester Hundred
8a = Epwell (Dorchester Hd.)
8b = South Stoke (Dorchester Hd.)
9 = Thame Hundred
10 = Lewknor Hundred
11 = Ewelme Hundred
12 = Pirton Hundred
13 = Langtree Hundred
14 = Binfield Hundred
14a = Caversham parish

O = Oxford

B1 = Shilton Berks.
B2 = Langford, Berks.
G1 = Shenington Glos.
G2 = Widford, Glos.

Berkshire (Abingdon Division)

15 = Ock Hundred
16 = Hormer Hundred
17 = Moreton Hd.
17a = Ashampstead, Basildon, Streatley (Moreton Hd.)

BAMPTON HUNDRED

[f. 1r, single column. This list is of the Ministers, Churchwardens, Constables and Overseers of the Poor who took the Protestation Oath at Woodstock on 14th February 1641, as mentioned in the Introduction. Such officials gathered at Woodstock (for Wootton Hundred, see page 139) and other market towns, such as Banbury (see page 72), though no similar lists survive for other Oxfordshire hundreds. Compare instead those for the Berkshire divisions of Abingdon (page 173) and Newbury.

The list is very inaccurate. Names as they appear on the parish returns, when they differ, are shown in square brackets.]

Hi officiar' et cler' protest. Apud Woodstock xiiii Febr. 1641.

Bampton Hundred in Com. Oxon.

Rice Jones esqr, one of the Justices of peace.
John Moore gen',
John Yate gen', *cap' con'* for the county aforesaid

Bampton and Weald
Wm Hodges,
Fr. Dring,
Edw' Joye, *Cler'*
Rich. Enstone, *Churchwarden*
Humphry Carter, *Overseer of the poore*
Wm Hall,
Jo. Sedwell [John Sidwell],
Rich. Greene, *Const'*

Aston & Coate
Tho. Fryme, *Const'*
Jo: [John] Patient, *Churchwarden*
Tompson Haucks [Hauckes], *Overseer*

Shifford et Chimney
Jo. Bennitt [John Bennet],
Jo: [John] Williams, *Const'*
Tho: Harris [Harrys],
Jo: Martin [John Marten], *Ch'*
Tho: Sperring [Perrin?], *Over'*

Hardwick et Elford [Yelford]
Robert Lydwell [Lydall], *Cler'*
Thom. Aldworth, *Con'*
Roger Hawkins,
Thom. James, *Ch'*

Standlake et Brittenton
[Brighthampton]
Nich. Shorter, *Cler'*
Rob. Wyett [Robert Wyatt],
Wm Townsend, *Const'*
Allex. Temple [Alexander Tempell],
Rich. Weale, *Ch'*
Xpofer [Christopher] Harris,
Gyles Coles [Giles Barnes], *Over'*

Ducklington
Thom' Wyatt [Wiat], *doct' divinit'*
Jo: Muttler [John Mutloe], *Const*
Rich. Ballowe [Ballow],
Jo: [John] Slaymaker, *Ch'*
Wm Hughes,
Tho. Tanner, *Over'*

Witney
Thom. White, *Cler'*
Ric. Ockley [Okeley],
Tho. White, *Const*
Wm Wood,
Jo. Parmee [John Parme], *Ch'*
Henr' White,
Wm Compton,
Edw. Garnor [Gardiner], *Over'*

Hayley et Crawley
Jo: Crofts [John Craftes],
Wm Howford [Holford], *Con'*
Jo: Hampsheire [John Hamshir], *Ch'*
Jo: Yate,
Rich. Taylor,
Geo. Darby, *Over'* Witney parish

Curbridge
Geo. Hart [Harte], *Const'*
Arthur Kite [Keite], *Ch'*
Tho. King, *Over'*

Lewe ['of Bampton', *added*]
Wm Beechee [Beechy], *Con'*
Wm Beechee [Beechy], *Ch'*
Thom. Shawe [Shaw], *Over'*

[f.2v]
Kelmscott
Jo: [John] Hughes, *Cler'*
Tho. Stephens, *Const'*
Phill'p Turner,
Willm Turner, *Ch'*
Thom. Hulls, *Over'*

Grafton
Robt Maysey [Meysey], *Sen' Con*
Jo: Maysey [John Meyey],
Henr' Kibble [Keeble], *Over'*

Clanfield
Fatnell [Phatnell] Denton, *Cler'*
Salomon Clark [Solo: Clarke], *Con'*
Jo. White [Whit], *Ch'*
Thom. Blagrove, *Ch'*
Jo: Chapman [*not identified:* Yeatman *or* Laffen?],
Robt Turner, *Over'*

Black Bourton
Edw. Joye, *Cler'*
Jo: Humphryes [John Humpheris]
Tho. Monke, *Const'*
Jo: Palling [John Pawlinge], *Ch'*
Sym. Dudson [Symon Dudsonne],
Jo: Pencott [John Pencotte], *Over'*

Alvescot
Ferryman [Ferriman] Twittie, *Cler'*
Robt Gladden, *Const'*
Sym. Hux,
Tho. Yarneton, *Ch'*
Tho. May,
Mihill Turfery [Michael Turfrey], *Over*

Brize Norton
Martin Raise [Royse], *Cler'*
Jo: [John] Moulder, *Cont'*
Edw. Boule [Edward Boole],
Jo: Fletcher [John Flecher], *Ch'*
Rich. Norden,
Robt. Fletcher [Weston], *Over'*

Astoll et Astall Eye [Leigh]
Thom. Pearson, *Cler'*
Thom. Barrett *[not identified]*, *Const'*
Wm Williams,
Jo: Sanders [John Saunders], *Ch'*
Lewis Bawer [Baker],
Rich. Haynes, *Over'*

Burford
Xpofer Glynne [Christopher Glyn], *Cler'*
Jo: [John] Clark,
Jo: [John] Hughes, *Const'*
Symon [Simon] Ward,
Rich. Vaysey [Veysey],
Henry Hayter,
Jo: Pearse [John Peirce], *Ch'*
Edw. Allen,
Wm Hayter, *Over'*

Upton et Synett [Signet], part of Burford
Thom. Marten [Martin], *Const'*

Hollwell et Westwell
Wm Davys [Thomas Davis], *Cler'*
Tho. Cooke, *Con'*
Tho. Fletcher,
Jo: [John] Bye, *Ch'*
Jo: Yeagles [John Eagles], *Over'*
Wm George,
Francis Ferneham [Vernum], *Const'*

Kencott
James Fritherne [Frethern], *Cler''*
Fr. Turner, Jun', *Const'*
Henry Gooddynough [Goodnoughe],
Adam Turner, *Ch' et Over'*

[f.2r]
Broughton [Poggs]
Thomas Hornesey [Hornsey], *Cler'*
Robt Burduxx [Burdocke], *Con'*
Rich. Humphryes [Humfrys],
Henry Thomas, *Ch'*
Edward Elderton,
Andr. Jefferyes [Jeffry], *Over'*

Bradwell et Filkins
Jo: [John] Field, *Cler'*
Jo: Burduxx [John Burdocke],
Walter Harper, *Const'*
Fr: Willett,
Thom. Turner, *Ch'*
Will' Stephens [Stevens],
Jo: Stuart [John Steward], *Over'*

Radcott
Robt Clarke, *Const'*
Geo. Cleeter, *Over'*

ALVESCOT

[f.3. In two columns. This is one of the rare parishes with signatures or marks for all listed. Marks are shown with asterisks, the others all being signatures.]

The names of all those within our parish of Alvescot that have taken the protestation. [58]

[f.3r, column 1]
Ferriman Twittie
Tho. Hales
Martin Turfery
Alexander May
Richard Prior *
Simon Hux Junior *
Henrie Francklin
Thomas Ditch *
Steven Huffam *
George Williames Sen' *
Thomas Tannan Jun'
Robert Wheelor *
Henry Church
Adwen Williames *
Robert Gladden *
Michael Turfrey
Anthony May
Alexander Hux
William Wheelor *
Thomas Wheelor *
Richard Calin *
George lliams*[sic]*
Thomas Radborne
John Dawes *
William Goodinough *
[f.3r, column two]
William Cooke *
Wall[ter?] Bushe
Thomas Prior *
Hugh Dunckley *
Andrew Henly *
Henry Tanner
John Hauskinnes *
Thomas Yarneton *
Peter Keene *
Roger Snell *
Robert Lynsee *
Thomas Afflett *
John Church *
James Taylor *
Henry Baker *
John Abday *
Thomas May
Simon Huxe Sen' *
Jane Maye widdow *
Thomas Cosinnes *
Thomas Clarridg
Thomas Henly *
William Clarridge *
Thomas Newberry *
George Parrott *
Richard Hinton
Henrie Briscoe *
[f.3v]
David Cove
William Masey
Henrie Crippes
William Bartlitt
John Widdowes
William Wheelor

Refusers, none.

*[The **Assessment** for Alvescot was on one of the decayed membranes and is lost.]*

ASTHALL [151]

[f.4r]
***Astall** in the Countie of Oxon*

A True bill of returne of the names of all Popish sectaries or Recusantes [3] which refuse to take the Protestation Commended by the house of Commons, being above the age of 18 years in the Parrish of Astall dated the 22th of Febr. 1641

Edward Saunders
Marye Saunders uxor eius
Elizabeth Cooke wid.

[f.5r, in three columns]

A True bill of the names of all those, who have taken the Protestation Commended by the house of Commons beinge above the age of 18 yeares in the parrish of Astall dated the 22th Febr. 1641 [148]

[f.5r, col. 1]
Nicholas Bartlett
Robert Pebworth
John Deanes
John Fellowes
Richard Jorden
William Clearke
Harman Fletcher
Edmund Surmon
William Bradley the younger
John Bradlye
Henery Fawckner
Giles Ritton
Richard Boyse
Zatheus Coxhead
Timothie Coxehead
Richard Stiles
Katherin Stiles
Marye Williams
Elizabeth Williams
Elizabeth Staight
Roger Williams
Anne Knight
Richard Wickens
Thomas Wickins
Richard Wickins the younger
Robert Weston
Richard Tomsen
William Bradlye
Robert Toolye
Edith Toolye
Florence Redburne
Lewis Baker
Thomas Whitinge
John Wickins
Thomas Toolye
Anne Townsen
Anne Haynes
Anne Coxehead
Edith Pebworth
Marye Hitchman
Joane Whitinge
Elizabeth Coxhead
William Kendall
Anne Kendall
Alice Fletcher
[f.5r, col. 2]
Elizabeth Deanes
Edward Farmer
Marye Farmer
Bartholomewe Howse
Thomas Cooke
Robert ap Robert
Margerett Wickins
Francis Neate
William Payne
William Staight
Marye Staight
Anne Franklin
Catherin Butcher
Anne Bradlye
Katherine Farmer
Agnes Wickins
Anne Jorden
Anne Bradley the younger
Raffe Cockerell
Marye Cockerell
Katherine Bowld
Anne Stiles
Bartholomewe Fawkner
Parnell Humffries
Mr. Martine Rathbone
Thomas Silvester
Robert Busbye
Marye Pebworth
Gilian Howse
Marye Pearson
Mstris Jane Silvester
John Kendall
Richard Sperrine
Thomas Staight
Joyce Hitchman
Marye Cooke
Raffe Rowles
Robert Riccotts
Thomas Wickens
Alice Rash
Alice Busbye
Lucie Wyatt
Joane Riccotts
Marye Clearke
Elinor Fawkner
Martine Radburne
Roger Wyatt
Anne Hodges
Elizabeth Hodges
Katherine Harris
Joane Wickins
Alice Rowles
Marye Wickins
[f.5r, col. 3]
John Bowld
Joane Fawckner
Alice Davis
Anne Amyas
Katherine Varnye
Elizabeth Hedges
Anne Staight
Abigaile Surmon
Marye Whitehouse
Barnabye Butcher
Thomas Hitchman
William Wickins
Elizabeth Wickins
William Pebworth
Edward Coxe
William Coxe
Richard Coxe
Elinor Fawkner
Alice Boyse
Barbara Harper

Marye Coxe
Marye Boyse
Margaret Barret
Richard Harris
Francis Bowld
Nicolas Rowles
Richard Harper
Humffrye Stiles
John Carter
John Saunders
Thomas Harris
Frizo Saunders
Margerett Bartlett
Winiffride Saunders
George Bushnell
Joane Bushnell
Anne Androwes
Andrewe Varnye
Joane Fawckner
Thomas Bishoppe
John Hedges
Francis Ebsworth
Joane Wickins
William Kendall
Joane Wickins

Tho: Pearson, *Vicar*
William Williams et John Saunders, *Churchwardens*
Richard Haynes et Lewis Baker, *Overseers*

*[**Assessment.** Membrane 13, following on from Brize Norton.]*

Astoll [Asthall] ***and Asthol Lye*** [Asthalleigh]

Rice Jones, Esqr., £2.18s.4d.
John Saunders, & Edward Saunders, for the farme they hold of Mr Field, £1.10s.2d.
Sr. Robert Cooke, £1.4s.8d.
Sr. John Lacy, 4s.
William Stayte, 7d.
Edmund Surman, 3s.6d.
Richard Haynes, 1s.9d.
George Bushnell, for the land he holds, 1s.9d.
William Kendall, 4s.8d.
John Deanes, for the land he holds, 1s.2d.
Thomas Hitchman, 1s.
Henry Deanes, 1s.
Harman Fletcher, 4s.1d.
William Bradley, for his goods, 1s.6d.
Nicholas Bartlett, 4s.1d.
Richard Jurden, for the land he holds, 4s.1d.
Joyce Hitchman, 7s.3d.
John Kendall, for the land he holdeth, 5s.10d.
Richard Townsend, 3s.6d.
Thomas Whiting, for the land he holdeth, 4s.1d.
Joane Falkener, vid., 10d.
Richard Harris, 8d.
John Harris, 6s.
Henry Cowburrowe, 1s.9d.
Edmund Cox, for the land he holdeth, 4s.8d.
Ralph Cockerell, 6d.
Thomas Barrett, 4s.8d.
William Williams, 7s.3d.
Francis Neate, 5s.10d.
Edward Saunders, recusant, for his goods, 3s.4d.
John Saunders, for his goods, 2s.
Thomas Whiteing, 1s.
John Kendall, for his goods, 1s.
Lewis Baker, for his goods, 1s.
Martine Radborne, 6d.
Gyles Written, 6d.

Soma total £12.0.0.

Edward Saunders, recusant, his surplusage, 3s.4d.
Mary Saunders, his weife, p poll, 2s.8d.
John *[blank]*, servant to Edward Saunders, p poll, 2s.8d.

BAMPTON

[f.9r, in three columns.]

Bampton [409]

A catalogue of all that have taken the Protestation within the parish of Bampton, consisting of the towne of Bampton, the Hamletts of Weald, Lew, Aston-&-Cote, Shifford, Chymney, and Bright-hampton.

1. Towne of Bampton [102]

[f.9r, col. 1]

Richard Rippon
Edward Blagrave
Leonard Carter
John Pettiver Jun.
Anthony Cromwell
William Hanckes
Robert Jones
Walter Castell
Anthony Staunton
William Collingwood Sen'
William Collingwood Jun'
Richard Greene Jun
Thomas Collingwood
Philipp Collingwood
Andrew Hanckes
Richard Pettiver
John Pettiver Sen'
Richard Sanford
Alexander Pettiver
Robert Carpenter
William Allen
Henry Iving
John Fisher
Tobias Hawkins
John Hill
Edward Carter
William Drewet Sen'
Henry Cooke
John Clarke
Roger Hill
John Ward
Richard Beconsell
Henry Aldworth
Thomas Carter Jun'
Richard Greene Sen'
Thomas Enstone
Robert Carpenter Jun'
Richard Orpwood

[f.9r, col. 2]

William Orpwood
Edward Cooke
Thomas Trew
John Trew
Richard Carpenter
Edward Ward
Thomas Willear
William Willear
John Luckins
John Lisset
Arthur Showell
Edward Ditton
Roger Carter
John Window
Thomas Window
James Brayne
Rodolph Clinton
Simon Carpenter
John Carpenter
Richard Lisset
Thomas Lisset
John Yong
William Edwards
John Carter
Robert Carter Sen'
Robert Carter Jun'
Thomas Carter Sen'
Thomas Townesend
Daniel Warwicke
Edward Richardson
John Richardson
Simon Basset
Richard Quarrier
Robert Hues
Nicholas Cooke
John Orpwood
William Drewet Jun'
William Pettiver
William Hill
Andrew Drewet

[f.9r, col. 3]

Thomas Burdocke
Henry Akers
John Dring
Edward Dring
John Drewet
Henry Poole
Thomas Drewet
Robert Drewet
Humphrey Carter Sen'
Humphrey Carter Jun'
John Carter Jun
Alexander Akers
Richard Ayser
Matthew Skinner Sen'
Matthew Skinner Jun'
Leonard Harrys
Robert Harrys
Alexander Draper
William Beechye
John Eagles
Thomas Drewet
Hercules Tayler

Refusers, none

Attest:
Richard Greene,
John Sidwell, *Constables*
Richard Enstone,
Humphrey Carter, *Collect'*

*[For the **Assessment** for Bampton and other places in the parish, see pages 10-12.]*

2. Weald [101]
[f.9v, col. 1]
John Palmer
Henry Coxiter
Richard Coxiter
John Trinder
Edmond Crips, natu maximus
John Gillet
Thomas Williams
William Clarke
Edmund Crips, natu minimus
Thomas Townesend
Richard Harrys
Robert Crippes
William Sadler Jun'
Edward Sadler
William Sadler Sen'
John White
Richard Almond
John Wayne
Thomas Wayne
John Baggot
Mariot Shepherd
Thomas Saunders
John Yong
George Harrys
Anthony Yong
Edmund Crips, natu medius
Anthony Horne
Thomas Crips; medius
Thomas Crips; Sen'
Thomas Crips. Jun'
Robert Wright
Thomas Wiblin
William Crips
Tobias Pawling
Richard Chayre
Richard Horne
William Wickins
William Lee
Thomas Laurence
Richard Gardiner
Stephen Watts
William Hews
[f.9v, col. 2]
William Watts
Thomas Hannes
Robert Ford
Alexander Cooper
Anthony Hore
John Evans
Thomas Bennet
William Fowler
Thomas Fillys
William Fillys
Edward Seary
Robert Crips
Maurice Smart
Francis Pullen
Joseph Castell
William Kibbel
Edward Rowland
Thomas Miles
Francis Perin
John Snoswell
Thomas Gervase
Edward Jones
Henry Denton
Philipp Cooke
Henry White
Thomas Erpen
William Goddard
Richard Stokes
John Quench
Leonard Wayte
Thomas Hickeman
Richard Orpwood
John Colet
William Trippe
Thomas Strange
John Puddell
John Pierson
Richard Arnold
John Dowglasse
William Eltham
John Russell
Edward Field
Timothy Joyes
John Joyes
Walter Steward
Robert Mace
Richard Haynes
[f.9v, col. 3]
Nicholas Norris
John Carter
Thomas Jones
Thomas Almond
Richard Crips
Lawrence Webb
Edward Ansell
Edward Waynewright
Richard Simmes [and] William Sadler of Haddon
Moses Wiblin,

Refusers, none

Attest:
Anthoni Young, *Collector*
William Hall, *Constable*

3. Lew [34]
[f.10r, col. 1]
William Wise
Richard Richins
William Beechy
Richard Beechy
John Pitt
William Brooke. jun'
John Collingwood
William Bedford
John Stutter
Edmund Garne
William Brooke Sen'
William Yong
Richard Wenman
Edward Moulder
John Harryson
Wiliam Harryson
Roger Harryson
Thomas Chamline sen'
Thomas Chamline Jun'
Thomas Startup Sen'
John Startup
Thomas Startup jun'
William Beechy jun'
Thomas Shyrman
Robert Kyte
Alexander Ellins
Ferdinando Shepherd
Thomas Geeves
William Geeves
John Sadler
Thomas Shaw
Thomas Withers
Henry Allye Sen'
Henry Allye jun'

Refusers,none

Attest:
William Beechy, *Con'*
William Beechy, *Chur'*
Tho: Shaw, *Collect'.*

4. Aston and Cote [113]

[f.10r, col. 2]

Sr. Thomas Hord
Henry Medhop
Timothy Sparrowhauke
William Margery
Henry Wickins
Rodolph Burnet Jun'
Richard Westly
Ralph Thomas
William Yong
Thomas Yong Sen'
William Hone
Edward Butler
John Fox
John Robenson
Christopher Kerne
Edward Galloway
John Yong Sen'
John Brooke, Sen'
John Brooke, Jun'
William Hyatt
John Cooke
Robert Wallys
Thomas Seary; Sen'
Thomas Seary: Jun'
William Startup
William Clevely
Rice Carpenter
William Ford
John Clarke
Edward Orpwood
John Rickards
Edward Rickards
Thomas Franklin
John Basson
Stephen Hill
John Rowland
William Cowlye
Richard Fletcher
Edmund Turke

[f.10r, col. 3]

Edmund Matthew
James Matthew
George Cooke
Edward Castell
John Startup sen'
John Startup jun'
John Walter
Alexander Towse
Nicholas Humphrys
Richard Moore
John Slattor
Bartholomew Slattor
William Sparrowhauke
John Waterman
John Yong jun'
Ralph Burnet sen'
Edward Merryfield
Thomas Yong, jun'
Robert Carter
Robert Radbon
Thomas Coxiter
Andrew Denton
William Aldworth
John Whitlocke
William Thomas
Richard Thomas
John Butler
Gowen Butler
John Gillham
Richard Beechy
Robert Townesend
Richard Townesend
Robert Patient
Thomas Brant
William Carter
John Radford
William Bishop
Richard Robinson
Thomas Moore
Henry Coxe
Andrew Davys

[f.10v, col. 1]

Richard Edwards
John Clarke
John Newman
Henry Newman
Thomas Newman
Robert Newman
Edward Tanner
John Stubbes
Richard Elridge sen'
Richard Elridge jun'
Robert Shepherd
Richard Clinch
Thomas Tayllor
Richard Patient
Roger Townesend
William Lindsey
Edward Purbrecke
Thomas Lindsey
Robert Lindsey
Thomas Coxiter Sen'
Richard Coxiter
John Williams
Robert Dale
Anthony Edwards
John Prior
Thomas Humphryes
Thomas Aldworth
Robert Gardiner
William Startup

Refusers, none

Attestant
Tompson Hauckes, *Collector*
Thomas Fryme, *Constabell*
John Patient, John Williams, *Churchwardens*

5. Shifford [28]

[f.10v, col. 2]
Richard Keene
Clement Ford
George Bartlet
Henry Harrys
William Bennet
John Bennet
Richard Farre
Thomas Perin
John Stone
Robert Farre
Robert Darbye
William Wayte
Richard Badnell
Robert Battin
Robert Bennet
John Bennet
Lawrence Ford
Francis Eaton
William Clarke
Roger Newman
Simon Tomkins
Richard Curson
Christopher Wilkes
William Sparrowhauke
John Willson
John Bennet jun'
Nicholas Ford

Refusers, none

Attest:
Tho: Harrys, *Churchwarden*
John Bennet, *Constable*

6. Chymney [15]

[f.10v, col. 3]
Robert Veisey sen'
Robert Veisey jun'
William Stampe
Edmund Martin
Henry Minshaw
James Tubbe
Henry Newbery
Simon Holland
John George
John Martin
Thomas Stampe
Thomas Tomline
John Walter
Walter Tawman

John Marten, *Constable and Churchwarden*

7. Brighthampton [17]

[f.11r]
Richard Thrift
Robert Bennet
John Tanner, Sen'
Robert Hozyer
John Tanner, jun'
Walter Lake
Thomas Ellys
Richard Miles
John Harrys
Robert Farmer
Thomas Stone
Edward Curson
Thomas Curson
Edward Bennet
Thomas Weald
Samuel Harrys

Refusers, none

Attestant:
Tho: Stone, *Constable*
Humphrey Flexney, *Churchwarden*

To all these aforenamed, *id est*, to all my parish, I have tendered the Protestation, and they have taken it; accordingly as is testifyed by the Constables, Church-wardens, & Collectors of each Hamlet, -respectively.

Wm. Hodges: Vicar in the first of the three vicaridges of Bampton; (& the only resident).

Febr. 26, 1641.

*[**Assessment.** Membrane 5, following on Aston and Coate.]*

Bampton, Weald, Haddon and Elford

[Yelford is in fact recorded separately with Hardwick, page 23.]

[blank] Ba....[?], and his Tenants[?] for Elford, *[? sum]*
Toby Hawkins, *[? sum]*
Widdow Stainton, & her daughter, 5s.
William Drewett, for the land he holdeth of John Mayott, gen., 11s.
Thomas Willyer, for the like, 6s.
Mathewe Skynner, for the like, 8s.6d.
Anthony Horne, for the like, 10s.
Richard Greene, 6s.
Roger Hill, and his mother, 8s.6d.
John *[illegible]*, 5s.6d.
Richard [....?kle], *[? sum]*
Richard Lisset, 10s.[?]
[illegible entry]
Edward Carter, for the land he holdeth of Mrs Clinton[?], 12s.
Richard Enstone, 6s.
Edmund Cripps, 13s.
Thomas Carter, sen., 3s.
Robert Carter, 3s.
Humphry Carter, jun., 3s.6d.
Humphry Carter, sen., for the land he holdeth of Thomas Ward, 7s.
Symon Carpenter, [?]s.6d.
John Windowe, *[? sum]*
William Hill, *[? sum]*
[The next three entries are very faded]
William W.....[?], & his Tenants, *[? sum]*
William H[ank]s[?], *[? sum]*
Mrs Jane H[anks ?], for the p'sonage & other lands which her Tenants farm of her, 12s.
Allexander Pottifer, & his mother, 5s.
John Siddwell, 4s.
William Collingwood, 8s.
Richard Greene, Taylor, 6s.
Thomas Collingwood, 4s.6d.
Leonard Carter, 1s.
John Lissett, 5s.
Thomas Burdock, 2s.6d.
Henry Alder, 2s.6d.
Roger Carter, 2s.6d.
[blank] Collingwood, vid., 4s.6d.
[Membrane 6]
Robert Mace, 1s.6d.
John Snowswell, 2s.6d.
Thomas Webb, 1s.
Edward Cooke, 2s.
Nicholas Cooke, 2s.
Symon Bassett, 1s.
William Edwards, 1s.
John Trewe, 1s.6d.
Henry White, 1s.6d.
William Pettifer, 1s.
Sr. Edward Yate, Kt., recusant & his Tennants for Haddon, £6.
Richard Drewe, gen. *[no sum noted]*
Richard Leader, gen., and their Tennants for pt. of the p'sonage, £3.10s.
Thomas Southby, gen., & his Tennants for pt. of the p'sonage, £1.8s.8d.
William Hodges, cle., for his Tythes, £1.
Sr. Thomas Hoard, £2.5s.
[blank] Wilson, gen., for Tythes, £1.10s.
John Palmer, gen., £2.5s.
John Jorden, gent., & his Tennt's, £1.
John Trynder, 18s.
Edmund Cripps, de Barsgate, 8d.
Edmund Cripps, de Upwell, 8d.
[blank] Saunders, gen., & his Tenn'ts, 3s.
William Sadler, for the land he holdeth of *[blank]* Joye, gen., & Richard Blower, gen., for Bampton & Weald, 16s.
Anne Sadler, vid., 3s.
Anthony Younge, for Bampton & Weald the land he holdeth there, 16s.
Robert Wright, 8s.11d.
Thomas Cripps, 6s.
Toby Pauling, 7s.
Richard Horne, & his mother, 8s.
William Fowler, 1s.
John Evans, & Nicholas Norris, 4s.
Roger Hill, 2s.9d.
William Hall, 9s.
William Goddard, 3s.
Richard Arnold, 2s.
William Wells, gen., & his Tennant, 2s.6d.
William Waynwright, & Edward his son, 9s.
Henry Coxeter, gen., 6s.
John Baggett, 1s.6d.
John King, & his Tennant, 2s.
Joseph Castle, 2s.6d.
Edward Blagrave, 2s.6d.
William Drewett, jun., 10d.
William Watts, 1s.
Thomas Saunders, 1s.
Robert Foord, 1s.
Thomas Lissett, 2s.
Edward Searey, 1s.
Richard Eysey, 2s.
Stephen Watts, 1s.
John Clarke, 2s.
Richard Anman, 2s.
Richard Arpind[?], 4s.

Soma Total £45.0.0.

Sr. Edward Yate, Kt., recusant, Surplussage for his land at Haddon, £6.

Lewe

*[**Assessment.** Membrane 7 continued, following on from Brighthampton. This section of the membrane is stained by damp and parts are illegible, though if examined under ultra-violet light it is possible a little more might be deciphered with persistence.]*

Edward Wil[son], cler.[?], for his pt. of Tythes there, £6.12s.
Thomas Southby[?], gen., for pt. of the Tythes, 5s.
Richard ...... the land ... *[several illegible entries, bracketed with]*
Ann Waynman, £1.10s.
...... elder for the like, 5s.
....hie, for the like, 5s.
....uce, for the like, 15s.
Made[?] ......, &
John Baston, for ......ke, 5s.
...., for the land he holdeth *[bracketed with]*
...... Mathew, 6s.3d.
...... Beechie, jun., 3s.
....ne Beechie, wid., 1s.6d.
...... Beechie, 1s.8d.
...... Collingwood, 2s.6d.
[Wi]lliam Wise, 15s.
William Brooke, 10s.
Thomas Chamlin, sen., 5s.
Thomas Jeeves, 15s.
John Sadler, 5s.
William Moulder, 8s.
[Tho]mas Shawe, 4s.6d.
Thomas Startup als. Thomas Bartlet, 1s.6d.
...aude Shephearde, 1s.
William Bedford, 1s.
Henry Medhopp, gen., for his sheepe pastured in Lew heathe, 2s.

Sum £8.0.0.

Aston and Coate

*[**Assessment.** Membrane 5. Membrane 4, presumably including the start of Aston and Cote, is missing.]*

Thomas Clinch, & Margery Clinch, & Roger Townesend, 2s.2d.
Edward Tanner, [?]1s.1d.
John Williams, jun., 6s.6d.
John Williams, sen., 6s.8d.
Alice Newman, 6s.9d.
John Newman, 4s.6d.
John Passume, 1s.1d.
Henry Medhopp, 2s.8d.
Tompson Haucks, 2s.11d.
Ralph Burnett, 2s.2d.
Richard Westly, 1s.1d.
Ralph Thomas, 5s.6d.
William Younge, 8s.6d.
John Foxe, 4s.
Xpofer Keene, 10s.8d.
John Younge, 2s.3d.
John Brookes, 9s1d.
William Hyatt, 2s.2d.
Thomas Searey, 3s.1d.
Robert Wallis, William Bishop, and Elizabeth Ripon *[bracketed together]*, 6d.
John Clarke, 2s.2d.
John Baston, 6s.9d.
John Riccotts, 10s.10d.
John Rowland, 18s.6d.
John Walter, 3s.3d.
Edmund Startupp, 2s.3d.
John Startup, 4s.6d.
John Slater, 13s.6d.
Bartholomewe Slater, 4s.6d.
Robert Carter, 6s.6d.
Edmund Younge, 4s.6d.
Ralphe Burnett, sen., 14s.
Robert Redburne, 2s..3d.
William Aldworth, 2s.3d.
Edith Thomas, 4s.6d.
Thomas Fryme, 2s.3d.
Robert Townesend, 6s.8d.
John Brickland, 9s.
Margery Fryme, 9s.
William Thomas, 9s.
Henry Coxeter, for Docter [William] Osburne [Osborne], his viccaridge
Robert Linsey, 2s.6d.
Richard Clinch, 1s.
Robert Passume, 2s.
Thomas Younge, sen., 2s.
William Hoane, 1s.
Roger Surman, 3s.
William Startupp, 3s.
William Foard, 2s.
Edmund Turke, 2s.
Edmund Mathewe, 1s.
George Cooke, 1s.
Allexander Towse, 2s.6d.
Nicholas Humpryes, 2s.
William Sparrowehawke, 1s.
John Younge, jun., 2s.
Thomas Younge, jun., 2s.
Ric. Carpenter, 1s.
John Radford, 1s.
John Edwards, 4d.
Robert Sheapherd, 4d.
Jane Haucks, 8d.

Sum total £20.0.0.

Shifford

*[**Assessment.** Membrane 6 continued, following on from Yelford and Hardwick]*

Robert Vaysey, gen., for his land there, £2.
William Hodges, clr., for his Tythes th:, 12s.6d.
Thomas Surby, gen., for his Tythes there, 12s.6d.
Richard Keene, £1.7s.
Clement Foord, 4s.
Thomas Harris, 5s.
Margaret Harris, vid., 5s.
Elizabeth Guillett, 3s.
Robert Bartlett, 13s.
John Carter, 3s.
Henry Harris, 7s.
John Bennett, jun., 1s.
John Stone, 10s.
Thomas Sperryn, 14s.
Robert Farr, 13s.4d.
Robert Darby, 2s.6d.

[Membrane 7]

R[obert] Bennett, 10s.
J[ohn] Bennett, sen., 10s.
W[illia]m Wayle [Wayte], 10s.
Richard Farr, 10s.
William Bennett, 5s.
Francis Yeadon [Eaton], 8d.
Roger Newman, 6d.

Soma Total £11.0s.0d.

Chimney

*[**Assessment.** Membrane 7 continued, following on from Shifford.]*

Robert Vaysey, sen., of Chimney, gen., £5.11s.
William Hedges, cle., for his Viccaridge here, £1.2s.
William Stampe, £1.3s.6d.
Edmund Martine, £1.3s.
Robert Dale, 11s.6d.
Henry Minchin, 11s.6d.
Anne Vaysey, vid., 7s.
Robert Vaysey, jun., 5s.
Henry Newberry, 2s.6d.
James Tubb, 2s.6d.

Soma total £11.0s.0d.

Brighthampton

*[**Assessment.** Membrane 7 continued, following on from Chimney.]*

Francis Dring, gen., for *[blank]* Wilsons viccaridge there, 14s.1d.
Thomas Surby, gen., for his Tythes there, 7s.8d.
Thomas Weale, 16s.
Richard Hosier, for *[blank]* Hopkins, gen., his land, 10s.10½d.
John Tanner, 7s.10½d.
John Yate, & Joane Cordiwell, 3s.4½d.
John Yate, for Joane Hicks, her land, 3s.4½d.
Thomas Stone, 10s.1½d.
Robert Bennett, 7s.1½d.
Alice Bridgman, 6s.
John Edward, 7s.6d.
Thomas Bennett, 4d.
Edward Curson, 10s.
Richard Thrift, 6s.4½d.
Thomas Curson, 5s.3d.
Anne Bennett, & Edward Bennett, 9s.9d.
John Tanner, jun., 2s.
Robert Hosier, & Richard Hosier, 2s.

Soma total £7.0s.0d.

[See also page 27.]

BLACK BOURTON [64]

[f.12r, in two columns]

Blacke Borton

The names of the Inhabitants of Blacke-Borton which have taken this protestation upon the: 21th day of this present February 1641.

[f.12r, col. 1]

1. William Trotman: gent
2. Symon Dringe: gent
3. Humpherie Smith: gent
4. Edward Trotman
5. Robert Gefferis
6. William Garret
7. Richarde Boos
8. William Stewarde
9. John Turner
10. Henry Kirbie
11. William Lawrence
12. Robert Tayler
13. Thomas Dudsonne
14. Thomas Whitinge
15. Robert Dringe
16. Thomas Maysy
17. Symon Maysy
18. James Maysy
19. Symon Winter
20. Richarde Winter
21. John Rogers : se:
22. John Rogers: ju:
23. Roger Rogers
24. William Rogers
25. Richarde Coomes
26. John Eaton
27. Richarde Pawlinge
28. Andrew Yeatman
29. Symon Hopkins
30. William Hopkins
31. Tobie Hopkins
32. Thomas Barnes
33. Nicolas Kynch
34. John Pawlinge ju.
35. Antony Coone [Coome]
36. John Edwards
37. John Monke
38. John Pencotte: se.
39. John Edmunds
40. Thomas Goovers
41. Thomas Cowles
42. Antony Cosens
43. Henry Cosens
44. John Curre
45. William Curre
46. Symon Turferie
47. William Robinnes
48. John Whittwaye
49. Roberte Hickes
50. William Smith
51. James Raynolds: se.
52. James Raynolds: ju.
53. Symon Kynch
54. Richarde Ellett
55. John Jordan
56. William Weeneway
57. John Sare
58. William Tumblesome

Churchwardens

1. Thomas Monke: se.
2. John Pawlinge: se.

Collectors

3. Symon Dudsonne
4. John Pencotte: ju.

Constables

5. John Humpheris
6. Thomas Monke. Ju

These six men beinge officers for the above namned Townde of Blacke-Borton did take the protestation before his majesties Justices at Woodstocke the: 14th day of this present February Anno : 1641.

*[**Assessment.** Membrane 11, following on from Kelmscott. This is from a detached scrap, very decayed and mostly illegible.]*

Black Burton

...... Hungerford, Esqr., £6.10s.
...., Doctor of Divinitie, £1.
[William] Trotman, gen., £2.15s.
Margery[?] Smyth, vid., 10s.
...., gen., 10s.

[The assessment for Black Bourton probably continues on Membrane 12. However, the top half of this is very decayed, faded and mostly illegible. Some names might be legible, but the decay is too bad to transcribe them.]

Sum. £20.0.0.

BRADWELL or BROADWELL

[f.13, in three columns]

***Bradwell** Com. Oxon*

The names of the Inhabitants of the parish of Bradwell Comt. Oxon and of Philkins and Holwell in the same parish, that hath taken the Protestation [121]

[f.13, col. 1]
John Field
William Stevens
Richard Goodinough
Wm. Dawes
Richard Fletcher
Thomas Cripps
Francis Allan
Wm. Vernum
John Allin
Oliver Welseburne
Francis Whiting
William Woodard
Ralphe Hughson
Thomas Brant
John Vernum
George Callis
Francis Day
Wm. Day
John Parsons
Thomas Neale
Thomas Hall
Robert Vernum
Thomas Callis
Richard Bowle
Thomas Maverley
Anthony Lanchberry
Ambrose Hickes jun:
Edward Winchcombe
Richard Vernum
Thomas Turner
Richard Simpson
Simon Hamlin
John Giles
John Huckes
Wm. Morton
Robert Allin
Richard Adams
Thomas Merry
Thomas Radburne
John Merry
Wm. Merry
Richard Merry
Simon Galloway
Richard Genner
James Fisher
Edward Hickes

[f.13, col. 2]
Edward Walrond
John Tuckewell
Thomas Woofe
Wm. Hickes
John Tey
Thomas Farmer
Silvester Giles
Wm. Goodinough
John Cripps
John Wooffe
Thomas Foard
Robert Hamlin
Francis Baily
Giles Larner
Wm Hulet
Simon Maverley
Wm. Stickle
Richard Bagget
James Charleton
Martin Turner
John Steward
John Galloway
Wm. Robinson
Robert Hamlin
Sim: Hamlin Jun:
James Purbreake
John Hughes Sen:
Wm. Burbage
Thomas Bromfield
John Hamlin
John Pullin
Hugh Robinson
Ambrose Hickes sen:
Wm. Callis
Richard Charleton
John Hames
Thomas Giles
Simon Maberley sen:
Thomas Woodward
Walter Bush
Edward Turner
William Turner sen:
Wm Turner jun:
Roger Pierson
Thomas Hulet
Thomas Bartlet
Thomas Goodinough

[f.13, col. 3]
Francis Maverley
Thomas Franklin
John Day
Thomas Mooring
Thomas Pierse
Wm. Tailor sen:
Wm. Tailor jun:
Humfry Keene
Wm. Coppin
Wm. Blocksome
Wm. George
Nathaniel Brooke
Robert Tailor
Henry Cooke
Thomas Mosse
James Tailor
Francis Vernum
Thomas Henly
John Beame
John Steward
Robert Richins
Richard Corke
Christopher Kilby

James Frethern, *Vic.*
Francis Willett
Tho: Turner
John Burdocke
Walter Harper

Bradwell

*[**Assessment.** Membrane 3, following on from Clanfield]*

William Henshall Esqr. for his lands in Bradwell, 15s.
Thomas Hampson Esqr., £1.11s.6d.
Mrs Martha Hampson, vid., £2.16s.3d.
Mary Goodinough, vid., £1.7s.
Margery Whiting, vid., 11s.3d.
Elizabeth Goodinough, vid., 6s.9d.
Elizabeth Day, vid., 3s.6d.
Elizabeth Steward, vid., 2s.3d.
Elizabeth Startupp, vid., 4s.6d.
Ann Steward, vid., 2s.3d.
Jane Parsons, vid., 2s.3d.
Walter Bush, 9s.
John Burdock. 9s.
Robert Burdock, 5s.
John Allen, 2s.3d.
Thomas Woodward, gen., 6s.
Henry Goodinough, 5s.
Edward Goodinough, 10s.
Walter Harper, 2s.6d.
William Vernam, 2s.
Ralph Hewson, 1s.6d.
Richard Dawes, 2s.
James Fritherne, clr., 6s.
Francis Willett, and Edmond Sirrill, for pt. of the parsonage, 6s.8d.
Ambrose Sacheverill, gen., for pt. of the same parsonage, 13s.4d.
Francis Willett, 11s.3d.
Anthony Lainchbory, 4s.6d.
Francis Hawkins, clr., 9s.
Thomas Hall, 2s.6d.
Martha Symmons , vid., 8s.
John Burdock, 2s.

Some totall is £14.0.0.

Holwell

*[**Assessment.** Membrane 13, following on Asthall and Asthalleigh.]*

Thomas Hampson, Esqr., 9s.2d.
Charles Trinder, gen., £1.6s.6d.
William Taylor, 3s.
Symon Yarneton, 6d.
John Godfrey, gen., 6s.5d.
Elizabeth Cleveley, 5s.5d.
Thomas Peirs, 3s.
Henry Cooke, 3s.
William George, 3s.

Soma total, £3.0.0.

Filkins

*[**Assessment.** Membrane 3 continued, following on Broughton Poggs.]*

James Fritherne, clr. of Filkins, 6s
Thomas Hampson, esqr., 4s.8d.
Francis Willett, gen., & *[name erased]*, gen., [?]14s.
Thomas Turner, [?] *[figures are faded for this and subsequent entries]*
James Purbrick, [?]s.8d.
Robert Burdock, [?]s.8d.
Thomas Woodward, gen., [?]s.8d.
Mary Charleton, vid., [?]s.8d.
William Merry, 2s.4d.
Martin Turner, 2s.4d.

[End of membrane 3. Membrane 4 is missing. It probably contained the assessments for the remainder of Filkins, possibly two other places, and the commencement of Aston and Cote.]

BRIZE NORTON [86]

[f.14r, in three columns]

Brise-Norton
Feb. 24: 1642

The names of the parishioners of Brise-Norton, alias Norton-Broyne, in the County of Oxon, that have taken the protestation:

[f.14r, col. 1]
Martin Royse: *Clarke*
John Moulder *Constable*
Churchwardens:
Edward Boole,
John Flecher
Over-seers of the poor:
Richard Norden,
Robert Weston
These are householders:
Toby Summers
William Bowle
Thomas Humfris sen:
Leonard Forde
Thomas Bolt
John Beckingsayle
George Eatman
William Greene
Thomas Howse
John Rutter
John James
Thomas Haseley
Thomas Allen
Thomas Whyting
Thomas Huggins
Thomas Wayte
Andrew Dixe
William Lake
Richard Hony
John Robbinson
Henry Humfris sen.
Henry Humfris jun:
John Gladden
George Acres
David Eatman
John Cotmore
John Parret
Roger Dodswell
Henry Cockhead
Steaven Dolton
William Buckingam
Richard Tackly
William Miles
[f.14r, col. 2]
Henry Cotmore
John Creeke
William Bartlet
John Humfris
John Greeneaway
John Tanner
Thomas Smith sen:
Thomas Smith jun:
Robert Rose
Hen. Bolt
Henry Anston
Thomas Humfris jun:
William Butler
John Haukeings
John Warde
William James
William Hibbert
Robert Hibbett
Henry Wheler
Christopher poulton *[sic]*
Robert Battin
Edward Bolt
Anthony Collet
These are householders sonnes:
Roger Summers
John Bolt
Richard Cotmore
William Rose
Thomas Beckingsayle
Charles Eatman
George Eatman jun:
Thomas Humfris min'
Robert Banham
Thomas Tommas
Henry Smith
Rowland Maxwell
Richard Anston

[f.14r, col. 3]
These are their Servants:
John Tayler
John Curre
William Westly
John Hickes
Richard Wayte
Robert Greeneworth
Richard Harison

The Names of the parishioners of Brise-Norton that refuse to take the protestation.

Mr. Thomas Greenwood Sen
Mr. Thomas Greenewood jun
Mr. Richard Todkill
William Linee
These 4 are recusants

*[**Assessment.** Membrane 12, following on from Black Bourton. Although the top part is very decayed, the lower part, covering Brize Norton, is in much better state and legible.]*

Brize Norton

The Lady Ann Wenman, £2.10s.
Thomas Greenwood, gen., recusant, £5.12s.
Thomas Greenwood, predict, for the ....[?] he farmeth of Mr Tempest, 10s.
Mr Doctor Wood, £2.4s.
[blank] Smyth, gen., 18s.
[blank] Hollyday, gen. 6s.
Richard Tadkine, recusant, for his goods, 3s.
[blank] Pokings, gen., for the like, 4s.
Richard Norden, 12s.
Robert Weston, 8s.

Thomas Humphry, 4s.6d.
Thomas Boult, 3s.
Edward Boule, 9s.
John Beckinghall [Beckingsayle], 5s.
[blank] Halesley, vid., 1s.6d.
Robert Glading[?], 4s.6d.
Thomas Howse, 1s.6d.
[blank] Cotmore, vid., 1s.6d.
[blank] [..]urst, vid., 1s.
William Greene, 1s.6d.
Tobias Summers, 8s.
Henry Cotmore, sen., 1s.
William James, 1s.
[blank] Enston, vid., 1s.6d.
John Fletcher, 1s.
John Rutter, 2s.6d.
William Bartlett, 1s.
William Bowle, 1s.
John Ward, 1s.
Henry Humphry, jun., 1s.

[Membrane 13. In contrast to membranes 7 to 12, this is in good condition and legible throughout.]

George Yateman, 6d.
Thomas Huggins, 6d.

Soma total £16.0.0.

Thomas Greenewood, gen., recusant, his surplusage money, £6.2s.
Richard Tadkine, gen., recusant, 3s.
Ellin Messenger, servant to Mr Greenwood, her surplusage & p poll, 2s.8d.
William Lyngin, servant the like, 2s.8d.
Thomas Greenwood, Jun., gen., recusant, p poll, 2s.8d.

[Broadwell - see page 14]

BROUGHTON POGGS [38]

[f.15r, single column]

***Broughton Poggs** in Bampton Hundred Oxon:*

These have taken the protestation

Drew Greenhalft
Robert Thomas
John Hathaway
John Greene
Richard Pearson the elder
Thomas Clarke
John Newberrie
Thomas Arden
Richard Thomas
Thomas Allen
John Legg
James Wallinger
John Stoakes
Richard Cox
John Parrat
Thomas Compton
Richard Foreshewe
Thomas Thomas
Thomas Cox
William Overberrie
Richard Pearson thyonger
Thomas Jeffry
Henrie Newberrie
William Clare
John Russell
Francis Kinge
Thomas Allen thyonger
John Greenhalft
Thomas Tuckwell
Richard Waine
Francis Bignell
Henrie Simson

Tho: Hornsey, *Rector*
Henry Thomas, Rich Humfrys, *Churchw'*
Edward Elderton, Andrew Jeffry, *Overseers*
Robt Burdocke, *Constable*

*[**Assessment.** Membrane 3, following Bradwell.]*

***Broughton** [Poggs]*

Arthur Mowse, esqr., of Broughton, £2.10s.
John Fettiplace, esqr., for Leamill farme, £2.10s.
[*name erased* - Thomas] Hornesey, clr., for the p'sonage, £1.3s.6d.
Ambrose Shepperd, gen., 3s.
Robert Burdock, 5s.
Robert Thomas, 5s.
Richard Pearson, 5s.
John Newberry, 4s.
Drewe Greenhalf, 3s.
Alce Jefferyes, vid., 4s.
William Turner, 4s.
John Hathaway, 1s.6d.
Thomas Allen, 2s.6d.
Richard Thomas, 1s.[?]

Suma total £8.0.0.

BURFORD (incl. **Upton** and **Signet**) [373]

[f.16r, in three columns]

Burforde

A catalogue of the Names of All the Inhabitants in the towne and parish of Burford in the Countie of Oxon' being males from 18 years old and upward who have taken the Protestation.

[f16r, centred]

Christopher Glyn, *Vic:*
Richarde Veysey, Henry Hayter, John Peirce, *Churchwardens*
John Hughes, John Clark junior, *Constables*
Ed: Allen, Willm Hayter, *Overseers*
David Hughes sen', George Watkins, *Bayliffes*
Thomas Silvester
William Barthollomew
Paule Silvester
John Clark senior
Nathaniel Noble
Simon Ward, *churchwarden*
Edmond Semely
Richard Sindry
John Tayler

[f.16r, col. 1]

East W[ard] [98]

Thomas Silvester Jun'
John Jelliman
Tho: Powell
Symon Cowborne
John Crosse
Henry Huggins
John Dallinn
Richard Andrewes
John Andrewes
Robte Andrewes
Roger Daniel
Robte Haynes
Tho: Silvester Jn'
Paule Silvester
Joseph Nichols
Nathan Seaborne

John Lyfollie
John Hanns Jun'
Tho: Baggs
Wm: Kelby

John Huntt
Tho: Silvester tayler
Wm. Peisley
Tho: Barton
John Knight
Michael Knight
Richard Bartholomew
Wm. Preedy

[f.16r, col. 2]

Abraham Bartholomew
John Batholomew
Tho: Minchin
Henry Williams
Symon Haynes
Tho. Parsons
Richard Thorpe

Richard Yate
Robert Serrell
Martin Belcher
Francis Mihaell
Robert Davis
Tho: Haynes sen'
William Norgrove
Tho: Morris Jun'
Richard Hauks Jn'
John Hardinge
Daniel Dicks
Christopher Hayward
Richard Harris
Michael Nicholls
Richard Miles
Richard Syndry Ju'
Tho: Syndry
Wm. Kempe
Rice Cooke

[f.16r, col. 3]

Robert Newman
Symon Francklin
William Tayler
Jonathan Tayler
Tho: Francklin
Wm. Hobbs
Richarde Yates vic.
Stephen Yates
John Kempster
Richard Crosse
John Nunney
Symon Hayter
Robert Goffe
Richard Hiatt
Richard Buckingham
Wm. Buckingham
Tho: Perry
Richard Haucks sen'
Tho: Horssman
John Hawcks
Tho: Tayler shepard
William Sessions
Griffin Dubber
Robert Straford
John Jessett
Thomas Tunckes
John Thorpe
Tho: Grundy

[f.16v, col. 1]

Symon Partridge
John Dawson
John May
John Thomas
Edward Norgrove
Richard Dawson
John Wells
Richard Cripps
Symon Hughes
Andrew Davis
Ralph Hickes
Nicholas Carter
John Tayler
Robert Hardinge
John Wilkins
Robert Symons

98

Westwarde [92]
[f.12v, col. 1 continued]
Richard Thorne
John Bray
John Westmacote
Geo: Greenhill
Edward Greenhill
John Combes
John Tayler
Humfrey Greene
William Foster
John Savage
John Legg
Robert Pattricke
Thomas Bray
Willm Rodes
Symon Rodes
Richard Gladden
Wm. Kinge
Wm. Minchin
Wm. Lardner
Zachary Jelliam
John Eve
Tho: Eve
Andrew Lyfolly
Wm. Baylies
John Scriven
John Bradford
Robert Symons
John Hodges
Richard Rose
Edmund Appleton

[f.16v, col. 2]
Miles Denton
Samuel Miller
Ambrose Berry
Richard Grimshawe
Robert Tayler
Richard Wiatt Jun'
Tho: Gardner sen'
Symon Smyth
Willm Smyth
John Kinge
John Bennett gent
Leonard Gardner
Tho: Smyth sen'
Tho: Smythe jun'
Tho: Randolph
Symon Randolph
William Peacock
Richard Wiatt sen
Richard Maule
John Midwinter
Anthony Biggnell
Michael Penistone
Robert Harper
John Farmer
John Saunders
Thomas Elkes
Wm. Kempster
Alexander Cooke
Walter Waker
Symon Bradshawe
John Collier
Henry Francklin

John Maior
Ansell Blanch
Robert Yates
John Goffe
Richard Tayler
Tho: Tayler
John Williams
Tho: Wilkins
Willm Lardner
Richard Carricke
Jeremiah Jelliman
Wm. Williams
Edw: Emmett
Edmund Eve
Tho: Daniel
John Daniel
Richard Levett
[f.16v, col. 3]
David Berry
Wm. Tayler sen'
Wm. Tayler surgeon
Benjamin Sessions
John Younge
Richard Peake
Alexander Stokes
Jo: Jorden Butcher
Edw: Ward
Richard Bucknell
George Thorpe
John Edwards
William Horssman
91

[f.16v, col. 3 continued]
Churchward [84]
Walter Veysey gen'
John Jorden gent
Richard Haynes
John Winstone
Edward Allen
Edmund Hickes
Ralph Holloway
Robte Hayter
John George
Wm. Jorden
Tho: Jorden
Tho: Willett
John Bennett
Edm: Munday

Henry Panter
John Woodward
Willm Weaver
John Wheeler
Richard Hayter
Phillipp Palmer
Wm: Greenway
Wm: Haynes
Tho: Cossam
John Coldinge
Wm: Veysey
Tho: Sondley sen
Tho: Sondley Jun

[f.17r, col. 1]
Richard Hewer sen'
Richard Hewer jn
David Davis
Symon Belcher
Geo: Hide sen
George Hide Jun'
Francis Sperke [?Sperks]
Symon Ward
John Warde
Francis Steward
Ralph Fletcher
John Coxe
George Palmer

Churchward *continued*
John Sanders
Wm: Sumner
Richard Hedges
Jo: Buckingham
Symon Harris
John Hiatt
Edmund Eeles
John Mason
Leonard Yate
Daniel Muncke Ju'
Wm. Lewis
James Strafford
Richard Norgrove
Mathew Winckfeild
Willm Eeles
George Hush
Wm. Faireford
John Morris
Geo: Peisley
Tho: Helme
Daniel Muncke
John Rose
John Maule
Robte Grey
Richard Lyfollie
Tho: Osman
Willm Hedges
Wm. Neale
John Osman
Richard Berry
Willm Gravanor [?Grovenor]
Tho: Danielson
Henry Hiatt
Willm Berry
Robte Berry
Tho: Keene
John Baker
Nicholas Sansam
[f.17r, col. 2]
John Boise
Tho: Smyth
Wm. Blackman
Wm. Scott
Tho: Huntt
Richard Tayler
81

[f.17r, col. 2 continued]
St. Johns warde [46]
Richard Sessions
Willm Bolton
Henry Overbury
Richard Wakefeild
Wm Coles
Richard Winstone
Robte Jorden
Phillipp Griffith
Henry Hayter
John Bolton
Tho: Miles
Edmund Badnol
Tho: Walker
Wm. Lambert
Edmund Pebworth
John Jelliman
James Burnett
Stephen Smyth
Phillipp Collins
Walter Panter
Wm. Jorden butcher
Robt Perry sen'
Robt Perry Jun'
John Hannes
Edmund Hinton
Edmund Pope
Tho: Jelliman
David Hughes Jn'
Wm. Jelliman
George Sondley
Richard Sondley
Richard Smyth
Wm. Marshall
Henry Sondley
Wm. Jorden sen'
Edmund Heminge
Michael Bancks
Francis Dukes
Edmund Younge
[f.17r, col. 3]
Giles Corbett
Tho: Jelliman
Tho: Gardner Jun'
Tho: Ricketts
Tho: Nichols
Edmund Dier
Tho: Smyth app'ntice
44

[f.17r, col. 3 continued]
Signett [9]
John Pearce
Richard Chamberlaine
Willm Tayler
Geo: Woodbridge
Tho: Archer
Robt. Hinton
John Whittington
Tho: Dawes
Robt. Richins

[f.17r, col. 3 continued]
Bury Barnes [13]
Symon Yate
Robte Yate
Tho. Sherman
Wm Carpenter
Richard Collier
Edmund Appleton sen'
Edward Freeman
Tho: Brush
Nicholas Francklin
John Francklin
Richard Francklin
Richard Eeve
Edward Newland

[f17r, col. 3 continued]
Upton [13]
Edwarde Wallis
Francis Turner
Wm. Turner
Edmund Beacham sen'
Edmund Beacham Jn'
John Hinton
Lawrence Younge
Christopher Kempster
Wm. Dumbleton
Tho: Haynes
Tho: Keare
Bartholomew Crasse
Tho: Martin, *Constable*

*[The **Assessment** for Burford was on one or more of the decayed membranes and is now lost.]*

CLANFIELD

[f.18r, in three columns]

Clanfield
the 23th of February 1641

We do certifie that according to your direction we have given the protestation with the names of all those that have taken it not anne one refusing it in witness whereunto we have for our hands the day and yeare above whriteth [95].

[f.18r, col. 1]
Hundred de Bampton

Francis More [?Mores]
Leonard Smith
Water Bennet
Richard May
John Sperinke
Antho: Pauling
John Tailer
Antho: Stevens
Syman Pauling
John Yeatman
Solo: Yeatman
John Stevens
Tho: Stevens
John Stevens
Adam Turner
Henry More [?Mores]
Henry Adames
Tho: Adames
Robert Turner
Nicolas Yeatman [sen'?]
Nicolas Yeatman [Jun'?]
Richard Yeatman
Richard Laffen
Alexander May
John May
John Laffen
Robert Laffen
John Booth
Tho: Booth
John Whithorne
Francis Whithorne
John Pearson
Tho: Pinnock
Francis Pinnock
William Wood
Simon Dier
John Goodinnough
[f.18r, col. 2]
William May
Alexander May
John Pauling
Tho: Waine
Will: Stevens
Will; Clarke
Will: Blagrove
Tho: Winchcom
Rich: Winchcom
Solo: Carpenter
Adam Heges
Rich: Goff
Siman Pauling
Tho: Curties
Solo: Clarke
Ralph Simans
Rich: Clarke
Tho: Lucket
John Lucket
Will: Porter
John Arnald
John House
Edward Duber
Tho: Duber
Roger Crass
Solo: Crass
John Tull
Will: Pauling
Ro: Franclin
Nicol: Carpenter
Tho: Carpenter
Rich: Veysey
John Sheaperd
Tho: Coles
Will: Coles
Tho: Lake
John Waine
Will: Waine
Rich: Pencot
Simon Cench
[f.19r, col. 3]
Nicholas Hules
Will: Hobbs
John Gun
Solo: Arnald
James Hill
John Lensey
Rich: Francis
John Harris
Tho: Temple [?]
Will: Yeaton
Robert Lauder
John Arnald
Tho: Barnes
Richard Hamand

Wittnesses
Phatnell Denton, *vic*
John More
Tho Blagrove, Jo: Whit, *Churchwardens*

*[**Assessment.** The transcript runs from Membrane 3. Membranes 1 and 2 were decayed and although now repaired remain almost illegible. The name of the place is lost, but comparison with the Protestation Return shows it to be Clanfield.]*

Hundred of Bampton:
Clanfield

William Taylor, 2s.2d.
John More, gen., and John Stevens, sen., for the land they held of James Saunders, 14s.7d.
Phatnell Denton, viccar, 17s.6d.
William Hedges, viccar of Bampton, 8s.9d.
Thomas Cripps, 2s.3d.
Thomas Wayne, 1s.
John Linsey, 2s.
John Wayne, 2s.
James Hill, 1s.6d.
William Porter, 3s.
Symon Pauling, jun., 1s.
John Pearson, 1s.
John White, 1s.

John Harryson., 1s.
Thomas Booth, 1s.
Robert Francklyn, 1s.
William Clarke, 1s.
Richard *[blank]*, 1s.
Thomas *[blank]*, 1s.
Richard Winchcome, 1s.
William Line[?], gen., 2s.
Thomas Addams, 2s.
John Arnold, 1s.
William [?Wai]ne, 1s.
Richard Yateman, 1s.
Henry More, 2s.2d.
Symon Pauling, 3s.2d.
John More, gen., for the land he holdeth of Sr. Edward Yates, recusant, 13s.1d.

Some totus £25.0.0.

Sr Edward Yate, Knight, recusant for this land holden by John More, gen., for surplusage money, 13s.1d.

COKETHORPE, HARDWICK and YELFORD

[f.19r, in three columns]
Cockthorpe, Hardwicke & Elford
Feb: 20th An. Do. 1641

A note of the names of every person above the age of 18 years, inhabitinge in Cockthorpe and Hardwicke & Elford in the County of Oxon whoe have taken the protestation tendered unto them by
Robert Lydall, *Minister*,
Thomas James,
Roger Hawkins,
Churchwardens. [88]

[f.19r, col. 1]
Michaell Rogers & Jone his wife
John Rogers & Elizabeth his wife
Richard Edwardes
John Bullocke Senior
John George & Anne his wife
Thomas Rawlins & Alice his wife
John Filkins & Elizabeth his wife
Francis Saunders & Martha his wife
Robert Whiteinge & Dorothy his wife
Thomas Rogers Junior
Leonard Edgerly & Anne his wife
William Edwardes & Martha his wife
Thomas Saunders & Anne his wife
Dennis Edwardes wid:
Elinor Bayly wid:
Moses Alder
Elizabeth Bayly
Thomas Alder senior
Thomas Alder junior
Elinor Alder
William Bullocke & Mary his wife
Robert Bullocke senior
Anne Bullocke
Alice Rogers wid:
Thomas Rogers senior
Mary Rogers
Hugh Ellis
Thomas Beale & Katherine his wife
[f.19r, col. 2]
Roger Hawkins & Elizabeth his wife
Jone Ellis
Jone Shurrey widd:
Margaret Bradley
John Bullocke Junior & Jone his wife
Thomas Bullocke
Robert Bullocke
William Wilkes & Jone his wife
Humphrey Slatter & Elizabeth his wife
Elizabeth Slatter wid
William Wilkes Senior & Joane his wife
Thomas James & Elizabeth his wife
Edward Templer & Elizabeth his wife
Robert Smith & Anne his wife
Marrian Hussie
Abraham Whiteinge & Elizabeth his wife
Anne Cockerell wid:
Thomas Bayly
Anne Peirson
Mary Edwardes
Margaret Smith Widd:
[f.19r, col. 3]
Thomas Camden
Margaret Hobbs
Thomas Blackhurst

[f.19r, col. 2]
Cockthorpe
John Shurry & Jane his wife
William Shurry & Sarah his wife
Thomas Smarte & Margarett his wife
Alice Smarte wid:
James Hussie & Christian his wife
Jone Hussie
[f.19r, col. 3]
John Coles
Margery Peart

*[**Assessment.** Membrane 6 continued, following Bampton and Weald.]*

Yelford and Hardwick

Ambrose Shepherd, gent., for his land there, £1.10s.
Bryan Smyth, Rector of Yelford, 3s.4d.
Richard Bayley, Esqr., 6s.
Thomas Wyatt, Doctor of Divinity, 6s.
John Franklyn, 6s.
Alice Rogers, vid., 3s.
Thomas Alder, 6s.
Francis Saunders, 6s.
William Edwards, 6s.
Thomas Rawlins, 3s.
John Rogers, 6s.
Richard Edwards, 1s.6d.
John Saunders, 1s.
Humphry Slatter, 2s.
John Bullock, sen., 4d.
John Bullock, jun., 1s.6d.
William Bullock, 1s.
John Muntayne, 2s.
Thomas James, 1s.6d.
Roger Hawkins, 1s.6d.
Bartholomew Brodley, 6d.
George Baddnoll, 6d.
Robert Whiteing, 1s.
John George, 1s.
Robert Bennett, 1s.6d.
Robert Falkoner, 1s.
Robt. Smythe, 4d.

Soma total £5.0.0.

DUCKLINGTON

[f.20r, in three columns]

Ducklington
Feb. An' Do. 1641

A note of the names of every person above the age of 18 yeares whoe have taken the protestation tendered unto them by Thomas Wiat Rector of Ducklington & Richard Ballow & John Slaymaker Churchwardens [153]

[f.20r, col. 1]
Richard Bayly & Mris Anne his wife
Thomas Wiat DD and Elizabeth his wife
Mris. Elizabeth Bayly wid:
William Bayly gent
Richard Sawyer gent. and Jane his wife
Walter Tanner and Joane his wife
Alice Trindall
William Waight and Elizabeth his wife
John Mutloe & Elizabeth his wife
Thomas Quinny Junior & Christian his wife
John Taylor & Anne his wife
Edward Dubber & Anne his wife
Robert Hughes & Martha his wife
Thomas Johnsonne & Anne his wife
Richard Tanner & Alice his wife
Bridgett Knight
William Taylor & Elinor his wife
Richard Steptoe & Elinor his wife
Henry Richardsonne & Alice his wife
John Morris & Alice his wife
Elizabeth Sexton
Joanne Cornish
William Cousens & Elizabeth his wife
[f.20r, col. 2]
Edward Allen & Dennis his wife
Jane Lydall
Charles Milton & Elizabeth his wife
Edith Sexton wid:
William Hughes senior & Margery his wife
William Hughes junior & Margarett his wife
Edward Harris & Jane his wife
Robert Harris & Dennis his wife
Thomas Burnett & Lettice his wife
Thomas Cornish & Margarett his wife
John Slaymaker & Jane his wife
William Harris & Margery his wife
Edmund Harris & Margery his wife
Phillipp Locton & Dorothy his wife
John Sissons & Anne his wife
Henry Ballowe
Richard Ballowe & Constance his wife
Arthur Steptoe
Thomas Tanner & Mary his wife
Elizabeth Steptoe
William Steptoe
Martine Johnsonne
Gillian Johnsonne
[f.20r, col. 3]
John Daye & Margery his wife
Steeuen Parloe
Edward Deane & Rebecca his wife
Edward Green & Silvester his wife

William Cornish & Joane his wife
Edward Tanner & Elizabeth his wife
Thomas Quinny senior & Barbara his wife
Richard Hopkins & Anne his wife
Nicholas Hopkins & Martha his wife
Edward Thorneton & Blanch his wife
Phillipp Lane & Katharine his wife
John Quinny
Mris. Martha Wiat
Henry Greene
Thomas Rowman
Katherine Outfeild
Margery Tanner wid:
Thomas Stockly
Hester Harris
Mary Pope
Simon Ives
Alexander West
William Cockerell
Gilbert Curson
Thomas Cornish Junior
Laurence Tanner
Thomas Tanner Junior
Mary Rawlins
[f.20v]
Christopher Lord & Elizabeth his wife
John Powell & Susanna his wife
Thomas Lord & Margarett his wife
William Tawman
James Paulin
Thomas Mitchell
Elizabeth Wilkes
Thomas Sadler
Mary Bennett
Barbara Dyer
Anne Danbury
Thomas Taylor
Thomas Burdsey
Richard Alder
Anne Quinny
Elizabeth Bull
Margery Dringe
John Thomas
Elizabeth Coxe
Elizabeth Prater
John Locton
Anthony Mooreton
Ursula Norton
Elizabeth Sadler
James Maior
Edmund Bartlett
Sibbilla Cooke
Katherine Harris
Barbara Harris
William Smith
Henry Allin

[f.21, blank]

*[The **Assessment** for Ducklington was on one of the decayed membranes and is now lost.]*

[Filkins - see page 14]

GRAFTON and RADCOT

[f.22]

Grafton and Rotct [26]
February the 18th 1641

Hundred de Bampton

According to your direction I have given the protestation with a not of their names not anie one refusing it in witness where unto I have sett my hand:
John More

Robert Meysey
John Meyey
Henry Keeble
Robert Meysey
Robert Meyey
William Ford
William Ford
Sacharia Hall
Tho: Keeble
John Keeble
Tho: Meyey
John Meysey
Tho: Blagrove
John Francis
John Francis
Francis Rallins
Robert Broad
Tho: House
Robert Francis

Rotcott

George Cleeter
John Cleeter
Francis Cleeter
John Meyey
Robert Clarke
John Bayley

*[The **Assessment** for Grafton and Radcot was probably on one of the decayed membranes and is now lost.]*

[Hardwick - see page 22; Holwell - see page 14.]

KELMSCOTT

[f.23r, in two columns]

***Kelmescot** in the parish of Bradwell Cont' Oxon'*

The names of the Inhabitants of Kelmescott that have taken the Protestation [35]

[f.23r, col. 1]
John Hughes, *Curat*
Phillip Turner
Thomas Stevens
Daniell Warwicke
Francis Simmes
William Turner
Daniel Warwicke
Francis Graine
Thomas Hulles
William Farmer
Thomas Coxe
Thomas Davis
John Glaze
Richard Turner, senior
John Hucks
Richard Turner
Edward Hucks

[f.23r, col. 2]
William Turner
John Snowshill
Thomas Baily
William Smith
William Lewis
William Davis
William Francis
Edward Hall
Henry Edwards
John Linne
Zachary Hall
Edward Govers

Non refused this protestation

James Frethern, *Vic:*
John Hughes, *Curat:*
Phillip Turner, William Turner, *Churchwardens*
Thomas Stevens, *Constable*
Thomas Hulls, *Overseer of the poore*

Non refused this protestation. 1641

*[**Assessment.** Membrane 11. Kelmscott follows Kencot, and concludes this badly decayed membrane. Its entry is all too decayed to read, but there is a detached scrap, also decayed, from which the following is partially legible.]*

Kelmscott

Thomas ......, *[?sum]*
Thomas S[tevens], *[?sum]*
Francis[?] Ramlas[?], *[?sum]*
John French, the elder, *[?sum]*
William Feare[?], *[?sum]*
John Taylor, ..., Chapman, *[?sum]*
Thomas Cox, *[?sum]*
[Za]ch[ery] Hall, 2s.6d.

Suma total £8.0.0.

KENCOT

[f.24r, in two columns]

***Kencot** Coun' Oxon' February 16 1641*

The names of the Inhabitants of Kencot that have taken the Protestation [32]. Here are the names of all the Inhabitants of Kencot Coun' Oxon', above the age of eighteene yeares.

[f.24r, col. 1]
Anthony White
John Blagrove
Francis Tailor
Robert Breakespeare
John Kerse
Richard Goodale
Edward Scolter
John Monke
William Turner Jun:
William Hulet
Adam Turner Jun:
Richard Gilman
Thomas Haines
Phillipp Breakespeare

[f.24r, col. 2]
Christopher Pawlin
Thomas Smith
Christopher Aire
James Godman
Robert Quinch
William Cowly
Thomas Monke
John Tailor
William Tailor
John Kilby
William Turner Sen:
Andrew Pierse
William Yateman

James Frethern, *Parson*
Francis Turner, *Overseer*
Henry Goodnoughe, Adam Turner, *Churchwardens*
Francus Turner, *Constable*

*[For **Assessment**, see page 26.]*

*[**Assessment.** Membrane 11, following Standlake. This part is in very poor condition.]*

Kencott

James F[rethern][?], *[?sum]*

[The next four surnames are torn or faded]
John ......, *[?sum]*
James ......, *[?sum]*
Francis ......, *[?sum]*
F..... ......, *[?sum]*
Henry Goodenough, *[?sum]*
Addam Turner, *[?sum]*
John Ker[se], *[?sum]*
John Beck...[?], *[?sum]*
William ......, *[?sum]*
Anthony ....., *[?sum]*
Xpofer Pauling, *[?sum]*

Suma tot *[illegible]*

STANDLAKE

[f.25r, in two columns]

The names of all such as have taken the protestation set forth by house of Commons in our parish of Stanlake [130]

[f.25r, col. 1]
Mr. Peter Yate
Thomas Gascoigne
John Yate
John Greene
Edward Smith
Gyles Barnes
Thomas Huckwell
Robt. Fawlkner
Wm. Baker
Edward Huckwell
Robt. Floyd
Edward Shipreeve
Nicholas Walker
Wm. Perry
Wm. Bennett
Bostock Clincott
Edward White
Thomas Pawlin
Anthony Giles
Thomas Strange
John Wheeler
John White
Gyles Beacham
Richard Wright
Robt Gilbert
Allin Hill
Thomas Branch
Walter Heath
Edward Reeve
John Michell
Christopher Hosyer
Henry Green
Richard Newman
John Arbadge
Henry Brostock
Anthony Fisher
Humphrey Eaton
[f.25r, col. 2]
Robert Hilliard
John Cusson
Thomas Cusson
Peter Rowland
Richard Lamnet
Wm. Brookes
Edward Bridgman
Wm. Hart
John Mosse
Edward Tayler
Thomas Barnes
Wm. Hutchins
John Boseley
Wm. Bedwell
John Bankes
Walter West
Nicholas Huckwell
James Lucky
Henry Longworth
John Baker
James Baker
Michaell Baker
Wm. Baker
John Wheeler
John Temple
Thomas Harris
Thomas Hatt
Ralph Walker
Robt. Walker
Joseph Pawlin
Wm. Bacon
Thomas Swift
John Greene
Richard Perry
Toby Collier
Richard Wait
Richard Pawlin
John Alder
August: Dod
[f.26r, col.1]
William Mylls
William West
Nicholas Gerring
Henry Parmee
Wm. Reeve
Humphrey Allin
Thomas Bullock
Wm. Allridg
Wm. Hart Jun:
John Munting
Richard Dod
Peter Townsend
Richard Tucker
Hugh Pead
Stephen Allin
George Calcott
Arthur Quench
Hugh Smith
John Yate
Leonard Walker
John Myles
Wm. Crips
Henry Hall
Nicholas Sherife
John Hanwell
Thomas Mawll
Francis Richins
Hugh Saunders [?Sawnders]
Richard Smith
Thomas Walker
John Edgerly
William Keinton
Thomas Huggins
John Hale
Edward Townsend
Jeffray Cooke
Edward Mayne

James Luckey
John Danvers
Robt Bryan
Phillip Allen
Richard Allen
John Carter
John Impe

[f.26r, col. 2]
recusants [who] have taken it:
Richard Hyde
William Wind
Jane Geare

All these whose names are above written have taken the protestation set out by the house of Commons neither doe we know any in our parish that refused it.

Nicholas Shorter, *Minist:*
Robert Wyatt, *Constable*
William Townsend, *Const:*
Christopher Harris, Giles Barnes, *Collectors*
Alexander Tempell
Richard Weale

*[**Assessment.** Membrane 10, lower half. The upper half is faded and illegible, as are the preceding two membranes.]*

Standlake and 'Brittenton' *[Brighthampton, but see also under Bampton: Brighthampton, page 12]*

The lady *[blank]* Stonehouse, for her land here, £3.5s.
Sr. Edward Cross[?], recusant, 3s.
Mr *[blank]* F.....ock[?], 15s.
Mr *[blank]* Rowen[?], gent., £1.10s.
Samuell Du..e, gen., 10s.
Richard [Hyde], gen., recusant, £1.15s.

[The next seven entries are badly faded and illegible, except for the sums collected: 15s., 9s., 3s., 2s., 4s., 3s., 3s.; the eighth entry, also illegible, is 'for goods, 6d.'; staining and partial legibility continues for the next few entries.]
...... Perry[?], 1s.6d.
...... Allen, 6d.
Thomas H[uck]well, 3s.
William Roberts[?], for goods, 1s.
Walter Heath, for goods, 1s.
Joan Quench, 1s.
Thomas Branch[?], 2s.4d.
Samuell Heath, 2s.
Thomas Harris, 2s.3d.
Edward Huckwell, for goods, 1s.
Robert Churchill, 3s.
Richard .....he[?], for goods, 1s.
John Greene, for goods, 1s.6d.
John White, for goods, 6d.
...... West, for goods, 1s.
Edward Taylor, for goods, 6d.
Phillip Allen, 2s.
John Carter, 6s.6d.
James Luckey, 6d.
Robert Wyatt, for goods, 3s.
Edward Smyth, 4s.
Richard Weale, 1s.6d.
Henry Weale, 2s.6d.
Mathew Larke[?], 8d.
Peter Townsend, 9d.
John Bennett, 9d.
[blank] Pawling, gent.[?], 2s.
Gyles Barnes, 1s.
Edward Mayne, gen., for goods, 3s.
Margery Townsend, 2s.
John Hopkins, 12s.
Mrs [*blank: probably* Dorothy] Gascoigne, for goods, 3s.6d.
Nicholas Gerring, for goods, 10s.6d.
William Mills, for goods, 6d.
Richard Dodd, for goods, 3s.
Peter Yate, gen., 5s.
Alexander Temple, 1s.
Alice Broadstock, 1s.
Jeffery Cooke, 3s.
Allen Hill, for goods, 6d.
Richard Church, 2s.
Richard Tanner, 3s.
William Perry, for goods, 1s.6d.
Xpofer Hosier, 1s.6d.
John Yate, for goods, 2s.

[Membrane 11. This is torn, faded and stained.]
[torn] Townsend, 1s.
[torn] Saunders, *[? sum]*
[torn] Yate, gen., 1s.
[torn] Saunders, 6d.
[torn: Robert?] Falk[ener], 1s.6d.
[torn] Gi...., 1s.6d.
...topher *[may be Christian name]*, 3s.
[torn] Dau..., 2s.
Willm. Aldridg, 1s.
Richard Farr, 6s.
[faded] Wayt, 1s.
[faded] Tanner[?], 2s.
...., 6d.
...... Barford[?], *[? sum]*
...... Co...., 6d.

Suma total £16.0.0.

[The remaining part of this membrane becomes progressively more decayed, torn, faded, stained and illegible.]

Sr. Edward Yate, Kt., recusant, his ... *[? sum]*
Richard Hade, gen., recusant, *[? sum]*
William Wind, recusant ..., 2s.8d.
Richard Hide[?], ... *[? sum]*
Jane G[eare], recusant, servant to Mr C....

WESTWELL

[f.27r. Single column.]

***Westwell** in the County of Oxo' & Hundred of Bampton*

The names of those which upon Wednesday (after evening prayer) took the Protestation in the Parish Church of Westwell being the 23rd of Febr. Ao. Dni. 1641 [33]

Being the full number of all mankind above the age of 18 yeares in the whole Parish.

Thomas Davis, *Curate*
William Swayt
George Peesly
Thomas Parrham
John Coppine
David Cooke
David Berry
William Alder
Robert Gossen
John Bye
Thomas Wiggins
Walter Sessions
John Clarke
Thomas Cooke Jn:
Edmund Wallis
Thomas Sessions
George Bagget
William Whitehead
Giles Wright
Henry Nappe
Edward Eagles
John Hancockes
Thomas Parrham iun.
Richard Webbe
John Humfreyes
Robert Berry
David Chadwell
Anthony A Bevan *[the 'A' may imply a second name]*
Robert Offlet
Thomas Sansam

None refusing

In the presence of
Thomas Fletcher, *Church-warden*
Thomas Cooke, *Constable*
John Eagles, *Overseer for the poor*
Who all tooke the Protestation before Justices at Woodstock.

*[**Assessment.** Membrane 13, following on Holwell.]*

Westwell

Richard Gardener, Doctor of Devinity, 10s.
Charles Trynder, gen., 16s.
William Swayte, 6s.
Ellinor Berry, 4s.1d.
George Peisley, 2s.
Thomas Fletcher, 2s.
Thomas Parham, 3s.4d.
John Coppin, 2s.4d.
David Cooke, 1s.8d.
David Berry, 2s.
John Eccles, 1s.
Symon Wynter, 3s.
Richard Lapworth, 1s.11d.
John Bye, 3d.
Thomas Wickins, 5d.
William Alder, 5d.
Thomas Cooke, Sen., 10d.
Walter Sessions, 1s.8d.
Thomas Sessions, 1s.
Robert Goffe, 4d.

Soma total, £3.0.0.

WITNEY

[ff.28-32, in two columns

***Witney** in Com' Oxon'.*
Feb.28.1641

These whose names are underwritten have taken the Protestation in Witney, Hayley, Crawley, Curbridge. [610]

[f.28r, col. 1]
Mr. Robert Brice
Mr. William Brice
Francis Wiltshire
Richard Peisly
Tho: Chandler
Will: Watson
Tho: Werge
Richard Brice
Moses Peirson
Tho: Durbridge
Adam Buttler
Edward Broaderton
Isaac Mayow
Stephen Burges
Andrew Rooke
James Darby
Jo: Rancle
Timothy Greene
Henry Giles
George Busby
Tho: Badnall
Tho: Kerse
Alexander Wood
William Taunt
Rice Carpenter
George Crump
Luke Davis
Robert Wily
Tho: Crofts
Francis Feild
Richard Abell
Jo: Fatherson
Richard Oakly
Tho: Bowman
George Parret Se:
George Parrett ju.
[f.28r, col. 2]
Simon Parrett
Francis Davis
William Purnill
Robert Bryan
Bostocke Bryan
Anthony Larden
Simon Larden
Tho: Turner
Jo: Bakers
Robert Hamlin
Richard Egerly
Tho: Munday
Ed: Ward
Tho: Ward
Hen: Constable
Rich: Hughes
William Hodson
James Hodson
William Hedges
William Smith
Charnell Horne
William Buckingham
Francis Buckingham
George Buckingham
Hugh Hill
Edward Ashfeild
Rich: Ashfield
Jo: Palmer
Edward Baldwin
Robert Tomlins
Jo: Crofts
Tho: Purton
Hen: White
Andrew White
Nathaniel Tims
Mr. Rich: Bates
[f.28v, col. 1]
Mr. George Bragg
Mr. Jo: Martin
William Gun
Ed: Goode
Tho: Kerse
Jo: Parmee
Edward Franklin
Isaac Greenoway
Richard Perkins
Francis Gibberd
George Penson
Tho: Wright
Tho: Parmee
Hen: Gardner
Tho: Lewis
Will: Lewis
Ed: Lewis
Roger Broaderton
William Carter
Walter Cowell
Rob: Wright
Francis Crosse
Jo: Townsend
George Fatherson
Abraham Robinson
Andrew White
William Stanford
Andrew Johnson
Christopher Lucas sen:
Christopher Lucas iun:
Hen: Lay
Tho: Mosely
James Mells
William Sallis
William Faulkner
Paul Hanchurch
Jo: Robinson
Rich: Showell
John Gould
Tho: Harris
Rich: Showell
Will: Showell
[f.28v, col. 2]
William Dirrill
Will: Giles
Jo: Harris iu'
Jo Lissutt
William Ballow
Tho: Steptoe
Rich: Lay
Nicholas Werge
Tho: Ditton
Jos: Gibbons
Jo: Combes
Jo: Harwood
Rob: Terry
David Sparrowhauke
Tho: Sparrowhauke
Tho: Foster
Jo: Peake
Will: Warcroft
Simon Povey

Edward Acres
Will: Page
Tho: Page
Nicholas Page
William Martin alias Varney
Will: Lardner
Phil: Box
Will: Russell
Edward: Gardner
Edward Gardner
Tho: Brice
Will: Lucas
Edw: Simmons
Will: Aram
Jo: Bishop
Rich: Bishop
Will: Wood
Jo: Purser
Rich: Harwood Sen
William Harwood
William Paine
Rob. Yate
[f.29r, col. 1]
Rich: Harwood iu'
Rich: Bud
Tho: Bedwell
Matthew Horne
Jo: Greene
Jo: Burcott
Tho: Horne
Rich: Parker
Hen: Gould
Tho: Saunders
Ed: Tipper
Hen: Wheeler Sen
Hen: Wheeler iun
Leonard Morris
Edward Haines
Walter Jefferies
Ed: Baker
Anthony Beesell
Rich: Gray
Jo: Dyer alias Humphreys
Tho: Harris
Jo: Blake
Ed. Blake
Jo Collett
Tho: King
Hen: Batson
Tho: Fettiplace
Jo: Hill
Jo: Bishop
Will: Canning
Tho: Jorden
Matthew Boyse
Stephen Cotes
Jo: Burkett
Will: Oakley
Rich: Purvill
Nich: Peirson
Tho: White
Tho: Brice
[f.29r, col. 2]
Henry Humphreyes alias Dyer sen:
Henry Humphryes iun:
Rich: Humphreyes
Humphrey Beacham
Will Saunders
Jo: Saunders
Rich: Ashfeild
Hen: Ashfeild
Ed: Ashfeild
Rich: Ashfeild
William Beacham
Will: Hitchman
Rob: Werge
Walter Fanch
Rich: Cotes
Jo: Church
Will: Levitt
Rich: Purser
Tho: Gadbury
Jo: Maior
Rich: Baker
William Purser
Rich: Rawlins
Tho: Hill
Will: Wilton
Tho: Wilton
Hen: Breakspeare
Peter Paine
William Paine
Simon Hill
Leonard Slattford
Jo: Baker
Jo: Cleaver
Ed: Cleaver
Nicholas Constable
Jo: Wright
Will: Constable
Jo: Gun
Jo: Buttler
Tho: Andrewes
Rich: Ford
[f.29v, col. 1]
Rob: Baker sen:
Rob: Baker iun:
Jo: Kimble
Jo: Crosse
Tho: Stratton
Walter Clerke
Richard Werge
Jo: Osman
Ralph Werge
Tho: Hudson
Rich: Cheyny
Michael Martin
Tho: Martin
William Webly
Tho: Deacon
Jo: King
Will: Compton
Rich: Slatter
Tho: Collier
Rob: Meese
Justinian Hicks
William Smith
Richard Wainewright
Tho: Dudly
Ed: Druce
Ed: Hawkins
Jo: Paine
Tho: Paine
Tho: Sexton
Rich: Wiatt
Will: Rawlins
Simon Whithorne
Rich: Wheeler
William Biffin
Rich: Lewis
Rich: Stanford
Roger Wright
Jo: Dix
Rich: Nurth
Richard Slatter
[f.29v, col. 2]
Leonard Cox
Roger Cox
Andrew Cox
Mr. Tho: Granger
Mr. Lanc: Granger
Edward Granger

Tho: Crips
Edward Rider
Tho: Purnill
Hen: Werge
Ed. Bull
William Hunt
Rob: Faulkner
Rob: Buttler
Jo: Williams
Ed: Williams
Tho: Craknell
Tho: Yate
Jo: Read
Tho: Price
Jo: Augustin
William Dutton
Rich: King
Rob: Pytt
Tho: Hodson
Jo: Horton
Jo: Steare
Tho: Sturridge
Tho: Ditton
Jo: Harris. Sen
Jo: Harris. iun
Will: Cove
Jo: James
Rich: Sheapheard
Ed: Rudgate
Jo: Kimble
Jo: Tanner
Jo: Thomas
Simon Ensor
Tho: Tanner
Francis Stanford
Tho: Smart
Nicholas Robinson
[f.30r, col. 1]
Jo: Garlike
Jo: Rybone
James Blew
Tho: Peirson
Rich: Bechee
Richard Day
Will: Randall
Tho: Rimes
Will: Eleman
Hen: Bird
Jo: Thomas
Justinian Armsden
Edward Hanchurch
Nicholas Cuff
William Cuff
Tho. Hanchurch
Tho: Dutch sen
Tho: Dutch iu
William Werge
Rich: Dutton
Rob: Patricke
William Varney
William Dutton
Jo: Boyse
Hen: Neale
Tho: Rudge
William Hodson
Richard Lawrence
Jo: Shaw
Rich: Lawrence
Rich: Purnill
Rich: Hames
Tho: Titcombe
Tho: Taylour
James Hodgskin
Rob: Hodgskin
Tho: Collier
Simon Arthur
Stephen Basely
[f.30r, col. 2]
Peter Rancle
Griffin Hayes
Ed: Fathery
Jo: Webly
Jo: Collett se.
Rob: Meares
Jo: Buttler
William Wright
Tho: Buckingham
Jo: Stephens
Jo: Bud
Will: Stephens
Rich: Ditton
Will: Selman
Ed. Martin
Roger Hunt
Tho: Hemmings
Giles Hart
Philip Potter
Tho: Walker
Rich: Day
Rich: Smith
Mr. Francis Brice
Will: Colin
Rich: Hodson
Jo: Peach
Mathew Bull
Anthony Hollyman
Tho: Baker
Rich: Ashfeild
Rich: Long
Leonard Goode
Nicholas Shorter
Jo: Shorter
Hen: Ayres
Jo: Harris
Rob: Bryan sen
Will: Bryan
Tho: Bryan
Rich: Fuller
Jo: Yower
[f.30v, col. 1]
Michael Foster
Tho: Werge
Ed: Hankes
Jo: Powell
Nicholas Peirson
Giles Selman
Jo: Parker
Ed: Cleaver
Tho: Webly
Will: Chamberlane
Will: Surrill
Jo: Hemming
Marke Tims
Rob: Wright
Tho: Cracknell
Tho: Yate
Hen: Ward
Rich: Johnson
Jo: Garlike
George Ward
Nicholas Cunny
Ed: Williams
Francis Impe
Jo: Trinder
Tho: Buckingham
Jasper Hicks
Jo: Humphreys
Francis Hone
Jo: Colsborne
Mr. Tho: Yate
Charles Brambsby
Rob: Joyner
Rich: Randle

Rich: Farmer
Francis Farmer
Andrew Dolton
[f.30v, col. 2]
Francis Old
Richard Eves
Nich: Hopkins
Rob: Greene
George Giles
Rob: Coles
Will: Webb
Andrew Hore Sen:
Andrew Hore iun:
Tho: Moulder
George Hart
Arthur Kite
John Wright
Richard Wright
Will: Wright
Alexander Richardson
William Tanner
Tho: Langson
Jo: Fisher
Will: Skinner
Humphrey Skinner
Jo: Mills
Will: Steward
George Crosse
Arthur Adams
Jo: Herring
Robert Harris
Jo: Giles
Leonard Greene
Rob: Hawkins
Mr. Stephen Brice
Richard Smith
James Gunnis
Mr. Jo: Hampshire sen
Jo: Hampshire iun
Ed: Prince
William Kimble
Mr. George Darby
Hugh White
[f.31r, col. 1]
William Holford
Tho: Holt
Ed: Dicks
Giles Eldridge
Michael Jones sen:
William Ballow
Rich: Plat
Mich: Jones iun
Richard Jones
Henry Selman
William Wright
Rich: Wright
Hen: Terry
George Jones
Will: Pennington
Ed: Fitchett
Hen: Shurly
Simon Lardner
Tho: Pennington
Tho: Hawkins
Jo: Smith
Tho: Pennington
Rich: Cambridge
Jo: Harris
Jo: Taylour
Jo: Gouers
Tho: Jones
Tho: Alder
Beniamin Rowles
Hen: Cotton
Anthony Rowles
Will: Cope
Tho: Petty
Jo: Belcher
Tho: Horseman
Edward Day
Tho: Gibberd
[f.31r, col. 2]
Hen: Terry
Will: Gould
Charles Gould
Hen: Fitchett
Humphrey Smith
Tho: Sparrowhauke
Will: Poulton
Rich: Wells
Rich: [?] Bowman
Christofer Savory
Tho: Hitchman
Tho: Fletcher
Hen: Horne
Jo: Partlow
Jo: Crofts
Jerome Wearing
Hen: Wearing
Rob: Allen
Will: Fisher
Tho: Horton
Will: Wayte
Rob: Wayte
Hen: Horne
Nath: Horne
Francis Crosse
Hen: Hawkins
Jo: Dorne
Ed: Williams
Tho: Norton
Jo: Fitchett
Mr. Jo: Yate
Mr. Walter Yate
Jo: Miles
Hen: Smith
Ed: Maior
Rob: Letherland
Jo: Smith
Hen: Smith
[f.31v, col. 1]
Will: Smith
Jo: Smith
Ed: Constable
Tho: Nevill
Jeremy Biggars
Jo: Crofts
Rich: Allen
Rich: Bignell
Rich: Smith
Jo: Holloway
Jo: Veale
Hen: Smith
Will: Smith
Tho: Michell
Alexander Michell
Richard Smith
Rich: Hiatt sen:
Rich: Hiatt iun:
Jo: Horne sen:
Jo: Horne iun:
Edward Horne
Richard Horne
Richard Brookes
Jer: Gould
Nicholas Vellis
William Harris
Jo: Bew
Jo: Lockton
George Fuller
Jo: Kary
Nick: Purnill
Ed: Jacob

Jo: Godfrey
Tho: Fletcher
Jo: Millard
Rich: Taylour
[f.31v, col. 2]
Will: Collyburne
Rich: Butler
Jo: Clerke
Jo: Hartshorne
Ed: White
Stephen Ring
Tho: White
Justinian Hicks
Tho: Pulley
Francis Pye
Rob: Slaymaker
Will: Ayres
Roger Gunday
Tho: Sheldon
Ed: Cotes sen:
Ed: Coates iun:
Rich: Crofts
Christopher Irons
Francis Edden
Jo: Pentecroft
Christofer Fulford
Rich: Phillis
Walter Phillis
Rich: Keele
Tho: Horton
Jo: Meddops

[f.32r, in two columns]
These whose names are underwritten did not take the Protestation

[f.32r, col. 1]
Leonard Pytt: he is sicke
Ed: Pytt, sicke
Rich: Martin, sicke
Will: Foster, sicke
Rich: Galloway, lame
Alexander Gardner, lame
Ed: Stepto
Jo: Smith, old & lame
Jos: Peirce
Adam Buttler, lame
Roger Lane, old & lame

[f.32r, col.2]
Peter Rider
Jo: Babbs, sick
Ed: Hames
Tho: Gould, very old & blind

Rob: Binks, old & lame
Jo: Cotton, blind
Phil: Norton, sicke
Henry Fitchett, old & lame
Mr. Walter Yate, lame
Mr. Jo: Pridie, sicke
Mr. Francis Rathborne, Recusant

We whose name are underwritten do testifie the premises to be true.
Tho: White, *Rect: de Witney*
Thomas White, Richard Okeley, George Harte, William Holford, John Craftes, *Cunstab'*
John Parme [Parmee], William Wood, John Hamshir, Arthur Keite, *Churchw'*
Jo Yate, George Darby, Hen: White, William Compton, Richard Taylor, Edward Gardiner, *Collectors*

[f.33 blank]

*[**Assessment.** Membrane 7 continued, following on from Lew.]*

Witney

Rich[ard] Slater, & John Hams, 1s.
...... Howes, for his howses & close, 2s.6d.
Richard Wyatt, 2s.6d.
John Payne, 8d.
Stephen Brice, 8d.
[blank] Horton, wid., 7d.
Thomas Turner, for his Tenem'ts, 1s.9d.
Thomas Collyer, 8d.
Marke Tymms, 1s.
Leonard Canden, for a howse, 1s.
Richard Slater, jun., 1s.6d.
William Giles, 1s.9d.
the Lady Ann Waynman, 7s.5d.
William Compton, 3s.
Thomas Beddall, 2s.
John King, 6s.
Thomas *[blank]*, 2s.6d.
Edward Greene[?], 1s.5d.
William Surrel, 1s.
Thomas Bishopp, 2s.6d.
William Webley, 3s.
John Williams, 3s.6d.
Thomas Price, 3s.
John House[?], 1s.
George Darbye, for his howse, 7s.
Richard Johnson, 2s.4d.
George Ward, 8d.
Henry Jones, gen., & his Tena'ts, 1s.
Richard Shepherd, 1s.
John Horwood[?], a howse, 1s.2d.
...... Clifford[?], of St. Giles p'ish in Oxford..., 7d.
Edward ......, 8d.
Richard ......, 1s.2d.
Francis Crosse, 8d.

[End of membrane 7. Membranes 8, 9 and the top of 10 are torn, faded and illegible. Membrane 8 continues with Witney, and possibly part of Clanfield, though see membrane 3. Membrane 9 contains Curbridge and probably Crawley, perhaps continuing on membrane 10.]

BANBURY HUNDRED

CHARLBURY

[f.34r, in three columns]

The names of those in and belonging to this Towne of Chorleburye wch have taken the Protestation. [191]

[f.34r, col. 1]
Robert Jenkinson
Charles Lee
Edward Jenkinson
Richard Eyans. sen'
Richard Eyans. Jun'
Richard Mansell
Alexander Harris. sen'
Thomas Harris
John Dutton
Thomas Joyner
John Greye
John Biggs
Thomas Ransome
Nicholas Harris
Edmund Margrets
George Roffe
Alexander Smith. sen'
Thomas Carter
John Lucas
John Harris
John Tenant
John Townesend
Thomas Fowler
William Margrets
John Viol
William Harwood
Thomas Tesler
Richard Weaver
Robert Brookes
Robert Collier
Alexander Smith Jun'
Edmund Harris
Edward Sanders
Thomas Beckingham
Adrian Fairebrother
William Strenght
Henrye Lardner
Thomas Griffin
Thomas Boureman
Christopher Dod
Richard Sheafe
Thomas Gatfeild
Thomas Pinfold
Thomas Sutton
Drue Carter
John Hastings
Edward Boyles
Thomas Fillis
John Brewer
George Tenant sen'
Robert Townesend
George Tenant Jun'
William Crawley
Anthonye Joyner
Richard Fletcher
William Rymond
Richard Anstee
John Eaton
Edmund Hedges
Edmund Prentice
Richard Charles
John Harwood
Thomas Mills
John Fletcher
Hugh Lardner
John Spur
John Lanchburye
Richard Clare
John Harben
Raph Loe
Swithun Therman
Edmund Harris
William Chapman
Joseph Ball
[f.34, col. 2]
Richard Locke
John Cotes
Thomas Bowell
John Pridee
Richard Roffe
Thomas Kerrye
George Bowell
William Boureman
Robert Hancocke
Edmund Fowler Jun'
John Greene
Richard Wright
Robert Leeke
Richard Cooke
Richard Joyner
Angel Roffe
William Stranght
Richard Harris
Gregorye Horseman
John Sherlye
Alexander Harris Jun'
Isaiah Cowling
Hugh Knot
Henrye Fletcher
Walter Robinson
Anthony Grey
William Rymond
Anthonye Fiddler
Thomas Sympson
William Roffe
William Barnes
Richard Barnes
Henrye Loe
John Fisher
William Townesend
John Thomas
Robert Lyne
John Daye
Henrye Mosse
Richard Pitt
Hugh Daye
Bartholomew Downeing
Roger Briscoe
Walter Boyles
William Beckingham
Alexander State
George Boureman
Ralph Brayne
Thomas Kench
Nicholas Leeke
William Greene
Edward Million
Walter Rymond
John Jones
John Lewis
Thomas Bishop

Ralph Wilshyre
John Turtle
Henrye Shad
Francis Strenght
Paul Clarye
Edmund Shad
Richard Cooke
William Fletcher
Anthonye Hollowaye
Edmund Roffe
Nicholas Harris
Alexander Harris
George Bustion
Richard Sheapard
Michael Deynes
William Cooke
William Hickes
Simon Taylor
William Rymond
Richard Boyles
[f.34, col. 3]
David James
William Lardner
Thomas Trueman
Richard Beckets
Robert Brookes
Thomas Smith
Charles Greye
John Greye
Nicholas Brinckefield
John Shad
John Hastings
Alexand'r Shad
William Wilkins
William Disleing
Acton Drake
John Lynne
Arthur Bromfield
Thomas Bennet
John Barnes
Mathew Hill
Francis Reynolds
Richard Weaver
John Burnam
Anthonye Bridges
William Barrel
John Ward
Michael Tucke
Robert Gilbert
John Warcus
Robert Townesend
John Gregorye
William Smith
Ralph Nolson [*or* Notson]
Robert Gaskin

Anthonye Tenant of the sayde Towne refuseth to take the Protestation.

John Phippes of the sayde Towne simply refuseth not, but demurres upon it as pretending not to understand what is meant by the true reformed Protestant Religion.

William Blackeburne. *Vicar*
Edmond Fowler
John Browne
William: Colle*[sic]*
Thomas Predie

*[**Assessment.** Membrane 9r, following on Prescott (Cropredy).]*

Charlbury

The Right Honble. the Earle of Danby [Sir Henry Danvers], 30s.
The Lady [Anne] Lee, 31s.10½d.
William Blackborne, gen., 22s.4d.
Richard Evens sen., 49s.2½d.
Richard Evans jun., 18s.6d.
George Tenante, 11s.5½d.
Alexander Harris, 10s.1d.
Thomas Priddy, 10s.1d.
John Coates, 10s.6d.
Edmund Rawlins, 8s.2d.
Edmund Hedges, 4s.1½d.
John Priddy, 5s.½d.
David Daux, 7s.4d.
The Widdow Hacker, 6s.10d.
The Widdow Harris, 8s.3d.
Edmund Prentice, 5s.6d.
Robert Townsend, 6s.5d.
William Coale*[sic]*, 4s.7d.
John Gray, 1s.10d.
Richard Gray, 1s.10d.
Richard Roffe, 3s.8d.
William Roffe, 2s.3d.
John Lanchbury, 2s.3d.
Edward Miller, 1s.4d.
The Widdow Joyner, 1s.4d.
John Dutton, 4s.7d.
William Trevis, 9s.2d.
Thomas Mosse, 1s.10d.
Thomas Bowell, 5½d.
Richard Harris, 11d.
The Widdow Lake, 1s.10d.
Thomas Kyte, 1s.4d.
William Chapman, 5½d.
John Spinne, 1s.10d.
Angela*[sic]* Roffe, 5½d.
Alexander Smyth, 5½d.
The Widdow Fairebrother, 11d.
William Strength sen., 5½d.
William Strength jun., 11d.
John Lucas, 5½d.
Edmund Harris, 5½d.
Richard Sambidge, 5½d.
George Rowell, 5½d.
Thomas Keinsham, 1s.10d.
Richard Cooke, 5½d.
Thomas Truman, 5½d.
Thomas Bowerman, 5½d.
George Roffe, 5½d.
Thomas Brisco, 5½d.
Austen Williames, 5½d.
Edward Sanders, 5½d.
William Brewer, 3s.8d.
Thomas Harris, 9s.2d.
Thomas Clemans, 4s.7d.
Widdow Priddy, 2s.3½d.
Thomas Rooke sen., 6s.5d.
Thomas Prentice, 3s.2d.
Robert Prentice, 11d.
John Smyth, 3s.8d.
Philipe Cowlinge, 11d.
Edward Corsey, 5½d.
John Browne, 15s.11½d.
Edmund Fowler, 5s.6d.
Thomas Joyner, 4s.7d.
Mathew Hill, 2s.3½d.
John Tenant, 2s.9d.
Thomas Teasler, 1s.4½d.

Richard Charles, 2s.3d.
Symon Tayler, 11d.
William Riman, 1s.10d.
John Hastinges, 11d.
John Bigges, 5½d.
Thomas Fowler, 11d.
Richard Fletcher, 5½d.
William Greene, 5½d.
Edmund Margetts, 11½d.
Henry Lardner, 5½d.
Adrian Fairbrother, 5½d.
The Widdow Hedges, 5½d.
Thomas Kerry, 5½d.
Anthony Gray, 5½d.
Alexander Shad, 5½d.
William Mosse, 5½d.
Anthony Buston, 5½d.
The Widdow George, 5½d.

Sum £19.1s.9d.

Recusants of Charlbury

Elnor the Wife of Thomas Clemants, 2s.8d.
Anthony Tenant and Joane his Wife, 5s.4d.
Philipe the Wife of Ralfe Brayne, 2s.8d.
Alice the Wife of Edmund Harris, 2s.8d.

for recusants money in Charlbury 13s.4d.

FAWLER

[f.35, column 2]

The names of those of the Towne of Fauler in the Parish of Charleburye that have taken the Protestation. [22]

Richard Badcocke
John Joyner
Sedrack Townesend
Timothye Jeffes
Robert Gislinge
Edward Hunt
Richard Cooke
Thomas Bumpas
Francis Reekes
John Williams
John Tombes
John Pridee
Thomas Bumpas
Richard Pacye
Edward Spurre
William Edden
John Hedges
Thomas Clinch
James Lardner
Richard Hedges
Richard Sambuch
Richard Rippingale

[f.35, column 2]

William Blackeburne, *Vicar*
Edmond Fowler
John Browne
William Coll*[sic]*
Thomas Predie

[Assessment. *Membrane 7r, following on Banbury.]*

Fawler

John Deinton Esqr., 38s.4d.
John Pridie, gen., 33s.10d.
The Widdow Hedges, 19s.3d.
Edward Hunte gen., 12s.8d.
George Pridie, 9s.½d.
Thomas Spadman*[sic]* gen., 6s.7d.
Thomas Bumpas. 13s.5d.
John Hedges, 11s.4d.
Thomas Pridie, 2s.4d.
Thomas Lord, 2s.8d.
Richard Hedges, 1s.4d.
Robert Gislinge, 8d.
Richard Sambridge, 1s.7½d.
Tymothy Jeffes, 7½d.

[f.35, column 2]

The Lady [Anne] Lea, 7s.6d.
Mr William Blackborne, Cler., 4s.
Alexander Harris, 2s.½d.
[membrane 7v]
Robert Townsend, 1s.1½d.
Thomas Harris, 1s.4½d.
Widdow Lake, 7d.
William Trevis, 2½d.
William Greene, 2½d.
Richard Roffe, 3d.
Edmund Fowler, 4d.
Richard Fletcher, 5½d.
Thomas Mosse, 8d.
William Brewer, 1½d
John Bidges*[sic]*, 8d.
Richard Irons, 2½d.
John Coates, 2½d.
John Dew, 5s.5d.
William Hedges, 5s.3d.
Hugh Kirke, 3s.1d.
Edmund Couper, 1s.2d.
Robert Osborne, 4d.
Widdow Coates, 4d.
Richard Coates, 3d.
William Larner, 11d.

Sum £9.10s.5d.

FINSTOCK

[f.35r, column 1]
The names of those of the Towne of Finchstocke in the Parish of Charleburye wch have taken the Protestation. [58]

Richard Joyner
Elias Hancocke
William Weaver
John Warcus
John Hedges
Anthonye Joyner
Edmund Joyner
Ferdinando Dixon
Richard Joyner
William Hastrings
William Cotes Sen
William Oake
Richard Wickins
John Buggo
William Cotes Jun
Thomas Wethisbyrry[?]
James Ivring
George Prudeman
John Cooke
William Crosse
James Weaver
William Daye Sen'
William Daye Jun'
William Warner Sen'
William Hill
Thomas James Sen'
William Warner Jun'
George Gyles
Thomas Jagurs
Thomas James Jun'
William Hill
James Wilkins
Leonard Lardner
Thomas Camden
Thomas Halloway
Robert Daye
William Camden
John Hunt
Richard Warcus
Richard Wickins
John Daye
Francis Parsloe
Richard Hunt
Humphrey Cowling
Leonard Camden
William Fillis
Thomas Warcus Sen'
Thomas Halloway
Thomas Warcus Jun'
Jeffrey Cowling
John Heskins
John Ivringe
Richard Cooke

William Blackeburne, *Vicar*
Edmond Fowler
John Browne
William Coll*[sic]*
Thomas Predie

*[**Assessment.** Membrane 7v, following on Fawler.]*

Finstock

John Priddy *[this name probably added later]*, 1s.6d.
Mr. [William] Blackborne [Blackburn], Cler., 4s.
Mr Thomas Martin, 57s.3d.
Richard Joynor, 13s.7½d.
Richard Badcock, 6s.6d.
Edward Hunte, 11s.6d.
Thomas Spadman*[sic]*, gen., 8s.6d.
Thomas Bumpas, 1s.3d.
George Priddy, 3d.
Thomas Hedges, 6s.10½d.
Widdow Harris, 6d.
Richard Wickings jun., 1s.6d.
Austen Fletcher, 1s.6d.
Robert Thacker, 7s.6d.
Thomas Holloway, 5s.4d.
Fardinando Dickson, 6d.
William Fills, 9d.
John Whorrod., 6d.
Jeffry Coleney, 3s.9d.
John Day, 1s.
Alice Bradshawe, 1s.3d.[?]
William Warner, 6d.
William Day, 1s.3d.
John Haskings, 3d.
William Weaver, 2s.3d.
Thomas Camden, 5s.
William Coates, 1s.6d.
Humphry Colinge, 1s.9d.
Thomas Jakewayes, 1s.3d.
William Oake, 1s.3d.
Margarett Warcos, 6d.
Leonard Larne, 1s.6d.
Thomas Wharcos, 6d.
James Wilkins, 1s.1½d.
Thomas Withby, 1s.
John Hunte, 7s.9d.
Richard Wickus sen., 5s.
Thomas House, 2s.6d.
Hugh Carter, 7s.6d.
George Prowdman, 2s.
George Gyles, 2s.
The Lady [Anne] Lee, 7s.6d.
Elizabeth Hedges, 6d.

Sum £9.10s.

[See also Shorthampton, Chilson and Pudlicote, page 98.]

BANBURY

[The Protestation Return for Banbury borough and parish does not survive.
Assessment. *Membrane 6.* ***Banbury Hundred****, commencing with Banbury Borough; for Neithrop and the remainder of the parish, see page 40. Bloxham Hundred is recorded on the first five membranes. For preamble, see page 206.]*

Banbury Borough

[membrane 6r]
Henry Foxe, 3s.6d.
Zachary Hams, 8d.
Rowland French, 2s.6d.
John Mumford, 6d.
William Clifton, 6d.
Mr Nathaniel Vivers, 5s.
The Widow Stokes, 6d.
Samuel Ward, 2s.
Robert Lamprey, 8d.
William Bloxham, 1s.
Mr Nathaniel Hill, 5s.
Abraham Gascoynes, 6d.
Mr Anthony Ansley, 4s.6d.
Mary Hill, 5s.
Widow Greenhill, 1s.
George Keynton, 6d.
John Bourman, 6d.
Thomas Bell, 6d.
Samuel Penn, 2s.
Richard Bloxham, 6s.
John Merrik sen., 1s.
John Walmsley sen., 6d.
Widdow Crooke, 6d.
Thomas Hickill, 8d.
Mr Richard Halhead, 20s.
James Fletcher, 3s.
William Buttler, 3s.
Thomas Ward, 3s.
Mr Anthony Hall, 5s.
Richard Warner, 1s.
William Pilkington, 6d.
William Jonson, 8d.
Thomas Reynalls, 2s.
Widdow Bradford, 1s.
James Worrall, 1s.
Elizabeth Hall, 6d.
John Wise, 2s.
Widdow Reynales, 1s.
Henry Smyth, 1s.6d.
Thomas Jackman, 1s.
John Walmsley jun., 6d.
Mathew White, 2s.6d.
Thomas White, 1s.6d.
John Heele, 6d.
Joseph Smyth, 1s.6d.
Thomas Pilkington, 5s.
John Rickeets, 8d.
Nicholas Stokes, 1s.6d.
James Wagstaffe, 3s.4d.
Mr Ayres, 14s.
Thomas Middleton sen., 6d.
Henry Glover, 8d.
Mrs Crosley, 2s.
Richard Hill, 2s.
Samuel French, 1s.
Jobe Robinson, 1s.
John Haines, slatter, 1s.3d.
Thomas Handes, 6d.
Mr Epiphany Hyll, 6s.
John Warner, 2s.
Isaack Wallton, 1s.6d.
John Tymes, 2s.8d.
Richard Fauson, 2s.
John Newland, 4s.
Richard Sloath, 6d.
Thomas Gibberd, 1s.
Nathaniel Kimbell, 2s.
Mr William Hall, 5s.
John West sen., 5s.
John West jun., 2s.
Widdow Welles, 1s.
Widdow Kimbell, 6d.
Thomas Smyth, baker, 1s.6d.
Widdow Lane, 2s.6d.
Widdow Dodson, 3s.4d.
Widdow Kight, 2s.
Joseph Awsten, 3s.4d.
Rowland Youick, 6d.
William Heynes, 5s.
Richard Richards, 2s.6d.
Thomas Oulds, 6d.
John Youick, 4s.
Mr John Awsten, 5s.
William Pagegett*[sic]*, 8d.
Robert Heywood, 8d.

Martine Canninge, 1s.6d.
Lawrence Steward and his son, 2s.
Mrs Goodwin, 2s.6d
Mr Aholiab West, 6s.8d.
Richard Sheldon, 2s.
Thomas Hammond, 2s.
Michael Ginkes, 8d.
Walter Norton, 6d.
Francis Weston, 8d.
Edward Leister, 6d.
William Taylor, 1s.[-]d.
William Goodber, 6d.
Richard Webb, 1s.
John Fausten, 8d.
John Wise, 8d.
Walter Wise, 1s.
John Yeats, 2s.
[membrane 6v]
Widdow Knibb, 1s.6d.
Mr Martine Tustian, 13s.4d.
Mr Robert French, 6s.8d.
William Wilkins, 1s.6d.
Simon Unitt, 2s.6d.
Mrs Wallyne, 3s.4d.
Mrs Halhead, 5s.
Edward Weston, tailor, 6d.
John Hall, 1s.
Mr Richard Downes, 2s.6d.
Mr Nathaniel Wheatly, 5s.
William Walsall, 4s.
Mr Robert Archer, 3s.4d.
Mr George Phillips, 5s.
John Tomes, 2s.
John Kinge, 3s.4d.
Gabriel Gubbin, 6d.
James Ricketts, 6d.
Widdow Reasinge, 9d.
Thomas Newman, 1s.6d.
Richard Jumpson, 6d.
Widdow Burrowes, 6d.
John Hall, baker, 18s.
Thomas Perkins, 2s.6d.
John Knibb, 2s.6d.
Robert Gascoyne, 3s.6d.
Widdow Gullyver, 1s.
Widdow Pettyfer, 4s.
William Savage, 1s.
John Scott, 8d.
John Butterie, 8d.
Manases Plumpton, 1s.
John Bentlye, 4s.6d.
William Robins, 4s.6d.
Thom. Crooke, 8d.
John Hanes, mercer, 5s.
William Maunder, 2s.
Mr Robert Benbowe, 1s.6d.
Thomas Judde, 2s.
Laurence Blieth, 3s.
Edward Welchman, 5s.
William Warner, 8d.
Stephen Walker, 8d.
Tytus Buckhingham, 2s.
William Perrin, 2s.
Tymothy Sherwood, 8d.
Thomas Pettiver, 8d.
Thomas Dumbleton, 6d.
Henry Yowick, 2s.
Mr Orgaine Nicholls, 5s.
John Cale, 1s.
John Kerwood, 8d.
Rice Yeats, 2s.
John Thomas, 6d.
John Tranter, 2s.6d.
Anthony Couper, 8d.
John Wheeler, 2s.6d.
Mr Richard Hall, 6d.
Mrs Terry, 1s.
Gamaliel Nicholls, 4s.
John Tomkins, 2s.
Mr Thomas Pim, 5s.
Mr William Pim, 4s.
Tymothy Laurence, 1s.
Roger Marchall, 2s.
Cressant Fly, 6d.
Richard Crockett, 1s.
Mathew Bently, 6d.
Mr Price, 3s.4d.
Edward Langham, 4s.6d.
Widdow Maunder, 2s.
Mr William Wheatly, 5s.
Mrs Wheatley, 5s.
Richard White, 2s.6d.
Izaack Pyner, 1s.6d.
Mr Edward Edens, 3s.6d.
James West, 4s.
Mr Edward Russell, 5s.
Thomas Addames, 3s.6d.
John Haines, shoemaker, 1s.6d.
John Awsten jun., 1s.
Rowland Haues, 4s.
Robert Gould, 6d.
William Reasinge, 6d.
Henry Bell, 6d.
Izaack Gascoynes, 6d.
Samuel Tatum, 8d.
Robert Basse, 6d.
William Gilkes, 4s.
Mr Edward Beale,. 4s.
Mr Richard Vivers, 40s.
Samuel Blackwell, 5s.
Mr John Vivers, 6s.8d.
Mrs Bently and Mathew Bently her son, 5s.
Obadiah Lord, 4s.
George Maunder, 1s.6d.
William Hawkins, 4s.6d.
Mr Thomas Halhead, 6s.
Widdow Turton, 2s.6d.
[membrane 7r]
Mr Thomas Robins, 6s.
Widdow West, 6d.
Zachary Stronge, 1s.6d.
Henry Westmocott, 1s.
Thomas Midleton jun., 6d.
Edward Weston, 8d.
Mr William Knight, 6d.
Edward Basse, 3s.
John Orall, 6d.
Widdow Dingly, 3s.
Thomas Middleton, 4s.
Thomas Steward, 3s.6d.
Widdow Gulliver jun., 1s.
Robert Wise, 1s.6d.
Mr Thomas Abraham, 2s.
William Turton, 4s.
John Haines, baker, 5s.
Mr John Webb, 4s.
William Stokes, 15s.
Mr William Allen, 8s.
Thomas Tomes, 2s.
Mathew Richards and his mother, 4s.
Thomas Deacle, 2s.6d.
William Ingram, 1s.6d.
Richard Steward, 6d.
William Whinge, 3s.4d.
Clemant Williames, 2s.
William Haughtin, 2s.
Joane Blackwell, 6d.
Mr Feild, 5s.
Mr Harford, 5s.

Mr Barker, 3s.4d.
John Roades, 1s.
William Hancocke, 6d.
John Bradly, 6d.
William Coxe, 6d.
Symon Willkins, 6d.
John Baker jun., 6d.
Daniel Sherwood, 6d.
Thomas Glover, 6d.
Richard Archer, gen., for his houses, 10s.
Mr Fox for his houses, 3s.
Robert Lampry for his house, 1s.6d.
Mrs Cross for her house, 1s.6d.
John Wise for his house, 5s.
Widdow Rennalls for her house, 1s.6d.
Henry Smyth for his house, 2s.6d.
Widdow Hall for her house, 2s.6d.
Richard Hill for his house, 2s.
John Newland for his house, 2s.
Mr William Hall for his house, 2s.6d.
John Steward for his house, 1s.6d.
Walter Norton for the house st.*[sic]*, 1s.
Mr Boodle for his house, 2s.6d.
William Goode for his house, 2s.
Mr Organne Nicholls for his house, 4s.
John Cale, plummer, for his house, 1s.6d.
Roger Marchall for the house st., 4s.
Edward Langham, Mr Price and Mr Smyth for the houses they live St., 4s.
Mr Nutte for his house, 3s.
Mr Whicars for his house, 6s.8d.
Thomas Perkins for his house, 2s.6d.
William Savage for his house, 1s.6d.
Thomas Robins for his house, 2s.
Mr William Allen for his house, 3s.
Mary Gulliver for her house, 3s.4d.
William Jonson for his house, 2s.6d.
John Heele for his house, 2s.
Richard Warner for his house, 1s.
Thomas Pettiver for his house, 1s.6d.
[the above nine entries are duplicated]
William Perrin for his house, 1s.6d.
Widdow Page for her house, 1s.
John Merricks for his house, 1s.6d.
Edward Weston for his house, 2s.
Samuel Tatum for his house, 1s.6d.

Sum £36.3s.9d.

*[**Assessment.** Membrane 8v, following on Wardington.]*

Neithrop, Calthorpe, Hardwick and Wickham

Thomas Chamberlayne Esqr., £5.7s.6d.
Mrs Elizabeth Chamberlayne, £1.
Doctr. William Turner, 5s.
Mrs Mary Hawtaine and her son, £3.5s.
The Lord Viscount Say and Seale, 7s.
Robert Barbar, gen, £1.12s.6d.
The Lady Elizabeth Cope, £8.
John Crew Esqr and Mr Hill, 14s.
Mr Richard Vivers, £1.11s.6d.
Mr Robert Vivers and Bishop of Ox[ford], £2.3s.
Mr Daniel Hires and Mr Bezaliel Knight's heirs, £2.6s.
William Ligon, gen., 6s.8d.
Richard Halhead, 9s.6d.
Thomas Halhead, 1s.6d.
Joane Kimbell, widow, and her sons, 1s.6d.
William Callcott, 8d.
Robert Marriage, 8d.
William Pinder, 8d.
John Shepherd, 8d.
Richard Foster, 6d.
Richard Jordan and his mother, 6d.
John Sparkes and Lanslet[?] Sparkes, 1s.
Mr Martine Tustian, 15s.
Richard Archer, gen., £3.13s.4d.
Mr Kinton, £1.
Mr William Thorpe, 7s.6d.
Robert Youicke, 8s.4d.
William Calcott and his son, 7s.6d.
John Richards and his son. 4s.8d.
Mathew Longe, 8s.
John Kimbell, 8s.
Mr Horton, 2s.6d.
Widow Coales, 2s.4d.
Joseph Awsten, 6s.
Mr William Wheatly, 7s.6d.
Ralph Winter, 2s.8d.
Mr Robert Harris, cler., 1s.3d.
Richard Southam, 7s.6d.
Edward Walford, 1s.6d.
Nathaniel Youick, 1s.4d.
Rowland Southam, 6d.
Richard Coale, 8d.
[blank] Cornacke of Neithrop, 6d.
Thomas Midleton, 2s.8d.
Humphry Robins, 1s.
Richard Collinges, 7s.6d.

Sum £38.1s.4d.

38.5s.6d.

sum £36.3s.9d.

CLAYDON

[f.36r. In two columns. This, like Mollington, and with the same curate, is one of the rare places with signatures or marks for all listed. Marks are shown by asterisks, the others all being signatures. See frontispiece.]

Vicessimo die Februarii 1641 Cleydon in Com' Oxon et in parochia de Croprey.

Wee whose Names are subscribed Have in the p'sence of Almightie God, before John Tipelre Clarke our Minister, togeather with our sayd Minister made our severall Protestacons the day & yeare aforesaid, according to the Tenor and effect of the Protestation here unto anexed. [62]

[f.36r, col.1]
John Tiplre, *Curat*
Geo: Butler
Thomas Neale
Richard French
Thomas Knibbe
Esay Parry
Anthony Shawe
Henry Goode
Nathanil Savage
Anthony Shaw *
William Knibb
Richard Basley [*or* Bastry?] *
John Millington *
John Francklin
Charles Hatton
Thomas Richards
John Knibb
William Hatten
William Rhoodes [?] *
Richard Wady
Anthony Neale
Oliver Stockley
Nicholas Sharman
Georg Robins *
Robert Webb *
William George [?]
[f.36r, col.2]
John Stockley
William Turner
Francis Ward *
William Pratt *
Thomas Norton *
John Harbert *
John Boreman *
Nathaniell French
John Camden *
John Welch *
John Harewood *
Edward Astell
John Stockley *
John Welch *
John Miller *
Thomas Neale *
Richard Knibb *
Edmund Robins *
Thomas Shawe *
William Jarvise *
[f.36v]
William Mason
William Saunders *
Francis Yeomans *
William Nicholls
Edward Palmer *
John Sharman *
Arthur Harrington *
John Borman
William Hawton
Felix Stockley *
Daniell Bourman *
Thomas Web

Theise are to Certifie you that the whole Inhabitants (of the Towne of Cleydon aforesaid) of Men from Eighteene yeares of age to the Oldest have made their protestations and subscribed their Names.

John Tiplre, *Curat*

Thomas Knibb,
William Hatten,
Churchwardens
John Knibb, *Overseer*
John Bourman, *Constable*

*[**Assessment.** Membrane 8r, following on Cropredy.]*

Cleydon

Sr. James Enyon, Knt., £2.12s.
Henry Boothby, gen., 10s.8d.
Thomas Boothby, gen., 16s.
Mr Doctr. Brunker, 4s.
Mr [John] Typler, 2s.8d.
George Buttler, 4s.
Thomas Knibb, 8s.
William Ladkins, gen., 5s.4d.
John Freckleton, gen., 7s.4d.
Richard French, 5s.4d.
John Knibb, 5s.4d.
John Stockley, 2s.8d.
William Nicholls, 3s.4d.
Robert Brockes, 2s.8d.
George Knibb, 2s.8d.
Francis Ward, 2s.
William Hattons, 2s.
Thomas Webb, 1s.4d.
John Bourman, 8d.
John Millars, 8d.
Henry Goode, 8d.
Alice Gardner, 8d.
William Jarvis, 8d.
John Sammons, 8d.
Widdow Robinson, 8d.
Elizabeth Sharman, 8d.
Anthony Shawe, 8d.
Thomas Wray, 8d.

Sum £7.4s.

GREAT and LITTLE BOURTON

[f.37r, in two columns; as there is a separate return for Cropredy, this is probably just for Great and Little Bourton.]

The Catalogue of all those that made the protestation of the inhabitants of Cropredy and Bourton according to the order of the Justices 15 February 1641 before Mr. Theophilus Lord minister there. [75]

[f.37r, col.1]
Mr. Edward Taylour
Mr. William Hall
George Gorstelow
George Devotion alias Dier
Willm. Jackman
Thomas Coleman
John Maunder
Bushell Maunder
Robt. Atwood
Willm. Coxfeild
Richard Sherley
James Fletcher
Thomas Fletcher
John Clifton
John Richardson
John Robinson
Willm. Plant
John Winckles
Thomas Hunt
Rich: Bachelour
Willm. Adkins
Willm. Loynes
George Gardner
Edward Gardner
George Bredon
John Hunt
Richard Breedon
John Perney
Willm Gims
Richard Claridge
Willm Saul
John Hands
Ambrose Claridge
John Willcoxe
Thomas Vosse
Henry Adkins
Willm Elkinton
[f.37r, col.2]
Jonathan Gardner
Willm Shatswell
John Smith
Thomas Judland
Robt Lord
Samuel Lord
Anthony Peirson
Robt Wiat
Nehemiah Haselewood
Nehemiah Maunsill
Thomas House
John Basse
Willm Fifeild
Thomas Neale
Rich: House
Jonathan Gard'ner
Edward Robinson
John Tarver
Thomas Parsons
Thomas Parsons*[sic]*
John Tarver*[sic]*
Willm Watts
Edward Matcham
Samuel Larden
Thomas Swaine
John Sabin
Basford Gardner
Willm Times
Thomas Hitchman
John Hill
Thomas Harberte
Thomas Hall
Joh Gulliver
John Arledge
Thomas Checklye

William Tomes,
Richard Densie,
Church-Wardens

*[**Assessment.** Membrane 8r, following on Claydon.]*

Bortons
[Great and Little Bourton]

The Bishop of Ox:[ford], 3s.
Mr Docter Brunkerd, 5s.4d.
Mr Richard Vivers, 37s.
Mr Clarkson, 15s.
Edward Taylor, gen., 5s.4d.
Mr Allen and
Josias Gardner, 10s.8d.
William Bourton, 6s.8d.
Richard Luckock, 2s.8d.
George Ranes, 1s.9d.
Mr Ambros Holbeth*[sic]*, 1s.4d.
Mr Warner, 1s.8d.
Mr Aholiab West, 2s.8d.
William Ricketts, 3s.3d.
Mr Webb, 1s.3d.
John Coales, 8d.
Mr Francis Grevill, 8d.
The Widdow Howes, 1s.4d.
Mr Webb of Hawes *[sic: ?Hanwell]*, 2s.8d.
Nehemiah Mancill, 1s.4d.
Samuel Lord, 8d.
John Gardner, 9s.
Thomas Hitchman, 9s.8d.
Thomas Hall and
Andrew Hall, 4s.2d.
John Cross, 8d.
Thomas Jarvis, 8d.
Thomas Vaughan, 2s.8d.
Annis Sherman, 1s.
Tymothy Coxe, 8d.
Thomas Gill jun., 7s.8d.
George Breedon, 8d.
Richard Sabin, 1s.2d.
Edward Holloway, 5s.4d.
Richard Claridge sen., 1s.
Richard Claridge jun., 4s.4d.
John Gulliver, 8d.
Robert Atwood, 1s.4d.
Edward Watts, 4s.4d.
Thomas Claridge, 1s.
William Hall, 8s.
Thomas Gill, 2s.

William Hall, 8s.
Thomas Gill, 2s.
James Hall, 2s.10d.
Nathaniel Gardner, 1s.
Thomas Plante, 8s.
William Elkington and
Thomas Chickly, 8s.4d.
William Cherry, 4s.
Robert Bull, 5s.4d.
Richard Gill, 4s.
Thomas Goodwin, 2s.
Moses Gardner, 3s.
Thomas Maule, 2s.
William Enock, 3s.4d.
George Bagly, 1s.4d.
William Townsend, 1s.4d.
Richard Batcheler, 1s.2d.
John Arlidge, 2d.
William Martin, 8d.
William Batcheler, 6d.
Thomas Kimbell, 6d.
George Gardner, 6d.
Richard Hall, 6d.
Thomas Holloway, 8d.
William Taylor, 8d.

Sum £11.2s. 6d.
[*corrected to* 11.2s.10d.]

CROPREDY
[of] Oxon'

[f.38r, in three columns]
The names of such as subscribed to the protestation in the [Countie] parish of Cropredie: June the 20th 1641: [158]
Edward Brunker, *Vicker.*
Thomas Andrew, *Curatt.*

[f.38r, col.1]
Peter Wayntworth
John Willmore
Edward Tayler
William Hall
Richard Cartwrite
John Blagrave
William Townsend
Thomas Swayne
John Miller
Thomas Hall
Samuell Lord
Arthur Allin
Thomas Gardner
Thomas Gill
William Enock
Richard Sabin
Robert Bull
Thomas Jarvice
Thomas Goodwin
George Breedon
Thomas Fletcher
Rob Hasellwood
Samuel Hands
John Bostock
Richard Watts
Michaell Crosse
Henry Bagley
John Tayler
Edward Austen
Richard Knibb
Thomas Gregory
William Bachiler
Thomas Hawkes
Nathaniell Savage
Richard Austen
James Bostock
John Adkins
John Hasellwood

[f.38r, col.2]
William Jervice
Robert Hans
John Pecke
Richard Bryan
Jonathan Haslewood
John Crosse
William Trusse
John Marston
Georg Gardner
Thomas Watts
William Gibbs
William Stanton
Thomas Gregory
Thomas Nibb
Edward Mole
Thomas Hitchman
William Howse
Thomas Stockley
Nehemiah Garner
Thomas Blackwell
Thomas Rawlins
Samuell Larding
Samuell Brockle
Nehemiah Hasellwood
Richard Gulliver
Thomas Mole
Isaby Bornham
George Bagley
William Hudson
William Cherry
Joseph Palmer
Richard Gorstelow
Thomas Gorstelow
Robert Crowley
William Hall
John Franklin
William Tayler
John Drake

[f.38r, col.3]
Martin Tims
Mathew Gill
Thomas Gill
John Wyatt
Thomas Hall
Thomas Mald [*or* Mold?]
Thomas Elkinton
John Hawkes
Richard Hall
William Wiatt
Edward Cox
Thomas Fletcher
Thomas Wiatt
John Richards
Thomas Hasellwodd
John Boarman
Francis Emmans
William Saunders
John Orton
William Suffolke
John Hawkes

Mathyas Barnes
Thomas Orlidg
Edward Lawrence
Anthony Elkiton
Nehemiah Mannsell
Thomas Pallmer
William Martin
William Lucas
Mathias Stanton
Thomas Vauhan
William Shatswell
Richard Gill
William Mason
Edward Pratt
William Cleridg
Richard Timmes
Georg Cleridg
Edward Hawtayne
Edward Howse
Edward Mole
[f.39r, col.1]
William Reade
Nathaniell Gardner
Moses Gardner
Thomas Hunt
Thomas Kimble
Manasses Plivie
John Warren
John Hunt
Richard Cooke
John Hill
Andrew Hall
William Bench
Peeter Arice
Basford Garner
Robert Hitchman
Richard Hedkins
Thomas Wadie
John Jeffes
[f.39r, col.2]
Valentine Hucksley
Thomas Elderson
Richard Hitchman
Henry Smith
James Hall
Edward Draper
John Clifford
William Langley
Thomas Laurance
James Batchiler
Thomas Howse
John Hunt
George Watts
William Ball
John Sabin
Christopher Rawlins
William Reade

William Tomes,
Richard Denzey,
John Arlidg,
John Gulliver,
Church Wardens

*[**Assessment.** Membrane 7v, following on Finstock.]*

Cropredy

Sr. Thomas Pope, Knt., 2s.
Thomas Boothby, gen., £1.17s.6d.
Henry Boothby, gen., £2.11s.
William Hall, 10s.
Joseph Palmer, 5s.
Thomas Gorstelow, 3s.9d.
Margery Broughton and Thomas Hawes, 5s.
Mr. Walker, 3s.9d.
Mr Docter Brunkerd*[sic]*, 3s.9d.
John Willmore, 12s.6d.
Richard Gorstelow, 5s.
George Dyer, 2s.6d.
William Reade, 2s.6d.
Alice House, 1s.10d.
John Wyatt, 1s.6d.
John Orton, 1s.6d.
Richard Denzy, 1s.

Mr Henry Boothby for Clattercott Groundes, £6.

Sum £13.10s.1d.

*[**Assessment.** Membrane 9r, following on Neithrop.]*

Prescott

William Goodwin, gen., £4.9s.6d.
Mr Goodwin, 12s.
William Sleath, £1
John Maunder, 10s.
Richard Denzy, 11s.
Richard House, 8s.
Richard Gorstelow, 9s.6d.

Sum £8.

MOLLINGTON

*[Although the parish of Cropredy, of which Mollington was a chapelry, mostly lay in Oxfordshire and the Hundred of Banbury, Mollington itself was divided between Oxfordshire and Warwickshire, and the Oxfordshire portion was in the Hundred of Bloxham (V.C.H. Oxon. **9**, p.3; **10**, p.2 (map), p.197). Nevertheless, the Protestation is filed under Banbury Hundred.*

[f.40r. In two columns. This, like Claydon, and with the same curate, is one of the rare places with signatures or marks for all listed. Marks are shown by asterisks, the others all being signatures.]

Vicessimo die Februarii 1641 Mollington in Com' Warr' et Oxon', et in parochia de Cropredye.

We whose names are Subscribed, have in the presence of Almightie God - before John Typelere Clarke our Minister Togeather with our said Minister made our severall Protestations the daye and yeare aforesaid according to the tenor and effort of the Protestation hereuntoe annexed. [78]

Joh Tiplre, *Curat*

[f.40r, col.1]
Anthony Wodhull
Richard Wodhull
Fulke Wodhull
Anthony Wodhull
Anthony Leycester
John Gorstelowe
Richard Gorstelowe
John Gorstelowe
Thomas Wodll*[sic]*
William Russell *
Richard Robins *
Edward Woodhull *
Richard Holloway *
John Adkins *
Edward Tymes *
John Bull
John Cosbrooke *
Anthony Robins *
Richard Chillds *
Edward Cammell *
Edward Corbett *
William Osburne *
John Warine *
John Gibbert
[f.40r, col.2]
Anthony Benfield
Thomas Claridg
Richard Coleman
Anthony Elkington *
Nicholas Downes
Thomas Staunton *
Richard Staunton *
Anthony Greenewood *
Richard Norton
Edward Elkinton *
Richard Elkinton *
John Massye
Richard Claridge
Richard Russell *
William Russell *
Francis Russell *
William Elkinton *
Embry Blicke *
Edward Day *
George Tyms *
Ambrose Child *
Thomas Sandivere *
John Corbett *
William Sandivere *
William Coleman
William Robins *
Phillip Coleman *
[f.40v]
Nathaniell Brookes *
Samuell Knight *
Robert Clements *
Richard Gullever
Richard Pettifere *
John Stanton
William Bray *
Anthony Kilby *
Francis Elkinton *
Robert Gilbert *
Robert Hands *
Thomas Tapportoe *
John Times
Robert Hands *
Joseph Elkinton *
William Knight
Richard Sandisan
William Napton *
Thomas Whithead *
John Tymes *
Edward Gubbine *
Thomas Sandivere *

Theise are to certifie you that the whole inhabitants (of the Towne of Mollington aforesaid) of Men from Eighteene yeare of Age to the Oldest have made theire protestations and subscribed theire Names except Mr. Ambrose Holbech, Mr. Richard Greville & Thimothie Harris whoe are all at London

John Tiplre, *Curat*
Richard Robins, *Churchwar:*
Edward Elkinton, *Overseer*
William Knight *Con:*

*[**Assessment.** Membrane 4r, Bloxham Hundred, following on Drayton.]*

Mollington

Anthony Woodhull, sen., Esqr., 57s.
George Raleigh, esqr., 7s.8d.
Thomas Boothby, esqr., 7s.8d.
Edward Brunker, Dr of Divinity, 3s.10d.
Thomas Woodhull, gent., 9s.1d.
Willm Russell, 5s.
John Massey, 4s.5d.
Edward Corbett, 18d.
Anthony Kilby, 2s.5d.
Anne Bull, widd., 1s.11d.
Edward Elkinton, 3s.11d.
Robert Croley, 2s.10d.
John Adkins, 18d.
Anthony Robbins, 6d.
John Bull, 12d.
Richard Clarridge, 6d.
John Corbett, 2s.
Joseph Elkington, 6d.
Ambrose Childs, 6d.
Willm Elkington, 18d.
Embre Blicke, 12d.
Richard Robbins, 5s.5d.

Sum: £6.2s.

SHUTFORD

[f.41r, in two columns]

***Shutford** Bill,*
Feb: 21st 1642

Wherein you have all the names of those parties that have taken this late protestation according to the appointment of that honorable assembly of Parliament. [54]

Thomas Griffin, *minister*
Robert Tayler,
Thomas Alcoke,
Churchwardens
Nicholas Alcoke,
John Austine,
Ov'seers of the puere
Edward Winter,
Constable

[f.41r, col.1]
Richard Nicholas
Robert Austine
Richard Turner
John Tayler
John Smith
Thomas Alcoke
William Hierne
Luke Cooke
Thomas Starlet
Hugh Turner
William Huet
Hugh Cooke
Richard Deene
Jonas Millard
William Nicholas
Thomas Clarke
John Haukes
Thomas Newell
Thomas Itchcoke
Thomas Tayler
Edward Wilkins
William Nethercot
Edward Tayler
Thomas Nicholas
Richard Nicholas
Joseph Nicholas
Samuel Nicholas
George Widley
Joseph Wilkins
[f.41r, col.2]
John Haukins
Robert Tayler
Salomon Deene
Christopher Deene
John Deene
John Alcoke
Richard Perkins
Edward Wallington
William Haukes
Raph Winter
William Smith
Richard Smith
John Alcoke
Robert Haukes
Thomas Shelsewell
John Nicholas
John Davies
Antony Kerby
Wallter Ancocke

*[**Assessment.** Membrane 9v, following on Williamscote (Wardington).]*

Shutford

The right honble. Viscount Saye and Seale, £5.2s.
Mr [Thomas] Merriott, Cler., 8s.8d.
Richard Nicholls, 13s.
John Austen, 10s.10d.
John Allcoke, 7s.7d.
Nicholas Allcocke, 6s.6d.
Edward Winter, 7s.3d.
Robert Tayler, 7s.7d.
Robert Tayler, 7s.7d. *[sic]*
Thomas Alcocke, 4s.4d.
John Potten, 4s.4d.
Soloman Deane, 2s.3d.
Edward Wilkins, 2s.
John Allcocke jun., 2s.2d.
Thomas Allcocke, 1s.3d.
Edward Wellington, 1s.
Ralph Winter, 1s.10d.
Widdow Winter and her Daughter, 2s.
William Sheldon, 8d.
William Ellitt, 4d.
Richard Turner, 3d.
Thomas Hitchcoxe, 2s.2d.
John Hawkes, 1s.8d.
Thomas Shelswell, 4d.
Joseph Willkins, 3s.3d.

£10.2s.[?]

SWALCLIFFE (incl. **Sibford Ferris** and **Sibford Gower**)

[f.42r, in two columns]

The names of all such Persons in the Parish of Swalcliffe, Sibford Goure & Sibford Ferris wth. in the Countie of Oxon' as have taken the Protestation required by the House of Commons in the Honble Court of Parliamt. [163]

[f.42r, col.1]
Thomas Merriot, *Vicar*
Edward Wykeham
Humphry Wykeham
Alexander Hollbrook
John Loggin
Robert Loggin
Edmund*[sic]* Litley
William Hopkins
Richard Lamb
Thomas Calcot
Robert Hale
William Gibbert
William Rowse
Edmund Gunne
Richard Constable
John Burrowes
John Litley
William Coles
William Soden
Richard Lamb
John Payne
Richard Geereing
Richard Gilks
Jeofrey Tredwell
Peter Harrice
James Kinge
Nicholas Austin
Richard Soden
John Cartar
Alexander Tredwell
Edward Clanfield
Richard Hale
William Gilks
William Bagget
William Berries
John Hawks
William Hopkins
Edmund Jakeman
John Newman
John Soden
John Gibbert
Jeofrey Gilks
William Tredwell
William Gilks
Jerome Lamb
George Gilks
Richard Jefkins
[f.42r, col.2]
John Gilks
Thomas Coles
Georg Crafts
John Bolding
Timothy Gilks
Christopher Padberry
William Wyat
Jerome Line
George Bloxam
Richard Calcot
John Hopkins
Georg Gilks
Michael Harrice
Georg Gilks
Richard Messenger
Nicholas Rickers
William Davis
Henry Denny
Georg Dumbleton
Francis Dumbleton
William Dumbleton
William Moult
Richard Bagget
Richard Burrowes
William Calcot
Robert Wilkins
Thomas Greene
John Allen
Edward Butler
Richard Calcot
James Calcot
Walter Fipps [?]
Richard Lord
Jeofrey Gilks
Nicholas Beale
Tho. Beale
Jeofrey Gilks
William Gilks
Erasmus Heynes
Richard Goodwin
Joseph Harrice
Jeofrey Tredwell
Georg Gilks
Henry Hopkins
William Soden
Joseph Gilks
[f.42v, col.1]
Richard Tredwell
William Heynes
Charles Heynes
Thomas Gilkes
John Whitley
Moyses Boucher
William Gibbs
Richard Tuscot
Humphrey Lenton
James Calcot
Thomas Gilks
John Drinkwater
William Gillet
William Simms
Richard Colegrave
Jonas Burrowes
Georg Coles
Robert Browne
Erasmus Adkins
Richard Howse
Tho. Heynes
John Greene
Richard Gilks
Tho. Lamb
William Perryn
Tho. Bloxam
Mathias Bannister
William Tooly
John Soden
Ferdinando Bagget
William Faxon
John Rowdag
John Hopkins
John Plesto
William Bonner
Richard Ennock
William Harrice
Edward Clark *[name struck through]*
Nicholas Leigh

Samuel Pettifer
John Taylaur
Tho. Manning
Richard Bloxam
Josias Tredwell
Samuel Hurtwell
Edward Clark the yonger
Richard Payne
Thomas Howse
William Harris
William Chese
Thomas Gilks
Richard Gilks
Aaron Hieron
[f.42v, col.2]
Samuel Hieron
Edward Crowley
William Gilks
John Hopkins
Tho. Hadland
Richard Walford

Thomas Butler, *Churchwarden*
John Butler & John Saule, *overseers of the poore*
Samuel Baggett, *Constable of Swalcliffe*
Mathias Edwards, *Churchwarden*
John Harris, *overseer of the poore*
Edward Clarke, *Cunstable of Sibford Ferris*
Thomas Caulcott & Richard Hobkins, *Churchwardens*
Richard Gibbard & John Bagget, *overseers of the poore*
William Litty*[sic]*, *Cunstable of Sibford Goure*

[f.43 - blank]

*[**Assessment.** Membrane 9v, following on Shutford.]*

Swalkliffe *[Swalcliffe]*

Thomas Chamberlayne Esqr., £5.2s.
Humphry Wickham, gen., £2.6s.8d.
Mr Thomas Merriott, Cler., *[sum obliterated]*
Thomas Longwise Esqr, £5[?].10s.
John Loggin, gen., £1.8s.4d.
Mr Addames, 10s.
William Gibson, 10s.
[The remaining entries are very rubbed and faded:]
John Buttler, 5s.
John Haule, 5s.[?]
Ralph Winter, 5s.
William Messenger, 1s.
Widdow *[illegible]*, 4s.
Henry[?] *[illegible]*, 1s.
Samuel Baggett, 6d.
Thomas Buttler[?], 1s.6d.
The Widdow Baker, 1s.6d.

Sum *[? no entry, or illegible]*.

[Membrane 4r, Bloxham Hundred, following Alkerton.]

Sibford Gore *[Gower]*

[Sibford Gower and Sibford Ferris were hamlets in the parish of Swalcliffe, itself mostly in the Hundred of Banbury. Despite this, the Sibfords were for taxation and other purposes considered part of the Hundred of Bloxham, though they were included under Banbury Hundred in the Protestation Returns (V.C.H. Oxon, ***9****, p.3).]*

John Hawkes, 4s.6d.
John Baggitt, 3s.4d.
John Gilkes, 7s.6d.
Richard Gibbert, 8s.2d.
Nicholas Austen, 8s.10d.
Richard Tredwell, 9s.2d.,
John Hopkins, 10s.6d.
John Soden, 4s.6d.
William Litley*[sic]*, 6s.
Thomas Gilkes, 8s.10d.
Joane Tredwell, 6s.
Jeffery Gilkes, 9s.4d.
William Soden, 13s.6d.
William Gilkes, 3s.2d.
William Soden*[sic]*, 12d.
Edward Litley*[sic]*, 2s.10d.
Richard Jeffkins, 1s.8d.
William Hoppkins, 18d.
Richard Walford, 6s.2d.
William Hoppkins, 4s.10d.
Thomas Calcott, 4s.6d.
Richard Calcott, 4s.8d.
Nicholas Beale, 12d.
William Rowse, 5s.5d.
Richard Lambe, 2s.6d.
William Faxon, 6s.
William Hoppkins, 9s.
Richard Molt, 2s.
John Whitley, 18d.
William Messenger, 6d.
Charles Haynes, 3s.
Thomas Haynes, 12d.
Richard Soden, 5s.
Thomas Merriott, Cler., 18d.
John Loggins, gent., 24s.
Mr Griffith, 12d.
John Wilkins, 18d.
William Symmes, 6d.
Richard Constable, 6d.
Anne Gilkes, 7d.
Thomas Hawkes, 2s.
William Gilkes, 12d.
Thomas Hadland, 8d.
Alexander Hadland, 12d.
Jerome Lambe, 8d.
Richard Carter, 8d.

Sum: £10.4s.

[Membrane 4v, following Sibford Ferris.]

Sibford Ferris

Symon Coleman, 8s.
Mathew Edwards, 5s.3d.
George Gilkes, 9d.
Richard Enocke, 3s.
Edward Harris, 15d.
William Coles, 2s.3d.
Edward Clerke, 6s.6d.
John Harris, 4s.6d.
Richard Walford, 15d.
Peeter Harris, 3s.6d.
Jeffery Tredwell, 2s.3d.
Samuel Pettipher, 2s.9d.
Willm Harris, 6s.6d.
Thomas Hale, 3s.
Erasmus Adkins and Widd. Howse, 18d.
Adkins for George Gilkes, 2s.
John Tayler, 3s.
James Kinge, 2s.1d.
Josias Tredwell, 1s.9d.
Geffery Gilkes, 12d.
Richard Calcott, 2s.8d.
Michael Harris, 6d.
Richard Howes, 18d.
William Gilkes, 9d.
Sarah Carter, 12d.
[blank] Whatcott ye Miller, 3s.6d.
John Loggins, gent., 13s.6d.
George Gilkes, 12s.6d.
Richard Gilkes, 5s.

Sum £5.2s.

WARDINGTON (incl. **Williamscott** and **Coton**)

[f.44r. Single column; f.45r, two columns. Some signatures.]

Wardington

A Note of the names of those tht have taken the protestation within the parish of Wardington Wil-liamscott & Cotes. [112]

Richard White, *Minister*
Joseph Coleman
Richard Humpfris
Thomas Pargeter
Edward Eden
John Burrows
Thomas Welchman
Will Gill
Esay Mosse
Edward Sabin
John Tredwell
Willi Corbitt
Nic' Bigges
Hue Harris
Daniell Fifeild
Ric' Peadell
Tho' Gardner
Tho' Beadell
Andrew Adkines
Thomas Torshell
Nicholas Bull
John Richarson
Walter Lane[?]
John Townsend
Peeter French
Thomas Chapman
William Lambert
Tho: Shorte
John Hyarns
John Randell
William Kench
William Gardner
John Price
John Goodman
[f.45r, col.1]
John Webbe
Thomas Torshell
Will' Budde
Ric: Peedle
Alban Bull
Will. Ball [Bell, Bull ?]
Rob: Stacy
Tho: Peedle
Richard Peedle
Will' Grime
Thomas French
William Wall [*or* Webb?]
William Malcher
Joseph White
Fulke Bailey
Nicholas Andrewes
Tho' Abits
Tho' Dolton
Alexander Harris
Henry Pincord
Timothy Dagger
John Wilkins
Jeames Steward
Willi' Gill
Ric' Glasse
John Goodman
Anthony Drake
Tho' Ward
Hue Flecher
Tho' Gibbes
John Rogers
Willi' Clarke
Georg Humfris
Georg Osburne
Willi' Jacson
John Swetman
John Webbe
Willi' Gardner
Tho' Stockly
[f.45, col.2]
Robert Margits
Edward Mayo
John Russell
Ric' Cole
Ric' Swetman
Samuell Gulbin*[sic]*
Sam' Woodcoke
John Sabin
Gabrill Rogers
Ric' Marriot
John Blackemore
Samuell Gardner
Ric' Cole
Willi' Healy
Ric' Wilkins
Edward Healy
John Gardner

Edward Crooke
Willi' Stacie
George Sharman
Nic' Maulcher
Micaell Bayly
Randell Bull
Ric; Gill
Tho' Page
John Wady
Sameull French
Hugh Sabin
Thomas French
Calcot Gardner
Morgan Muddin
Joseph Calcott
William West
Richard Calcott
Steven Gees
Edward Richardson
Gualter Baker
Edward Giles
Richard Andrewes

*[**Assessment.** Membrane 8v, following on the Bourtons.]*

Wardington

George Chamberlayne, gent., 3s.4d.
Mr Feild, 18s.8d.
Mr Docter Brunkerd, 13s.4d.
Mr Coleman, 10s.8d.
Richard Coale, 8s.
William Healy, 6s.8d.
Edward Giles[?] *[no sum]*
Edward Taylor, 4s.
John Coale, 4s.
Thomas French, 1s.4d.
Peter French, 2s.8d.
John Tymes, 5s.4d.
Michael Bennitt, 2s.8d.
Mris. Elnor Bleck, 10s.8d.
John Gardner, 9s.4d.
Samuel Gobbin*[sic]*, 5s.10d.
Cresant Heley, 2s.8d.
Albon Bull, 4s.
William Webb, 4s.
John Webb, 5s.4d.
John Cay, 2s.8d.
Thomas Lambert, 1s.4d.
Thomas Pargeter, 1s.4d.
Edward Eden, 2s.8d.
Thomas French, 6s.8d.
William Gardner, 4s.
Samuel French, 9s.4d.
John Blackmore, 5s.4d.
William Kinch, 9s.4d.
Richard Wickins, 5s.4d.
William Corbitt, 8d.
John Waday, 1s.4d.
Thomas Short, 4s.
John Hirons, 2s.
Thomas Torshell, 8s.
Richard Piddill, 2s.8d.
Mr Thomas Robins, 5s.4d.
John Fayrefoxe, 5s.4d.
Edward Sabin, 8d.
Hugh Sabin, 8d.
Thomas Chapman, 8d
William Kinch, 9s.4d.
William Glasse, 1s.4d.
Robert Kinge, 1s.4d.
John Burrowes, 1s.4d.
John Hunte, 5s.4d.
John Marrett, 1s.4d.
Richard Plestow, 1s.4d.

Sum £13.18s.

*[**Assessment.** Membrane 9v following on Charlbury.]*

Williamscott

Mr Docter Brunkerd, 3s.
Edward Taylor, gen., 46s.
John Ditchfield, 6s.
Samuel Sord [?], 1s.6d.
James Steward, 6d.
[blank] Gardner, 6d.
Thomas Stone, 6d.
Richard Plestow, 1s.
John Coales, 1s.
John Goodman, 1s.6d.
John Tredwell, 1s.
Mr Vivers, 1s.
Mr Chamberlayne, 2s.
Edward Taylor, 8s.
John Ditchfield, 2s.
The Goodwife Birch, 6d.
Tobias Calcott, 6s.
William Grine, 1s.
Isaiah Mosse, 4s.
Mr Vivers, 7s.
Goodman Gill, 2s.6d.
Robert Fifeild [?], 1s.
Thomas Lomberd, 1s.
Michael Bayley, 3s.
John Blackynore, 6s.
John Busby, 2s.
John Kinge, 2s.
Edward Eden, 1s.
Richard Willkins, 1s.
Richard Andrewes, 1s.
Richard Marriatt, 1s.
Albon Bull, 6d.
Richard Plestow, 2s.

Sum £6.3s.

BINFIELD HUNDRED

CAVERSHAM [73 and 101]

[Caversham is missing from the returns of parishes in Binfield Hundred at the House of Lords. However, the late Brigadier F.R.L. Goadby identified two lists in the earliest Caversham parish register (now at the Berkshire Record Office, as Caversham was transferred to Berkshire in 1911) as probably having been prepared in connection with the Protestation Oath.

The earlier is on a blank page following baptisms for 1641, prepared by the Perpetual Curate, William Brice, and records 73 names headed by his own. Many are signatures or have 'marks' which appear to be original. Partly because of the signatures, often in unlettered hands, as well as some fading, many of the names in this list are difficult to identify with certainty. The names are in two main columns with a third short column, all on the verso of a folio contemporarily numbered '8'.

The second list, several folios later (following burials for 1641), has 101 names. It is in a different hand, the same throughout, and much easier to read. There appear to be no signatures and, although those who signed by mark are indicated, the 'marks' themselves are careful copies, not the originals.

An article by Goadby together with a rearrangement of the two lists in one alphabetical sequence appeared in 'The Oxfordshire Family Historian', 3, 7 (Spring 1985), pp. 229-30. In this he suggests that the first list, perhaps incomplete, was written by Brice in Summer 1641, in accordance with the original Parliamentary Bill of 6 May; and that the second was copied into what was then a new register started by his successor (probably Richard Lloyd) soon after his arrival, consequent on the issue of the Proclamation itself in January 1641/2. The page preceding this second list has written at the foot: 'Wee whose Names are heare subscribed' and a series of trial initial letters. The list is in two columns on the recto and one on the verso. Also on this verso is a marriage entry for Allan Zouch Esqr. of Woking, Surrey, and Katherine Hubbart relict of James Hubbart, dated 1st March 1642.

For the purpose of this edition the lists have been retranscribed and appear in their original order, with asterisks indicating those who signed by mark (both originals and copies).]

[First list, f.8v, col. 1]
William Brice, *Curate*
Henry Daniell
Thomas Vachell
Nich. Tatnall
William Clarks
John West
William Wheeler
Thomas Aldworth [Aldridge]
William Berry
John Castell
Latton Welbecke
Thomas Blackall
Ephraim West
William Atkins
Mathew Payne [?]
Richard Castell
Robert Loveiey
John Salter
John Smith *
William Smith
Hugh Stockes
John Young *
William Phillipps
Edmund Fernhed [?]
John Hicks
Atowell Bastook [?] *
Thomas Louioy *
William Ridgnalfe [?]
Latton Welbecke *[a different signature to that above]*
...... *[? faded]* Salter
[f.8v, col. 2]
Richard Nash
John Kent
John[?] Gage
Umpheri Simmes *
Thomas Young *
William Cotten
John Dunt
Henri Sharpe *
Thomas Read
Abraham Cotten
William Louejoye * [Loueioy]
William Lee
Henry Curtis *[an obliterated mark before this name was interpreted by Goadby as 'Sir', but this seems unlikely]*
Richard Robinson *
William Soundy [Sowndie]
Robert Read [Reed]
Henry Whitehill
Roger Ireland

John Read [Reed]
Hue Coster
Richard Ireland
Richard Mylson
William Grenwod *
[Greenwod]
John Boshnell [Bushnell]
John Bradlye [?] *
Steven Wallis *
William Pery
Nicclle[?] [Michael] Bolte *
Peter Boshnell [Bushnell]
John Benn-e [?] *
John Barnod * [Barnard]
Thomas Boshnell *
[Bushnell]
Thomas White *
John Kent *
William Quelche *
Robert Williames *
[Williams]
[f.8v, col. 3]
Thomas Wells
Richard Benwell *
Nicolas Coles [?]
Gorg Vernhead *
[Fernhead]
Robert Pigat [Piggatt]
William Percy
William Blackeman

[Second list]
'Wee whose Names are heare subscribed'

[col. 1]
John Crockford
John Crockford *[sic]* *
Anthonie Wheler *
John Nevell *
Henrie Loveioye *
Richard Berry
Raulph Stevens *
William Kent *
William Sowndie *
Robert Reed
Henrie Whittle
Roger Ireland
John Reed
Hugh Cotton *
Richard Ireland
Richard Millson
William Greenwod *
John Butler *
John Bushnell *
John Broadly *
Stephen Wallis *
William Percie
Michaell Boult *
Peter Bushnell *
John Benham *
John Barnard *
Thomas Bushnell *
Thomas White *
John Kent *
William Quelche *
Robert Williams *
Nicholas Carter *
Robert Piggatt *
Georg Fernhead *
William Percie
William Blackeman *
Thomas Brigham
Edward Clarke
Earth & Ashes Gradnum
John Loueioy
Thomas Moeman *[? - the third letter is faded and could be 'r']*
Cristopher Brounsmith
[col. 2]
Augustine Loueioye
Robert Fissher
William Loueioy
Henrie Jeffry
John Farrar
Edward Duntt *
Henrie Curtis
Robert Huntt
William Willis *
William Robinson *
John Loveioy *
Henrie Butler *
John Pacie *
John Simmons
Walter Stevens
Thomas Wytell
Bernard Piggot *
Peter Bushnell *
Francis Binfield *
Robert Makins *
Robert Benham *
Peter Nitingale *
John Waite *
Roger Sowndie *
Edward Reed
Raulph Stevens Junior
John Binfeild *
Andrew Binfeild *
John Banister *
Philadelphia *[blank]*
Peeter Brea..
[verso]
John Daie *
William Hatte *
Raulph Seaward
Richard Benwell
William Ireland
John Benham Junior
Heiden Brigham
John Harrisse
Henrie Loveioye *
Francis Slater
Joseph Curtis *
John Loveioye
Edmond Bullock *
William Nitingale *
Silvanus Paine *
William Duntt *
Robert Reed
Richard Bushnell *
Thomas Aldridge *
[Aldworth]
Thomas Duntt *
John Parker *
William Haule *
Francis Holoway *
Richard Lawrence *
Edward Willis *
William Bye *
John Moseden *
Nicholas Salter *

'These are to Certifie'

HARPSDEN

[f.46r, single column]

A note of all those that subscribed to the protestation in the parish of Harpsden. [32]

Mr. William Farrowe
William Simons
Richard Payn
Thomas Roberts
Richard Beard
Nathaniel Reade
Parslowe Reade
Thomas Heyward
John Stanbrooks
William Towers
Solomon Seawell
Samuell Seawell
William Shermer
John Coussins
Thomas Payn
William Harris
Edward Seawen
Robert Curtes
Ellis Stanbrook
John Jennings
Rodophus Paine
Tho: Darbie
Edward Benfield
John Round
William Pearman Se:
William Pearman Jn:
Edward Bushe

Tho: Johnson, *Curate*
Henrie Round, *Sidesman*
John Hunt,
Sebastian Douse,
overseers
Simeon Parrat,
Tithing Man

HENLEY on THAMES [718]

[f.47r, in two columns]

The Names of those of the Parish of Henley that were either sick or out of towne when the Protestation was taken by the rest of the sayd Parish

[f.47r, col. 1]
Mr. Hester
Augustine Valentine Junior
Will: Crace
Fran: Round
John Baldwin, sick
Thomas Jackson
Thomas Greene
John Blackall, sick
John Hide
Mr. Hill
Robt Hunt
Willm Sanders
Mr. Tomson

[f.47r, col. 2]
Walter Savage
Toby Lancaster
Miles Stile
Robert Coudry
Edward Katherines
Edward Cock, sick
Ferdin: Ward, sick
William Winter
Sackvill More
Thomas Beast
John Primmer
Griffin Tull
Robt Meakins
Richard Winter

[f.47v]
Gabriel Arnold
Peter Hayward
Th: Crace
Ab: Carter
Will: Spratt
Goodman Waters
Goodman Cleare
Roger Miles
William Wade
Christopher Woodeson
Goodman Usher
Th: Barrett
Isaack Parker
John Munday
Th: Burges
Will: Pennaker
Humphry Foord
John Flood

[f.48]

Which Protestation, as it was not refused by any to whom it was tendered, so I am confidant it will readily be taken by all those that are now absent when it shall be tendered to them.

Robt Rainsford, *Parson of Henly*

[f.49r, in two columns, with many signatures]

Henley

[f.49r, col. 1]

Francis Stevens, *Warden*
Robert Rainsford, *Parson*
Robert Munday,
Richard Edmonds,
Churchwardens
William Finch, *Constab:*

Richard Facie
Henry Boler
Richard Beard
Andrew Gibbs
Francis Crace
Walter Barfoote
Wm Pulley
Andrew Powell
Raphe Reade
Abraham Pocock
John Farmer
Ambros Freemantl
Edward Raunce
Raphe Frith
William Howse
Nicholas Farenbarrow [?]
William Lane
Symon Story
Edward Rock
John Gray
Raphe Hale
Tymothy Heacraft
Robart Mosly
John Symsonn
John Anderwes *[sic]*
William Reading
John Toovey
William Lingar
Samuel Stockwell
Philip Nash
John Basse
Thomas Paynter
William Veere
William Floyde
Thomas Keene

[f.49r, col. 2]

Thomas Trenley
Will. Serman
Lamech Cove [?]
Thomas Froste
Will' Flod
Thomas Woodgate
John Froste
John East
Henry Jordan
Thomas Percy
Richerd Barnes
Robt Alloway
John Damsell
Roger Bowler
William Beard
Francis Arnolld
John Joy
Willm Butler
William Weeden
William Westley
John Wright
Matthew Tomson
John Sussex
William Grove
John Grove
Nathaniel Yate
William Joy
Francis Tiler
Willm Felpes
John Morgan
Jeffery Brookes
Thomas Brookes
Edward Heath
Thomas Butler
William Goodwin
Simon Benwell
Edward Dapwell
Simon Benge
Andrew Floyd
Thomas Hester
Richard Wheeler
Thomas Haynes

[f.49v, col. 1]

Thomas Nash
Edward Hambledon
Burcket Hale
John Fortune
Richard Parye
Andrew Browne
Robert Lock
Thomas Wheeler
Thomas Butler
William Thomas
William East
John Veer
John Bradway
Thomas Veer
Thomas Kelley
John Eales sen:
William Johnson
John Eales Jun, 100
Thomas Percy
Christopher Newbery
Henry Freemann
Richard H---ne [?]
Bartholomew Carter
John Adames
Robert Clarke
Edward Kent
William Veanmore [?]
Robart Douglass
William Wilkes
Roger Forest
Andrew Bolt
John Maine
John Smeeton [?]
Robert Alloway
Simon Loueioy [Lovejoy]
John Haward
John Grant
Ralph Allman
Richard Hatch
William Reade
Thomas Hatch

[f.49v, col. 2]

Edward Lynney
Richard Nyx [?]
Robert Pengrove
William Carter
Thomas Sedgrove
Humphry Parkes
Richard Stonor
Thomas Widdeson
John Sallett
William Fatt
Zachary Barnes
Richard O--n-s [?]
Henry Osborne
Humfary Nubery
Nathaniel Lorchin
Robert Frith
William Sandars
Edmund Hunt
John Transome
William Tull

Richard Loueioy [Lovejoy]
Daniel Jemmatt
Edmund Sturmy
Leonard Godfery
Rice Sanders
Henary Whitside
Edward Coles
John Robinson
Ralph Spurr
Henry Emery
Roger Hayes
Salomon Dubbar
Clement Woodrofe
Ralph Blackall
Richard Fatt
John Browne
John Browne *[sic]*
John Sallet
Henry Barret
John More
[f.50r, col. 1]
Henrie Cullen
Humphry Douglas
Samuel Robinson
John Techin
Richard Webb
William Sneade
Thomas Williamson
John Carter
John Clarke
Bennet Kent
Leonard Robinson
William Read
Tomas Grifen
Henry Smith
Antony Butcher
Andrew Baylie
John Brian
Thomas Caster [?]
Thomas Britten
John Pusey
George Eemes
Edward Parish
Augustine Weeden
Roger Foster
Robert Tamlin
Bartholomew Godfrey
John Lancaster
James Maynard
Adam Springall
Timothy Lavington

John Gibbs
Edward Tuffy
Thomas Ford
Robert Kente
Antony Yong
Thomas Shephard
Thomas Peters
John Rockhall 200
Richard Deane
William Lane senior
[f.50r, col. 2]
Fran: Littlepage
William Leaver

by mee Samuell Trotman of Stankamb in the parish of Stunchkumb & Cunty of Gloster.

[f.50r, col. 2, continued]
Robert Gibbs
Richard Grant
William Jeninges
Oliver Slater
Simon Orie [?]
Humphrey Milam
John Hams [?]
Zachary Howse
Steven Beard
Williame Web
John Michell
John Cutturnes
Michell Floud
William Gibbs
Andrew Gibbs
William Prat
William Lorchin
Thomas Downing
Thomas Messenger
Abram Carter
Thomas Evet
Richard Seaver
William Barnes
Robart Emeat
John Moore
Thomas Handly
William Atkines
William Read
John Meay
Richard Wade
Thomas Bolton

George Messinger
John Shipwash
Robt Cooper
Francis Browne
Edward Burgesse
Richard Comme
Richard Whitesid
John Lane
Henry Smyth
Robart Browne
totall 246
[f.51, col. 1]
Richard Lorchin
Richard Phillipes
John Phillipes
Ellis Skynner
William Adkines
Edward Earvai
John Gibbe
Thomas Whitngton *[sic]*
Edward Meades
John Digwood
Walter Smeth
Andrew Powell
Roger Sutten
Isack Thakam
John Hunt
Robert Burges
John Patron
Robert Tomsin
Thomas Skiner
John Gimets
William Gests
John Rackstraw
William Rackstraw
Richard Sharp
John Edmans
John Morhin
Richard Westen
Thomas Cornish
Henery Greener
Will. Fearmer
Henry Monday
Thomas Clayton
Will. Brooke
Will. Strafford
George Greener
David Mallet
Tho' Wickens Junior
William Howse
Robert Bland

Will. Butcher
John Pocock
John Direct
Thomas Stone
John Bell
Thomas Wickens
[f.51r, col. 2]
Jeames Steevens
Richard Hall
Thomas Talior *[sic]*
Robert Lamden
Richard Taylor
Thomas Arn--- [?]
Jeremy Direck
Hugh Floyd
Jeames Lane
Thomas Barret
John Hud
John Yovens
John Prior
Christopher Avery
Isack Harison
James Duglas
Richard Ells
Seth Smyth
George Pocket
Rice Nyx
John Tyler senior
John Wheeler
John Tyler
John Goade
John Greene
Jacob Harrison
Edward -k-cut [?]
Thomas Beret
Roger Fortin
Richard Matingley
Henry Pennington
John Cooke
John House
Edward Brian
Michael Sharpe
Thomas Lea
Edward Wildow
Francis Kent
John Warner
Henry Clayden
Miles English
John Ashby
Job Hobbins

[f.51v, col. 1]
William Nix
William Collier
Richard Anstill
Nathaniel Yate
Humphrey Fortune
John Fisher
Richard Russell
John Chapman
Henry Cope
Walter Cottrell
Thomas Meade
John Goswell
Francis Smith
Thomas Bray
Nicolas Savage
Thomas Corneon
Raphe Norris
William Seare
William Dwight
Robert Mecock
Richard Foxe
Luke Welles
Christopher Munday
William Woodrofe
William Ward
Robt Munday
Andrew Primmer
Michael Harrison
Thomas Eeles
James Collins
Edward Dalls
William Bodkin
John Huntt
Thomas Brooke
Henry Boswell
John Stapers
William Boswell
Thomas Boswell
[f.51v, col. 2]
Richard Whiteside
Humphrey Compton
William Harris
Thomas Clarke
Thomas Goade
Joseph Goade
Thomas Heyes
Griffin Dwight
Jerome Embris
Richard Floyd
Nicholas Bell

Isaack Keene
John Nash
Jerome Dry
Richard Fruin
Rodulph Elmes
Robt Simmons
Henry Slade
William Damsell
William Morehen
Thomas Cornish
Thomas Coles
Philip Price
Thomas Smith
John Britten
Richard Ssyemer
William Bird
Samuel More
Richard Ward
John Stapers
John Harris
Andrew Buck
Robt Guile
Rombelow Morehen [?]
Willm Dwight
John Walters
Richard Browne
James Thackam
Richard Collins
Henry Cheney
George Jennings
Rich: Ward
[f.52r, col. 1]
Daniel Hayward
Roger Miles
Thomas Sharpe
William Smith
John Davis
Daniel Stockwell
John Canfield
Tho: Carter
Tho: Wright
Tho: Weston
John Savage
John Clarke
Francis Powel
John Knatt
Rich: Butterfield
Math: Stirrup
Gab: Gardner
John Chare
James Guile

John Buckett
John Harris
Richard Cater
John Harris
Henry Perkins
Edward Jennings
John Wells
Ed: Reason
Will: Jennings
John Parker
Willm Compton
Rich: Holland
Raph Tiler
Edward Luce
George Tiler
Giles Harding
John Collyer
William Bucket
William Lea
Austen Chapman
John Jennaker
Richard Bennet
John Woodrofe
Daniel Hobbins
[f.52r, col. 2]
Richard Whittington
Edward Hide
John Barrett
Francis Bush
Thomas Clark
James Hayward
Henry Pratt
Ferdinando Warner
Richard Hatch
William Jemmatt
Thomas Astill
Simon Linney
William Coleman
Philip Paty
William Chaney
Richard Farr
John Cooper
Thomas Cule
Philip Savage
William Andrewes
Robert Arnold
Henry Briarhurst
Augustin Hackett
[f.53r]
William Hawkins
Jeremy Atkines
Robert Robbinson
Rafe Burneham
Arthur Carver
Thomas Hance
John Dry
Robert Steavens
Thomas Fawly
Bartholomew Deane
Simon Loveioye
Edward Ennion
Roberte Webb
John Nutt
Hennery Noier
Ritchard Tiler
Peeter Parker
Franncis Prince
Tho: Hussey
William White
Thomas Parslow
John Granger
Samuell Cock
Ralphn Perkins
Thomas Elbery
John Griffin
Thomas Aurie
William Mathew
Anthony Noyer
Nathanewell Parkins
William Dee
Frances Farmer
Edward Bland
[f.54, col. 1]
Willyam Rackstraw
Robert Willyams
Edward Hide
John Smyth
Larence Carver
Edward Milam
Thomas Merit
Robert Younge
Georg Smyth
Thomas Messenger
Henry Sturrope
William Goade
George Munday
John Woode
Floris Linne
John Phillips
John Edmance
Ralph Messenger
Richard Alline
Robert Shearee
Thomas Browne
Thomas Flooyde
Na: Ward
Rich: Brian
Richard Cox
Mykiele Boulte
Richard Girdler
Roger Burnam
Dorian Floyd
John Clarke
Francis Longe
John Dabs
Tho: Combe
George Damsell
Richard Theede
John Mylam
Hen: Coopper
Daniell Wolde
Ralph Bartlet
Joseph Noblet [or Noblee?]
Thomas Wise
Barnadine Allawaye
Thomas Randall
Phillip Alvere [?]
Thomas Est
Willyam Johnson
[f.54r, col. 2]
Richard Floyde
Robert Sharpe
John Griffin
Richard Faro
William Almon
Richard Cookeman
Gerramy Dericke
Francis Dericke
Oliver Hester
Simon Loveioye
Cristopher Bisshope
John Granger

ROTHERFIELD GREYS

[f.55r, in three columns]

Rotherfeilde Grays

A returne of the names of all such as have taken the protestation within the parish of Rotherfeilde Grays, of Binfeilde hundred, in the County of Oxon, wich freely, and voluntarily made that protestation, whch the members of the Honble house of Commons in Parliament assembled made the 3 day of May 1641. [111]

[f.55r, col. 1]
John Hollins, Rector
Edward Web sen:
Edward Web iu:
Forester Elmes
Richard King
William Summer
Artois Winter
Francis Powell
Henry Osborne
Thomas Woolle
Philip Apsblon
Edward Heywood
Richard Redford *[name struck through]*
Thomas Shard
Richard Hill
Roger Sharde
William Reade
Thomas Campfeilde
Henry Bolt
Samuell Cooke
Andrew Costard
Edward Costard
Robert Costard
Richard Redman
Thomas White
Raphe Simons
Henry Lea *[name struck through]*
Augustine Granger
Richard Morris
Thomas Lucy
Walter Williams
James Rogers
Thomas Milborne
Richard Curtis
[f.55r, col. 2]
Charles Vere
Humphrey Paine
Adrian Norman
Robert White
John Kent
John Mayne
Thomas Williams
Robert Williams
Raphe Farrow
James Wigmore
William Willis
Mathew Fisher
Alexander Barnard Sen
Richard Barnard
Alexander Barnard iu
John Clarke
Gilbert Bayly
George Williams
George Ameris
John Coles
Richard Coles
Robert Browne
John Darby
Samuell Audry
Thomas Lucy
Daniell Cocke
Robert Norman
John Brookes
Richard Browne
George Browne
Bartholomew Whitehorne
Richard Bond
William Kent
Thomas Kent
[f.55r, col. 3]
Walter Kent
Nicholas Champion
George Jones
William House
John Edwards
John Nott
Thomas Bacchus
Thomas Shipway
Raphe Shipway
Robert Holder
Richard Neues [Neves ?]
Abraham House
John Smart
Edward Drewe
John Eest
John House
Thomas Clisbee
John Boyer
Raphe Boyer
Christoper Rakestraw
Robert Boyer
William Page
Raphe Page
Thomas Stiffe
Christopher House
Henry Redburne
John Dolton
Raphe Golder
William Butler
Thomas Alexander Se.
Thomas Alexander iu:
John Butler
Zachary Sarnye
William Alexander
John Godwin
Francis Fox

Ita testamur
Johannes Hollins, *Rect'*
Alexand Barnard,
Thomas Bacchus,
Joseph Stanes
Churchwardens

These 3 bargemen, Henry Lea, Henry Lum, Richard Redford, are absent, but being communicants, we presume they will not refuse it, when it is tendered to them.

ROTHERFIELD PEPPARD

[f.56r, in two columns]

Rotherfeilde Peppard

A returne of the names of those persons which have taken the protestation. [52]

William Graye, *minister*
Edward Clark, *Constable*
William Benwell,
John Kent,
Churchwardens
Walter Blackall,
William Corderye,
Overseers

[f.56r, col. 1]

Francis Benwell
John Benwell
John Sone
James Vergo
Richard Nash
Walter Clarke
Richard Clarke
Richard Ward
Richard Curtise
Thomas Curtise
John Blackall
Edward East
John Dolton
Henry Brian
John Clarke
William Warner
Augustine Kent
Raph Kent
Ambrose Inglis
William Filby
John Benwell
Robert Hedges
Henry Blackall
Raphe House

[f.56r, col. 2]

Francis Dolton
Theophilus Dolton
Richard Parker
Richard Lucy sen
Richard Lucy
Thomas Whiting
Robert Norman
Henry Benwell
Robert Godfrey
John Page
Augustine Knappe
William Cordery
William Cordery
Henry Browne
Thomas Golder
William Parker
Richard Ilsley
Thomas Apleton
John Bynfeild
Richard Crookes
Thomas Moore
John Barnes

SONNING

[f.57r, in two columns]

Feb: 20 1641

The names of them who have taken the protestation in the parte of the parish of Sonninge wch is in the Coun' of Oxon' [118]

[f.57r, col. 1]

Thomas Saxbe, *vic ibid*
Matthew Paine
John Simons
Walter Keene
Robert Binfeild
Charles Breach
George Asey [*or* Hey ?]
William Paine
Thomas Stevens
Edward Broune
Edward Rose
James Cope
Giles Blith
Thomas Champion
William Steere
Edward Tailor
John Frewin
John Broune
John Frewin *[sic]*
Edward Reade
William Simons
Anthony Lovejoy
Anthony Percy
Thomas Paine
Robert Cosens
Anthony Percy
John Townsend
Robert Wigmore
William Simons
Richard Gray
Henry Simons
Roger Sonndey
Richard Sonndey
Nicholas Webbe
Henry Sadgrove

[f.57r, col. 2]

Thomas Druce
John Purchase
Robert Glasse
Thomas Seaward
Michael Minson
Henry Thorne
Joseph Sonndey
Richard Horne
Thomas Wildgoose
John Booker
John Percy
Luke Lovejoy
Nicholas Richardson
Henry Champion
John Chamberlaine
Richard Sprules
John Groute
Thomas Stevens
Thomas Rose
William Jackson
Richard Parnes
Edward Nash
Jasper Winter
Martin Cannon
William Seaward
William Paine
Anthony Saunders
Henry Tailor
Henry Sparrow
Tho: Paine
John Hall
Tho Hall
William Button

[f.58r, col. 1]

Thomas Hutchins
Tho: Steevens
William Paine
Tho: Marlow
John Steevens
James Witshead
Edward Yonge
William Yonge
William Lovejoy
William Yewin
William Ford
John Morton
Tho: Kemble
Ralph Stere
Peter Wright
George Percy
Richard Barnes
John Pearcy
George Neles
Tho: Simons
Richard Binke
Edward Breach
Solomon Lovioy
John Wright
Lenard Nichols
Thomas Seaward
Walter Perrin
William Simons
John Simons
John Barfoote
John Knight

[f.58r, col. 2]

Tho: Seward
Richard Seward
Ralfe Kinge
John Lucas
Humfrey Loveioy
Tho: Heafield
Mechil Bolte
Abraham Kinge
Richard Hartwel
Tho: Geffery
John White
Tho: Nichols
John Martin
Robert Keene
Clement Sale
John Swaine
Robert Perrin
Roger Paine
John Pither
William Broune
John Simons Jun'
Robert Geffrey
Charles Jones

[The following note, as f.57a, is attached to the second sheet]

Sonning Parish:

A return of the names of them that wee warned to A Pear John Clith Constabel of ay[Eye] and Donsdon Thomas Marlo Church Warden Francis Tailor and Richard Breach overseers Thomas Huckin t[ith?]ingman

BLOXHAM HUNDRED

ADDERBURY EAST

[f.59r. In three columns.]

Feb 26th: 1642 [sic]
A catalogue of all the names of those that tooke the protestation of Adderbury the East. [114]

[f.59r, col. 1]
Mr. Oldish [William Oldys], Vicar
Mr. William Danvers
Mr. Richard Rowell
Mr. John Coles
Robert Gardner
Henry Gardner
John Adkines
John Rendall
Michaell Bellow
Hugh Wiatt
Thomas Wiatt
James Baseley
Francis Yeamans
John Mathewes
Robert Hayward
Robert Sammon
Richard Pittes
Edward Hide
Richard Bunker
Richard Boodle
William Eagles
John Gardner
Christopher Sammon
Thomas Harris
William Wheeler
Edward Griffin
Robert Sayle
Thomas James
Thomas West
Michaell Daniell
John Harris
Thomas Gaskin
Robert Lester
John White
John Wiatt
John Giles
John Burbery

[f.59r, col. 2]
Richard Spencer
Thomas Tustion
John Lake
Thomas Kinge
Richard Bootes
Richard Harris
John Price
John Robinson
Richalie Busbee
Anthony Burbuy
John Gilbert
Thomas Watts
John Tomolines
Robert Richards
Henry Penn
William Phillips
Moses Francklen
John Gardner
Richard Savige
Richard Maule
William Litchfield
Henry Carpenter
Thomas Jakeman
Richard Grantham
William Meades
Thomas Baker
Jonathan Hancoke
Richard Bloxham
Richard Jeffes
Thomas Carter
William Carter
Edward Cricke
William Higges
Henry Scott
James Maiyo
Henry Hunt
John Dunkeley
Simon Westly
Richard Child

[f.59r, col. 3]
Thomas Litchfield
Thomas Cox
John Cox
Thomas Cox *[sic]*
John Harris
William Crossley
Richard Bull
William Carter
Daniell Wooddert
William Pittes
Thomas Pittes
William Trafford
Richard Hall
Thomas Crosse
John Burlinge
Richard Horseman
Thomas Lictfield *[sic]*
Robert Baseley
William Webb
Simon Webb
John Gibbs
Richard James
Thomas Rooke
Anthony Adkin
Thomas Lester
William Lester
Simon Judd
Thomas Judd
Richard Bull
Richard Parish
Robert Kinge
Robert Baker
William Meades
Thomas Bunker
John Robinson
Richard Blinko
William Dolly
Robert Janson

*[**Assessment.** Membrane 1v, following on Milcombe.]*

Adderbury the East

The Lord Willmote, £5.12s.6d.
Sr William Cobbe, Knight, £3.15s.
Robert Gardner, 15s.
William Danvers, 3s.9d.
Henry Gardner, 7s.8d.
John Adkins, 11s.6d.
John Kendoll, 3s.9d.
Robert Sammon, 3s.9d.
Richard Pitts, 1s.11d.
John Gardner, 9s.5d.
Christopher Sammon, 2s.
John Gardner *[sic]*, 3s.9d.
Widd. Ranes, 5s.
[Membrane 2r]
Avis Dumbleton, 2s.6d.
Mathew Wyse, 3s.9d.
William Pitts, 5s.4d.
Thomas Crosse, 2s.
Mr Coles, 2s.6d.
Thomas Lester, 2s.
John White, 5s.
Robert Lester, 7s.
John Wyate and Widd. Wyate, 6s.4d.
Richard Spencer, 6s.
Anthony Burbery, 2s.
William Carpenter, 2s.6d.
Thomas Watts, 12d.
John Robinson, 12d.
Joane Jackeman, 9s.5d.
William Litchfeild, 3s.
Moses Frankline, 3s.9d.
Mris Bustard, 10s.
Symon Westly, 2s.4d.
Mathew Wyse jun., 6s.
Mathew Wyse sen., 1s.3d.
William Wheeler, 1s.3d.
Mary Coursey, 12d.
Thomas Gascoigne, 12d.
Thomas Cope, 3s.9d.
Widd. Upton, 1s.10d.
William Eagles and Eliz. Eagles, 1s.8d.
Thomas Hull, 2s.
Mary Hull, 2s.
James Basely, 6d.
Thomas Blincoe, 4d.
John Eagles, 4d.
Michael Barker, 1s.9d.
Widd. Sammon, 5s.
John Coxe, 1s.8d.
Edward Griffin, 4d.
Mr [William] Oldis, 12s.6d.
Mr [Richard] Rowell, 3s.4d.
John Price, 4d.
Samuel Goodwin, 2s.6d.
Mris Pymme, 12d.
Elizabeth Collins, 2s.
Dorothy Collins, 12d.
Anne Madge, 2s.
William Dalby, 1s.8d.
William Bayley, 4d.
Richard Grantam, 6d.
Thomas Carter, 3d.
Henry Hunt, 15d.
Robert Kinge, 9d.
William Lovesey, 3d.
John Dunkeley, 4d.
Henry Carpenter, 15d.
Richard Maul, 3d.
Henry Penne, 6d.
John Huckes, 6d.
James Mayor, 6d.
Richard Bookes, 6d.
Richard Harris, 6d.
Thomas Kinge, 2d.
Thomas Tustian, 3d.
John Myte, 6d.
Joyce White, 6d.
Richard Bull, 6d.
Widd. Crosse, 3d.
William Judde, 3d.
Thomas Litchfeild, 2d.
William Leister, 6d.
Richard Horseman, 12d.
Robert Sale, 4d.
Thomas Harris, 4d.
Hugh Wyate, 3d.
Thomas Wyate, 3d.

Sum £20.8s.

ADDERBURY WEST

Adderbury West

[f.61r, in three columns]
The names of those wch take this predistation [61]

[f.61r, col. 1]
John Doyley
Tymothye Dalbie
William Barbar
Tymothe Poulton
Thomas Swaine
Anthony Mathew
Thomas Upton Sen'
Thomas Upton Jun'
Thomas Adkins
Richard Blee
Hendey Chinner
Hugh Lathberry
John Tibbes
John Parsons
William Poulton
Richard Calcote
Edward Bratford
Richard Clarke
Thomas Maule sen'
Thomas Maule jun'
John Deane
[f.60r, col. 2]
Christopher Jackman
Richard Crooke
Roger Horsman
Thomas Bachiler
John Croker
Michaell Bankes
Christopher Doyley
Michaell Chambers
Charles Danvers
Mathew Higges
Henry Stenton
Richard Leachman
Thomas Walker
William Illiman
William Tanner
Robert Adkins
John Adkins
John Nibbes
Bowet Line
[f.60r, col. 3]
Richard Bellow
Michael Bellow
Robart Tayler
Edward Parishe
Nicholas Herrod
Nicholas Harris
Thomas Smith
Thomas Gauderne
John White
Roger Maule
Thomas Line
Thomas Harris
Richard Wackton
Nicholas Maule
Richard Gardner
John Childe
Richard Tibbes
William Densey
John Watson
William Wincott
William James

*[**Assessment.** Membrane 2r, following on Adderbury East.]*

Adderbury the West

Sr William Cobbe Kt, 22s.6d.
Robert Barber, gent., 15s.
Mr [William] Oldish, 5s.
Mr John Doyley and his mother, 22s.
Mr William Danvers, 4s.6d.
Mr [Richard] Rowell and George Danvers, 10s.
Mr [Michael] Bankes, 10s.
Mr Christopher Doyley, 1s.6d.
William Polton, 12s.6d.
Richard Belloe, 5s.
Robert Lester, 2s.6d.
Christopher Jakeman, 8s.
John Childs, 7s.
Richard Gardner, 4s.
[Membrane 2v]
Thomas Westly, 6s.3d.
Thomas Maul, 2s.6d.
William Densie, 2s.6d.
Thomas Lyne, 2s.
Thomas Kingstone, 6s.
Mr [Henry] Standard, 5s.
Thomas Hall, 6s.
Tymothy Poulton, 2s.6d.
Richard Gill, 2s.6d.
William Jakeman, 15d.
Widd. Yeomans, 5s.
Widd. Lyne, 2s.
Thomas Upton, 15d.
Henry Carpenter, 1s.6d.
Robert Westly, 5s.
William Coxe, 2s.6d.
Richard Tibbs, 9d.
Martin Swift, 5s.
Mr Tringe, 2s.6d.
Edward Deene, 5s.
William Wincott, 5s.
Widd. Barrett, 2s.
Thomas Yett, 6d.
Hugh Lathbury, 1s.6d.
Willm Rimell, 2s.6d.
John Adkins, 6d.
Willm Tanner, 6d.
Dorothy Collins, 1s.6d.
Widd. Phippes, 7d.
Mr Lydiate, 2s.6d.
Timothy Dalby, 2s.
Thomas Adkins, 18d.
Anthony Mathew, 2s.6d.
Robert Maul, 18d.
Michael Wyate, 18d.

Sum £11.1s.

ALKERTON

[f.61r, in two columns.]
***Alkerton** bill*

The names of all those that have taken theire protestation being all the men in our parrish [29]

[f.61r, col. 1]
Christopher Lidyat
Beniamine Goodwine
William Lidyat
Henrie Hancock
Tymothie Knibb
James Swarbrick
Edward Clifford
John Ell
Richard Hyron
John Lidyat
Mihill Potipher
William Guy
Richard Collins
John Collins
Jesper Barton
Thomas Goodwine
Joshua Goodwine
Thomas Yate
John Renolds
[f.61r, col. 2]
Henrie Ward
Richard Avelin
John Smart
Robert Cliffort
Richard Walker
Robert Hopper
William Meakes
William Yats

Henrie Hancock,
Edward Clifford,
Churchwardens
William Clifford,
Constable

*[**Assessment.** Membrane 4, following on Mollington.]*

Alkerton

Mr [Thomas] Lydiate, Cler., 16s.
Robert Burden, 16s.
John Goodwin, 16s.
Beniamyn Goodwin, 16s.
Christopher Lydiate, 18s.
William Lydiate, 16s.
Robert Hopper, 8s.
Jasper Barton, 2s.
Widd. Barton, 2s.
Thomas Slye, 2s.

Sum: £6.2s.

BARFORD ST. JOHN

[f.62r, single column.]

The names of All those persons as have taken the protestation that was enjoined them by the houses of parliament to be taken The which protestation was taken the 18th day of February 1641 first by William Oldish Vichar of Aderbury in Coun' Oxon and by Anthony Holton and John Hues Churchwardens and Robert Poulton Constable and Thomas Taylor and Thomas Flintt overseers for the pore of Barford Saynt Johnes in the parish of Adderbury aforesayde and afterwardes by them given to the rest of the Inhabitantes of the Sayde Towne whoose names are underwritten [35]

Householders

William Boudell
William Poulton
Richard Taylor
Lawrence Curnocke
Anthony Hawkenes
John Belcher
Thomas Poulton
Thomas Curnock
Christopher Meares
William Meares
Richard Ireones
John Betts
John Leechfeild
John Eezley
John Tredwell

Menes sones and servants

Abell Taylor
Nehemiah Pryne
John Poulton
Richard Bunting
Edward Parish
Thomas Poulton
Gyles Peake
Francis Bull
John Claridge
Robert Baker
Robert Lovedrene
Richard Hawkenes
Edward Baseley
Edward Betts
James Browne

and none of all those persones that did refuse but did all very willingly take it at the sayd time.

*[**Assessment.** Membrane 3r, following on Milton.]*

Barford St John

William Oldys, Cler., 15s.6d.
Thomas Edmonds, gen., 18s.6d.
Willm Bowdle, 13s.6d.
John Belcher, 12s.11d.
Thomas Tayler, 9s.
Willm Poulton, 4s.6d.
John Hughes, 5s.2d.
Thomas Poulton, 3s.6d.
Anthony Houlton, 3s.6d.
Anthony Hawkins, 2s.7d.
Richard Tayler, 3s.6d.
Thomas Cornocke, 2s.7d.
Thomas Flynte, 2s.7d.
Robert Poulton, 3s.6d.
John Litchfeild, 12d.

Sum £5.2s.5d.

BLOXHAM

[f.63r, in four columns.]

***Bloxham** in Count' Oxon'*

A note of all those that have taken the pitestation: not any of the towne refusinge to take the same [213]

[f.63r, col. 1]

John Griffith Esq.
John Lyne
William Kendall
Joseph White
Jeremiah Counser, generosus
Martin Bates
Thomas Meers
Richard Gascoigne
Thomas Gascoigne
Thomas Pangburne
Samuell Cleaver
William Bruce generosus
William Lovell senior
George Grime
John Drake
John Westly
Robert Greene
John Lovell
Robert Potter
Thomas Allen
Robert Richards
Timothy Parrish
Thomas Baseley
Robert Stranke
Jonathan Newell
John Hawkes
George Hawkes
Edward Richards
Edward Burrose
Thomas Haukes
John Bilson
William Pratt
Thomas Makins
Jonathan Churchill
Thomas Payne
Henry Johnson
Michaell Johnson
Michael Ball
Thomas White
William White
Thomas White
William Lamley
Robert Squire
George Bennett
Richard Simkins
Richard Cleaver
Robert Cleaver
William Bloxham
Hugh Hadland
Edward Hall

[f.63r, col. 2]

Richard Hilton
William Hall
Peeter French
Thomas French
John Rasken
Robert Carter
John Richards
William Nevell
William Ward
John Aston
Samuell Aston
George Aston
Robert Payne
Roger Jakeman
George French
Robert Bowers
Batholomew Hudson
Thomas Hudson
William Gardner
Thomas Sturman
Thomas Mayo
George Mayo
James Cakebread
Thomas Biggs
Thomas Farrent
Thomas Samon
Thomas Reighnolds
Richard Marshall
William Randoll
Thomas Aris
William Bloxham
John Turner
Timothy Gabell
Thomas Mayo Junio'
Jonathan Upton
Robert Taylor
Thomas Huckell
John Bignell
Thomas Hilton
Thomas Plestoe
Thomas Hickman
Tymothie Marsh
Hugh Parrish
Samuell Lovell
Richard Harrod
William Dolton
Hugh Sturman
Vallentine Keaver
William Lovell Junio'
John Parsons sen'
John Parsons jun'

[f.63r, col. 3]

Richard Samon senio'
Richard Samon
John Web
Edward Robinson
Beniamin Robinson
William Maule
Nickolas Beale
Richard Samon
John Battman
John Robinson
James Norton
Thomas Lovell
Thomas French
Robert Cleaver senio'
John Cleaver
John Blunt
John Clifton
Henry Hitchman
Thomas Hitchman
John Smith
Thomas Allen
Thomas Cattell
John Cattell
Richard Tylor
Samuell Tylor
Robert French
Thomas French
Mathew Whitaker
John Crannidge
Henry Barnes
Ralph Barnes
John Andros
John Cooke

George Greene
Hugh Lane
Thomas Taylor
Thomas Willetts
John Uwick
Robert Hilton
William Balyes
Robert Steynton
Thomas Gabell
John Wollams
John Gascoigne
William Gascoigne
William Hilton
Richard Samon
Thomas Merrivall
George Giles
Edward Leonard
Barnabee Gardner
Richard Emans
William Hitchman
[f.63r, col. 4]
Thomas Nickoles
John Nickoles
Thomas Nickoles Junio'
Thomas Padburie
John Freeman
Richard Basely
Nicholas Cricke
Nathaniell Cheese
Thomas Cheese
Robert Samon
Henry Rigsbie
John Halle
Robert Mesey
William Dalbie
Thomas Stranke
Richard Newell
Jonathan Newell
Joseph Newell
Gregory Peck
Daniell Lovell
John Lovell Junio'
John Palmer
Robert Pulton
Richard Guest
John Beck
William Beck
John Parsons
Robert Randoll
Thomas Penson
Thomas Hartley
John Barnes
John Goffe
Robert Coliat
Thomas Mall
Magnis Marden
Thomas Marden
Edward Sharpe
John Turner
William Randoll
Thomas Randoll
Tymothie Crakar, *Clerke*
Thomas Partridge
John Partridge
John Warren
John Plumer
Francis Drake
William Colsburne
Thomas Clemens
John Clemens
Walter Fiefeild
John Fiefeild
Richard March
Edward Lyne

Heerunto doe testifie
George Beenett, William Maull, *Churchwardens*
Roger Matthew, *Clerke*
Robert Richards, Henery Hitchman, *Constables*
Thomas Nicholes, William Lovell, *Ov'seers of the poor*

*[**Assessment.** Membrane 1, following on preamble.]*

Bloxham ps. Borealis
[i.e. North]

Thomas Chamberlayne esqr., 36s.
John Griffith esq., 36s.
Mr [Wm.] Bruce and Elizabeth Huckell, wid., 16s.
Roger Mathews *[sic]*, clerke, 15d.
Mr Jeremy Councer, 8s.9d.
Richard Hilton, 7s.6d.
John Lovell, 5s.
William Lambley, 10s.
George Bennet, 7s.6d.
Robert Potter, 8s.9d.
Mary Huckell, wid., 4s.5½d.
Alice Lovell, wid., 2s.6d.
William Lovell, 2s.6d.
Samuel Lovell, 7½d.
Widd. Parrish, 5s.
Thomas Plestowe, 7½d.
Timothy March, 7½d.
Thomas Huckell, 9s.5½d.
Thomas Reignolds, 5s.
Widd. Forren, 5s.
Widd. Dorwood, 15d.
Bartholomew Hudson, 15d.
Robert Payne, 5s.7½d.
Widd. Bloxham, 3s.9d.
George French, 8s.9d.
Thomas Dalby, 15d.
Dorcas Greene, 15d.
Widd. Phipps, 15d.
Timothy Parrish, 15d.
Thomas Payne, 15d.
Peeter French, 7½d.
Thomas Mayoe, 15d.
Widd. Kendoll, 7½d.
William White, 3s.9d.
Timothy Dalby, 15d.
William Turner, 15d.
Edward Hawten, 5s.7½d.
Gregory Pecke, 15d.
Thomas Lovell, 2s.6d.
John Westly, 3s.9d.
Robert French, 7½d.
Edward Robbins, 6s.3d.

Thomas Gabell, 1s.10½d.
Thomas Gascoigne, 15d.
Widd. Munt, 8½d.
John Gascoigne, 15d.
Anne Huckell, 15d.
Robert Measy, 12½d.
Francis Drake, 7½d.
John Gabell, 7½d.
Widd. Sammon, 15d.
William Bloxham, 7½d.
Widd. Mudwin, 15d.
The heirs of Ralph Carter, 7½d
William Ward, 3s.1½d.
Robert Richards, 2s.
Thomas Mankes *[sic; probably misreading for* Stranke], 6d.
Thomas Meakins, 12d.
Thomas Hudson, 15d.
Henry Sly, 12d.
Edward Burrowes *[Par. Reg.:* Burrose*]*, 2s.
Thomas Biggs, 6d.
George Mayoe, 12d.
George Grime [*Par. Reg.:* Ginne *or* Greene], 12d.
John Richards, 12d.

Sum: £12.13s.2d.
[Added below, presumably by auditor:] 12.14s.5d.

[Membrane 1v]
Bloxham ps. Australis
[i.e., South].

John Cartwright esqr., £4.
Roger Mathew *[sic]*, Clerke, 6s.3d.
Mr Jeremy Councer, 8s.1½d
Richard Gascoigne, 16s.
Thomas Nicholles, 12s.3d.
William Lovell sen., 6s.10½d.
Richard Sammon sen., 6s.3d.
John Westly, 12s.6d.
Richard Basely, 4s.4½d.
Henry Rigsby, 1s.10½d.
Gregory Pecke, 2s.6d.
Robert Sammon, 15d.
Henry Hitchman, 1s.10½d.
Widd. Gascoigne, 15d.
Edward Robbins, 15d.
Willm Maul, 2s.6d.
Willm Hilton, 1s.10½.
Richard Sammon jun., 7½d
Richard Newell, 7½d.
James Lovell, 15d.
Anthony Matthew, 7½d.
Samuel Gittins, 8s.1½d.
Widd. Stranke, 1s.10½d.
Thomas French, 15d.
Thomas Reignolds, 2s.6d.
Widd. Dorwood, 7½d.
Bartholomew Hudson, 7½d.
John Smith, 7d.
William Gascoigne, 7½d.
Widd. Cooke, 15d.
Robert Potter, 15d.
Elizabeth Councer, 5s.
John Cooke, 3s.6d.
John Goffe, 2s.6d.
John Warren, 12d.
Robert Hilton, 15d.
Thomas Willett, 12d.
James Norton, 15d.
John Parsons, 6d.

Sum: £10.4s.10d.

BODICOTE

[f.64r, in two columns.]
The names of the Inhabitants of Bodicott in the Countie of Oxon' who have taken the protestation in the twenties day of februarie 1641. [91]

[f.64r, col. 1]
William Burling
Thomas Hall seyn:
Mathew Cherrie
Richard Gileat
John Gileat
Richard Gileat Ju:
Willm Aris
John Smith
Saunders Pettie
John White
Sammuell Greene
Samuell Franklinne
Thomas Hancock
Willm Wise
Nathaniell Warde
William Barnes
Thomas Venne
Thomas Eden
Thomas Bellew
Sill: Bunker
Mathew Wise sey
John Penne
Willm Ryton
Joseph Grant
Thomas Mercer
Richard Rowsam
Edward Dumbleton
Willm Webb
Thomas Grant
Richard Ryton

[f.64r, col. 2]
Aleys Hansbury
Henrie Ward
Willm North
John Wheler
Mease Hall
William Gileat
Henn: Aris
Thomas Warde
Willm Grante
Richard Grante
Edward Sutton
Cornelius Phips
Antonie Lawrens
John Warde
Robert Wise
Henrie Wise
Mathew Wise
Leonard Hall
Richard Colleman
Willm Burling Jun:
Thomas Pettepher
Thomas Hall
Thomas Lukins
Thomas Webb
John Webb
Edward Robins
John Bellowe
Thomas Webb Jun:
Raphe Philips
Thomas Bradford
Willm Bradford
[f.64v, col. 1]
John Robins
Mathew Wise
Robert Whing
Willm Bradford
Mathew Ryton
Thomas Handes
Willm Holloway
Thomas Penne
Thomas Clifford
Thomas Francton
Mathew Dale
Mathew Goodwine
John Ritonn
John Awcock
[f.64v, col. 2]
John Bratford
John Webb
Mathew Wise
Thomas Wills
Edward Wheler
Richard Grimley
Robert Wise
Jonathan Webb
Nicholas Busbie
Robert Dale
Thomas Merrie
John Webb
Willm Grimley
Will: Goafe
Will: North
Edw: Houghton [*or* Stoughton?], *Curat ibim*

*[**Assessment**. Membrane 2v, following on Adderbury West.]*

Boddicott

Sr William Cobbe, Knight, 32s.
Willm Oldish, Clerke, 7s.8d.
Mr Heyres, 11s.6d.
Mr Howes, 8s.8d.
Mr Lucan, 2s.10d.
Mr Vivers, 11d.
Mr Hawtrey, 5s.
Willm Bradford and his sonne Thomas, 15s.4d.
Willm Burlinge and his daughter, 12s.6d.
Henry Ward, 9s.7d.
Willm Graunte *[or* Grannt(e) *here and below]*, 4s.4d.
Thomas Hall, 2s.4d.
Joseph Graunt, 1s.10d.
Willm Writen, 2s.
Thomas Hall and his sonne, 5s.9d.
John Wheeler and his sonnes, 3s.10d.
John Penne, 13s.5d.
Thomas Webbe and his sonne Thomas, 19s.
Widd. Penne, 3s.10d.
Mathew Wyse sen., 5s.6d.
For Adderbury Towne land wh. Richard Coleman Farmes, 5s.4d.
Henry Wyse, 3s.10d.
Robert Wyse, 18s.5d.
Robert Wyse and his sonne, 5s.6d.
Widd. Wyate, 5s.9d.
Thomas Wills, 2s.
Willm North, 3s.10d.
Thomas Graunte, 1s.
Richard Graunte, 12d.
John Webb, 9d.
Mathew Wyse jun., 11d.
Edward Pittome, 12d.
Willm Penne, 1s.10d.
Robert Wyse jun., 8d.
Nathaniel Ward, 1s.6d.
Robert Winge, 6d.
Willm Barnes, 12d.
John Robins, 12d.
Henry Aris, 6d.
Mathew Cherry, 6d.
John Smith, 6d.

Sum £11.12d.*[sic]*

BROUGHTON (including North Newington)

[f.65r, in two columns]
Jann: 16. 1641

Comitat. Oxon' the names of those that have taken the protestation in Broughton and Newington. [75]

[f.65r, col. 1]
Raphe Taylor, *minister ibid*

John Fiennes *[probably a signature, added after the main list was compiled, in the space above the second column]*

Josiah Slader
William Lampith
John French
Edward Holloway
Francis Stafford
Clement Rogers
Solomon Nicks
Joseph French
Symon Mourby
Edward Rowly
Jonathan Rowly
William Page
Thomas Buller
Thomas Wilkins
Edward Thomson
Francis Thomson
Symon Thomson
Richard O-ers[?]
Thomas Watts
Samuel Watts
Thomas Moore
Samuel Homes [*or* Howes?]
Richard Gittway
Richard Harris
John Baul
Thomas Alcocke
William Rawlins
Thomas Dadwell
John Roberts
John Roberts *[sic]*
Richard Luccocke
Solomon Gide[?]
Andrew Daulby
John Woodfeild
Henrie Williams
John Averie
Roger Jackman
Francis Bull
John Pearch
Thomas Roberts
Edward Matthew
Robert Barton

[f.65r, col. 2]
Richard Symonds
Richard Beale
John Lecke [*or* Kecke]
William Watts
Thomas Watts
John Ellyman
William Hastings
Samuell Graunt
Richard Dumbleton
Thomas Knowles
John Sconce
John Parkins
Richard Hastings
Jeffery Lecke [*or* Kecke]
Thomas Leck [*or* Keck]
Daniel Strange
Joseph Lecke [*or* Keeke]
John Varnan
Richard Varnan
William Hartlett
William Alken[?]
Solomon Androse
Edward Williams
William Rush
John Rush
Thomas Wills

John Wilkins, *Cunstable*
Alexander Jackson,
Anthonie Tustian,
Churchwardens
Richard Morrie,
John Hicks, *Overseers for the poore*

*[**Assessment.** Membrane 5r, following on Wroxton.]*

Broughton and Newton
[North Newington]

The Lord Viscount Say and Seale, £8.5s.7d.
Mr James Fennis, £5.5s.8d.
Mr [Raphe] Tayler, Cler., 10s.
Mr Slater [?Slader], 5s.
John French, 13s.
John Ball, 11s.
John Woodfeild, 2s.
Mr [Clement] Rogers, 3s.
Andrew Dalby, 2s.3d.
John Nicholls, 4s.
John Hicks, 3s.
Richard Gittaway, 5s.
Margaret Gibbert, 12d.
[Membrane 5v]
Thomas Watts, 3s.6d.
Thomas Alcocke, 12d.
Alexander Jackson, 12d.
Richard Luckocke, 5s.
Edward Rowley, 12d.
Sollomon Nicholles, 3s.
Willm Lampitt, 3s.
Edward Hollowell, 3s.
John Roberts, 3s.
John the Londer *[sic]*, 12d.
Edward Tompson, 12d.
Symon Morby, 12d.
Richard Samson, 5s.6d.
Richard Symmons, 12s.
Symon Coleman, 7s.
Anthony Tustian, 18d.
Richard Varnan and his sonne John, 10s.
William Watts, 10s.
Richard Hastings, 10s.
Richard Dumbleton, 12d.
John Sconce, 4s.
John Leeke, 8s.
Thomas Leeke, 12d.
John Ellimore, 4s.
William Allen, 3s.
Mr William Goodwin, 8s.

Sum £22.2s.

DRAYTON

[f.66r, in two columns]
A note of the names of all the Inhabitants of Drayton which have taken the protestation 22 day February 1641 [35]

[f.66r, col. 1]
***Drayton** Inhabitants:*
Mr. Thomas Lodg [Lodge], *Minister*

Thomas Goodwin
Brett Goodwin
Luke Davis
Thomas Mole
Thomas Austin
Richard Austine
Edward Fewterer
Richard Saule
William Maior
Richard Maior
John Bratford
William Jarvice
Edward Jarvice
Richard Farden
Richard Tayler
Edward Whitbee
John Potter
Robert Muddin
Nathaniell Claridg
Simon Piner
Richard England
John Draper
[f.66r, col. 2]
Edward Welles
Nathaniell Mole
Daniel Bratford
Thomas Davis
Robert Hackwood
Thomas Saule
Gamaliell Mole
Thomas Mole
Thomas Moore
William Whitbee
John Howkins
Nicholas Arice

***Note.** For **Epwell**, see Introduction, page xiv*

*[**Assessment.** Membrane 3v, following on Horley.]*

The right honble. the Lord Say & Seale, £4.8s.4d.
Mr James Fennys, 5s.8d.
The Lady Elizabeth Cope, 27s.4d.
Mr Robert Austen, 33s.4d.
Mr Willm Thorpe, 5s.8d.
Mr Cotten and Mr Millett, 8s.
Mr Willm Wheatlye, 7s.4d.
William Jarvis, 4s.
Michael Hardinge, 4s.8d.
John Bradford, 12d.
William Maior, 8d.
Richard Saule, 3s.
Thomas Austen, 2s.
Nathaniel Mole, 18d.
[Membrane 4r]
Daniel Bradford, 2s.
Gamaliel Mole, 18d.
John Potter, 2s.
Richard Farden, 2s.
Luke Davies, 18d.
Grivell Hiberdine, 18d.
Mr [Thomas] Lodge, cler., 18s.

Sum: £11.6s.

HANWELL

[f.67r, in two columns, grouped as shown.]

Hanwell

The names of those, who have protested [51], are as follow

[f.67r, col. 1]
William Norbury
Thomas Norbury
Edward Cox
Nathaniell Cox
Timothy Cox
William Cox
Peter Stainton

John Claridge
Richard Grant
Thomas Bowers
John Lucas

William Lucas
John Mumford
Thomas Claridge
James Claridge
Michael Mayoh
Richard Grant
William Grant

William Buller
Thomas Buller
Edward Buller
Thomas Haines
George Haines
William Borton
Edward Borton
John Haslood sen'
[f.67, col. 2]
Nathaniell Osborne, *Constable*
William Rickets
Laurence Watkin
John Haslood jun'
Thomas Haslood
John Hawks
William Glaze
Samuell Glaze
Thomas Smalley
John Davis
George Claridge
John Gardner
Jonas Haslood
Thomas Grant
Robert Yates
Thomas Prat
John Prat
Thomas Bradford
John Muddin
John Claridge
Joseph Grant

The residue have already made their protestation at Banbury Febr. 15. Before the right w'pfull his Majesties Justices of the Peace, met there for that purpose.

[The next four names inserted at the foot in different handwriting:]

Samuel Bowars
Thomas Graunt
Samuel Plorrier[?]
Edward Graunt

These have protested, nor know I of any who refuseth in this place.
Rob: Harris. *Rector*

*[**Assessment.** Membrane 3, following on Barford St. John.]*

Hanwell

The Lady Elizabeth Cope, 55s.
Robert Harris, Cler., 20s.
William Norbury, 4s.6d.
Edward Cope, 9d.
Anthony Claridge, 18d.
Thomas Hickes, 18d.
Richard Graunte [*or* Grannte, *and below*] jun., 1s.1½d.
Stephen Dowe, 2s.7½d.
Thomas Bowers, 3s.
John Lucas, 4d.
Willm Mumford, 3s.
Thomas Claridge, 5s.[?]
Michael Mayowe, 4½d.
Thomas Mumford, 18d.
Richard Graunt sen and his mother, 2s.3d.
Willm Graunt, 3s.
Willm Buller, 6s.
Thomas Haynes, 2s.10d.
Willm Borton, 4s.
Edward Wootton, 11s.
Edward Borton and his mother, 18d.
Nathaniel Osborne, 3s.8½d.
John Haslewood, 2s.3d.
Willm Ricketts, 4s.
Edward Graunt, 2s.7½d.
John Gardner, 3s.
Jonas Haslewood, 2s.9d.
Thomas Graunt, 3s.
Peter Staynton, 4d.
John Mudwin, 12d.
Robert Yates, 18d.
John Claridge, 4d.
Stephen Dowe, 12d.
Thomas Pratt, 4d.
George Claridge, 4d.
William Glaze, 8d.
Thomas Smalley, 6d.
Widd. Blakesley, 4d.
Thomas Haslewood, 6d.
Lawrence Watkins, 6d.
Willm Coxe, 6d.

Sum: £8.

HORLEY

[f.68r, in two columns.]

The names of those tht tooke the protestation in the parish of Horley, feb: 21: Anno Dom:1641 [47]

[f.68r, col. 1]
Mr. Anthony Danvers
John Clarson
Thomas: Clarson
John: Goodwin: ju:
John: Clarson: jun:
William: Kine
John: Kench: jun'
Valentine: Parker
William: Dry
John: Bradford
Thomas: Watson:
Alexander: Garner
Thomas: Saul
Thomas: Blackwell
John: Kench: se:
Henry: Parker
Peter: Mumford:
Richard: Cooke
William: Kench
Edward: Kench
William: Nichols
Amfrdg: [*altered to* Humfrydg] Locke
Richard: Holloway
James Bottomly
Christopher: Wheeler
John: Rainebow
Henry: Robins
William: Merry
Richard: Highhorne
[f.68, col. 2]
John: Bankes
Christopher: Cooke
Richard: Pratt
William: Saul
John Goodwin: se:
Thomas: Kench
John: Mumford
Samuell: Dey
Thomas: West
John: Ancorne
John: Parish
Thomas: Bankes
Jonathan: Bartlett
John: Westbury
William: Bowers
Michaell: Pratt
Thomas: Arlidge
William Blackwell

*[**Assessment.** Membrane 3v, following on Hornton.]*

Horly

Anthony Danvers, gent., 23s.
Willm Coleman, 18d.
John Clarkeson, 13s.9d.
Richard Holloway, 7s.
Thomas West, 5s.
John Anker, 7s.
John Bratford, 2s.3d.
Richard Coleman, 18d.
John Kinch, 6s.6d.
John Goodwin, 5s.
Henry Parker, 9s.6d.
William Bowler, 7s.
Thomas West, 2s.3d.
William Nicholls, 11d.
Beniamine Lovell, 3s.
Richard Pratt, 2s.
Willm Blackewell, 12d.
Willm Bowers, 18d.
Willm Kinch, 3d.
Richard Hixe, 3d.
Peter Mumford, 5s.6d.
Christopher Wheeler, 18d.
John Saul, 4s.
Gregory Walline, 1s.10d.
Mary Carpenter, 2s.
Mary Saul, 1s.3d.
Valentine Gardner, 2s.3d.
Avis Saul, 4d.
Richard Sharman, 1s.2d.
Edward Pratt, 14d.
Phillip Wasburne, 3d.
William Tibitts, 6d.
John Mumford, 3d.

Sum: £6.2s.9d.

HORNTON

[f.69r, in three columns.]

The names of all the Inhabitants of Hornton wch have taken their Protestation [73]

[f.69r, col. 1]
William Osburne, Curate
William Ladkines
Richard Croftes
William Mister senior
Richard Sharman
Richard Box
Richard Hix
Edward House
Thomas Hyern senior
Richard Greene
Richard Banwell senior
Richard Adames
John Eaborne
John Walker
Thomas Banwell
William Payne
George Manning
Henry Treeve
Thomas Smith
Richard Grime
John Symkines
William Collet
Richard Gylkes
John Randell
William Bagger
[f.69r, col. 2]
William Goodwin senior
Richard Denny
John Grime
William Mister Junior
Thomas Sharman
Thomas Hix senior
Walter Eaborne
Thomas Hitchcock
Thomas Hyern Junior
John Hix
Richard Banwell Junior
Thomas Gylkes
Jeffery Juskines
William Robbines
Henry Hitchcock
Richard Hawtin
William Hutchines
Richard Arne
John Garner
Hugh Gyles
John Palmer
Robert Mayow
John Tayler
John Letch
Erasmus Symmons
[f.69r, col. 3]
William Goodwin Junior
John Hitchcock
William Bird
Walter Nix
George House
Thomas Hix Junior
Philip Wasburne
Thomas Letch
George Browne
[John Symkines, *deleted*]
Thomas Greene
Thomas Croftes
Robert Browne
Henry Gaskines
George Burwell
Umphery Ray
Joseph Hyern
Henry Denny
John Denny
Foulke Lampery
John Hill
Thomas Garner
Leonell Barfoot
Christopher Bird

*[**Assessment.** Membrane 3v, following on Hanwell.]*

Horneton

William Goodwin, 19s.6½d.
Richard Letch, 13s.6d.
Richard Sharman and his mother, 14s.8d.
Richard Arne, 22s.5½d.
Richard Croftes, 12s.
William Mister, 13s.
Walter Enborne, 14s.1d.
Philip Wasburne, 10s.9½d.
Thom' Hixe jun. and John Hixe, 5s.5d.
John Palmer, 5s.3½d.
Edward Howse, 2s.4d.
Thomas Hix, sen, 6s.8½d.
Thomas Greene, 6s.6d.
George Howse, 3s.2d.
John Gyles, 9d.
Elizabeth Gilkes, 9d.
Richard Gryme, 2s.3d.
Elizabeth Phipps, 2s.1d.
Isaak Symkins, 6d.
Foulke Lampery, 16d.
William Badger, 12d.
Willm Bird, 12d.
Richard Boxe, 12d.
Henry Treeve, 12d.
Richard Hixe, 12d.
John Denny, 6d.
Joseph Hyron, 6d.
Walter Nixe and his sonne, 15d.
Leonell Barfoot, 6d.
Widd. Hawten, 6d.
Erasmus Symmons, 6d.
Richard Banwell, 12d.
Thomas Letch, 3s.5d.

Sum: £8.10s.

MILCOMBE

[f.70r, single column.]

All the inhabitants of Milcombe have taken the protestation whose names are here subscribed. [44]

Mr. William Reive,
Curate ib[id]em

George Dalby, gentleman
William Bonner, gentleman
John Dalby
Robert Gibbeard
Phillip Potter
John Roberts
George Haughtin
Richard Potter the elder
John Russell
Edward Bucher
Thomas Burchall
William Sale
Thomas French
John Eagles
John Norton
William Browne
Richard Hicman
Robert Hicman
Thomas Stranke
Robert Treadwell
Humfrey Twoyeareold
William Tustin
John Buckingame
Robbert Potter
Richard Potter the younger
Phillip Bucher
John Turbut
Chrystopher Smith
Beniamin Ward
James Coper
Alexander Venson
Edmund Davis
Andrew Stranke
Water Barlett
Thomas Vincles
John Phipes
Richard Boughton
Robert Scot
Samuel Roberts
John Austin
Hugh Sterman
Thomas Walter
Thomas Bloxam
William Pritchet

taken the 21th of February 1641

*[**Assessment.** Membrane 1v, following on Bloxham.]*

Milcombe

John Cartwright esqr., 15s.
Rowland Baugh, gent., 30s.
William Bonner, gent., 12s.6d.
George Dalby, gent., 40s.
John Dalby, gent., 10s.
William Reeve, Clerke, 2s.
Mr Thomas Holloway, 5s.
Phillip Potter and Edward Belcher, 5s.4½d.
Richard Potter, 6s.3d.
John Roberts, 5s.
Susanna Stranke, vid., 5s.
Robert Tredwell, 2s.6d.
Thomas Burchall, 3s.9d.
Joane Hickman, widd., 2s.6d.
Joane Hickman, widd. *[sic]*, 2s.6d.
John Hartwell, 1s.3d.
Mr Ambrose Holbidge [Holbeche?], 3s.9d.
John Carpenter, 5s.
Robert Gibberd, 7s.6d.
Samuel Lovell, 7½d.
Thomas Walter, 2s.6d.
George Hawten, 5s.
Richard French, 18d.
John Norton, 3s.
William Sale, 18d.
Thomas French, 2s.
John Eagles, 2s.6d.
William Browne, 2s.6d.
John Russell, 3s.
Robert Hickman, 9d.

Sum £9.10s.

MILTON

[f.71r, in two columns.]

Oxon' ***Milton*** *in the Parishe of Adderbury.*

The names of those that have taken the Protestation at Milton aforesaid [41]

[f.71r, col.1]
Robard Swifte
Thomas Westley
Richard Neale
John Bellow
Robart Turner
John Turner
Thomas Cox
Simon Cox
Martine Swifte sen'
William Cox
William Webb
Samuell Cox
Josias Cox
John Liddiate
William Maule
George Maule
Caneman Flecman
Edward Swifte
William Bayley
Edward Wootton
[f.71r, col. 2]
John Wyatt
Richard Gill
Willia Chaplen
John Gibbes
Richard Nevell
Anthony Nevell
Robart Maule
Christopher Swifte
Martine Swifte Jun'
William Nevell
John Mayo
William Halle
Thomas Deane
William Turner
Thomas Turner sen'
John Turner
Thomas Turner Jun'
Thomas Maule
Anthony Turner
John Turner sen'
John Turner Jun'

There are none that denie this protestation within my libertie.

*[**Assessment.** Membrane 2v following on Bodicote.]*

Milton

Mr [Henry] Standard for land yt William Bayle, Martin Swift and Richard Neale Farme, 12s 6d.
Willm Oldis, cler., 12s.
Mr Tayler, 4s.8d.
Mr Christopher Doyley, 8s.4d.
Mr Cricke, 5s.
[Membrane 3r]
Mr Brunie [*or* Bruine], 3s.
Thomas Hall for land that William Turner, Symon Cox, Richard Neale and Richard Gill Farme, 12s.
Willm Coxe, 3s.
Thomas Westly, 6s.6d.
Willm Coxe *[sic]*, 6s.6d.
John Lydiate, 5s.4d.
William Maul, 5s.4d.
William Turner, 4s.6d.
Richard Neale, 3s.6d.
Thom's Turner, 3s.6d.
Thom's Maul, 3s.4d.
Robert Swift, 3s.
Widd. Mayowe, 3s.
Edward Swift, 2s.
Christopher Cope, 2s.6d.
John Bellowe, 2s.
John Turner, 12d.
Widd. Phippes, 6d.
Christopher Swift, 6d.
Richard Nevill, 6d.
Anthony Nevill, 2d.
William Bagle *[sic, but ? for* Bayle*]*, 2s.
Richard Gill, 18d.
Martyn Swift ye younger, 18d.
Symon Cope, 18d.
Thom's Cope, 12d.
Martyn Swift sen., 4d.
Samuel Cope, 8d.
Josias Cope, 4d.

Sum £6.2s.6d.
[Added below, presumably by auditor:]
£6.3s.0d.

Sibford Ferris *and* ***Sibford Gower****: see under* ***Banbury Hundred (Swalcliffe)****, pages 48-49.*

TADMARTON

[f.72r, in two columns.]

The Bill of the parish of ***Todmorton*** in the County of Oxon' [80]

[f.72r, col. 1]

Ambrose Saycheverill, *Clarke*
Thomas Browner, *minister*
John Potter, Ewen Anderton, *Churchwardens*
John Pittway, *Cunstable*
Robert Pargeter, John Ward, *Collectors*
Thomas Bloxham
John Potter Junior
Daniell Lord
Richard Hartlett
Henry Profitt
Robert Best
John Bourton
Edward Hawten
James Hawten
William Samman
William Slamaker
Thomas Austen
Richard Gunne
Thomas Potter
Organ Nicholles
John Greene Senio'
John Greene Junio'
Isaak Greene
Timothie Samman
John Freeman
Robert Lord
John Coales
Richard Butler
Thomas Baynard
John Dumbleton Senio'
John Dumbleton Junio'
Thomas Hiron
Richard Hiron
Organ Dumbleton
Thomas Hiron *[sic]*
Richard Hiron *[sic]*
Organ Dumbleton *sic]*
Thomas Broderton
William Bloxham
Richard Ward
Samuell Ward
Samuell Hiron
William Hawten
Henry Lynnett
Thomas Tredwell

[f.72r, col. 2]

John Spratly Senio'
John Spratly Junio'
Robert Dabson
John Benson
Thomas Chubley
James Slade
William Lovell
William Nibbs
Frauncis Grivell
John Oliver
Richard Hawten
Robert Hawten
Henry Hawten
Edward Hawten
Frauncis Tayler
William Hedges
John Baker
Raphe Carter
John Blacwell
John Broderton
John Smith
William Dumbleton
Thomas Warde
Henry Warde
John Weston
William Smart
William Wesbury
John Hawten
Robert Hawten
John Spratly Junio'
John Dumbleton Junio'
Ferdinando Dumbleton
John Clarke
Thimothie Clifford
David Pargeter
John Simkins

All these are of our parish of Todmorton above the age of eighteene, And they have all taken the protestation according to the order appointed, the xxiiih day of February 1641.

*[**Assessment.** Membrane 4v, following Sibford Ferris.]*

Tadmerton

Ambrose Sacheverill, Cler., 33s.
Erasmus Sacheverill, gent., 8s.
Thomas Bloxham, 5s.
Anne Plestowe, Widd., 3s.
John Potter, 7s.
Alice Bayley, Widd., 14s.
Daniel Lord, 6s.
Robert Pargittor, 3s.
John Bourton, gent., 20s.
James Hawten, 3s.
William Sammon, 2s.
John Dumbleton, 6s.
Edward Hawten, 6s.
Thomas Austen, 5s.
Richard Gunne, 5s.6d.
John Pittway, 6s.6d.
Timothy Sammon, 12d.
Thomas Potter, 12d.
John Greene, sen., 6d.
Mary Mason, Widd., 12d.
Timothy Hiron, 12d.
Richard Hartlett, 12d.
Thomas Baynard, 5s.6d.
John Ward, 3s.
Alice Dumbleton, Widd., 4s.
Organ Dumbleton, 12d.
Thomas Hiron and his sonne Richard, 10s.
Katherine Gibbert, 5s.
Owen Anderton, 3s.
Richard Bloxham, 8s.
Katherine Hucks, widd., 12d.
Susanna Austen, Widd., 12d.
William Potter, 3s.
Joyce Ward, Widd., 4s.
Richard Ward, 4s.6d.
Samuel Hyron, 8s.
William Hawten, 5s.6d.
Margery Baker, widd., 5s.
Henry Lynnett, 2s.
Thomas Tredwell, 4s.
John Spratley and his sonne Thomas, 5s.
David Pargittor, 6d.
Sum £6.8s.

WIGGINTON

[f.73r, in two columns.]

Wee whose names are heare underwritten of the parish of Wigginton have taken the protestation on Saturday the 19th of February 1641. [41]

[f.73r, col. 1]
Thomas Holloway min'r
George Blount
Thomas Tayler
Thomas Croftes
Bartholomew Robines
George Box
Richard Allin
William Box
John Tayler
James Shealer
Frauncis Hiatt
Mathew Harrod
John Box
Thomas Wickens
William Lamburd
Thomas Kerrod
James Callcot
Humphrey Haull
Richard Wiatt
William Yates
John Wickens
William Scooler
William Callcot
William Harris
Frauncis Shealer
Richard Calcote
Richard Hall
George Broadstocke
[f.73r, col. 2]
John Croftes
Thomas Giles
Walter Calcote
John Allin
John Baker
William Haull
John Callcote
John Haull
Richard Haull
John Newell
Roberd Price
John Newell
John Wesbury

*[**Assessment.** Membrane 4v, following Tadmarton.]*

Wigginton

Thomas Holloway, Cler., 22s.6d.
George Blunt, gent., 13s.
Richard Hall sen., and William Hall, 10s.
Widd. Wesberry, 3s.9d.
Richard Harris, 15d.
James Calcott, 6s.3d.
Frauncis Shealer, 5s.
Humphry Hall sen. and Richard Hall jun., 3s.9d.
Widd. Boxe, 15d.
Mathew Harwood, 2s.6d.
[Membrane 5r]
William Lambert, 3s.9d.
Widd. Gyles, 3s.9d.
Humphry Hall jun., 5s.
Thomas Crofts, 6s.3d.
Widd. Newell, 2s.6d.
John Newell, 3s.9d.
John Calcott, 7½d.
John Hall, 5s.
Thomas Tayler, 3s.9d.
Richard Calcott, 5s.
Frauncis Hiate, 2s.6d.
Thomas Dumbleton, 7½d.
William Lovell, 15d.

Sum £5.13s.

WROXTON and BALSCOT

[f.74r, in three columns.]

Oxon' Bloxh'

The names of all those that have taken the protestation the 22th of February 1641 of Roxton and Balscott as followeth [108]

[f.74r, col. 1]
Sr Thomas Pope
Anthony Litchfeilde
Henry Aldingeton
Edward Holloway
Richard Grant
Thomas Taylor
Henry Coleman
George Cox
Christopher Cox
Edward Lucas
Thomas Ingram
Luke Wooten
John Carter
John Carter *[sic]*
Thomas Coleman
Richard Coleman
Edward Foukes
John Cox
Henry Cowpere
Henry Battes
William Williams
Richard Corbett
Richard Busbey
Robard Garner
[f.74r, col. 2]
Samuell Aldingeton

Malachy Aldingeton
William Lucas
John Lucas
John Holloway
William Buckeland
William Carpenter
Tymothy Carpenter
Thomas Johnson
Thomas Johnson *[sic]*
Robard Greene
Henry Farman
Henry Holloway
William Carpenter
Thomas Chetell
John Hayes
Simon Lentton
Edward Lucas
John Webb
William Cleridge
George Tasker
William Ellys
William Parker
Richard Hancocke
[f.74r, col. 3]
Richard Gibard
John Hayes
William Samon
John Hayes
William Holloway
John Smyth
Vallentine Johnson
Thomas French
John Mumforde
John Hewes
John Wates
William Muncke
Simon Mumforde
Thomas Grante
Thomas Wayte
James Wauker
Thomas Greenwoode
Robard Coleman
William Greene
Edward Wayte
Edward Handes
Arthur Hale
John Deane
Richard Hartelett
Thomas Bowller
Jonathan Bartlite

Balscott

[f.72r, col. 1]
Francis Webb, 'geit.'
Robard Burden
Vallentine Garner
Thomas Sly
Henry Adkins
Henry Plum
Robard Ingram
John Bayer
Humfrey Dick
John Plum
John Dicke
[f.72r, col. 2]
Edward Adkins
Richard Adkins
William Tayler
Barnebe Mathews
Edward Gurman
John Robins
Edward Nyxes
John Garner
Robard Hanley
John Ingram
Henry Clarke
[f.72r, col. 3]
Ambrose Taylar
John Reynolds
John Brateforde
Jeffery Hanley
Abram Furins
Daniell Pinfolde
Richard Clifford
Richard Taylar
Richard Adams
Thomas Brateford
John Smedly

Thomas Taylar, *Cunstable of Roxton & Balscott*

*[**Assessment.** Membrane 5r following on Wigginton.]*

Wroxton and Balscott

Sr Thomas Pope, Knight, £6.8s.
Anthony Litchfeild, 11s.6d.
William Carpenter, 3s.8d.
Thomas Tayler, 9s.2d.
Robert Coleman, 5s.6d.
Richard Holloway, 5s.9d.
William Greene, 4s.7d.
Luke Wotton, 4s.7d.
John Carter, sen., and John Carter jun., 4s.10d.
Edward Wayte, 1s.10d.
Valentyne Johnson, 1s.2d.
Symon Mumford, 1s.10d.
John Mumford, 3s.8d.
Richard Hancocke, 7s.11d.
Elizabeth Bartlet, 3s.8d.
Anne Bartlet, 1s.10d.
John Lucas, 1s.2d.
Richard Graunt, 6s.5d.
Edward Holloway, 10s.11d.
Thomas Ingram, 4s.10d.
George Coxe, 1s.10d.
William Lucas, 4s.2d.
Edward Lucas, 1s.10d.
Thomas French, 1s.10d.
Christopher Coxe, 1s.10d.
John Mills, 4s.11d.
William Holloway, 4s.10d.
George Tasker, 1s.2d.
Henry Holloway, 1s.2d.
William Sammon, 1s.2d.
Henry Aldington, 4s.7d.
Samuel Aldington, 4s.7d.
Timothy Carpenter, 11d.
Henry Forman, 7d.
Anne Roberts, 1s.2d.
Mris Webbe, 1s.2d.
Robert Burden, 17s.5d.
Valentyne Gardner, 9s.8d.
Edward Adkins, 9s.2d.
William Tayler, 9s.2d.
Ambrose Tayler, 11s.3d.
John Ingram, 3s.
Richard Adkins, 3s.8d.
Henry Plombe, 3s.8d.
Henry Clarke, 1s.2d.
John Reignolds, 4s.7d.
William Elletts, 4s.
Samuel Bradford, 5s.6d.
Jeffery Horly, 1s.3d.
Richard Ingram, 1s.2d.

Sum £18.4s.
[£18.4s.4d.]

CHADLINGTON HUNDRED

ASCOTT-UNDER-WYCHWOOD [81]

[f.75r, in two columns.]
The names of all the Inhabitants of Ascott under Whichwood in the Countie of Oxon' that made the protestacon the 20h of Februarie Anno domine 1641 according to the Order from the Parliamt

[f.75r, col. 1]
John Fryers
Nicholas Perrie sen'
William Fletchar iun'
Peter Poole
Thomas Winchester
Fulke Chaundie
Richard Palmer
Nicholas Clarke
Thomas Gill
Charles Hamonde
George Peisler
Thomas Whyting
Henry Brookes
Thomas Hickes
William Whyting
George Henlowe sen'
Edward Dunford
Richard Hedges sen'
Willm Bridgman
Richard Hickes
Willm Fletchar sen'
John Fletchar sen
George Whyting sen'
George Whyting iun'
Robert Fletchar
Richard Greene
Joseph Bridgman
Christopher Daie
William Washington
John Newland
Edward Edgerton
William Mourton
William Carter
Thomas Williams
Richard Slatter
Nicholas Mathewes
John Bayneham
Robert Browne
William Odie
John Buntinge
Nicholas Carpenter
Thomas Henlowe
[f.75r, col. 2]
Florence Hamonde
John Hamonde
Edward Clarke
John Fletcher sen'
Willm Cole
George Ryman
Thomas Fletchar
Richard Harris
Elizabeth Seelie
Barbara Norcott
Thomas Kewe
Robert Thomas
John Whytinge
Richard Castell
Thomas Townsend
William Norcott
Anthonie Gardner
Richard Dunford
George Hickes
Nicholas Perrie iun
John Fletchar iun
Anthonie Wie
Henrie Clinch
Samuell Sandle
Richard Harris
Robert Chapman
Richard Hedges iun'
Thomas Fletchar
William Gardner
Richard Burbura
Robert Newland
Henry Bridgman
Robert Greene
John Webley
George Henlow iun'
Fulke Franklin
Fulke Carter
William Johnsonne
William Fletchar iun'

BRUERN [27]

[f.76r, single column]
We of Brewern whose names are heare under-written have taken the Protestation.

Robert Harris, *ibidem Minister*
John Draper
Elias Jackman
Edward Reileigh
Peter Tenannt
Robert Saunders
Robert Pound
Thomas Chandelor
Thomas Sandells
Richard Hodges
William Myles
John Smith
William Atkins
Thomas Crump
Mathew Martyn
James Godfrey
Michaell Wheeler
Thomas Ricketts
Richard Ricketts
Stephen Norgrove
Timothy Norgrove
Thomas Norgrove
Richard Tayler
Thomas Morton
Richard Foster
Thomas Ebsworth
James Holloway

CHADLINGTON [109]

[f.77r, in three columns.]
Chadlington
Februarie 23th 1641

The names of those who have taken the Protestation.

[f.77r, col. 1]
John Osbaston Esq.
Elias Garner Esq
John Boxe
Ralfe Arkle
William Braine

Henry Osbaston Gent
Maxmilian Osbaston Gent
Thomas Drake
John Drake
John Osbaston
John Tooly
Humphrey Hall
Richard Drake
James Sheiler
Arther Washington
Tho: Crosse
Richard Lorde
Tho: Lorde
Tho: Lorde *[sic]*
Anthony Carter
John Rimill
William Titmos
Tho: Haugtin
[f.77r, col. 2]
Michaell Drake
John Lorde
Elias Harris
John Bishoppe
John Carter
Tho: Laudar
Richard Crosse
Hercules Crosse
Tho: Halloway
John Newman
Richard Newman
Tho: Hadduck
Hendry Drake
Anthony Crosse
Comfort Yeats
John Boxe
Edmund Spooner
Paul Crosse
William Crosse
John Crosse
William Garner
John Drake
Tho: Launndr
Isaak Launchbury
John Launchbury
[f.77r, col. 3]
John Cooke
Edward Fullwell
Lawrence Crosse
John Crosse
John Boulter
Tho: Crosse
William Crosse
Richard Geoyner
Richard Alwin
William Bennet
Tho: Bennet
Richard Robbins
William Andrews
William Heighed [?]
Richard Cooper
William Cooper
Richard Hide
Tho: Harry
Richard Poole
John Weighton
John Normon
John Normon *[sic]*
Richard Tipin
Richard Scey
[f.78r, col. 1]
Robert Hide
Humphrey Hide
Joseph Reeve
Tho: Jurden
Richard Normon
John Smith
Tho: Scey
Michaell Staple
Steeven Nickholds
Richard Hudsonne
John Adee
James Robbinsonne
Humphrey Harris
Tho: Poole
Robert Taplin
Steephen Coling
Anthony Staple
Richard Taptoe
Tho: Staple
William Staple
Frauncis Drinkewater
Arther Staple
John Scey
John Smith
William Haile [?]
[f.78, col. 2]
Hendery Bikey
Hendrey Brookes
James Mansell
Simon Barnes
Richard Walter

There are none wch refuse to take this Protestation.

Witnesse
William Albright, *Minister*
Robert Carter, William Mason, *Churchwardens*
Hercules Launchbury, Thomas Wheeler, *Constables*
Robert Carter, Thomas Bishop, *Overseers*

CHASTLETON and BROOKEND

[f.77r, in two columns]
The names of all the men inhabitinge within the Parish of Chastleton & Brookend from eighteene yeares old & upwards, who have all taken the Protestation. [42]

[f.77r, col. 1]
Henrie Jones Sr: Esqre
George Greenewood sen: Gent
John Widdowes
Hugh Williams
Anthonie Williams
Nicholas Phelpes
Robert Rede
William Greene
John Wakefield
John Bromehill
John Hale
Robert Bromehill
John Arkill
John Newman
Henrie Newman
Edward Widdowes
William White
John Mace

[f.77r, col. 2]
Arthur Jones Gent
George Greenewood iu:' gent
Thomas Jones gent
Thomas Cradučke
Henrie Jones ju'
Randall Butcher
Richard Hughes
Richard Dumbleton
Robert Durran
John Smith
John Boareton
Steven Collins
John Williams
Isacke Williams
Thomas Canninge
Austin Taylor
Thomas Roberts
William Gardiner
William Venvill
Edward Phipps

Daniel Greenwood, *parson*
Robert Turner, *Curat*
John Widdowes, *Churchwarden and Collector for the pore*
John Hale, *Constable*

CHIPPING NORTON

[f.80, in three columns.]
A Returne of the names & Surnames of all such persons as have taken the protestation within the towne of Chipping Norton in the County of Oxon' according unto direction given theron: February 14th Anno Domini 1641 [281]

[f.80r, col. 1]
Baylieffs:
Mr Henry Cornish,
Mr Robert Berry
Burgesses:
Mr Thomas Fawler
Mr John Higgons
Mr John Davies
Mr William Dyson
Mr Thomas Fawler Jun'
Mr Philip Cave
Mr John Crispe
Mr Mathew Eldridge
Mr Richard Grove
Mr Robert Berry

William Thomas *[inserted later]*

Mr Nathaniell Stainforth
Mr Richard Elsinge
Bernard Powis
Edward Wilde
William Carter
Thomas Huggins
Edward Hinds
Phillip Wisdome
Robert Walbridge
Richard Edkins
William Gubbins
Thomas Thrist
Thomas Painter
William Barton Jun'
Walter Coleman
Henry Baker
John Biggs sen'
Simon Newman
Alexander Alcock
John Browne, carpenter
Thomas Paty
William Paty
Richard Croker
William Moorton
Thomas Hollans
John Righton
Robert Beamont
John Cooke
John Bostock
Stephen Coleburne
William Minchin
Thomas Cooke
William Weston
Elizeus Linders
Thomas Rowland
John Biggs Jun'
[f.80r, col. 2]
Michaell Shadwell gent
Robert Wharton Gent
John Hannell
Mathew Clements
Richard Phillaps
George Lord
William Coleman Jun'
John Trowte
Mathias Trowt
John Hunt
John Kerry
James Trowte
Thomas Hyatt
Thomas Coleman
John Cornish
Thomas Frame
John Stoit
Hugh Fisher
Thomas Newman
Michaell Cornish
Jonathan Ordway
Thomas Taylor
Thomas Somerton
Richard Letch
Thomas Fletcher
William Braine
Richard Dannc [?]
Edward Butler
Richard Needle
Robert Sheerley
John Newman
Francis Hutchins
George Butler
Robert Davies
Henry Colebarne, taylor
William Coleman
Thomas Bates
Christopher Turner
William Arnold
John Edkins
Mathew Braddish
Edward Bell
Richard Edkins
Edward Hutchins
William Tidmarch
James Coleburne
James Goodwin
Thomas Heath
[f.80r, col. 3]
John Bennett
Thomas Wilkes
Gyles Bromley
Thomas Sweetlad [?]
Robert Cockrell
Richard Taylor
Richard Tyler
Richard Anston
John Par
William Knolls
Thomas Trowt
Richard Marshmoore
Edward Johnson
John Shepheard
Richard Lake
William Darrow
Edward Sims
Richard Hedges
Richard Tomes
John Plevie
William Colman sen'
William Austen
Thomas Pierce
Andrewe Watts
Raph Walter
John Crosse
William Greene
John Horwood
Thomas Minçhin
William Barton
John Tidmarsh
Thomas Andrews, mason
Thomas Crosse, mason
William Thrist
Thomas Broadhurst
Francis Banaster
George Emonds
Richard Watson
James Hawkins
Thomas Crosse, carpenter
Randall Court
William Turner
John Simes
William Harris
Clement Fisher
Thomas Bell
[f.80v, col. 1]
Nicholas Massinger *[this name in a different hand]*
Richard Cooke
John Fawler
John Smart
Henry Meekes
George Hadden
John Higgons jun.
Stephen ap Hugh
George Colburne
Richard Norton
John Cowley
Robert Edkins
Thomas Moore
John Brookes
Richard Arnold
Anthony Wilkes
John Potter
John Wilkes
William Trowte

Nathaniell Maunder
Richard Hutchins
James Marshall
Richard Perry
Richard Dall
Nicholas Holton
Thomas Stephens
Simon Mander
John Goodwin
John Butler
Stephen Tidmarch
William Nicholls
William Fletcher
Thomas Rose
Richard Joyner
John Caricke
William Higgons
George Pary
William Butcher
Robert Wirge
Richard Jaques
John Wordly
John Alleme
John Clifton
Henry Tomason
John Wilkes, carpenter
Robert Edmonds
Thomas Whiting
John Diston
Thomas Emley
Robert Prestwitch
John Smith
Phillip Parr
Michaell Coleman Jun'
[f.80v, col.2]
Henry Fawler
Thomas Andrews Jun'
Henry Colburne Jun'
Nathaniell Adcock
Sampson Cox Jun'
Edward Meekes
Henry Simpkins
Henry Higgons
Phillip Eglinson
Thomas Denton
Edward Tinson

Stephen Sidmarch
William Bentley
Henry Kite
Sampson Copson
William Coleman
Edward Linders
Robert Bridgman
George Diston
Edward Linders Jun'
Edward Rowland
Samuel Rowland
Richard Batty
Giles Tidmarsh
Samuell Fulkes
Mathew Turner
Richard Belcher
Richard Tymes
Robert Goodacre
Robert Dunford
Thomas Gybbert
William Needle
John Austen
William Howlder
Edward Bentley
William Diston
John Berry
John Wildgoose
Richard Arnold jun.
Michaell Coleman sen'
William Collins
John Collett
Thomas Cooke
William Butler
Thomas Waringe [*or* Warnige]
Richard Huckvale
John Needle
Hester Roberts
Thomas Phillips
Zachary Stainfoorth

Thomas Androuse senior *[named added later]*
William Browne
William Browne *[sic]*
William Padgett
Richard Buller

Brain Potter
Thomas Gardner
Edward Trout Jun'
John Browne sheppard
William Gardner

[names added later:]
Simon Hathaway
Thomas Allin
Peeter Brawnis
Thomas Androsse Jun'
James Coleburne
William Harbert
John Yeardly
Thomas Clements
Henry Munchin
John Bastock
Thomas Panier
Brian Perrin
William Collins
Richard Allin
Thomas Brown

John Norgrove, *Vicar*
Thomas Reeve, *Churchwarden*
Richard Groves, Daved Dix, *Overseers*
Daniell Hurst, *Constable*

[f.81r]
A Returne of all such within the towne or Borrough of Chipping Norton in the County of Oxenford who have *not* tendered themselves upon warninge given, for to take the protestation.

Richard Fryers
Robert Candle *[deleted in original and initialled by the writer of the Return]*
Wm. Yarnall
Wm. Grainger
Tho: Eddkins

*See also **Over Norton**, page 95*

CHURCHILL

[f.82r, in two columns, with some signatures.]

The names of the Inhabitants of Churchill in the Countie of Oxon' that have consented to the protestation. [101]

[f.82r, col. 1]
Edmunde Glynn, *minister*
Giles Harris
George Morecroft
Will: Bridges
William White
Thomas Hacker
Thomas Jett
William Maunder
Austyne Williames
Charles Charles
Richard Ebbsworth
Thomas Heidon
Richard Brayne
Phillipp Tappan
Michael Tappan
William Mullington
Thomas Mullington
Robert Chamberlaine
Richard French
Thomas Harris
William Joyner
Wakham Broton
Edward Day
Michaell Day
Walter Mathew
Thomas Drue
Phillip Hunt
John Spurrier
James Joyner
John Crosse
Frannces Hale
William Brangman
Edward Brangman
John Savage

[f.82r, col. 2]
John Tappan
William Beaman
Henry Meadcroste
Thomas Sessions sen'
Thomas Sessions iun'
William Sessions
John Sessions Sen'
John Sessions iun'
James Brookes
John Cowlinge
Richard Bridgman
John Bridgman
Peter Minchin
John Ralphe
Richard Norton
Walter Norton
Thomas Bridges
John Jett
Richard Hunt
Richard Harris
Thomas Hicks sen'
Thomas Hicks jun'
Hugh Hickes
Richard Boxe
Richard Coates sen'
Richard Coates iun'
Maurice Mullington
Thomas Shurley sen'
Thomas Shurley iun'
Robert Davis
Richard Lucas
Thomas Glynne
Giles Sessions
Thomas Andros
Humfrey Truman
Antony Crosse

[f.82v, col. 1]
John Whitley
Thomas Whitley
Thomas Hiett
Henry Hiett
Richard Whitley
William Whitley
Henry Peirs
Thomas Minchin sen'
Thomas Minchin iun'
Thomas Greenhalfe
William Willson
John Harvy
Henry Bridges
George Dee
Thomas Heminge
William Crosse
Thomas Willkins
Richard Willkins
Humfrey Willkins
John Sparrie
John Maunder
William Hall
Richard Spurrier
Edward Spurrier
Richard Wisedome
John Denton
Richard Parmry
William Skay
John Birdsey
James Collins
John Ashbee

All have consented, none refused.
Edmunde Glynn, *minister*

[f.83 - blank]

CORNWELL [23]

[f.84r, single column.]
Oxon' February 24 1641:
The names of such persons within the towne of Cornwell as have taken the Protestation accordinge to an order made by the house of Commons in Parliament' bearinge date 5 May 1641.

Edward Wood
Thomas Dawson
Richard Yarnton
Thomas Spour [?]
Thomas Hastings
Henry Caple
John Weston
Anthony Freeman
John Freeman
Thomas Wiggins
Giles Hicks
Andrewe Tomkins
Richard Hellifax
John Castle
Anthony Haile
William Hinde
Paul Hicks
Edward Bartlett
Richard Hicks

In presence of
John Wilton, *Parson of Cornewell*
Robart [N-har?], Thomas Hallifax, *Churchwardens*
Richard Gordon: *Constable*

ENSTONE [124]

[f.85r, in three columns.]
A Catalogue of their names who have taken the protestation in the Parrish of Enston.

[f.85r, col. 1]
Neate Enston
William Miller
Tho: Newman
William Fortnam
Edward Fortnam
Arthur Wickens
Rich: Box
Phillip Bolton
William Garner
Silvester Whiteinge
Jennings Classen
Rich: Nobbs
Lawrence Hitchman
Thom: Edwinge
Tho: West
William Hunniman
John Silver
Steven Fortnam
Rob Collett
John Laston
William Bolton
Edmund Fortnam
William Fitchet
John Hardiman
John Tasker
Edward Barksdale
Robert Laston

Ludston [Lidstone]
Richard Sanders
Tho: Belcher
Roger Mace
Roger Varney
William Millen
Robert Classen
John Warland
Ralph Marten
William Fortnam

[f.85r, col. 2]
Church Enston
Nicholas Marshall
Francis Smith
Richard Turfrey
Tho: Gardiner
Roger Morris
Tho: Blake
Anthony Harris
Hugh Burroes
Phillip Margetts
Mathew Mirrick
Henry Ely
John Rawlins
William Rimond
Rich Allwinn
Will Varney
John PhippsRich Miller
George Phipps
Nathaniell Hodgkenson
John Renn
Robert Hart
William Fawdrey
William Burrough
Francis Butcher
Francis Bourne
Arthur Forde
William Lord
Rob: Millard
Hutchens Lord
John Mirrick

[f.85r, col. 3]
Radford
Thomas Marten
Richard Riman
John Marten
Tho: Jilkes
Rich: Riman iu'
John Riman
William Riman
Tho: Robins
Tho: Busby
Ralph Simpson
Rob: Clemmence
Rise Clemmence iu'
John Clemmence
Rise Clemmence
Jo: Barfoot

Gadgingwell [Gagingwell]
Robert Cooper
Henry Drinkewater
Edward Belcher
William Austen
Edward Collet
Tho: Waram
John Busby
George Andrewes
William Busby
John Drinkwater
Edward Drinkewater
Anthony Parker
John Busby

Clevely [Cleveley]
John Huggins
William Drinkewater
William Collett
William Sleamaker iu'
Richard Huggins
Edward Miller
John Riman
Edward Miller sen'
Edward Freeman
Edward Hill
Tho: Butcher
Rich: Busby
William Cockciter
Rich: Busby iu'
Rob: Drinkewater
[f.82v]
John Cooke
Tho: Ward
Tho: Longsteaff
William Sleamaker
Andrew Adams
William Collins

Chawford [Chalford]
Abraham Darrott
Lawrence Hitchman
John Box
Israall Slatter
Phillip Box

Ditchley
Rob: Larner
James Ellis
Tho: Freeman
Henry Holloway
Joshua Douglas

[f.86 - blank]

FIFIELD MERRYMOUTH [50]

[f.87r, in two columns.]
Fyfield merymouth
Feb 23 1641

[f.87r, col. 1]
Symon Parratt
John Percie
John Trinder
Richard Curteise
Ralph Whyting
Thomas Whytinge
Thomas Deringe
Richard Gillat
Thomas Hutton
Richard Preist
Giles Greenway
John Turner
William Spencer
James Traherne
Alexander Kene
Abraham Shaw
Alexander Seywell
William Greenway
Thomas Snossell
Edward Whiller
Edmond Cambrie
William Smyth
Thomas Godfrie
Richard Arters
Richard Colgrove
Thomas Goodenofe
Thomas Greenway
Thomas Baylye
Tobyas Peircie
[f.87r, col. 2]
Israel Minchine
William Hardinge
James Leech
Thomas Ellis
Richard Harrood
William Denton
Richard Peircie
Richard Shaw
Richard Cleaver
John Bayley
Thomas Cox
William Cambrie
Henry Kibble
Thomas Hutts
John Bridge
William Cleaver
Thomas Turner
Richard Phillips

The Protestacon was taken by parishioners of Fifield merimouth from Eighteene years upwards the day and yeare above written whose names are hereunto subscribed in the presents*[sic]* of us

Michael Mills, *Curat*
William Gillat, *Churchw'*
Simon Denton, *Constable*

FULBROOK [52]

[f.88, in two columns]
The names of all the Inhabitants of the Towne and parish of Fulbrooke in the Countie of Oxon' and the hundred of Chadlington who have made the Protestation

Coram Justicoiaris
Christopher Glyn, *Vic'*
Robert Francklin,
John Mawberly,
Churchwardens
John Taylor, *Constable*
Richard Symons,
John Collier, *Overseers*

Rich: Jordens
Robert Jorden
Robert Haines
John Batholomew Sen'
Richard Palmer
Henry Cosins
Thomas Hathaway
Thomas Smith
Edmund Pattricke
Francis Sympson
Robert Applegate
William Collier
Thomas Pattricke
Thomas Haines
Edward Bradley
Griffin Boreman
William Wilkins
Thomas Cowles
William Seely
Austen Hitchman
William Palmer sen'
William Hathaway
Thomas Cambray
William Cooke
William Lyddiatt
Miles Lambert
William Potter
Robert Collier
John Cooke
John Harris jun'
William Hedges
John Harris sen'
Henry Farren

[f.88, col. 2]
Giles Sharpe
Alexander Varney
Richard Collier
John Bartholomew Jun'
Walter Lewes
Nicolas Bayley
Henrie Simons
Robert Slow
William Palmer Jun'
Thomas Sessions
Robert Sessions
John Aplegate
John Davis

Coram nobis
C. Glyn, *Vic:*
John Taylor, *Constable*
John Maberley,
Robert Francklinne,
Churchwardens
John Collier,
Richard Simons,
Overseers

HOOK NORTON [197]

[f.89r, in three columns.]
Hooknorton Bill of the names of those men that have given their Consent to the protestation

[f.89r, col. 1]
Richard Paramoure Esq
Gerrard Croker Esq
Martin Malins
Richard Robins
James Calvert
Jarvase Sneth
Thomas Harbutt
John Crosse
John Clarke
John Pulchro
Ralph Armes
John Armes
William Coling
John Munday
Thomas Haynes
Anthony Tasker
John Tasker
Edward Mason
John Watkins
Robert Prue
Thomas Kerry
John Castile
Thomas Woodford
John Woodford
George Ludyatt
William Prue
John Harwood
John Parran
Robert Parran
Joseph Reynold
John Pitham
Richard Fipps
Edward Munchin
Zachariah Carter
Richard Clifton
William Clifton
James Pitham sen'
John Pitham
James Pitham jun'
Robert Butcher
John Clifton
Richard Ward Junior
John Gardener
Thomas Nibb
Thomas Harris
Simon Coling
Robert Austin
Giles Mosseter
Lewis Hickockes
Andrew Harbert
Richard Williamson

[f.89r, col. 2]
Phillipp Mourton
William Woodford
Rafe Fipps
Roger Rowse
Richard Hall
John Hall
John Pitham
Robert Stanley
George Blagrave
Richard Avery
James Fraine
William Elco
Richard Calkott
Matthew Sabin
William Cantes [*or* Cautes?]
Richard Hyerne
John Goffe
John Lawrence
John Argien [?]
George Wells sen'
George Wells Jun'
Thomas Greene
Richard Coling
John Coling
Richard Carter
Nehemiah Carter
Tobyas Gilkes
John Lamly
Richard Getfield
Richard Ward sen'
Moses Ward
John Ward
Richard Luckett
Thomas Walford
John Wilkins
Richard Fox
Richard Tasker
Giles Hambridge
Richard Wyatt
Simon Hyerne
Jonathan Churchill
Tymothy Potter
Nicholas Baldwing
John Coling
Richard Coling
Richard Young
John Ellyman
William Taylor
William Hall
John Geeves
John Hastings
John Churchill
William Pratt
[f.89r, col. 3]
John Goffe the Elder
William Goffe
John Goffe Jun
John Baldwing
Edward Washbrooke
George Goffe
John Goffe filli'
Thomas Goffe
Walter Calkott Junior
John Shreeve
John Preston
William Robins
Richard Barrow
John Gealing
John Guy
Richard Filkins
Richard Wytenn
William Moberly
Thomas Luckett
Thomas Beale
Simon Gardener
Gerrard Taylor
George Taylor
George Calkott
Alexander Calkott
Josias Goodson
Edward Smith sen'
John Smith
Edward Smith Jun'
Georg Clarke
William Geeves
Henry Gealing
Edward Gilkes
John Lamlee
William Hull
Robert Willmutt
John Willmutt
Thomas Cave
James Walker
Thomas Maule
Robert Pufforis
Matthew Wyten
James Beale
Richard Prescott
William Cooke
Richard Perkins
Thomas Weemadge
Richard Weemadge
William Venfeilis [?]
William Gilkes
Thomas Bell
[f.90r]
Robert Paine
John Gibbs
Edward Castile
Thomas Calkott
Thomas Castile
Thomas Baker
John Hull
Thomas Pufford
William Pufford
James Pufford
Rafe Pufford
Francis Abbott
Richard Young
William Scarlett
John Taylor
Nicholas Taylor
Edward Collett
William Allin
Richard Luckett
Alexander Luckett
William Marshall
Thomas Hynde
Thomas Fipps
Humfry Gibbs
Robert Cowley
John Luckett
Henry Carelesse
Alexander Fox
Daniell White
John Malins
John Weaver
John Mainard
Rafe Rawlins
John Wyton
William Luckett
Roger Luckett
Richard Snell
Paule Bartlett
Thomas Squirrell
Richard Parish

Signd'
Jo Hyron, *Constab'*
John Pufford

KINGHAM [101]

[f.91r, in three columns.]

Kingham infr' hund' de Chadlington in Com' Oxon'. The names of all those that have protested according to the protestation tendered unto them

Georg Morecroft, parson of Kingham in Com' Oxon':

[f.91r, col. 1]

Charles Morecrofte
Hercules Morecrofte
Thomas Loggin sen'
John Loggin
Thomas Loggin iu'
Edward Powis iu'
John Waters
John Harris
John Watts
Simon Dalbie
Thomas Smith
Michael Younge
Anthony Bromsgrove
Raphe Boulter
William Quatermaine
William Hadland
Henry Welshe
Thomas Hawten
John Dyer sen'
John Dyer iu'
Thomas Pathlow
Richard Ibell
Anthony Gisborne sen'
Anthony Gisborne iu'
William Horne
Francis Hugginson
William Hawten
John Haddon
John Newell
Thomas Newman
William Davis
Richard Hunyborne
Francis Hunyborne
Richard Boulter
John Boulter

[f.91r, col. 2]

Daniel Fynch
Richard Guilliams
James Boulter
John Gisborne
William Haddon
Richard Haddon
Edward Hunslow
Edward Pope
Robert Andrewes
Henry Forde
John Forde
William Watts
William Wilson
John Beacham
Edward Greene
Hierome Creswell
Thomas Eaton
Edward Powis sen'
Thomas Hulles
Robert Pearse
Richard Warde
William Warde
Richard Bradley
Edward Bradley
Henry Huckin
Thomas Huckin
Richard Forde
John Hale
John Crosse sen'
John Crosse iu'
Richard Crosse
William Eaton
Daniel Brayne

[f.91r, col. 3]

William Hale
Michael Miles
Andrew Keene
Thomas Hemming
Henry Dyslyng
Francis Stone
Nicholas Stone
Edward Collier
William Farrand
Robert Adams
Richard Ball gen'
William Strowde
Robert Hitchman
Richard Miles
Thomas Phillips
Raphe Quatermaine
Robert Pitham
Francis Allen
Robert Allen
John Wilson
Thomas Boulter
Gyles Bridge
John Shepheard
Thomas Miles
Thomas Spurrier
William Crosse
Edward Cooke
Thomas Eaton sen'
William Eaton iu'

William Boulter, *Const'*
Edward Gillet, *Church'*
John Allen, *Overseer*

[For Kiddington, see Wootton Hundred, page 130.]

LEAFIELD [73]

[f.92r, in two columns.]
The names of the Inhabitants of Lefield which have taken their protestation

[f.92r, col. 1]
Thomas Stevens
Edward Fisher
Thomas Rawlins
Thomas Browne
Richard Crosse
James Cove senior
James Cove Junior
Wacum Huchins
Addam Amsden
Richard Jeffery
William Spratly
Richard Dizlinge
Richard Wilson
Theoffilus Bridgman
Thomas Wilson
John Smith
John Hall
Edward Cowlinge
Henry Cowlinge
William Cowlinge
John Hamlin
Thomas Hamlin
Peeter Marsh
Nicolas Underwood
Matthew Underwood
Thomas Dickcox
William Hunte
Richard Hamlin
John Eales
Thomas Eales
John Busbie
William Dixe
Hercules Drinkewater
John Webbe
William Robbins
Bennet Peirce
Edward Rawlins senior
John Rawlins
James Rawlins
Edward Rawlins Junior
[f.92r, col. 2]
Henry Clifton
James Clarke
Robert Thecher
Robert Birch
John Ebsworth
Gyles Tharpe
Matthew Payne
Thomas Androus
John Harris Senior
John Harris Junior
Thomas Sparrow
Thomas Harris
James Greene
Francis Lorde
William Birdsy
Richard Varney
Edward Varney
Humfery Wilkins
Richard Hichman Senior
William Brayne
William Hichman
Thomas Goffe
Francis Clarke
Richard Hichman Junior
Robert Pratt
John Sparrow
Henry Smith
James Jones
Humfery March
Richard Whitinge
Steven Surman
Henry Booton
John Cowborow

LYNEHAM [44]

[f.93r, in two columns.]
The names of the Inhabitants of Lyneham that have taken the protestation

[f.93r, col. 1]
Augustin Sheyler
Marke Reeve
John Whythor
Arthur Whythor
Robert Felps
Henry Hiatt
John Brayn
Tho: Whyting
Chr: Whyting
John Hooper sen'
John Hooper jun'
Roger Harris
John Collins
John Brookes
John Snyth
Will Beard
Tho: Ebsworth
Rich: Aderton
Tho: Wells
Tho: Bennett
Tho: Castell
John Phyllips
Tho: Hunt
Tho: Bennett
Tho: Bennett *[sic]*
Tho: Ebsworth
Gregorie Ebsworth
John Benfeeld
Samuell Ball
Robert Dod
Richard Baker
John Baker
Edward Baker
Anthony Wickins
Marke Gilbert
John Fisher
[f.93r, col. 2]
John Bayleis
Tho: Lardner
Jesper Hare
Anthony Hale
Tho: Margatts
Symon Edwards
John Bayleis
John Cannion [?]

MILTON-under-WYCHWOOD

[f.94r, in two columns.]

Milton in the Parrish of Shipton under-Whichwood. The names of all the Inhabitants there dwelling that have taken there protestation [92]

[f.92r, col. 1]

William Foster
Francis Foster
William May
Henery Jeffoson
William Hicke
Samuell Mace
Edward Turton
Thomas Bell
John Mathewes the elder
John Mathewes
Thomas Rawlins
Edward Rawlins
William Parrett
William Greene
Andrew Sessions
Edward Lord
Richard Digger
Hener Willet
Robert Willet
Nicholas Cripps
William Cripps
Robert Wilkins
Edmond Gregory the elder
Edmond Gregory
Robert Mooreton
John Parrett
William Parrett the elder
Thomas Sich
Edward Hyet
Henery Cocke
Tobye Hyet
William Chapman
John Elkees
Thomas Burson
Richard Burson
Richard Michell
William Hucks
William Fowler
Thomas Fowler
Richard Hyet
John Baynum
John Tommes the elder
John Foster
William Tompson
Edmond Seacole
Richard Rush
John Hicke
John Hicke
William Hicke
Thomas Thorne
Lennord Grove
John Isher
Thomas Elees
William Widdowes
William Smyth

[f.94r, col. 2]

Thomas Sessions the elder
Thomas Sessions
William Pettypher
William Burson
John Smyth
William Collins
Robert Sammon
Richard Phelps
Richard Shewery
Robert Seacole
John Seacole
John Edees
Michaell Sessions
James Sessions the elder
Richard Miller
George Hollis
John Tommes
John Wayne
Thomas Collins
Robert Hunt
James Weaver
Thomas Bayles
John Wakefeild
John Rawlins the elder
John Rawlins
Richard Hucke
Thomas Barnes
William Willis
Thomas Hyet
William Lennet
William Edwarde
James Sessions
Richard Garner
Thomas Larawnce*[sic]*
Thomas Sessions
Richard Ebsworth
Richard Jonns

MINSTER LOVELL

[f.95r, in three columns.]
The Inhabitants of Minster Lovel in Oxfordshire all excepting [10]
Francis Ewre Esq'
Richard Ewre
Shellie Morgan
Margaret Ewre
Prudence Hubert
Ellen Ewre
Bridget Hatton
Bridget Mrs. Hubert's mayd
Paulina Hooper
Ann Palmer
have taken and consented unto the protestation there names being heere subscribed [98]

[f.95r, col. 1]
of men
Thomas King
Persival Bosewell
Henerie Hedges
Thomas Harris
John Baldwin
Robert Coates
Richard Line
William Day
Thomas Windle
Thomas Carter
John Lewis
John Robyson
William Robinson
Thomas Dislin
Robert Castle
Solomon Warner
Henerie Lighefolly
John Lock
George Cooke
William Brookes
Christopher Hawkins
John Rowles
Thomas Boorton
William Sanders
William Thomas
[f.95r, col. 2]
Henerie Steevens
William Steevens
William Palmer
Robert Palmer
Richard Lighfolly
Richard Harris
Edward King
John Cleaver
William Hawes
Henerie Dicks
John Bennam
William Wellman
Henerie Barret
Robert Wayte
Thomas Lighefolly
William Rush
Edward Debanks
Robert Whitar
Thomas Priors

[f.95r, col. 3]
of woemen
Jane Ewre
Elizabeth Dickinson
Mary Porter
Katherine Redman
Margarte Hewer
Joan Austin
Elizabeth Windle
An Carter
Joan Lewis
An Robyson
Ellen Smith
An Castle
Allice Pointer
Ellin Harris
Mary Harris
An Lock
Joan Cowell
Mary Brookes
Ellen Hill
Ellin Rowles
Ann Boorton
Ann Boorton *[sic]*
Joan Thomas
Alice Sanders
[f.96r]
Margaret Steevens
Dorothy Lighfolly
Elizabeth Palmer
Allice Bignell
Joan Harris
Ann King
Elizabeth Ward
Elizabeth Dicks
Sarah Hall
Allice Hall
Jean Bennam
Mary Wellman
Ellen Barret
Ann Rush
Ann Shaler
Malinda Wayte
Jean Munday

Soe testifieth
Edmond Dickinson, *Vicar*
Edmon Harris, *Constable*
William Hall, *Churchwarden*

NORTHMOOR [64]

[f.97r, in two columns.]
Northmore
Febr. 23d 1641

A List of their names that have taken the Protestation [62]

[f.97r, col. 1]
Henry Rawlins
Richard Steavens
John Smart
John Hadden
Thomas Ridge
Thomas Brabone
John Stone
George Turner
John Griffine
Stephen Dasen
Richard Carter
Richard Steavens
William Walwyn
Richard Ridge
Edward Ridge
John Dasen
Luke Woodlye
Samuell Bolton
Nicholas Roberts
Francis Kempster
Francis Batts
William Harris
Henrye Bedwell
Thomas Walter
James West
William Clanfeild
Thomas Cogs
John Rumnye
Francis Smith
Henrye Batts
Robert Bedford
Mihell Brooks
Humfrey Dasen
Edward Eaton
John Weale
Richard James
[f.97r, col. 2]
William White
William Fayrbeard
Justinian Fayrbeard
Walter Tanner
Thomas Shard
Umphery Prentice
Walter Adams
Gawen Champneys
John Playdall
Simon Smith
Thomas Harris
John Tounsend
Christopher Dod
George Harris
John Bagnoll
Henry Cleevely
William Bedwell
Stephen Alder
Richard Crips
Henrye Savorye
Henery Fayrbeard
Thomas Shaw
Henry West
John Fayrbeard
Henry Martine
Thomas Martine

Absent:
Henrye Greenway
Thomas Greenway

[f.98 - blank]

OVER NORTON

[f.99r, in three columns.]
A note of the names of all such persons that have taken the protestation being Inhabitants of Over Norton in the County of Oxenford Feb 24th 1641 [69]

[f.99r, col. 1]
Nicholas Busbie
Richard Brame
Anthony Robins
John Buckett sen'
Richard Bush
Edward Bickerstaffe
Charles Braine
William Fletcher
Thomas Scott
John Hutchins, taylor
William Gardner
Edward Hopkins
John Miles
Richard Braye, taylor
John Haukes
John Hutchins, shepherd
William French
Thomas Kite
Thomas Harris
William Braine, shephard
Nathaniell Busbie
John Buckett Jun'
Roger Profitt
George Turner
John Haukes Jun'
William Dier
[f.99r, col. 2]
William Huckvale
William Hopkins sen'
Walter Chawney
John Meekes sen'
Richard Shelfox
Richard Buckett
William Hopkins Jun'
Thomas Taylor
William Watson
Richard Nicholls
Edmond Braine
Thomas Hind
Richard Hutchins
George Durbridg
Richard Fletcher
Richard Hopkins
William Greenhill
John Busbie
Samuell Minton
William Busby Laborer
[f.99r, col. 3]
Robert Wheeler sen'
John Wheeler
John Meekes Jun'
Thomas Ingraham
Richard Ingraham
Robert Wheeler Jun'
Thomas Tymes
William Times
George Wesbury
William Busby sen'
William Busby
Thomas Smith
Thomas Neatson[?]
Thomas Litmas
George Greane
John Coper
Christtofar Scott
William Neale

John Norgrove, *Vicar*
Richard Berry, *Churchwarden*
John Freeman, *Cunstable*
William Fletcher, Richard Bickerstaffe, *Collectors for the poore*

There is not any person within the towne that hath refused ti take the protestation
John Freeman

RAMSDEN

[f.100r, in two columns.]
These are the names of the Inhabitants of Ramsden which have taken the protestation [40]

[f.100r, col. 1]
James Parsloe
Henry Newland
Richard Huse
William Dickson
William Lardner
William Collins
Thomas Lardner
Thomas Tasker
William Lardner
Richard Hickes
Humphrie Lardner
Richard Norris
William Bisship
James White
Roger Lane
William Joyner
John Mountaine
Richard Lardner
Water Woodward
Henry Mountaine
Elias Hayes
George Spur
William Roberson
John Bisship
Thomas Leech
William Baylie
Thomas Roach
William Darand[?]
[f.100r, col. 2]
Steeven Brice
Robert Powel
Humphrie Lardner
Richard Dickson
Thomas Bisship
Owen Lane
Humphrie Collins
Thomas Franncis
William Joyner
John Lea
Thomas Roach
Robert Stanford

GREAT ROLLRIGHT

[f.101r, in three columns]
Roleright magna in Coun' Oxon' Feb 23 1641

The names of all those persons which from the age of 18 yeares and above, have subscribed to the promise vow and protestation approved by the house of Commons concerning the doctrine of the true reformed protestant Church of England etc. [74]

[f.101r, col. 1]
William Sheapeard Esqr
Edmund Rouswright
Edward Hill
Rich Berry sen'
Rich Rouse
Rich Carter
Robt Baffin
John Bayly
Richard Hull
William Bradly
George Hilton
Simon Baffin
John Kerry
Rich Berry Jun'
Gyles Woodley
John Bradley
William Berry
Samuell Baffin
John Wardner
Robert Hull
John Baffin
Tho: Dickerson
Tho: Austen
John Gubbins
John Fullin
Tho: Carter
Thom: Wayne
John Curtes
John Morton
John Haynes Sen'
John Haynes Jun'
Rich Brayne
James Tasker
James Hands
Edward Wiet
Edward Prentice
Edward Carter
Fardinando Broomechan
[f.101r, col. 2]
John Tayler
Rich Cox
John Wilkins
Robt Greene
William Horsman
John Lihorne
Rich Harvie
William Smith
Anthony Barnes
John Masemore
Rich Masemore
Tho: Simons
William Carter Jun'
Rich Bayly
Alexander Hawten
Christopher Kendell
Tho: Endoll
Tho: Butcher
William Baughan
Henry Baughan
Tho: Smith
John Witt
Tho: Becket
Robert Broomecham
Phillip Crasley
Tho: Essex
John Spelsburie
[f.101r, col. 3]
William Freeman
Rich: Leatherland
William Lewes

Witness to this protest:
John Goodwin, *Rector ibidem*
Hugh Hopkins, *Constable*
William Carter,
John Gardner
Churchwardens
John Baughan,
Edward Warner,
Overseers

Nemo recusat

SALFORD

[f.102r, in two columns.]
The names of the Inhabitants of Salford that have taken the Protestation [55]

Edward Huckings not taking the protestation

[f.102r, col. 1]
William Walton
Richard Jorden
Charls Hyett
William Price
Thomas Hopkins
Thomas Hilton
John Jorden
William Ofnell
John Reeve
Walter Goodere
Thomas Phillips
Edward Surrell
William Boulter
John Paddocke
Richard Hadland
Thomas Arice
William Haddon
John Mynchin
Edmund Weston
John Haddon
William Key
Nicholas Harris
Edmond Hicks
William Spiser
Thomas Bushupp
Robert Weston
John Weston
[f.103, col. 2]
John Davice
Thomas Haddon
Edmond Franklin

Richard Johnson
George Hudson
Edward Phillips
John Phillips
John Bryon
John Heyward
Richard Arice
John Jorden
Ralph Fawdry

John Henly
Mathew Kings
Edward Herbert
Richard Hyett
John Davize senior
William Collins
William Arice
Edmund Hiorne
Thomas Tandy

Not any of the inhabitants of Salford refused to take the protestation
William Roberts, *Curat ibid:*
Henry Hyett, *Cunstable*
John Light[?], John Herons, *Churchwardens*
Henry Fitch,
John Boulter, *Overseers*

SHIPTON-under-WYCHWOOD

[f.103r, in three columns]
The names of the Inhabitants of Shipton that have taken the Protestacon. [104]

[f.103r, col. 1]
Rowland Laie Esquier
John Holland
Thomas Oven sen'
Willm Whyting sen'
Thomas Skey
Thomas Wisdome
Anthony Ashfeild
Thomas Reason iun'
Charles Bramsbie
Leonard Camborn
John Bockinsoll
James Whytinge
John Hawker
Thomas Wigmore
Edward Riccards
John Brookes
Richard Pinke
Thomas Rymell
Willm Coxe
Willm Colinge
Henry Mourton
Richard Colinge
Thomas Huxsen
Robert Hux
Willm Huxe
George Huchins
George Deene
Symon Colinge
Richard Shoringe
Richard Brookes
Willm Clarke
John Ashfeild
Peeter Kemmer
Richard Smyth
Richard Shayler
Thomas Hawten
Nicholas Shailer
John Chapman
Arther Smyth
Zacheus Smyth
Henry Wheeler

[f.103r, col. 2]
Thomas Ellins
Thomas Hobby
Willm Busbie
Willm Daniell
Willm Farmer
Willm Amsdon
Willm Collins
Willm Whyting iun'
Thomas Oven iun'
Henry Whytinge
Leonard Oven
John Dovie
George Price
Nicholas Beckett iun'
John Bishoppe
Thomas Wheeler
John Huxe
Edward Cooke
John Steevens
Nicholas Beckett
Willm Beckett
Willm Deene
John Greene
Symon Tomson
Thomas Rawlins
Thomas Shailer
Ralph Hastwell
John Wheeler
Edward Hastwell
Henry Greene
Edward Towslie
Willm Wisdome
Richard Hayter
John Williams
Willm Parratt
Richard Hickes

[f.103r, col. 3]
Thomas Sharpe
Willm Parrat
Willm Greene
Rowland Mills
Thomas Lawrence
Robert Berryman
John Andrewes
Richard Warde
Robert Mathewes
Henry Archard
Nicolas Jonnes
William Stow
Michaell Pope
Richard Elles

Richard Harris sen'
Richard Harris iun'
John Daie
John Lanchburie
Willm Wheeler
Richard Cooke sen'
Thomas Cooke
Willm Riche
Richard Cooke iun'
John Woodward
Robert Foster
John Foster
George Thomas

SHORTHAMPTON, CHILSON and PUDLICOTE

[f.104, single column.]
The names of all the Inhabitants of Shortampton, Chilson and Pudlicote which have made protestacion in the presence of the minister, Constable and Churchwardens [34]

Richard Harris
John Harris
Giles Harris
John Mawton
Richard Reeve
Richard Browne senior
Richard Browne Junior
John Brookes
William Harris
William Crosse
James Bennet
Robert Cole
Edward Lankfere
George Sparrowe
John Balies
Thomas Howze
Thomas Cowles
Owen Dowen
Thomas Fortman
Thomas Maior
Robert Charles senior
Robert Charles Junior
John Charles
William Kewine [*or* Kerine?]
Simon Church
John Brookes
William Pebworth
Michaell Harris
William Churchey
Thomas Cottrell
John Merimust
Humfrey Reeve
Richard Windowe
Edmond Rimell

SPELSBURY

[f.105r, in three columns]
We the inhabitants of the Parish of Spellesbury whose names are underwritten have protested the protestation first taken by the Honourable house of Parliament and since commanded to be taken by the Commons of the Kingdome Feb: 25: 1641 [118]

[f.105r, col. 1]
George Pickering
John Paty
John Tredwell
Willm: George
Valent. Ivings
Francis Riman
Hugh Duglas
Thomas Bennet
Thomas Rymon
Stephen Souch
Willm Souch
Robert Ryman
John Hawkins
Tho: Rooke
Rich: Claridge
Tho: Langford
Walt: Trinder
Robt: Prentice
Will: Tounsend
John Langford
Tho: Gardiner
John Bernard
Rob: Adomes
Abraham Harris
Abell Iserd
Rich: Hanwell
Rich: Mullis
Rich: Mullis *[sic]*
Rich: Hawkins
Ed: Dennel
Franc: Webb
Mathew Poulton
Tho: Minors
Robt: Clare
Oliver Kinderly
Mihil Hollowey
John Adams
John Biggs
John Crosse
Francis Sharpe
Willm: Sessions
Tho: Gibbs
Rich: Esell
Willm: Margetts
John Sansum
John Joyner
Tho: Souch
Rich: Cooke
John Joyner
Phillip Cowling
[f.105r, col. 2]
Andrew Robbins
Willm: Bridgeman
Henry Sansum
Henry Blagrove
Henry Trinder
Nathaniell Crosse
Henry Wadman
Edmound Coursy
John Westbery
Willm Claridge
Willm Rooke
Willm Spencer
Christopher Harris
Humphery Trinder
Henry Trinder
David Fletcher
Willm: Trinder
Robt: Guy
Willm Slutford
Christopher Miller
Tho: Townsend
Tho: Huckewell
Willm: Huckewell
Abell Iserd

Alexander Ryman
Rich: Taylor
Tho: Trinder
Abell Trinder
Willm: Spenser
James Westbery
Willm Rooke
John Wisdome
Tho: Rooke
Samuel Souch
Henry Ryman
Tho: Carter
Willm Smith
Robt Ryman
Tho: Tennant
Willm: Kerry
Roger Andrewes
Willm Freeman
Christopher Brewer
George Cowling
Edmond: Hopkins
John Crosse
Willm Sessions
Willm Collins
Tho: Brayne
Willm Brewer
Tho: Kerry
Tho: Kerry *[sic]*
John Hopkins
Tho: Kite
Willm: Tounsend
John Freeman
[f.105r, col. 3]
Anthony Crosse
Anthony Longford
John Webb
John Cowling
John Watts
Je: Cary

Jo: Ferriby [*or* Ferily?], *Vicar*
Tho: Prentise, Tho: Couling, *Churchwardens*
Edward Issard, *Constable*
Ed: Dennet, *[blank]* Ryman, *Overseers*

Who having taken it before the Justices were present at the time of these mens protesting.

SWINBROOK

[f.106r, single column; some signatures.]

Swinbrook

The names of all those that took the protestation [31]

Edward*[sic]* Fetyplace
Richard Croke
Rolandus Jones *Curat*
Richard Gyles
Thomas Bramley
John Cowles
Richard Hathaway
Edward Winchester
John Fletcher
Thomas Shailer
John Blunsden
William Scotte
Robert Cowles
Richard Cowles
John Simmons
Thomas Cooke
Richard Briers
Francis Tayler
John Harris
John Edwards
John Hathaway
Richard Hathawy Jun'
James Ellins
John Butler
Richard Giles Jun'
Robert Hedges
Thomas Cooke Jun'
Thomas Goodlocke
Richard Mabley
John Archard
Richard Arnold

TAYNTON

[f.107, in three columns]
Febr: 20 1641
Tainton Protestation in the Countie of Oxon' solemly and publickely made by they whose names are subscribed [69]

[f.107r, col. 1]
Hen: Fletcher
John More
Fran: Hampson
Stephen Gascoigne
Willm Veysey
Rob: Collier
Richard: Andrewes
Jo: Johnson
Jo: Simons
Willm Edwards
Jo: Lambert senior
Rob: Lambert
Tho: Rossell
Rich: Sparrow
John Thorpe
Hen: Fletcher iunior
Willm Hibberd
Jo: Lambert iunior
Andr: Gregorie
Edw: Clarke
Rich: Alflat
Willm Collens
John Bell
Jo: Sitman
Rich: Throughwood

[f.107r, col. 2]
Willm Freeman
Antho: Marchall
Tho: Payne
Tho: Baker
Willm Cockhead
Valen: Strong
Jo: Collier
Edw: Maddack
Hen: Fletcher senior
Rob: Fletcher
Tho: Edwards
Hen: Gillat
Ralph Baker
Willm Gregorie
Edw: Balbie
Willm Taplin
Rich: Mihell
Rich Hoare
Rob: Large
Rob: Sessions
Willm Burrowse
Antho: Panting
Humphrey Sich
Daniel Patrick

f.107r, col. 3]
Rich: Baker
Tho: Lambert
Jo: Fry
Jo: Clarke
Rog: Andrewes
George Andrewes
Watler Alflat
Tho: Maddock
Willm Cooke
Sam: Lambert
Tho: Garter
Tho: Greenaway
Tho: Bradley
Jo: Throughwood
Rich: Throughwood
Willm Dalby

The inhabitants of Tainton have with an unanimus Consent voluntarily made there Protestacon, not any one refusing to make the same vow. Witnesse they whose names are subscribed.

Hen. Fletcher, *Vic*
Will Veysey, *Constable*
Valentine Strong,
Edward Clarke,
Churchwardens

LANGTREE HUNDRED

GORING

[f.108r, in two columns.]
Oxon': The Returne of the names of the Inhabitants of Goring wch have taken the protestation in manner and forme as the Minister, Churchwardens, Overseers and Constable took the said Protestation before his maties Justice of Peace [128]

[f.108r, col. 1]
Robert Calton sen' Esqr
Robert Calton iu' gent
Edward Whistler gent
Robert Whistler gent
Richard Parslew gent
Richard Wylder yeom'
Henry Whistler yeom'
John Grace yeom'
Philip Hensloe gent
Thomas Wrench yeom'
George Henwood yeom'
John Symons yeoman
Henry Wylder Yeom'
William Platt yeom'
William Tovey
William Paslew gent
Thomas Wylde sen'
John Messenger sen'
Thomas Wheeler
Edward Busnell
John Sprules
William Mattingley
Thomas Wylde un:
John Toby
William Pocock
William Gray
John Grove
Thomas Hunt
Robert Dennis
John Aldridge
Jeffry Avery
James Whistler
Ralfe Wethredge
John Davy
John Gunnis sen:
John Greenoway
Barton Bushnell
[f.108r, col. 2]
John Wylder
Thomas Lewndon
Thomas Wellman
Nathaniel Bushnell
Robert Pincott
John Buy
John Russell
Henry Tub
John Gunniss iu:
Thomas Hodges
Richard Buy
Robert Hone
Thomas Druce
Hugh Wakelin
John Hawe [*or* Haue, Hane?]
Henry Clemans
John Hunt
John Woodly
Henry Davy
Henry Pauling
Richard Pottinger
Thomas Symms
Mathew Painter sen'
William Abery
James Higgs
John Chippe
William Moorecock sen'
John Jerman
Richard Wylder
Henry Avery
Thomas Montague
Charles Gash
Hen Pauling
John Avery
John Gash
Wm Grove
William Barratt
Ralfe Wylder
Robert Carter
[f.108v, col. 1]
Ralfe Lewndon
Henry Ayre
William Townsend
John Messenger iun'
John Moorecock
Edward Wild
Frances Hoames
Philip Esdell
Griffen Chayre
Thomas Miles sen'
Thomas Miles iun'
John Jervice
John Cripps
Edward Smith
Thomas Higgs
Philip Hoames
Thomas Whood
Leonard Bolt
[f.108v, col. 2]
William Montague
Richard Carter
William Crutchfeild
Mathew Avery
William Stonely
William Moorecock iun'
Richard Buy iun'
William Wiltshire
John Higge
John Brimmer
Wm Wylder
Thomas Woodly
William Novice
Robert Bolt
William Payne
Henry Lawrence
Mathew Painter iun'
Griffin Hyggs
Barton Hyggs
Thomas Luendon
Alexander Avery
[f.109r]
John Havell
Richard Fruewen
Richard Lewendon
Nathainell Butler
Fraunces Mattingle
William Bigges
John George

None of the Inhabitants have refused to take the within mentioned Protestation.

In witness whereof we have hereunto subscribed our hands this XXth of Feb. 1641

Jeremiah Wharton, *Minister*
Richard Wheeler, *Churchwarden*
Thomas Wrench, Henry Wylder, *Overseers*

John Messenger, William Platt, *Constables*

IPSDEN

[f.110r. This is the only return for which the names of those taking the Protestation Oath are not provided.]

Februarii 20 164

These are to testifye that all the parishioners of Ipsden in the County of Oxon' did willingly take the protestation the day and yere above written [4]

Ita testor Steph: Haxby
John Crutchfield, *Constable*
Matthew Allnutt, Henry Browne, *Churchwardens*

MONGEWELL

[f.111, single column.]
Oxon. hundred de Langtree

The Retorne of the Minister and the Constable and Churchwardens of the parish of Mungwell for the taking of the oath of Protestacion Februarii the 20th 1641 [17]

The names of all Inhabiting w'hin the said parish appoynted & required to take the said oath of protestation and performed by them the day and yeare above as followeth.

Rice Prichard, *Rector.*
Peter Attwell, *Constable,* & Robert Hutton, *Churchwarden* allready taken.

And all these following upon the day.

William Davis Senior
William Davis Junio'
Robert Coldre
Thomas Everard
Nicolas Loe
William Todmerten
Robert Ward
John Trendour

Servants
William James
Thomas Dyer
Francis Knolles
Robert Tucker
William Browne
Robert Lane
Nicolas Mowden

Rice Prichard
Peter Attwell
Robert Hutton

NEWNHAM MURREN

[f.112r, in two columns.]

Oxon' Newneham Murren in Langtree hundred

We the parishioners of Newnham Murren have taken the Protestation accordinge to the order prescribed in the said protestation February the 20th 1641 [32+]

[f.112r, col. 1]

Robert Fortie, *minister*
Richard Crocksford, *Constable*
Richard Ayres, *Churchwarden*
Richard Crocksford, *Churchwarden*

Edward Sadler and his family
John Higgs and his family
John Longe
William Knighte and his Sonne
Willm Bennett
Edward Clarke
Michaell Hancocke, his wife is a recusant
Thomas Ellis
John Woodly
Thomas Calcott
John Betteridge
Thomas Hood
William Clisbye
Roger Giles
Thomas Warnman [Waniman?]
John Ayres
William Holmes
Richard Moore and his sonne
Christopher Skinner
Thomas Costard and his sonne
Thomas West and his servants
Richard Turtle and his sonne
[f.112r, col. 2]
Mr. Wartoppe not at home, his servants all tooke the protestation.
Henry Reeves
William Cooper
Walter Avery

NORTH STOKE

[f.113r, single column. This is one of the rare returns with signatures or marks for all listed. Marks are shown with asterisks, the others all being signatures.]

Oxon' Langtree Hund.
The 22th of February 1641

A Returne for the Constabell of North Stocke to his Maiesties Justices of all those that hath taken a true othe of the protistacion with there seaverall names hear under written [28]

William Chapman *
Thom Stacey *
Thom Taylor *
John Arendon *
Frences Gothredge *
John Southwood *
George Borden *
Rech: Stone *
Henery Bristoe *
Richard Allnot *
Thom Smith *
Will Flyd *
Collines Cleeft *
John Stevenes *
William Browne [?] *
William Greenewaye *
Thom Smith Senio'
John Smith *
Mihill Radford *
John Hollmes *
William Shearman *
William Cogare *
John Heues *
Robart Galle *
George Robets *

Henry Bristoe & Henry Chayman, *Churchwardens*
Thomas Cox, *Constable & overseare for the pore*

PLOUGHLEY HUNDRED

*[No Protestation Returns survive for Ploughley Hundred. The documentary references are all, therefore, to the **Assessment**, P.R.O. E179/164/496A, starting on Membrane 2r.]*

***Hundred de Ploughley** in Com. Oxon. **North Division**.*

ARDLEY

Sr. Thomas Penyston, Knt. and Baronett, 27s.6d. *Affid.*
Thomas Drope, 22s.11d. *Affid.*
Thomas Grantham, 4s.7d.
Raph Ford, 11s.5d.
Thomas Kinge, 5s.
John Motley, 4s.
John Grantham, 4s.7d.
Richard Morton, 3s.9d.
John Greene, 3s.
Richard Bignell, 3s.
Mary Addams, 18d.
Avis Chilton, 5s.
Edward Tanner, 8d.
John Filpott, 8d. *Affid.*
Willm. Pusie, 4d.
John Linett, 8d.
John Smyth, 11d.
Lawrence Kinge, 2d.
John Tanner, 2d.
John Bishopp, 2d.

Sum £5.

BOYCOTT

[An Oxfordshire enclave near Stowe in Buckinghamshire. On m.4r, following Stoke Lyne.]

Paul Myller Esqr., £5.

*[Note. For **Caversfield**, formerly a Buckinghamshire enclave in Oxfordshire, see page 109 for Protestation Return.]*

BUCKNELL

Willm. Rawlinson Esqr., £4.4s.
Mr [Thos] Miller, R'cor, 40s.
Mr Clarke, 10s.
John Line, 19s.4d.
John Abbotts, 11s.4d.
Richard Antwisell, 10s.4d. *Affidavt.* Antwisell and Je..., Subcoll. ye xivvj'd.[?]
Edward Fesie, 6s.
Edward Kinge, 11s.4d.
Widd. Firkin, 18d.
Richard Jeffes, 13s.4d.
Willm. Brock, 11s.4d.
Richard Harris, 2s.
Robert Fesie, 5s.
Richard Line, 5s.
Mathewe Mey, 2s.
Robert Antwisell, 3s.
John Humfrys, 2s.
Thomas Steedman, 11s.4d.
Thomas Antwisell, 18d.
John Brue, 10d.
Willm. Antwisell, 12d.
Thomas Jesopp, 4s.
John Fesie, 2s.
Willm. Robinson, 12d.
Willm. Cleadon, 12d.
Thomas Gunnyman, 12d.
Leonard Fox, 2s.6d.

Sum £13.

COTTISFORD

D'cor [Michael] Reade, 7s. *Affid.*
Sr. Richard Fermor, Knt., 7s. *Affid.*
Mr Awstin, 46s. *Affid.*
Mr French, 20s. *Affid.*

Sum £4.

FINMERE

Finmore

Richard Horne, R'cor., 14s.
John Sutton, gen., 10s.
Willm. Keate, gen., 11s. *Affid.*
John Jeffes, 5s.
Willm. Wheatley, 2s.6d.
Thomas Bates, 6d.
Henry Tapping, 6d.
Thomas Waddopp, 4s.
Thomas Archer, 6d.
John Baldwin, 6d.
John Jones, 4s.6d.
Willm. Elyott, 4s.6d.
Thomas Watts, 4s.
Barnaby Chattwell, 2s.
Ambrose Heyton, 8s.
Willm. Neele, 6d.
Thomas Jarvis, 4s. *Affid.*
Thomas Smyth, 12d.
Thomas Bowes, 4s. *Affid.*
Edward Robins, 4s.
Richard Gardiner, 2s.6d.
John Warren, 3s.
Thomas Middleton, 8s.6d.
Thomas Baldin, 2s.
Edmund Paxton, 13s. *Affid.*
Henry Paxton jun., 5s. *Affid.*
John Yates, 3s.6d.
Charles Cranwell, 2s. *Affid.*
Willm. Aris, 4s.6d. *Affid.*
George Watts, 3s. *Affid.*
William Ellord, 3s.
Henry Paxton sen., 2s.
Henry Broughton, 3s.6d.

Sum £7.0s.6d.

[Note. Finmere is out of order on the roll and follows Fringford.]

[Membrane 2v]

FRINGFORD

[The first seven entries are very worn and faded:]
The Right hoble. the Lord [Broo]ke, £4.
Mr [William] Overton, 21s.
Edward Holton, 5s.6d.
Willm.[?] Quetys [?], 3s.
Willm. ---be, 3s.6d.
G----[?] Wesbery [?], 3s.
Richard Thorp[?], 3s.
Henry Oddington, 4s.
John Grantham, 4s.
John Dodwell, 3s.
George Hawtin, 2s.
Robert Ladyman, 12d.
John Allom, 12d.
Katherine Tredwell, 12d.
Roger Warner, 6d.
George Vaux, 2s.
David Lawley, 2s. *Affid.*
Lewes Finmore, 2s.
Willm. Smyth, 2s.
Thomas Finmore, 2s.
Robert Langley, 2s. *Affid.*
Widd. Peeke,
Robert Smewin, 2s.
Mris. Staunton, 5s.
Mris. Crosse, 2s.
Richard Tomlins, 5s.
Robert Stopp, 2s.
Thomas Stopp, 2s.
Richard Barker, gen., 3s.
Charles Thorpe, 6d.
Phillip Coles, 6d.
Richard Stevens, 18d.
George Finmore, 6d.
Henry Foster, 2s.6d.
Henry Jones, 6d.
George Molden, 12d.
John Shackerley, 18d.
Robert Bruton, 18d.
Thomas Pendon, 12d.
Richard Pendon, 12d.
Willm. Barrett, 2s.
Richard Perram, 6d.
Thomas Cox, 6d.
Thomas Barker, 6d. *Affid.*

Sum £8.

FRITWELL

Frittwell

Mris. [Mary] Barker, 33s.4d.
[blank] Dutton, Cler., 6s.8d.
Mr Barker, 19s.6d.
Richard Hobcroft, 5s.5d.
Richard Hickock, 6s.6d.
Gilbert Wells, 9s.2½d.
Margery Fox, 6½d.
Jeffery Harres, 6½d.
Willm. Hobcroft, 6s.6d.
John Hobcroft, 6s.6d.
Nicholas Gorge, 6s.6d.
William Horne, 6½d.
John Ridley, 6½d.
Giles Gasey, 6s.6d.
Mathewe Wise, 7s.7d.
Robert Kilby, 7s.5d.
Willm. Nickolson, 2s.6½d.
Mr [Thomas] Harding, 8s.8d.
Robert Kilby, 8s.8d.
Edmund Hobcroft, 19½d.
Thomas Heydon, 2s.2d.
Willm. Androes, 2s.2d.
Mris. Hatton, 2s.2d.
John Colly, 12½d.
Thomas Watts, 13d.
Nicholas Kilby, 5s.11d.
Richard Padgett, 2s.2d.
Beniamin Watts, 2s.2d.
John Padgett, 2s.2d.
Roger Fennymore, 2s.2d.
Willm. Grace, 2s.2d.
John Wise, 5s.5d.
John Tomkins, 2s.
Willm. Hobcroft, 2s.
Willm. Punter, 2s.6d.
Thomas Grantham, 2s.6d.
Thomas Addams, 2s.
John Orme, 8d.
Michaell Loveday, 8d.
George Harris, 12d.
William Kinge, 8d.
Phillip Hickocke, 4s.10d.

Sum £9.15s.

[Note. Fritwell is out of order on the roll and precedes Fringford.]

GODINGTON

Goddington

Willm. Line, gen., 2s.
James Benskin, R'cor., 20s.
Cadwallader Coker, gen., £3.5s.
John Henley, 55s. *Affid.*
Raphe Coker, gen., 27s.
Willm. Jerrard, 5s.6d.
Hugh Jackson, 25s.6d.
John Lambe, 5s.
Leonard Bruton [*or* Braton], 2s.
Willm. Joyner, 1s.
John Pyne, gen., 5s.
Richard Clyfton, 4s.
Humfry Baylis, 2s.
Thomas Chapman, 6d.
Edward Friday, 6d.
Richard Paxton, 6d.
Willm. Paxton, 6d.

Sum £11.12d.

HARDWICK

Sr. Richard Fermor, Knt., 15s.
Henry Daves, 7s.6d.
Widd. Mercer, 6s.6d.
Robert Ward, 6s.
Michaell Walker, 4s.6d.
Widd. Bishopp, 4s.6d.
Henry Davies, 13s.
Richard Combes, 7s.
Edward Hilliard, 7s.6d.
Richard Bish, 3s.6d.
Raph Thorneborowe, 6s.6d.
The Parsonadge, 18s.6d.

Sum £5.

HETHE

Heath

John Ryton, 6s.
Andrew Bradshaw, 6s.9d.
Willm. Cooke, 6s.4d.
Richard Watkins, 5s.3d.
Robert Creede, 4s.6d.
Richard Shackerley, 9d.
Dorothy Webb, 9d.
Richard Bish, 6s.
Henry Watson, 2s.3d.
Richard Herne, 9d.
Willm. Herne, 9d.
Willm. Phillips, 3s.
Mr Evans, 19s.3½d.
Anthony Quainton, 5s.8d.
George Verney, 18d.
Willm. Bilson, 4½d.
James Gauderne, 9d.
Thomas Pecke, 2s.
Alexander Petty, 2s.7½d.
Richard Saunders, 9d.
Henry Herne, 3s.
Edward Herne, 4s.3d.
[blank] Treatcher, 4s.6d.
Widd. Stanson, 12d.
Hugh Elmes, 2s.
Robert Whitehead, 12d.
George Evans, 18d.
Isaack Mesey, 12d.
Thomas Judge, 12d.
Thomas Webb, 12d.
Thomas Evans, 12d.
John Smyth, 6d.
Willm. Randall, 12d.
Richard Patten, 12d.
Richard Silver, 6d.

Sum £5.0s.4d

LAUNTON

Richard Okeley, £5.3s.
The Parsonadge, 53s.8d.
John Cottesford, gen., 21s.8d.
Willm. Deely, 7s.11d.
John Jones, 6s.2d.
Walter Allyn, 6s.7d.[?]
Henry Jarves [*or* Jarvis] jun., 7s.8d.
Willm. Freeman, 10s.9d.
Raphe Moore, 3s.1d.
John Bennett, 3s.1d.
John Deely, 3s.1d.
William Winslowe jun., 18d.
Thomas Coles, 23d.
Mr Evans, 7s.8d.
John Rand, 5s.
John Jarves [*or* Jarvis], 4s.
Henry Jarves [*or* Jarvis] sen., 2s.8d.
John Jarvis jun., 3s.
John Sly and Jane Mott, 4s.7d.
Richard Barnet, 9d.
Frances [*i.e.* Francis] Thomas, 8s.5d.
Isabell Paxton, 3s.1d.
Willm. Bigg, 10s.
Ann Henn, vidd., 3s.1d.
Richard Henn, 6s.8d.
Francis Maryatt, 6s.2d.
James Dodwell, 6s.2d.
John Bostock, 4s.7d.
John Coles, 5s.
John Prince, 3s.
Giles Sowtham, 18d.
Edward Freeman, 3s.1d.
Edward Clarke, 3s.1d.
John Abbott, 4d.
Mr Wilkinson, 3s.2d.
Margarett Jones, 4s.7d.
Thomas Freeman, 2s.
Willm. Hawkes, 12d.
John Duck, 6s.
Alexander Barnett, 12d.
Mr Oliver, 7s.
Anthony Trulock, 6s.
Ellin Jervas, 6s.8d.
Thomas Sannders [*or* Saunders], 3s.
Willm. Coles, 2s.
Richard Freeman, 5s.
Henry Basson, 5s.
Arthur Hudson, 6d.
Nicholas Hawkins, 6d.
Richard Chapman, 8d.
James Shirt, 3s.
Nicholas Jones, 12d.
Arthur Ladbrooke, 12d.
Richard Clysoon, 6d.
Edward Robins, 6d.
[Membrane 3v]
Willm. Wickens, 12d.
James Markeham, 3s.
Willm. Freeman jun., 12d.
Edward Hill, 2s.2d.
John Walsh, 4s.
Thomas Parslowe, 12d.
Willm. Woodbridge, 4s.
Willm. Gom, 6d.
John Henn, 12d.
John Smyth, 6d.

Sum £20.

LILLINGSTONE LOVELL

[former Oxfordshire enclave, now in Buckinghamshire].

Lillingston Lovell

Sr. Peter Wentworth, Knt., £6.16s.
Mr Salisbury, 26s.
Edward Bland, 18s.
John Billing, 10s.
Michaell Saunders, 9s.8d.
John Alnutt, 6s.
Peter Saunders, 4s.
John Spencer, 8s.4d.
Widd. Steere, 4s.
Elias Barfoote, 2s.
John Danser, 18d.
Willm. Harper, 18d.
Robert Hall, 12d.
John Bennett, 12d.
Widd. Coles, 12d.
Willm. Morton, 12d.
John Barrett, 12d.
James Hampe, 12d.
Thomas Tarry, 12d.
Henry Gascoigne, 12d.
Randoll Horroll, 12d.
Widd. Mawkins, 12d.
John Robins, 12d.
Richard Trotter, 12d.
Willm. Wells, 6d.
George Curtis, 6d.

Sum £12.

MIXBURY and FULWELL

Mixbury and Fullwell

Mris Philipp Sill, £7.
Mr Ford, 19s.8d.
Thomas Wellisom, 13s.3½d.
Elizabeth Riccard, 4s.8d.
Isabell Perkins, 2s.2d.
Eliz. Tredwell, widd., 4s.10d. *[interpolated]*
Willm. Creede, 4s.4d.
John Creede, 5s.9d.
Jane Wyton, 4s.9½d.
Richard Wyton, 5s.
Richard Creede, 9s.11d.
Symon Porter, 3s.2d.
Willm. Bradshaw, 2s.
Thomas Bateman, 6s.6d.
Thomas Hauke, 2s.8d.
Thomas Wheatley, 4d.
Sill Wellicom, 12s.9½d.
Nicholas White, 2s.8d.
John Maior, 6d.
Hugh Tredwell, 4s.10d.
Thomas Gibbs, 11s.8d.
Beatrice Bateman, 12d.
John Watts, 2s.10d.
George Gibbs, 6s.
Willm. Blunt, 9s.1½d
George Riccard, 6s.6d.
Richard Elliott, 4s.
Thomas White, 12d.
Richard Strange, 14d.
Christian Wheatley, 2s.2d.
Henry Coome, 8s.6½d.

Sum £15.5s.½d

*[See also **Willaston** or **Woolaston**, page 109.]*

[Membrane 2v, following Hardwick.]

NEWTON PURCELL

Newton Pursell

Richard Blower, Esqr., 20s.
The Lord Brooke, 8s.
Edmd. Paxton, 2s.
Mr Lawrence, 6s.
Joseph Lawrence. 4s.
Thomas Walker, 3s.6d.
Roger Marty, 3s.
John Alexander, 18d.
Stephen Duke, 12d.
Thomas Webb, 2s.
Robert Day, 2s.
[Membrane 3r]
Nicholas Finch, 18d.
Willm. Tapping, 2s.
Robert Warr, 18d.
Gabriell Androes, 6d.
John Seely, 6d.
John Assell, 6d.
Thomas Staley, 6d.

Sum £3.

[Membrane 4r]

SOMERTON

Henry Arundell, Esqr., £5.
Sr. Richard Fermor, Knt., 20s.
D'cor [Thomas] Walker, 40s. *Affid.*
Robert Appletree, 10s.
Thomas Hall, 30s.
John Hore, 10s.
Raphe Clyfford, 8s.
Walter Day, 7s.
Willm. Myne, gent., 5s.
Benedict Clyfford sen., 5s.6d.
Benedict Clyfford jun., 12d.
Nicholas Syms, 12d.
Francis Sleamaker, 12d.
Willm. Lovell, 3s.
Henry East, 6s.3d.
Willm. Saunders, 2s.
Humfry Francklyn, 5s.8d.
Mr Dutton, 3s.
Simon Hose, 4s.
George Griffin, 5s.
John Horne, 12d.
Widd. Lovell, 12d. *Affid.*
Willm. Hall, 4s.
John Tompkins, 2s.3d.
Widd. Hore, 12d. *Affid.*
Walter Lepington, 3s.3d.
John Gosling, 3s.3d.
Edward Bradford, 4s.3d.
Thomas Bowers, 12d.
John Hall, 3s.3d.
John Clarke, 12d.
Nicholas Hore, 12d.
Willm. Davies, 12d.
John Howes, 2s. *Affid.*
Thomas Tompkins, 12d.
John Harris, 4d.
John Martyn, 12d.
Henry East, 12d.

Sum £15.

SOULDERN

Soulderne** or **Sowlderne

John Weedon, gent., 43s.4d. *Affid.*
Bernard Weedon, gen., 20s.
Lettice Brograve, 20s. *Affid.*
Richard Walker, gen., 20s. *Affid.*
D'tor Watkins, 33s.4d.
Mr [Thomas] Harding, Rcor., 56s.8d.
Thomas Smyth, gen., 20s.8d.
Willm. Mynn, gen., 4s.8d.
John Dodwell jun., 18s.2d.
Ferdinando Gough, 18s.2d.
Thomas Dodwell, 12s.10d.
Robert Bignell, 14s.6d.
John Browne, 9s.10d.
James Browne, 6s.7d.
Willim. Bowers, 15s.
Robert Holt, gen., 3s.4d.
John Dodwell sen., 7s.4d.
Willm. Hayle, 7s.10d.
John Kinge sen., 4s.8d.
John Kinge jun., 4s.6d.
Richard Dodwell, 14s.
Richard Bignell, 8s.8d. *Affid.*
John Wise, 14d.
John Gough, 5s.9d.
Richard Bignell, 2s.4d. *Affid.*
John Hodges, 4s.6d.
Anthony Buckingham, 7s.4d.
Mathewe Wise, 6s.8d.
George Sowham *[probably mistake for* Sowtham*]*, 2s.4d.
John Dodwell, 21d.
Widd. Hickock, 17d.
[blank] Grantham, 12d.
Richard Davies, 8d.
Willm. Barnett [?], 6d.
Willm. Francklyn, 6d.

Sum £20.

STOKE LYNE

Stokelyne

Charnell Petty, gen., £4.6s.
Cadwallader Coker, gen., £3.18s.8d.
Thomas Holt, gen., 10s.
Mr White, 13s.4d.
Gilbert Watts, 5s.10d.
Giles Stuttesbury, 11s.2d.
Henry Stuttesbury, 8s.9d.
Christofer Rand, 7s.8d.
George Heydon, 5s.
Thomas Addams, 6s.8d.
Willm. Newton, 6s.1d.
John Bishopp, 6s.
[In margin:] Affid. for John Bishopp being Constable and having collected 40s. doth detaine it.
John Butcher, 2s.4d.
Edward Bruton, 2s.5d.
John Hewes, 4s.10d.
Raph Thorneberry, 2s.7d.
John Presloe, 8d.
Henry Davies, 2s.

Sum £13.

SHELSWELL

The Lady [Elizabeth] Cope, £10. *Affid.*

STRATTON AUDLEY

Edwd. Chamberlayne Esqr, 40s.
Willm. Woodward, gen., 24s.
John Sheusmythe, gen., 16s.
Henry Basson, 16s.
Chr. Parker, 7s.
John Tugwood, 6s.
Thomas Kinge, 2s.
Willm. Bignell, 5s.
Willm. Mortymer, 5s.6d.
George Willcox, 2s.6d.
[Membrane 4v]
Richard Clyfton, 5s.
John Brooke jun., 2s.
John Bignell, 4s.
Nicholas Mortymer, 5s.3d.
Peter George, 3s.
Willm. Perkins, 12d.
Robert Alday, 2s.
Edward Robins, 2s.
Edward Cary, 12d.
John Woollyn, 12d.
Robert Woolyn, 12d.
Thomas Dickenson, 12d. *Affid.*
Edmund Brooke, 6s.
Richard Berry, 6s.
James Beddyn, 16d.
John Brooke sen., 2s.
Thomas Lawrence, 10s.
Joane Toogood, 2s.
Robert Beddyn, 4s.11d.
Thomas Mortymer jun., 18d.
John Grace, 2s.
Nicholas Grace, 12d.
Robert Kinge, 2s.
Edmund Pyttham, 3s.
Thomas Grantham, 3s.
Mary Berry, 12d.
Richard Temple, 6d.
Mr Grymes, 18d. *Affid.*

Sum £10.

TUSMORE

Mr Henry Fermor, 9s.2d.
Henry Davies, £4.9s.4d.
Willm. Punter, 16s.8d.
Thomas Sowth, 10s.5d.
Richard Bisse, 5s.10d.
James Gautherne, 2s.7d.
Marke Kenton, 3s.4d.
Robert Ward, 2s.1d.
Raphe Swayne, 6d.

Sum £7.

WOOLASTON or WILLASTON

Wollaston
[in Mixbury parish]

Sr. Thomas Penyston, Knt. and Baronett, £4. *Affid.*

ADDENDUM

CAVERSFIELD

Although no Protestation Returns survive for Ploughley Hundred, they do for the neighbouring Buckingham Hundred across the county border in Buckinghamshire. Amongst these returns is one for Caversfield, a Buckinghamshire enclave in Oxfordshire close to Bicester.

Feb: 21th 1641.

The p'testation sett forth by the parliament 5 Maij 1641 was assented unto by the Inhabitants of the p'ish of Caversfield whose names are heere under written.

Mr Thomas Moyle
Edward Wells
Humphery Goodgame
Jeffery Towne
Thomas Kibble
Rich: Allom
John Higginson
Vincent Penne
Christopher Parker
Thomas Dumbleton
Thomas Eelly
Thomas Kinge
Edward Justice
Richard Oliver

All the males from 18 yeres & upwards have taken the p'testation, & it hath bin denied by none.

Rich: Grimes, *Vicar*

[Membrane 5r]

Ploughley Hundred: South Division.

BICESTER: MARKET END

Bister Market End

Mr [John] Bird, 10s.8d.
Thomas Clemens, 10s.4d.
Raphe Wall, 12d.
Thomas Wall, 6d.
Richard Mortymer, 5d.
Richard Grantham, 22d.
Willm. Blythe, 14d.
Willm. Cory, 6d.
Willm. Wynter, 3d.
Walter Baylis, 5d.
John Alexander, 14d.
John Pope, 18d.
Thomas Grantham, 22d.
Widdowe Androse, 3d.
Humfry Hunt, 9s.
Willm. Whiston, 20d.
Widdowe Turner, 7s.2d.
John Swynshead, 5d.
John Kerwood, 16d.
John Medcalfe, 7s.10d.
Richard Clemens, 4s.6d.
Edward Jackman, 3s.7d.
[In margin:] Affid. for Edw. Jackman, Subcoll. for £8.5s.
Edmund Duck, 2s.8d.
Daniell Barnes, 5s.11d.
Michaell Steele, 2s.
Henry Parker, 4d.
Willm. Linney, 4d.
the smyth, 3d.
Edward Clarke sen., 6s.10d.
Edward Clarke jun., 10d.
Mary Robins, 5d.
Willm. Baylis, 10d.
Willm. Lyne, 5d.
Robert Hawkins, 4d.
Willm. Swyft, 5s.5d.
George Clemens, 10s.9d.
Chr. Abbott, 6d.
Robert Bates, 8d.
Andrewe Saunders, 4d.
Thomas Francklyn, 4d.
Raphe Dibdale, 3s.4d.

Bister Market End

John Cooper, 3d.
Thomas Freeman, 4d.
Raphe Syms, 6d.
John Shillingworth, 6d.
John Sheppard, 3d.
Widdowe Bryan, 9d.
Mathewe Lillyatt, 18d.
Thomas Sherman, 12d.
John Bolton, 4d.
John Steward, 4d.
Widd. Ford, 11d.
George Sumner, 15d.
Lister Blount, gen., 4s.6d.
Nicholas Lock, 4d.
John Smyth, 2s.9d.
John Bess, 15d.
James Vortlowe, 10d.
Nicholas Jones, 15d.
Humfry Baylis, 4s.6d.
Willm. Shreeve, 4d.
Richard Clarke, 3d.
Thomas Sutton, 9s.
Mr Francklyn, 4s.6d.
Widd. Reading, 3d.
John Page, 22d.
Gabriell Cooke, 7s.2d.
Allen Woolton, 11d.
Thomas Kinge, 2s.9d.
Abell Bartram, 11d.
Francis Thomas, 4s.6d.
Raphe Thomas, 11d.
Widd. Sutton, 22d.
Willm. Freeman, 22d.
Samuell Cooper, 2s.8d.
John Baylis, 3d.
Anne Clemens[?], 22d.
Widd. Boat, 22d.
John Ellingham, 12d.
Willm. Petter, [?2s.] 11d.
[Membrane 5v blank; Membrane 6r]
Giles Sowtham, 6s.
Samuell Blackwell, 12d.
Thomas Burges, 3d.

John Burrowes, 2s.9d.
Welsborne Blount, 6d.
William Manly, 6d.
George Francklyn, 6d.
Richard Clarke, 11d.
Richard Crosse, 6d.
Thomas Hughes, 3d.
Widd. Paxton, 10d.
John Kinge, 14d.
John Dormer, 6d.
Luke Gurney, 6d.
Robert Baylis, 10d.
Thomas Bodycott, 18d.
William Bird, 4d.
Martin Chatterley, 3d.
Thomas Turner, 6d.
Paul Deane, 6d.
Robert Churchill, 3d.
Mr Coker, 14d.
George Clemens jun., 22d.
Mr Duck, 12d.
Richard Heyward, 2s.8d.
Robert Cox, 22d.
John Wilson and Thomas Beckley, 22d.
Henry Jervas and Thomas Beckley, 12d.
Mr Coker, 18d.
Christopher Irons, 2s.9d.
Thomas Sutton, 10d.
Thomas Roberts, 17d.
Henry Allen, 3s.3d.
Richard Grantham, 3d.
Humfry Baylis, 4d.
Richard Clarke, 5d.
Thomas Clemens, 4s.9d.
Willm. Potter, 11d.
John Pape [*or* Pope], 23s.5d.
Mr Yateman and John Tugwood, 15s.8d.

Sum £20.9s.1d.

BICESTER: KING'S END

Bister Kingsend

Cadwallader Coker, gent., 49s.6d.
Thomas Spencer, 49s.6d.
John Wilson, 3s.4d.
Raphe Clemens, 13s.4d.
John Triplett, 11s.
Robert Leaper and his Mother, 16s.6d.
Matthew Lillyatt, 5s.
Robert Cox, 10s.
[In margin:] Affid. for Ro: Cox subcoll. p. 49s.
Edward Leaper, 2s.6d.
George Clemens, 3s.4d.
Richard Grantham, 20d.
Thomas Beckley, 2s.
Christopher Hanwell, 3s.4d.
Arthur Hudson, 2s.6d.
John Baylis, 12d.
Willm. Thomas, 6d.
Willm. Linney, 12d.
Raphe Dibdale, 12d.
Richard Heyward, 12d.
Richard Tyms, 12d.
Willm. Wynche, 6d.
John Mukehill, 6d.

Sum £9.

BLETCHINGDON

Sr. Thomas Coghill, Knt., £9.6s.8d. *Affid.*
D'cor Swift, 5s.
James Chesterman, gen., 20s.
[*blank: probably* Thomas] Edgerley, 40s.
Robert Androes, 4s.
Giles Jinkins, 3s.
Widd. Bowden, 16s.
Thomas Judge, 7s.
Richard Prickett, 5s.
William Morton, 2s.
Mr Nickson, 2s.
[Membrane 6v]
[blank] Androse, 12d. *Affid.*
John Bedwell, 12d.
Edward Greene, 4s.
[blank] Parrett, 12d.
Richard Kent, 3s.
John Buckley, 3s.[?]
John Spinler, 3s.
Edward Silverside, 10s.[?]
Francis Brathwayte, 5s.
Robert Blower, gen., 4s.
the Parsonadge land, 15s.
Dawrenford Meade, 2s. *[Dornford Meadow is shown on the map in VCH, p.63]*
Edward Sea Esqr., 6s. *Affid.*
Mr Warburton, 14s. *Affid.*
Robert and Thomas Bowell, 15s. *Affid.*
Widd. Dabson, 12d. *Affid.*
Mr Merry, 3s.
Hugh Smyth, 12d.
John Francklyn, 2s.4d.
John Hilliard, 12d. *Affid.*
Willm. Collyer, 12d.
Willm. Clarke, 12d. *Affid.*
Thomas Burdett, 12d. *Affid.*
Willm. Allen, 12d.
Willm. Drake, 12d.
Richard Hanwell, 2s.
[blank] Varny, 12d.
Thomas Evans, 12d. *Affid.*
John Godby, 12d.
[blank] Goodson, 6d. *Affid.*
[blank] Dully, 6d.

Sum £23.
[Auditor's amendment:] £22.11s.

CHARLTON on OTMOOR

Charlton cum Membr.

The Parsonadge, 57s.10d. *Affid.*
Thomas Garth, Cler., 9s.2d. *Affid.*
Richard Alley als. Leverett, 24s.8d.
John Kirby, 12s.4d.
Raphe Kirby, 9s.3d.
Nathaniell Kirby, 9s.3d.
Edmund Thurston, 9s.3d.
Thomas Castell, 13s.10½d.
Mr Burrage, 3s.1d.
Michaell Bryan, 3s.1d.
Richard Brinkloe, 3s.1d.
Martin Bourne, 4s.6½d.
Simon Warner, 3s.1d. *Affid.*
Robert Gateman, 3s.1d.
Richard Pemerton, 3s.1d.
Widd. Shirt, 3s.1d.
Thomas Mynn, 6s.2d.
Oliver Pangburne, 6s.2d.
Henry Poole, 6s.2d.
Thomas Phillipps, 3s.1d.
Thomas Jarrett, 2s.4d.
Ladyes Meade, 4s.6d. *[Lady's Mead is shown on the map in VCH, p.85.]*
Widd. West, 18d.
Widd. Arpwood, 18d.
Thomas Maynard, 18d.
Thomas Pangburne, 12d. *Affid.*
Willm. Dukenson, 12d.
Christopher Peart, 12d.
John Daye, 12d.
Robert Cope, 12d. *Affid.*
Thomas Howes, 6d.
Elias Porter, 6d.
Thomas Poole, 12d.
George Gilder, 12d.
Richard Moore, 3s.
Vincent Yousters, 3s.
Thomas Sharpe, 3s.6d.
John Wyatt, 7s.6d.
Widd. Blake, 6s.
Thomas Wyatt, 6s.
Edward Coles, 13s.6d.
Robert Blake, 3s.
Richard Smart, 9s.
John Burrin, 3s.
Widd. Deely, 2s.3d.
Thomas Chillingworth, 18s. *Affid.*
John Parker, 3s.6d.
Henry Smart, 2s.
Thomas Darling, 6s.
Thomas Wyatt, 18d.
Willm. Pym, 18d.
Widd. Poole, 3s.
Robert Robins, 3s. *Affid.*
Thomas Davis, 7s.6d. *Affid.*
John Bignell, 5s.
Robert Gateman, 4s.6d.
Thomas Hollyer, 3s.
Willm. Poole, 6d.
Widd. Cooper and Richard Cooper, 6s.6d.
Widd. Bartlett, 3s.
Widd. Ellyott, 6s. *Affid.*
Richard Brinckloe, 3s.
Peter Kirby, 18d.
Andrewe Osburne, 2s.
Willm. Chittle, 12d.
Thomas Ryman, 12d.
Richard Carter, 12d.
Robert Flynt, 12d.
George Wyatt, 2s.6d. *Affid.*
George Blake, 2s.6d. *Affid.*
Henry Smarte, 12d. *Affid.* *[interpolated]*
Robert Robins, *[and]* Thomas Maynard, 6s.
Coplands, 6s.

Sum £18.12s.

[Membrane 7r]

CHESTERTON

Sr. Francis Norreyes, Knt., 21s.8d.
Mr [Philip] French, 7s.4d.
Mr William Mawnd of the Farme, 56s.8d.
Mr William Mawnd of the Grange, 21s.8d.
Thomas Mawnd jun., 11s.2d.
William Mawnd sen., 10s.
John Spittle, 11s.2d.
Thomas Mawnd sen., 9s.8d.
Richard Stevens, 2s.1d.
James Hicks, 5s.6d.
Widd. Hide, 7s.2d.
Richard Allen, 5s.6d.
Richard Jervas, 7s.4d.
Mris Bowell, 4s.9d.
Willm. Walton, 3s.6d.
Thomas Hawkins, 5s.6d.
Richard Smyth, 9s.6d.
Willm. Hawkins, 8s.6d.
John Bowell, 3s.6d.
Thomas Bartlett, 2s.6d.
Richard Porter, 18d.
Willm. Lowch, 12d.
John Jenkins, 16d.
Nicholas Faukener, 8d.
Oliver Hues, 2s.
Robert Rogers, 6d.
Richard Harvy, 6d.
the Parsonadge, 17s.
the Vicaridge, 13s.
Edward Spittle, 12d.
Edward Freeman, 18d.
Raph Hitchman, 18d.
Richard Cooper, 9d.
Willm. Hide, 12d.
Widd. Bartlett, 18d.
John Creeke, 4d.
Jasper Butler, 3d.

Sum £13.

HAMPTON GAY

The Lady Fermor, 50s.
Edward Say Esqr., £3.13s.4d.
Willm. Weedon, 5s.8d.
Widd. Triplett, 5s.8d.
Edward Belson, 2s.10d.
John Dennett, 2s.10d.

Sum £7.[0s.4d.]

HAMPTON POYLE

Sr. Henry Crooke, Sr. Waltr. Pye, 16s.
Sr. Robert Crooke, 42s.
Sr. Thomas Coghill, 6s.
Willm. Plastoe, gen., 30s.
D'tor [John] Tolson, 32s.
Humfry Greene, 6s.
Thomas Sawby, 2s.
Thomas Keat [? Kent], 9s.7d.
Willm. Steere, 3s.
Thomas Hanwell, 3s.6d.
Em London, John London, 8s.9d.
Stephen Dennett, 3s.6d.
[In margin:] Affidavt. Stephen Dennett, Sub Coll, 18s.9d.
John Jarvis, 3s.
[Affid. - deleted]
Richard Dennett, 3s.6d.
Bridgett Kempe and John Gaunt, 5s.3d.
Steven Scott, 2s.
John Ford, 4s.6d.
Richard Silverside, 6s.6d.
Willm. Sheene, 8s.9d.
Henry Lumbard, 5s.3d.
Woodstock land, 12d.
Alice Lumbard, 4d.

Sum £10.2s.5d.

LOWER HEYFORD

Heyford ad Pontem

Thomas Cole, R'cor, 37s.
Willm. Bruce sen., 19s.7d.
Gabriell Merry, 25s.
Willm. Bruce jun., 16s.10d.
Widd. Bruce, 5s.4d.
Horatio Merry, 4s.8d.
Henry Parker, 7s.
Robert Washington, 4½d.
John Sheeres, 9s.11½d.
Symon Merry, 3s.8d.
Samuell Merry, 4s.7½d.
Widd. Elkins, 3s.6½d.
Richard Elkins, 2s.8d.
Widd. Jorden, 3s.
Willm. Mynn sen., 3s.
Willm. Mynn, 18s.
[Membrane 7v]
Richard Peesly, 3s.1d.
John Elfred, 3s.1d.
Widd. Kinge, 4s.8d.
Henry Kinge, 4s.8d.
John Norton, 4s.8d.
Anne Cates, 12d.
Thomas Castell, 9s.10d.
John Lawrence, 3s.6½d.
Robert Barrett, 19d.
Henry Kinge, 2s.
Bartholomew Bird, 9½d.
John Giles, 2s.6d.
John Barrett, 2s.6d.
John Lawrence sen., 4½d.
Henry Bennett, 9½d.
George Merry, 4d.
Anthony Hedges, 6d.
Thomas Brooke, 6d.
Edward Varney, 6d.
Widd. Syms, 2s.
Mary Hathway, 6d.
John Merry, 6d.
John Whetton, 12d.
James Trepas, 6d.
Henry Whyton, 2s.
Gabriell Merry, 6d.

Sum £10.2s.

UPPER HEYFORD

Heyford Warren

Anthony Barker, R'cor., 30s.
Edward Ashworth, gen., 50s.
[In margin:] Affid. agt. Edw. Ashworth and Will. Rogers, Sub coll. p. 15s.
John Lawrence, 9s.
Willm. Heynes, 6s.9d.
John Hore, 6s.9d.
Widd. Meacock, 4s.6d.
Robert Barrett, 6s.9d.
John Hawkins, 9s.
Stephen Dockins, 12d.
John Fox, 6s.9d.
Robert Tanner, 6s.9d.
John Rogers, 10s.
Richard Gazey, 6s.9d.
Willm. Rogers, 13s.9d.
Thomas Lawrence, 6s.9d.
Robert Howes, 4s.6d.
Willm. Harbert, 12d.

Sum £9.

ISLIP

Islipp

Mr [Thomas] Gilder and
  Mr [John] Bancks, £3.10s.
Mr Gilder, 8s.
Mr Bancks, 10s.6d.
John Wrench, 3s.6d.
James Ford, 7s.
Jerome Cooper, 6d.
Widd. Pangburne, 2s.
Joseph Gould, 21d.
Roger Sandy, 21d.
Robert Perrye, 12d.
Raph Horwell, 7s.
Raph Rogers, 6d.
Willm. Ostwell, 3s.6d.
John Freeman, 3s.6d.
Thomas George, 12d.
Ben. Knight, 12d.
Nicholas Dye, 12d.
Christopher Hunt, 12d.
Mathewe Browne, 6d.
Widd. Bradley, 14s.
Mr Box, 18d.
Mr Marryatt, 3s.
Mr Violett, Rector, £3.3s.
Mr Francis, 3s.6d.
Thomas Stocker, 8s.9d.
Henry Bolt, 10s.6d.
John Greene, 3s.6d.
Thomas Craker, 18d.
Willm. Osburne, 2s.9d.
Raph Horwell, 3s.6d.
Richard Coles, 5s.3d.
Henry Davis, 21d.
Peter Littlefeild, 21d.
Robert Pryor, 3s.6d.
Jeffery Younge, 18d.
Raph Dagley, 2s.9d.
Richard Deely, 21d.
Thomas Gallway, 12d.
Mr Aston, 3s.6d.
Mris Pytts, 7s.

[Membrane 8r]
Thomas Durrant, 21d.
Leonard Bolt, 11s.
Willm. Bridgewater, 12d.
Thomas Penn, 12d.
Widd. Penn, 12d.
[blank] Augure, 12d.
Bartle. Bird, 12d.
Richard Stocker, 12d.
Thomas Bolt, 12d.
Thomas Freeman, 3s.6d.
Henry Druse, 2s.6d.
John Tredwell, 18d.
Peter Stiffe, 21d.
Thomas Tredwell, 3s.4d.
Henry Rooke, 3d.
Anthony Jeffreys, 3d.
Christopher George, 3s.6d.
George Penn, 12d.
Henry Fidler, 12d.
Widd. Verney, 12d.
Peter Flexney, 3s.
Thomas Savadge, 12d.
Thomas Hincks, 12d.
Thomas Dennett, 12d.
Edm. Crofts sen., 3s.
Edm. Crofts jun., 12d.
Joane Clarke, 12d.
Widd. Leverett, 12d.
Edmund Ewstace, 2s.6d.
Ben. Knight, 3s.
James Ward, 6d.
Widd. Barfoote, 12d.
Robert Standard, 20d.
Henry Bolt, 18d.
Mris. Pytts, 3s.4d.
Christopher George, 18d.

Sum £16.16s.7d.

KIRTLINGTON

Kirtlington cu. membr.
Henry Day, 17s. *Affid.*
Thomas Chamberlayne,
  Esqr., 10s. *Affid.*
Humfry Hide, Esqr., 8s.2d.
  Affid.
Stephen Augier, gen., 35s.
Richard Rayer, 14s.8d.
Joane Hall, 15s.6d.
  Affid. p. 5s. in pt.
Margarett Hawkins, 14s.6d.
  Affid. p. 9s.5d.
Richard Walker, 10s.½d.
Justinian Walker, Richard
  Walker, 3s.4d.
Thomas Turner, 2s.11d.
Anthony Slater, 5s.4d.
Margaret Hall, 12s.4d.
  Affid. p. 3s.10d. in pte.
Richard Martyn, 5s.8d.
Widd. Rayer, 6s.
Widd. Bryan, 3s.
Thomas Pryor, 5s.4d.
Richard Hall, 8s. *Affid.*
George Barrett, 3s.6½d.
James Morton, Richard Hall
  jun., 7s.8d.
Justinian Walker, 7s.
Widd. Younge, 2s.5d.
Christopher Fennymore,
  2s.9d.
Justinian Walker, 2s. *Affid.*
James Chamberlayne,
  14s.4d.
James Sleamaker, 3s.6d.
Jasper Butler, 12d.
Edward Dully [? Dally], 7d.
Richard Bathe, 2s.6d.
Clement Eyres, 4d. *Affid.*
Francis Walker, 4d. *Affid.*
James Morton, 6s.6d.
Widd. Swetnam, 6d.
Christopher Benson, 3d.
  Affid.
John Bathe, 7s.8d.
Richard Martyn, 8d.
Thomas Ewyn, 6d.
Widd. Mesey, 18d.
Widd. Milward, 18d.

***Kirtlington** continued*

Widd. Collingridge, 8d.
John Hall, 16d.
Francis Flight, 5s.
Andrewe Stranger, 15s.4d. *Affid.*
Richard Woodward, 13s.4d.
Hugh Smyth, 11s.8d.
Edward Hall, 6s.8d.
Giles Head, 3s.4d. *Affid.*
Mr Hide, 3s.4d. *Affid.*
[Membrane 8v]
Richard Jackman, 18d.
Willm. Finmore, 12d.
Richard Hall jun., 2s.6d. *Affid.*
Thomas Francklyn, 18d.
Willm. Annyson, 3s.
Robert Slater, 2s.
Thomas Jephkins, 2s.6d.
Henry Bull, 4s.
Raphe Bathe, 12d.
Thomas Tolly, 18d.
Anthony Hall, 18d.
Joseph Sutton, 2s.6d.
John Walton, 2s.6d.
Henry Ebburne, 6d. *Affid.*
Thomas Swetnam, 6d.
Edward Wootton, 12d.

Northbrook

Thomas Chamberlayne Esqr., 8s.4d. *Affid.*
Thomas Carpenter, 3s.4d. more, 12d.
Joane Hall, 20d.
Henry Kinge, 4s.
Rowland Bennett, 5s.6d.
Widd. Astell, 12d.
John Butler, 22d.
George Eliman, 7s.6d. *Affid.* 6s. in pt.
Widd. Chamberlayne, 6d.
Widd. Radford, 14d.
Thomas Hawkins, 5d.
Anthony Day, 4d.
Marmaduke Butler, 2s.6d.
Widd. Cosier, 12d.
Willm. Croughton, 18d.
John Willms., 12d.
Edwarde Kinge, 12d.

Sum £18.6s.3d.

MIDDLETON STONEY

Middleton Stony

Nicholas Harman, Esqr., 5s.6d.
Mr [Richard] Worrall, R'cor, 12s.
Michaell Hewes, gen., 10s.
[blank] Fitzharbert, widd., 26s.
John Land, 7s.6d.
Willm. Hide, 6s.
Symon Cony, 6s.6d.
John Smyth, 3s. *Affid.* p. 2s.
Widd. Nixon, 6s.6d.
Daniell Warner, 5s. *Affid.*
Barton George *[sic]*, 8s.
Thomas Smyth, 6s.
Nicholas Smyth, 12s.
Symon Hawkins jun., 6d.
Robert Cookoo, 6d.
Nicholas Tyms, 4s.
John Hedges, 9d.
Willm. Tanner, 12d.
John Luckett, 12d.
Widd. Land, 7s.
Richard Payne, 4s.
Richard Bedwell, 6d.
Thomas Bishopp, 6d.
John Gill, 9d.
John Tyms, 6d.
John Gardner, 6d. more, 6d.
Willm. Smyth, 4s.

Sum £7.

NOKE

John Irons, £5.12s.6d.
Hugh Holden, R'cor., 16s.
Mris Hatton, 5s.4d.
Hercules Quartermaine, 2s.8d.
John Mercer, 2s.8d.
Anne Warland, 3s.
John Day, 2s.8d.
John Flaxman, 2s.8d.
John Harper, 2s.

***Noke** continued*

Widd. Tomlins, 2s.
Daniell Bull, 2s.
Jozas*[sic]* Warland, 2s.
Thomas Johnson, 16d.
Widd. Kent, 16d.
John Howes, 16d.
Richard Dewe, 16d.
Thomas Norcott, 16s.
Widd. Mott, 12d.
[Membrane 9r]
Ellis Johnson, 8d.
John Fuller, 4d.
Leonard Androes, 8d.
Widd. Jesett, 4d.
Widd. Norman, 4d.
Roger Durant, 4d.
Thomas Hawkins, 4d.

Sum £8.6s.2d.

ODDINGTON

Edm. Chamberlayne, Esqr., 23s. *Affid.*
Thomas Craker, 7s.8d. *Affid.*
Widd. Bradley, 5s.9d. *Affid.*
Willm. Hanwell, 14s.5d.
Mr [Thomas] Browne, R'cor, 30s.8d.
Robert Berry, 14s.4d.
Robert Walcott, 19s.3½d.
Thomas and Robert Meadds, 22s.6d.
Richard Boswell, 20s.1½d.
Thomas Walcott, 13s.5d.
John Kirby, 6s.8½d.
Widd. Payne, 6s.8½d.
Phillip Sellenger, 5s.9d.
Widd. Meades, 3s.10d.
Thomas Pullen, 23d.
Richard Corbett, 12d.
Widd. Hixe, 23d.
Humfry Goodgame, 12d.
Willm. Vervine, 12d.

Sum £10.0s.12d.

WENDLEBURY

John Bird, Rector, 25s.
Mistris Hitch, 22s.
Mistris Bowell, 22s.
Thomas Moyles, Esqr., 4s.
Mr Hewes, 9s.3d.
Willm.Mawnd, 11s.2½d.
Thomas Roberts sen., 7s.8d.
Widd. Roberts, 4s.
Thomas Roberts jun., 8s.
Thomas Kinge, 16s.9d.
Willm. Fennymore sen., 2s.
Willm. Fennymore jun., 6s.4d.
Androwe Hide, 8s.4½d.
Richard Younge, 4s.
Gabriell Copland, 7s.
Gabriell Honor, 2s.
Robert Oakeley, 2s.6d.
John Oakeley, 5s.6d.
John West, 9s.
Mistris Lewes, 5s.
Edmund Lewes, 18d.
Willm. Mawnd, 20d.
Leonard Dymmock, 3s.
Thomas Quelch, 2s.
Thomas Batchelor, 2s.
Willm. Napton, 18d.
Mary Clarke, 12d.
Thomas Bartlett, 2s.
Richard Dawson, 2s.
Mr Wryte and Mr Richardson, 21d.

Sum £10.

WESTON on the GREEN

Weston

Sr. Francis Norreyes, Knt., £4.
Mr Mathewes, 5s. *Affid.*
Mistris Blower, 5s.6d.
Robert Jenings, gen., 2s.
Gabriell Merry, gn., 3s.6d.
Willm. Hanwell, 5s. *Affid.*
John Allen sen., 5s.
Willm. Porter sen., 6s.6d.
Chr. Stevenson, 6s.
Robert Blea, 4s.
James Harris, 3s.6d.
Thomas Lewes, 3s.
Anne Gibbs, 12d.
Andrewe Allam, 3s.6d.
John Allam, 3s.6d.
Edward Allam, 4s.6d.
Willm. Ladyman, 3s.6d.
James Woodward, 2s. *Affid.*
Willm. Allen[?], 2s.6d.
Nicholas Kilby, 6d.
Willm. Drake, 18d.
John Wise, 2s.
Henry Goodson, 2s.6d.
[Faded for rest of membrane]
Peter Worlade [?], 2s.6d. *Affid.*
Thomas Fox, 18d.
Thomas Androw [?], 12d., *Affid.*
Bartholomew Howes, 2s.6d.
Symon Davyes, 9d.
John Jerrard [?], 6d.
Robert Digwoodd [?], 6d.
Ursula Allen, 2s.
John Stratton, 4s. *Affid.*
Robert Webb, 2s.
Phillip Johnson, 2s.
[torn] Goodson, 18d.
[torn] ...son, 12d.
[torn] ...well, 3s.6d.
[torn Fa]wkener [?], 2s.
[Membrane 9v; first five entries faded.]
*[torn ...]*e, 2s.
[torn], wid. [?], 12d.
*[torn ...]*oole, 18d.
*[torn ...]*umde [?], 18d.
*[torn ...]*ward Lathbury, 6d.
Thomas Hanwell, 6d.
Thomas Mathewes, 12d.
Edward Andrewes, 12d.
Nicholas Mawnd, 4s.
Lawrence Fawkener, 9d.
John Langley, 9d.

Sum £10.9s.[?]d.

Recusants

Besides Recasants taxed to pay Suplusage money by the said Acte as followeth:

Bister Market end & Kings end

Henry Benson, 16d.
John Busby, gent., 27s.6d.

Bucknell

the wife of Henry Walcott, 16d.

Cottesford

Sr. Richard Fermor, knt., 7s.

Frittwell

Mris. Hatton, 2s.6d.

Hardwick

Sr. Richard Fermor, knt., 15s.

[Sum 44s.3d.]

Launton

Elizabeth wife of Willm. Winslowe, 16d.

Kirtlington

[The following five are bracketed with 'Affid.' written against them]
Mary Arden, wid., 16d.
Margarett Arden, spinster, 16d.
Margarett ux. Humfrd. Hide, Ar., 16d.
Eliz. ux. Henr. Daye, 16d.
Robert Smyth and Anne ux. eius, 2s.8d.

Sum 9s.4d.

Somerton

Sr. Richard Fermor, Knt., 2s.
Willm. Mynn, gen., 5s.
Widd. Smyth, 16d.
Ellen Smyth, 16d.
Anne Hall, 16d.
Mary Clyfford, 16d.
Benedict Clyfford, jun., 12d.
Dorothy Goslinge, 12d.
John Horne, 12d.
Alice Lepington, 16d.
Lucy East, 16d.
Christian Saunders, 16d.
Margarett Horbert, 16d.
Willm. Saunders, 2s.

Sum 41s.

Souldern

[Asterisked entries have 'Affid.' written against them.]
*John Weedon, gen., 43s.4d.
Bernard Weedon, gen., 20s.
Thomas Smyth, gen., 20s.8d.
*Elinor Weedon, 16d.
*Ignatius Weedon, 16d.
*Robert servant to Mr Weedon, 16d.
*Mary Loe, 16d.
*Rowland Dray[?], 16d.
*Mary Draper, 16d.
Roger Anstee, 16d.

Sum £4.18s.0d.

Shelswell

Edmd.(?) Hawley, gen. & ux., 2s.8d.

Stratton Audley

Juliana ux. Nich. Mortymer, 16d.

Tusmore

Mr Fermor, 9s.2d.
Mris. Fermor, 16d.
Mris. Middleton, 16d.
John Bosgate, 16d.
John Polton, 16d.
Anne *[blank]*, Chamber mayde, 16d.
Anne, Cooke Mayde, 16d.
Eliz., Dayry Mayde, 16d.

Sum 18s.6d.

WOOTTON HUNDRED

NORTH ASTON

[f.114, single column.]

The names of those that have taken the protestation [37]

Mr. Jo: Denton the elder Esq.
Mr. Tho: Denton
Jo: Warren, *Vicar*
Mr. Jo: Denton the yonger
Jo: Churchill
Ed: Wing
Jo: Hedger [Hedgee?]
Rob: Jefferies
Jo: Line
Rich: Stevens
Tho: Curtis
Will: Carpenter
Rob: Andrewes
Will: Geeves
Will: Cooper
Will: Rogers
Rob: Harris
Rich: Cooper
Tho: Borton
Rich: Poulton
Antony Bishop
Tho: Hickes
Jam: Littleford
Will: Wing
Will: Johnson
Tho: Nicholson
Jo: Sleamaker
Jo: Wing the yonger
Peter: Walkelet
Jo: Seden
John Winge
Thymothy Winge
Edward Winge
Robt Winge
Ed: Badger
John Times[?]
Richard Coleburne

STEEPLE and MIDDLE ASTON

[f.115r. In two columns. This is one of the rare parishes with signatures or marks for all listed. Marks are shown by asterisks, all others being signatures.]

The names of all the parishioners in Steeple and Middle-Aston who took the protestation February the 20 1641 [91]

[f.115r, col. 1]
Edward Wirley
Fran: Croke
William Belcher
Gabriell Copland
Edward Lamlee
John George
Michaell Barker
Edmund Marten
Henry Barker
John Hams
Henry Parsons
John Bayles *
John King
Timothy Parsons *
Robert George *
Richard Buckinghame *
John Cox
John Hanks *
Edward Carter *
William Geins *
John George the midle *
William Parsons *
William King *
William Peckaver *
Robert Hobcroft *
Robert Freman the younger *

[f.115r, col.2]
John Bates *
Henry Getley the elder *
John Rudson *
Richard Andrewes *, yeoman
Richard Banister *
Richard Rainolds *
Edward Pen *
Richard Stevens *
Tymothye Hickes
Thomas Fox *
Richard Phips *
James Payne *

[f.116r, col. 1]
Robt. Foxe *
Richard Hobcroft
William Hobcroft *
Henrie Batterson [*or* Batteson] *
Joh'is Large *
John Barker
Robert Orchard *
John Georg
Edward Stone *
Richard Feild
David Hawks
Joh'is Winge *
William Hawkins *
William Smith *
William Barton *
Walter Powell *
Henry Lamlee
Joh'is Payne *
Rici Crasse *
Robert Freeman
John Hobcroft *
William Hobcroft *, sheepheard
Henry Getley *
William Barret *

[f.116r, col. 2]
Thomas Quito [?] *
Giles Pen *
Nicholas Cox *
James Rose
Richard Andarns [?]
Richard Hix *
Thomas Read *
Christopher Deane *
Giles Beamond *
Steven Feild *
Horatio Stevenes
Giles Nicholson *
William Tredwell *
Robert Pen
Giles Pen the younger *
George Nicholson *
Thomas Hall *
William Beamond *
Thomas Sommerford *
Henry March *
Timothy Stevens *
John Nickolson

We whose names are heer subscribed doe testify and witnes that all the men parishioners from 18 years and upwards (as far as we can gather) have taken the protestation commended unto them by the high court of Parliament

Edward Wirley, *Minister*
Gabriell Copland, *Overseer of Steeple Aston*
Michael George *, Michael Barker, *Churchwardens*
Nicholas Cox *, *Oversee of Middle-Aston*
Henry Barker, *Constable of Steeple Aston*
James Rose, *Constable of Middle-Aston*

[f.117 - blank]

BARFORD ST. MICHAEL

[f.118r, in two columns.]
Barforde Saynt Michaelle
in Com' Oxon' [62]

For the Lordes of the Honourable High Courtt of Parliament The Honourable House of Comones his Maiesties Justices of the Peace, In the Countie of Oxon' aforesayd or to whomsoever It may Concerne We whoose Names are hereunto subscribed doe Certifie that all the male kinde from the age of Eighteene yeares olde and upwardes within our sayd parish of Barford abovesayde have made theire protestation according to the order prescribed from parliament.

Imprimus *[sic]* It was first made of Mr. Thomas Chapline vicar of our sayd parish and of George Rymell and John Hawten senior Churchwardens and of John Holloway and William Fortnam overseeres for the pore of our sayd parish of Barford sntt michael and afterwards of Them Given to the rest of the Inhabitants whoose names are underwritten.

Anthony Owen,
Counstable

[f.118r, col. 1]
Mr. William Shephard
George Pittam
John Newman senior
Richard Heynes
Richard Lovedreane senior
John Owen senior
John Owen junior
Thomas Nickoles
Anthony Collenes
John Rydall
Francis Jarvis
Richard Owen
George Wakefeild
Richard West
John Hawten Junior
William Morley
Thomas Parkines
Robert Lawnton
Thomas Caraway
William Pleevie
William Collenes
John Newman Junior
John Payne
Thomas Harding
William Gibbs
George Fortnam
Abell Pagett
Umphery Vaughan
William Gyles
John Fortnan
John Lovedrean
John Clevenger
Christopher Biggs

[f.118r, col. 2]
Francis Fortnam
Thomas Faekner
William Faekner
Thomas Fortnam
Richard Lovedreane
William Holloway
Martine Timmes
Samuell Rymell
William Hancock
Francis Weaver
Thomas Gibbs senior
Thomas Gibbs Junior
John Maning
Richard Ladbrooke
William Fortnam Junior
Philip Fortnam
Thomas Hawten
Richard Hawten
Edward Elketton
Edward Horseman
Richard Fortnum
Andrew Allder
Richard Carpenter

Mr. Tho: Chaplin, *Vicar ibid*
George Rymill,
John Hawtin,
Churchwardens
Antho: Owen, *Constable*
John Holloway,
William Fortnam,
Overseere

STEEPLE BARTON

[f.119r, in four columns.]
Steeple Barton *alias* ***Barton magna*** *in the County of Oxon'*

The names of all those persons above the age of eighteen yeares within the precincts of the said parrish, who on the 20 day of February in the yeare of our Lord God 1642 tooke the vow and protestation lately set forth by the honourable court of Parliament. [103]

[f.119r, col. 1]
Philip Turner
Isaac Peely
John Busby
Henry Busby
Antony Councel
John Dawby
William Dawes
John Busby
Hezekiah Egglestone
Robert Gubbin
John George
Robert Wilkinson
John Hanwel
Thomas Akers
Henry Adams
John Smith
Antony Councel youn.
Richard Herbert
William Wells
Richard Cooke
Edward Clarke
Henry Cooke
[f.119r, col. 2]
James Worcast
John Robbins
John Goldsmith
Robert Sexton
Henry Cooper
Thomas Johnson
William Hickes
Richard Hall
Oliver Dudson
Thomas Egglestone
Thomas Grexon
Henry Gibband
Edward Burham
Walter Kirby
William Green
John Gennins
Daniel Spicer
William Fox
John Stafford
Henry Barret
John Arnold
William Hanwel

[f.119r, col. 3]
Thomas Potter
Thomas Proud
William Arnold
William Kings
John Smith
Tymothe Bodenton
John Elmes
Thomas Parker
Giles Dines

Clement Arnold
Agnes Roberts
Anne Dawes
Anne Hanwel
Elizabeth Goldsmith
Josan[?] Wells
Agnes Goldsmith
Elizabeth Kirby
Anne Grant
Mary Writon
Sarah Armes
Alce Box
Dorothe Couch
Dorothe Gubbin
Elizabeth Allen
Anne Frankelin
[f.119r, col. 4]
Anne Johnson
Elizabeth Parker
Mary Dawby
Margery Cooper
Margret Lovely
Jone Busby
Dorothee Deely
Julian Clarke
Alce Cooke
Anne Egglestone
Katharine Sheepherd
Elizabeth Green
Anne Barret
Edith Cooke
Marget Worcast
Millescent Smith
Alce Barret
Mary Dawby

Elizabeth Burnham
Katharine Hanwel
Marget Hanwel
Elizabeth Busby
Prudence Sheepherd
Mary Cooper
Anne Councel
Dorothe Gennins
Elizabeth Hanwel
Elizabeth Wilkinson
Dorothe Jones

Mr. Raph Sheldon Gentleman and inhabitant within the precincts of Steeple Barton, with his family, whose names are underwritten, assented to the protestation so far, as it concerned the defence of the Kings Maiesties person and state, the priviledges of Parliament and the rights of the subject with obligation of their lifes and fortunes to defend them: dissenting onely, from one clause of religion standing in opposition to what they professe, being the religion of the Church of Rome. [5]
Johannes Yorke
Anne Tadnam
Elizabeth Baker
Katharine Baker

Ita testamur
John Couch, *Vicar of Steeple Barton*
Bartholomew Barret, *Constable*
Henry Cooke, *Churchwarden*
Edward Clarke, *Churchward'*

WESTCOTT BARTON

[f.120r, in two columns.]

***Westcott Barton** parish*
February the 27th An Dom'
1641

The Bill of Westcott Barton of the names of all the inhabitants [------ ------?] consented and assented unto the protestation wch was tendered and resceived by us from his Ma'ties Justices at Woodstock in manner and form following [46]

[f.120r, col. 1]
Imprimus Stiven Pole
Thomas Fourd
John Forbrother
[Fairbrother]
Edward Winter
Thomas Peirt sen
Thomas Winter
Jeffery Hickes
Robert Johnson
Samson Offeild
Richard Willis
Walter Heaydon
William Smith
Richard Gibbes
Richard Austen
Andrew Crasse
John Luces
Michaell Fiddler
John Cooper
[A---les?] Judge
Gyles Rushe
Gressant Parker
Henery Varney
Robert Hore
Polley Houle
John Offeild
John Buswell
George Little
Edward Welles
Humfery Houle
Willie Houle

[f.120r, col. 2]
Tuh--my[?] Westcott
Henery Blabey
John Love
Tho: Sutton
Thomas Pearte iunior
William Cries
Thomas Harris
William Harris
Richard Ford
Thomas Belcher Junior

In witnesse hearunto wee have sett our hanes *[sic]* in particular the daye and yeare above sayd
Tho: Belcher, *Rector eodeim Villiam*
Tho: Peirt and John Offeild, *Churchwardens*
John Forbrother, *Cunstable*
Tho: Fourd and Robert Hore, *Overseers of the poor*

BEGBROKE

[f.121r, single column.]
***Begbrooke** in the*
Countie of Oxon': 1641

A Returne of the names of the Inhabitants of the parishe aforesaid which have unanimously consented to the Protestation inioyned them by the high Courte of Parliament [20]

Vincent Coventree, *Rector*
John Fitzherbert Esq'
William Garret,
Richard Coxe,
Churchwardens
Vincent Coventree iun'
John Kinge
Nicholas Kent
George Cooke
Edward Davys
Christopher Younge
William Younge
Samuell Saunders
Edward Lowell
Edward Cripps
William Browne
William Whitinge
George Honey
John Cave
Francis Wiggins
Thomas Morgan

In testor
Vicentius Coventree
William Barrett
Richard Cox
Samuell Saunders,
Constable

CASSINGTON and WORTON

[f.122r, in two columns.]

Cassington and Worton

The names of those that have taken the protestation the XXVIIth day of February. [75+2]

[f.122r, col. 1]
Henry Egleandle, *minister*
John Cole, Gen'
Robert Greneway
Thomas Grenway
Richard Grenway
Richard Flexney
John Stayne
John Cherry
Robert Payne
John Hanwell
Robert Aiers
Thomas Bathe
Richard Greene
Henry Kench
Henry Burle
Thomas Croton
Georg Holloway
Walter Payne
Richard Geeves
William Godward
John Cosier
Rafe Fadey
Richard Fadey
John Greenway
Thomas Seale
Alix Slatford
Francis Boulter
Steven Seale
Steven Langford
Richard Grant
John Jonson
John Warin
Henry Harris
Peter Pangborne
Adam Bolgrove
John Martin Se
John Martin Ju

[f.122r, col. 2]
Steven Townsend
Jeames Townsend
George Townsend
Henry Phillips
Thomas Spooner
Richard Plesto
Edward Trendale
Thomas Whing
Thomas Smith
Robert Burle
Thomas Bathe
John Greene
John Bramsgrove
John Francis
Nicholace Bramsgrove
Nicholace Barker
Richard Franklin
Thomas Spooner
John Forty
Robert North
John North
Richard North
Henry North
Mathew Crips Se
Mathew Crips Ju
Owen Kirton
Thomas Kirton
Thomas Jeames
Thomas Potter
Sanders Painkes
Robert North
Richard Kirton
Steven Shadwell
John Collier
Thomas Laughton
Georg Payne
John Tuckwell
Thomas Tucwell

William Raynolds,
Edmond Raynolds,
Refuse being recusants

COGGES

[f.123r, in two columns]
***Coggs** in Oxon-Shire*

The names of all those that tooke the protestation set out by act of Parliament. This Protestation was taken by the parishioners of Coggs in the County of Oxon' on the 23 day of Februarie 1641 in the parish Church of Coggs [79]

[f.123, col. 1]
Bartholomew Crutchfeild
Richard Bartlet
Barton Crutchfeild
John Brookes
Thomas Munday
Lawrence Cunstable Sen'
Lawrence Cunstable iun'
Sampson Horne
William Townesend
John Roch
Leonard Gunnis
Richard Chruchfeild
William Ring sen:
William Ring Junior
William Johnsone
Robert Androse
Thomas Baylie
Thomas Dorne
James Nevill
Edward Shurley
Edward Mills sen'
Jonas Archer
Edward Young
John Thomas
William Wainman
Edward Harris
John Thornebury
Antony Tennant
Hardwicke Carpenter
Richard Butcher
John Butcher
John Androse: sen: gent
John Androse: jun: gent
Henry Androse: gent
John Teret *[for* Tenent*?]*
William Barber
Walter Linsey
Robert Davis
John Powell
William Brudenell
James Foster
John Rawlins
Richard Rawlins

[f.123, col. 2]
John Harris
Richard Love
John Foster sen:
John Foster: Jun:
Leonard Androse
William Swan
George Allen
Richard Wats
Nicholas Wats
Hugh Androse
John Androse
Nicholas Johnsone
Henry Johnsone
John Chany
John Lay
Walter Lay
Thomas Rawlins
William Flexney
Michaell James
John Cunstable
Henry Fletcher
Henry Paine
Thomas Harmer
Edward Miles iun'
Thomas Duffin
Christopher Johnsone
William Cunstable
Robert Evans
John Haines
William Thornebury
Francis Stone
Charles Tailor

Testamur:
Jacobus Parkinson, *Minister*
Richard Ballord,
John Bruer, *Churchwardens*
Thomas King

We have none in our parish which refused to take the Protestation.

[For Combe, see page 135]

DEDDINGTON

[f.124r. A very long sheet, in three columns.]

***Dedington** parish in the County of Oxon'* [304]

We (whose names are hereunder written) Inhabitants of the Parishe of Dedington aforesaid have in the Presence of Allmighty God promised, vowed & protested and by these presents doe promise vow and protest to maintain & defend as far as lawfully we may with our lives power and estates the true reformed Protestant Religion expressed in the doctrine of the Church of England against all Popery and Popish innovations within this Realm contrary to the same doctrine and according to the duty of our allegiance His Ma'ties Royall Person Honour and Estate; As allso the Power and Privileges of Parliament; The lawfull Right and Liberties of the Subiect and every person that maketh this Protestation in whatsoever he shall doe in the lawfull pursuance of the same. And to our Power and as far as lawfully we may we will oppose & by all waies & means indeavour to bring to condigne punishment all such as shall either by Force, Practise, Counsells, Plots, Conspiracies or otherwise, doe anything to the contrary of any thing in this Protestation contained etc.

[f.124r, col. 1]
John Duncombe Esq
Thomas Apletree Gent
John Lane Gent
Thomas Higins Gen'
John Welchman Gen'
Richard Manning
Simon Busby sen'
William Sturch
Peter Hall
William Glazebrooke
Richard French
Cornelious Bazely
John Robins
Thomas Wells
George Sparrow
John Jeafkins sen'
George Waterman
John Jewster
George Nursse
Richard Harris
Thomas Low
John Kerwood
William Pritchat
Bennet Smith
George French
John Margits
Thomas Gilkes
John Paine
Salomon French
Thomas Baal
John London
George Elkinton
William Lewes
John Sissell
Thomas Nicholson
John Meades
Thomas Baker
Timothy Gilkes
Thomas Durran
John Hopcrofte
John Hollier
William Ledlow
William Patten
John Swift
Michaell Cope
Robert Baldwin
Edward Manning sen'
Henry Randle
Ralfe Dry
Henry Featherton
John Tappertoe
James Manning
Edward Manning iun'
Edward Kempster
Robert Nicholson
Edward Parsons
William Jones
Henry Hawood
Richard Mercer
Francis Jewster
Stephen Humfris
William Pope
John Jakeman
John Tombs
John Minstrell
John Manning sen'
Richard Franknill
John Williams Sen'
Thomas Kerwood
William Kerwood
John Carter sen'
John Carter iun'
Thomas Robins
George Tredwell
Edward Parsons
Nicholas Triplet
John Busby iun'
John Browne
William Stone
William Hall
Francis Smith
Richard Tompson
Nicholas Rand
Walter Rand
Richard Gibbs
Richard Tompkins
Jonathan Jewster
Edward Turnor Sen'
John Kempster
Thomas Bates
Thomas Hollier
Norris Burdett
Thomas Triplet
Robert Pleastow
Edward Marshall
John Fellowes
John Franknill
William Turnor
George Turnor
Edward Turnor iun'
Nicholas Jones

John Hiorns
John Swift
John Rogers
Richard Large
William Eives Sen'
Thomas Swift Sen'
[f.124, col. 2]
Edward Gibson
Walter Bishop
Edward Manning Sen'
John French
John Reeve
Edward Hitchcoke
Richard Maynerd
William Fletcher
Thomas Wilkins
William Gibbs
William Trentham
Humfry Mills
Timothy Harris
Stephen Rimell
Thomas Ryley
Isaak Rimell
Thomas Swift
Thomas Rogers
William Forrest
William Busby
Thomas Ivitoe
Robert Mathew
Henry Vies
William Large
Richard Hunt
Justinian Churchill
William Pritchat
John Allin
John Richards sen.
Bennet Hiorns
Henry Beere
Edward Rand
Edward Price
Henry Wills
Woolstone Rogers
Robert Wellman
John Maynerd
John Tompson
Thomas Sellard
Thomas Nibbs
Thomas Pratt
John Williams iun'
John Winter
James Applebee
Richard Coles
William Forbesse
Richard Cox
John Harris
Anthony Riman
Thomas Maynerd
John Nicholson
Robert Fox
Thomas Slemaker
Edward Jennings
Thomas Gibbs
Wlliam Mathew
Thomas Horne
Timothy Bignell
Mathew Busby
Ralfe Johnson
Samuell White
William Cates
Thomas Swift Sen'
John Aris
Robert Harris
Thomas Chandler
Richard Rogers
Zachary Stillgoe
William Appletree
Thomas Fletcher
Richard Rimell
George Makepeace
Moses Davies
William South
Thomas Gibson
William Nurs
George Blackburne
Anthony Harris
John Wetton
Simon Busby
John Mason
Bartholomew Bett
Roger Maule
John Hopkins
John Cony
Marke Savage
Thomas Wyatt
James Taylor
Thomas Rowse
Thomas Smith
George Jakeman
Robert Bates
John Richards iun'
Robert Barret
Robert Turnor
Robert Hanwell
Anthony Maule
Michaell Knibb
Jonathan Winkles
Luke Bazely
Abraham Greene
Thomas Garner
Michaell Maynerd
Nathaniell Nutt
John Alderly
[f.124r, col. 3]
William Hall, *Clerk*
Edward Maynerd
Nevel Brome, Gent
Edward Bates sen'
Tredwell Bates
Edward Bates iun'
John Heritage sen'
Thomas George
Simon Busby
Thomas Lovedreame
William Tey
Thomas Tey
Richard May
Thomas Churchill
John Dyer
William Rand
John Daniell
Richard Burtonwood
William Warkworth
John Coney
Michaell Maynerd
Anthony Prentice
John Flint
Richard Potter
William Garrett
Anthony Lee
John Mercer
Jonathan Jeafkins
William Heynes sen'
William Heynes jun'
Samuell Bradford
William Calcot
Nicholas Swetnam
Churchill Carter
John Johnson
Thomas Swetenam
Henry Maunder
Philip Man
William Smith
John Swetnam

William Hanwell
William Ingram
Richard Smith
William Summers
Richard Loosley
Richard Browne
John Nutt
Jonathan Scroggs
Edward Harris
John Jeafkins iun'
Edward Gardner
Richard Fenn
John Manning iun'
Richard Nevill
James Batcheller
Hercules Aris
William Aris
Henry Bignell
Anthony Rimell
Nathaniell Ollibanes
Thomas Parrish
William Hauten
John Bignell sen'
John Bignell iun'
Thomas Stevens
William Sharman
Thomas Russell
William Bignell
Anthony Parker
William Wells
William Dry
Richard Tredwell
Edmund Bull
Richard Rawlins
Henry Sheapherd
Philip Sheapherd
Edward Lovedreame
Thomas Dry
John Dry
Thomas Harris
John Hauten
John Heritage iun'
William Fitchet

The names of the Constables, Churchwardens and overseers of the Poore of the Parrish of Dedington

Francis Busby,
Robert Forrest, *Constables of Deddington*
William Collins, *Constable of Clifton*
Anthony Bazeley, *Constable of Hempton*
John Maynerd, *Churchwarden*
Thomas Nutt,
Richard Hale, *Overseers of the poore of Dedington*
John Bignell, *overseer of the poore of Hempton*
John Busby, *overseer of the poore of Clifton*

The names of those that came not in to subscribe to the Protestation upon lawfull warning are these, namely [4]

Edward Smith of Dedington
Richard Cooke of the same
James Cooke of the same
John Aris alias Derry of the same

DUNS TEW

[f.125r, in two columns.]

A catalogue of all such of Dunstew in the County of Oxon as being above eighteen years of age did either deliberately read or hear read the protestation lately sent downe from the high court of parliament and did freely and willingly give their assent and consent to the same on the twentieth day of Febr: Anno domini 1641. [77]

[f.125r, col. 1]
Thomas Castell
Robert Castell
Richard Mitchell
William Fletcher
Thomas Galloway
William Collis
Anthony Burbery
John House
Thomas Heines
John Heines Sen:
William Payne
John Castell
Richard Barret
John Punker
Thomas Baker
Thomas Page
John Broune
John Randel
Robert Walker
Humphry Payne
Jonathan Orleige
Edward Waldin
William Burbery
Thomas Stephens
William Harris sen:
Henry Harris
William Cotton
John Lee
Stephen Feild
William Butler
Richard Hanks
John Heines jun:
William Dubber
Anthony Dubber
George Sumner
John Pimmerton
Richard Collines
Richard Dew
William Hartewell
John Timmes
George Baker
Giles Baker
Robert Coxe
John Tredwell
Thomas Wheeler
Stephen Buckingame
Joseph Fletcher
Thomas House
Thomas Judge
Jeffery Sparrow
Edward Carter
Thomas Smith

[f.125r, col. 2]
John Poulton
Richard Heines
Richard Feer
John Harris
John Baker
Richard Baker
Nicholas Cleuer
Samuell Cleuer
Richard Williams
John Nickolls
William Deen
Michael Tayler
Anthony Hopkins
William Harris Jun'
Henry Harris
Thomas Deen
Edmund Walker
William Collins

They whose names are above written did make that protestation above sayd in the presence of us the minister constables church-wardens and overseers of the poor of the parish of Dunstew above said, who did lately make the same protestaion being tendred to us whose names are here underwritten, and further we doe testify that ther was not any other in our parish that did gainesay the said pro-testation.

Nicholas Coxeter
George Raves,
Edward Dearle,
Churchwardens
Richard Galloway,
Richard Hickes,
Constables
John Crips,
Edward Chamberlaine,
Overseers of the poor

GLYMPTON

[f.126, single column.]
Glimpton

The names of those wch have taken the protestation in the parish of Glimpton [31]

Mr William Wheate esqr
Mr. William Woodward *Rector ecclesiae*
John Woodward, yeoman
Rich: Ellot, *Constable*
Rob: Terry, *Churchwarden*

Tho: Ricketts
Rich: Mason
Will: Tredwell
John Harrise
John Johnson
Rich: Johnson
Rich: Moulder
Henry Hull
Georg Barton
John Daulby
Tho: Joyner
Will: Prise
Joh: Zoanes [?]
Rich: Zoanes [?]
Simon Vicers
Tho: Twinam
Tho: Vicers
Joh: Vicers
Jeffery Smith
Edw. Davis
John Sperinck
Leanard Wilham
Edward Dexill
Rob. Benson
Tho: Wisdom
Tho: Roff

And these are all the men in the towne and parish above 18 yeares of age.

Wm. Woodward, *rector ecclesiae*
Rich: Ellot, *Cunstable, Churchwarden*
Rob: Terry, *Churchwarden*

HEYTHROP

[f.127r, single column.]
Febr. 23 1641

In the parish Church of Heythropp, According to the Order of the house of Commons the protestation was taken of these whose names are subscribed [10]

Gabriell Richardson, *Rect. Eccl.*
Thomas Chamberlaine Esqr.
Thomas Browne
Edward Fox, *Churchwarden*
William Heydon
Thomas Varney
Richard Prue
William Hunnie
John Carter
William Harrison

All that were present. None refusing.

KIDDINGTON

[The parish of Kiddington was split between two Hundreds, Over (Superior) Kiddington being in Chadlington whilst Nether (Inferior) Kiddington was in Wootton. The Protesation Returns for both, on one single column folio, 128r, are filed under Wootton Hundred.]

***Cuddington** alias*
***Kiddington Superior et inferior** in Com' Oxon'*
27 die februarii
Anno Domini 1641

The names of such persons wthin the precincts of this parrish who have taken the protestation sett forth by the honourable house of parliament. [46]

Kiddington Superior

Thomas Offeild
Richard Franklin
William Hancorne
John Rooke
William Widdows
William Franklin
Thomas Stiles
Lawrence Wells
William Hockson
Ralph Widdows
Robert Offeild
John Mawberley
Thomas Humphreys
Ciprian Fidler
Thomas Adams
John Payne
Vincent Franklin
Nicholas Franklin
Thomas Franklinn
John Busby
John Kerrey

Kiddington Inferior

Nicholas Twinam
Leonard Clarke
Thomas Campion
John Colegrove
Nicholas Slamaker
Richard Butcher
Thrustian Heards
Silvester Hancks
Edmund Booden
Walter Nicholls
John Boreman
John Swann
John Hemming
Edward Stacy
Henry Stacy
Rice Wisdome
Richard Deanes
Richard Lewis
Robert Barratt
Thomas Flint

These persons whose names are here underwritten doe Answere that they doe assent unto every branche and clause of the protestacion sett forth by the honourable house of parliament only the first branch excepted, it being repugnant unto the religion wch they now professe.

Mr. Peter Browne Esqr.
Servants:
Francis Winter
Thomas Battmason
William Flint
William Nicholls
Thomas West

Edward Plant, *Rector. ibid*
Nic' Twinam,
Ric Franklin,
Constables
William Hancorne,
Nic' Slamacker,
Churchwardens

[f.129 - blank]

KIDLINGTON

[f.130r. In three columns, very long, one sheet pasted below the other.]

***Kidlington:** this returne Februarie 23th 1641*

The names of all the Inhabitants of the parish of Kidlington: which have taken the protestation the daye and yeare above written [198]

As followeth
Richard Prideaux: *minister*
Churchwardens:
Richard Winch
Jo: Goodsonn
Jo: Bachelour
Overseers of the poore:
Woodhull Streete
Edward Allmont
Jo: Sargeant
Jo Houses
Constables:
Jo: Tustain
Jo: Shreeve
Jo: Bayley
Rich Hailes
Phillipp Doe

[f.130r, col. 1(1)]
Anthony Findall
Thomas Allene
William Frendall
John Bricknell
Robert Phillipps
Ralf Smith
Edward Halloway
John Wrinch
Alexander Halloway
John Allen
Thomas Allen Ju:
Robert Berrie
Nicholas Renolds
Thomas Smith
Richard Bayley
Will Hitchman
Richd Dennett
Richd Jones
Robert Wordsworth
William Cooke
[f.130r, col. 1(2)]
Robert Phillipps
Will Marsh
Richd Morlowe
Thomas Fortie
John Bayley
Thomas Houses
Griffin Holton
Laurence Wordsworth
Tho: Allsopp
Ralf Houses
Edward Albett
Tho: Carter
Francis Taylor
Jo: Taylor
Francis Gudgine
Edwarde Turner
John Hore
George Wayes
Thomas Haukins
Will: Abbetts
Will: Morrell
Bennet Wayes
John Sparrowhauke
Thomas Armsbye
Edward Humphries
Rich Hobbs
Tho: Wordsworth
Francis Bramsgrave
Richard Drinkwater
Richard Lambe
John May
John Forte Se'
William Kersie
Richard Francis
Christop'r Sandars
[f.130r, col. 2(1)]
Roger Brente
Thomas Sandars
Will Springall
George Dod
William Dod
Robert Weale
Tho: Teaslar
Ralf Galloway
Richd Sampson
Tho: Halloway
Edward George
John Symons
Geo: Brusse
Thomas Sutton
John Goodson
William Dod
John Sandars
John Halloway
John Fortie
Michaell Webb
John Hale
Daniell Sanders
Humphrie Bantinge
Richard Webb
Christopher Wilde
John Webb
Walter Allen
Christopher Fortie
Henrie Gilkes
William Savage
Edward Coles
John Allen
Richard George
Nathaniell Faukner
[f.130r, col. 2(2)]
Thomas Standare
Edmond Humphries
Henrie House
Robert House
John Smith
William Hutton
Edward Hutton
William Burgaine
Richard House
Henrie Wright
William Bachelour
Allen Prine
Robert Buckland
John Buckingame
Arthure Hauckins
John Hitchcocke
John Burname
Thomas West
Richard Bayley
Thomas Hillock
John Dod
William Pert
John Gibson

William Bramsgrove
John Teaslare
Edward Galloway
William Warland
Randall Webb
Robert Cave
Edward Weale
Christopher Sandars
Lewes Dyson
Thomas Hanwell
John Newman
Thomas Aires
Thomas Fortie
Christopher Coles
Christopher Sandars
[f.130r, col. 3(1)]
Samuell Sandars
Edward Bransgrave
William Coles
William Cosier
James Sandars
Richard Teaslar
Richard Reeve
Robert May
Stephen Winter
John Sandars
Christop'r Coxe
Nicholas Pert
John Carter
Edward Lacye
Robert Young
George Brusse
Henrie Teasler
Michaell Peake
Walter Forde
John Conye
Thomas Kent
Richard Webb
William Forde
John Galloway
Robert Hore
James Jurye
William Golde
William Bartlett
William Bayley
John Nevell
Francis Lath
Thomas Dorne
Stephen Nevell
Thomas Huggins
George Allen
John Smart
[f.130r, col. 3(2)]
Vencent Rey:
Humphrie Hammon
John Laude
Nicholas Morrish
Bartholomew Buckland
Thomas Enstones
William Savage: Ju:
Richard Swarbrooke
John Swarbrooke
Thomas Creake
John Teaslare
George Clare
William Cave
Richard Kemster
William Hart
James Scoott
John Forde Se'
John Forde Ju:
Christopher House
Samuell House

[For Ledwell see page 138]

NORTHLEIGH

[f.131r, in two columns.]
The Protestacion was administered to and taken by these whose names are here under written of North-Leigh in the county of Oxford the 23 day of Februarii Anno Domini 1641 [121]

[f.131r, col. 1]
Edward Parrott Esq
Henry Buckerfeild
Edward Johnson
Richard Holloway
Thomas Townend
Thomas Martin Sen gent
Thomas Martin Jun gent
John Hedges
William Hales
John White
George Barston
Robert Hart gent
Edward Busby
John Swift
Thomas Calcott
Edward Calcott
Simon Rolph
Edward Francklin
Thomas Francklin
Walter Tarrant
Thomas Kilbey
Richard Abergainy
Edmond Francklin
Edmond Francklin *[sic]*
Thomas Francklin
Thomas Shepherd
John Neale
William Collier
James Phipps
Hugh Rose gent
Andrew Ballow
James Brackspere
William Compton
Thomas Wheeler
Thomas Ward
Richard Clemens
William Harris
William Lamborne
John Palmer
Thomas Brooks
John Carver
George Morton
Edward Spurr
William Francklin
John Cambden
Henry Browne
Edward Browne

[f.131r, col. 2]
Thomas Haines
Edward Mason
William Mason
Richard Lawrence
John Townsend
John Wing
Robert Clemens
William Brush
Thomas Dowlin
Leonard Porter
George Hunslow
Humphrey Busby
William Harvy
Henry Gadfeild
Henry Phipps
James Puffet
Richard Brummingum
John Bruming
Richard Rogers
Henry Swift
Thomas Hales
William Lardiner
John Smith
William Roberts
Edward Playster
Roger Barford
Thomas Collins
William Brackspere
Thomas Collins
John Brooks
Thomas Shepherd
Martin Barfot
Richard Brackspere
Robert Bennet
Edward Cros
William Collier
James Lord
John Roberts
Thomas Phipps
William Hood
Robert Hood
William Phipps
John Folly
Abraham Busbey
William Collins
Stephen Cousens
William Miles
John Pomray
William Blackwell
John James
Francis Busbe

[f.132r]
John Francklin
William Richeston
Thomas Blackwell
William Waite
William Francklin
Thomas Thace
Tho: Smyth
John Horne
William Worcos
William Moris

The Protestacion given to these men & women of **Wilcot** in Comite de Oxon'

Ric. Alder
Dorathy Alder
William Andrewes
Tho. Horton
Mary Andrewes
Alse Bisely
Henry Baylies
Tho. Baylies
John Godard
Margaret Acres
John Acres
Margery Wall

The names of such of North-Leigh wch have refused to take the Protestacion [2]
viz. Mounser *[sic]* Dibinion, Recusant
William Pitman

[signed] William Willes, *Curate*

SOUTHLEIGH

[f.133, in three columns]
South Leigh

The names of all those who made the protestation the XXIIIth day of Februarie Anno Domini 1641 [148]
Inhabitinge within the parrish of South Leigh: in the presence of
Edward Smith, *minister*,
Francis Symmes, *Constable*,
Walter Hart & Richard Wastie, *Collectors*,
John Pye & Robert Wright, *Churchwardens*.

[f.133r, col. 1]
Marrian Wastie
Agnes Harris
Anne Symmes
William Sheephard
Richard Sheephard
William Collier
Hellen Collier
Joane Collet
William Collet
Judith Collet
Percivall Gibs
Dorothie Gibs
James Gibs
Elizabeth Tomson
William George
Susan George
John George
Julian Parme
Richard Parme
Raph Parme
John Cooke
John Foster
Elizabeth Foster
Thomas Foster
John Rose
Anne Rose
William Thomas
Margerie Thomas
Elizabeth Pye
Thomas Pye
Elizabeth West
William Evans
John Whitman
Judith Whitman
William Harris
Alice Harris
Elizabeth Coale
George Smith
Martha Smith
Elizabeth Smith
John Tidmarsh
Dioniz Tidmarsh
John Barfoot
Dorothie Barfoot
Jane Barfoot
Julian Smith
Steaven Smith
William Chruchis
Marie Gardiner
Agnes Evans
Elizabeth Hart
Marie Hart
John Symmons
Margarite Symons
John Frances
Thomas Parme
Agnes Parme
John Phips
Margarite Phips
Justinian Phips
Hellen Haycraft
Susan Clarke
William Hardinge
Marie Wright
Richard Trindar
Margarite Trindar
Hellen Trindar
Francis Cox
[f.133r, col. 2]
James Cookewoe
Margarite Cookewoe
Thomas Cookewoe
John Cookwoe
Richard Druet
Hellen Druet
John Druet
Alice Druet
Margarite Druet
John Folley
Agnes Folley
Richard Folley
Elizabeth Folley
Margarite Folley
Anthonie Cox
Elizabeth Cox
Richard Griffin
Marie Griffin
John Gunnice
Susan Gunnice
Steaven Taubot
Elizabeth Taubot
Marie Hart
John Hart
Agnes *[blank]*
Margerie Harper
Edward Franklin
Anne Franklin
Dorothie Franklin
Richard Price
Susan Price
Mathew Price
Margerite Price
Elizabeth Joyner
Edward Tesler
Elizabeth Tesler
Alice Mise
Hellen Mise
Richard Bowyer
Agnes Bowyer
Barnard Fanch
Agnes Faunch
Henrie Coleburne
Emme Coleburne
Philip Cox
Anne Cox
Christopher Butcher
Elizabeth Butcher
Richard Lord
Julian Lord
Elizabeth Lord
John Reeve
Marie Reeve
Thomas Bullocke
Joane Bullocke
Edward Allin
Dionize Folley
John Stebdow
Sislie Stebdow

Thomas Jackson
Frances Jackson
Edward Kinge
Marrian Kinge
Richard Druet

Robert Enston
Catherine Hanks
William Guyes
Joane Guyes

[f.133r, col. 3]
Thomas Guyes
William Coale
Thomas Smith
Elizabeth Smith
Robert Foster
Elizabeth Smith

(LONG) COMBE

[f.134r, in two columns.]
Com' Oxon'

A list of the severall inhabitants names whoe have taken the protestation within the parish of **Longe Combe**. Feb. 20. 1641 [176]

[f.134r, col. 1]
Richard Lloyd alias Joyner
Thomas Pokins Sen'
Thomas Pokins Jun'
William Marten
Richard Pokins
John Hurst sen'
John Pilkinton
Bradshaw Tayler
Richard Peirce
Richard Hardiman
William Satten
William Daniell
William Warden
Roger Caton alias Tayler
John Warde
Walter Payne
Richard Newman
George Warde
John Townsend
James Pope
William Austen
John Paine
William Ayres
William Bouden
Roger Hancks
Thomas Dennet
William Spurre
William Francklin
John Johnson
Edward Hurst
William Harwood

John Reade
Thomas Knight
Ralph Holland
John Bouden
Thomas Smith
Christopher Warde
Lawrence Bett jun'
Lawrence Bett sen'
Robt Warden
Roger Francklin
Christopher Smith
Thomas Tame
[f.134r, col. 2]
Thomas Payne
Robt Lanckford
Phillip Keene
John Dutton
Henry Browne
Ralph Hammon
George Bolton
Edward Robinson
Oliver Cadburie
John Smith
William Eates
Christopher Hough
Christopher Hill
John Hurst jun'
Robt Morris
Thomas Elliot
John Belcher
John Styles
Richard Key
Edward Davies
Edward Coxen
Edward Fathery
Richard Ashley
Henry Johnson
John Forrest
Henry Parthelowe
Henry Marten

John Carver
Edward Anyson
William Anyson
Thomas Riccards
James Becket
Richard Chamberlaine
Richard Denmore
Marke Tuchin
John Amsden
John Greene
Nicholas Judge jun'
John Sexton
Nicholas Judge sen'
John Bett
John Bouden
Charles Tuchin
[f.134v]
John Satten
Richard Tuchin
Edward Locke
John Hill
[f.135, col. 1]
Hester Pokins
Elizabeth Marten
Joane Forrest
Mary Bolton
Elizabeth Bouden
Katherine Ward
Alice Harwood
Elizabeth Varney
Margery Sexton
Alice Hurst
Elizabeth Chamberlaine
Elizabeth Davies
Katherine Hanckes
Mary Measle
Alice Locke
Daurathy Tuchin
Alice Ward
Alice Beckett

Elizabeth Caton alias Tayler
Mary Ashley
Anne Parthelowe
Susanna Johnson
Alice Hough
Elizabeth Payne
Joane Hill
Joyce Newman
Elizabeth Read
Edith Hill
Elnor Davie
Anne Eates
Anne Hamdon
Elizabeth Satten
Alice Carver
Alice Pokins
Sisly Abson
Elizabeth Daniell
Hannah Morris
Mary Tuchin
Margaret Dutton
Elizabeth Smith
Barbara Warden
Elinor Lanckford
Daurathy Judge
Jane Morris
Anne Coxen
Susanna Carver
Daurathy Pilkinton
Elizabeth Townsend
Elizabeth Belcher
Joyce Hutchins
Anne Belcher
Anne Ayres
Elizabeth Pope
Mary Smith
Katharine Forrest
Ellen Judge
Isabella Elliot
[f.135, col. 2]
Jane Francklin
Joane Bennet
Anne Anyson
Elizabeth Greene
Margery Hurst
Jane Forrest
Mary Wallis
Alice Varney
Elizabeth Bouden
Edith Bouden
Alice Judge
Alice Ayres
Elizabeth Smith
Joane Newman
Francis Pope
Margaret Dennet
Elizabeth Abson
Joane Hill
Francis Lanckford
Joyce Marten
Abbigall Marten
Alice Cooke
Mary Burges
Martha Tuchin

The above have taken the protestation before us underwritten.
Wm. Carver. *Minister*
Thomas Bouden, *Constable,*
John Newman, *Churchwardens*
Henry Hill,
John Morris, *Ov'rseers*

Recusants of the same
Mary Tayler
Wm Carver, *Minister*

Testibus
Tho: Bouden, *Constable,*
John Newman, *Churchwardens*
Henry Hill,
John Morris, *ov'rseers*

[For Middle Aston, see page 119]

SOUTH NEWINGTON

[f.136r, in two columns.]
The names of the Inhabitants of South Newnton in the County of Oxford which have taken the Protestation [72]

[f.136r, col. 1]
John Stranke and Timothy his man
William Buckingham
Humphrey Buckingham
William Baldwin
Richard Smith Senior
Richard Smith Junior
John Gunne
Tho: Buckingham
Tho: Soden
Humphrey Hall
Richard Keene
Richard Hatterly
John Hickman
Thomas Hitchman
John Meares
Richard Buckingham
William Tasker
Richard Childes
John Kinges
Anthony Mery
William Kerwood
Thomas Coates
Thomas Boulton
Edward Box
Thomas Smith
Samuell Kinges
Robert Smith
Richard Eedes
Thomas Ason
Richard Dale
Michaell Greene
William Stokes
Arthure Stokes
Philip Pen
Anthony Tayllor
Anthony Bennett

John Gardner
Jarett Morton
Francis French
William French Junior
Robert French
Richard Wyatt
John Buggin
John Parsons senior
John Parsons Junior
[f.136r, col. 2]
John Tayler senior
John Tayler Junior
William Hunt
Thomas Parsons
Richard Parsons
Edward Gould
Henry Smith
Richard his brother
William Tey
William Franklyn
Richard Tustian
William Campion
Robert Kerwood
William Nicholes
John Ryman
George Hall
John Payne
William Payne
William French senior
William Noune
Samuell Taplin
Thomas Lovell

None of our parish have refused.

Ista Protestatis erat recepta in praesentia nostrum.

Antonii Tayllorii, *ibiden Vicarii*
Humphrey Hall, *Constable*
William French, Francis French, *Ch' Wardens*

[For North Aston, see page 118; for Northleigh, see page 133.]

ROUSHAM

[f.137r, in one column; some signatures.]

The names of all such as have tooke the protestation within our parish of Rowsham in Wotton-deanery 1641 [45]

Will: Palmer, *minister*
Ral: True [?]
Simon Jefferson
Philemon Owen
Daniell Ownoh *[sic]*
Thomas Heasman
Symond Ridey
John Powell
Thomas Marten
William Follieott
John Dew
Edmund Peirson
Thom: Meese
[names of Churchwardens and Overseers are at this point]
Richard Trumpplet
Richard Proudman
Robt Ilbury
Thomas Creake
John Surrall
Thomas Peirson
Edmund Martynne
John Peitenne
John Coxe
Joh Baker
Nicholas Winslow
William Howse
John Clarie
[f.138r]
John Morris
Robert Bowton
Antony Winslow
Robt Hawkes
Edmund Archer
John Younge
Willm Hanwell
Thom: Merrie
Willm Milles
John Pearson
John Smith
Richard Millen
Timothy Pearson
Thomas Dodwell
Nicholas Meese

John Peirson, Henry Grymley, *Churchwardens*
Robt Fluxman, John Verney, *Overseeres of the poore*

SANDFORD ST. MARTIN

[f.139r, in two columns.]
***Sandford** Parish February the 23th An Dom' 1641*

The bill of the parish of Sandford of all those whoe have consented and Assented unto the Protestation wch have binn presented unto them the daye and yeare Above written [64]

[f.139r, col. 1]
Mr. Henery Crocker
Mr. John Crocker
Mr. John Parsons
Mr. John Marten
Richard Kings senior
Richard Kings Junior
Tho: Busbey
Mathew Gubbings
Robert Fox
Robert Rushe
Tho: Hitchman
John Bates
William Bates
Richard Kings
Robert Kings
Nicholas Tasker
William Tasker
William Bambury
Tho: Alline
Richard Rimon
Christopher Buckingm
Tho: Silver
Richard Sayer
John Buller Junior
Richard Loudey
Richard James
John Buller senior
Thomas Bates
John Griffin
[f.139r, col. 2]
John Cheles
William Kings
John Kilbey
William Heaydon
Edward Buller
William Mason
William Durwood
Henery Durwood
Samuell Browne
John Cox et James Busbey
Thomas Busbey Junior

Ledwell
William Aris
John Locke
Tho: Shealer
Humfrey Collings
Richard Busbey senior
Richard Busbey Junior
Thomas Mitchill
John Cox
Roberte Collings
Thomas Collings
Richard Kings
Edward Robbings
John Hedges
William Poole
James Meades
Mathew North
William Smith Senior
William Smith Junior
William Meades
George Wiate
[f.139v]
Henery Nushe
William Palmer
Mathew Pittum
John Coles
Jeffery Hitchman

In Witness hearunto Wee have Sett our hands the daye and year wthin named.
Tho: Belcher, *Vicar eadem villa*
Tho: Collings, *Counstable*
William Aris,
John Marten, *Overseers*
John Buller,
Tho: Shealers, *Churchwardens*

[f.140r]
The returne of Sandford Parrish

February the 23th An Dom' 1641

The returne of all those in our parish whoe have denyed to consent unto the the Protestation latly tendered unto them by wee whose name are hear underwritten.
Imprimis, Anthony Appletre
John Ludyeate
Alice Ludyeate wife unto the said John
All those are recusants.

In Witnes hearunto wee have sett our hands the daye and yeare Above Writtn.
Tho: Belcher, *Vicar eadem villa*
Tho: Collings, *Constable*
John Buller,
Tho: Shealer, *Churchwardens*
John Marten,
William Aris, *Overseers*

[ff.141-2 blank.]

[For Southleigh, see page 134; for South Newington, see page 136; for Steeple Aston, see page 119; for Steeple Barton, see pages 120-21.]

SHIPTON upon CHERWELL

[f.143r, in two columns.]
A just Catalogue of all the names of the male-sexe w'thin the parish of Shipton-Charwell from eighteene yeares & upward who tooke the same protestation wch wee tooke before his Ma'is Justices of the Peace at Woodstocke for the Countie of Oxon' & were by them requested to tender it to the Inhabitants of severall Parishs according to the order of the House of Parliament.
[29]

[f.143r, col. 1]
Robert Standard gent
William Slatter
Christopher Triplet
Ralph Claris
John Hayles
Richard Symons
Henry Forrest
Edward Frogley
John Stratton
Randolph Forrest
Thomas Jackson iun
William Smyth
Symon [?] Web
[f.143r, col. 2]
Edward Bayleys
Thomas Turner
Joseph Jackson
Richard Austin
Steven Harper
John Cate
Robert crofts
Robert Antwistle
William Stevens
William Stainton

Wee have none refuse to take the protestation.
Richard Warre, *Curate of Shipton*
Thomas Jackson, *Constable*
William Hicks, William Fletcher, *Churchwardens*
John Cicell, Justinian Pearson, *Overseers for the poore*

STONESFIELD

[f.144, in two columns.]
***Stunsfeild** in Comte' Oxon*

A list of all those wch have taken the protestation
[55]

Robert Loten : Richard Holloway, *Churchwardens*
John Dew, William Lardner, *Collect'*
John Morris, *Const'*

[f.144, col. 1]
William Cicill
George Weston
William the sonne of Robt Lardner
John Busbee
Thomas Horne
William Horne
Will' Woolridge
Will' Hedges
John Hedges
Thomas Hedges
Edward Cowper
Robt James
Robt Boxe
John Rowell
James Loten
John Loten
Thomas Loten
John House Sen'
Thomas Smith
Hugh Kirke
Nicholas Kirke
John Kirke
George Naishe
Richard Keates
[f.144, col. 2]
Richard Wase
William Lardner Jun' of Doggets
Edward Lardner
Richard Lardner
James Lardiner
Hugh Lardner
Robt Osbourne
John Osbourne
Richard Osbourne
Thomas Boulten
Daniell Boulten
Thomas White
John House Jun'
John Boyce
John Hedges
Will' Lardner sen' of Lincolnes
Will' Lardner Jun' of Lincolnes
Richard Baldwin
Robt Tanner
Thomas Fellowes
Ralph Greene
Robt Gray
Thomas Greene
Michaell Greene
William Swaine
Refusers none.

Fran: Abba, *Curat'*
John Morris, *Constable*
Roberte Laughton, Richard Holloway, *Churchwardens*
John Dewe, William Lardner, *Overseers*

STANTON HARCOURT

[f.145r, in four columns.]
A returne of the names of all those who have taken the protestation the twenty third of February 1641 before the Minister and Constables and Churchwardens and Overseers of the Poore of Stanton Harcort and Sutton [267]

[f.145r, col. 1]
Roberte Houendon gent
Mrs. Frances Houendon
Thomas Caple
Katherne Pencot
Agnis Angle
Ellian Ellis
Henry Smith gent
Mrs. Dorothy Smith
Roberte Blackaloe gent
Mrs. Mary Blackaloe
Thomas Flexney
Jane Flexney
Thomas Flexney
Margery Batin
Katherne Bedwell
Thomas Wood
Shusana Wood
James Wood
Dorothey Wood
John Perkins
John Androus
Thomas Flexney
Isabell Flexney
Katherne Flexney
Mary Flexney
Isabell Flexney *[sic]*
Katherne Flexney *[sic]*
Ann Reely
William Dixson
Thomas Lee
Francis Busbee
John Wood
Judeth Wood
Christian Wood
Joseph Flexney
Richard Beden
Edward Beden
William Haris
Gillion Sexton
John Walter
Margery Walter
Ann Walter
Henry Chadwell
Jone Chadwell
Ann Allinn
Margreat Allinn
Ann Allinn
Ann Sayer
Jone Secolle
Giles Michell
Margery Wood
James Sheares
Sissila Sheares
Edward Hankes
Jone Hankes
Elizabeth Hankes
Wiliam Allinn
Sissila Allinn
Henry Bates
William Flexney
Anne Flexney
Edward Burden
Elizabeth Burden
Richard Simons
Elizabeth Simons
Richard Fisher
Alce Fisher
William Pencot
Jone Pencot
John Smart
Dorothey Smart
Thomas Haris
Elizabeth Haris
Hercilus Bunce
Dorothey Bunce

[f.145r, col. 2]
William Chruchly
Elizabeth Smith
Laurance Milion
Ann Redborne
William Tanner
Ussila Pencot
Margreat *[blank]*
Thomas Taner
William Fisher
Katherne Fisher
John Crackeloe
Margreat Crackeloe
William Bayly
Sara Bayly
Margreat Parme
Ann Parme
Henry Boulton
Richard Weele
Elizabeth Withers
Thomas Redborne
Margreat Redborne
Robert Redborne
William Caple
Marrian Paine
John Hedges
Katherne Hedges
Judeth Barfote
Robert Foster
Margreat Foster
Richard Flexney
Margreat Flexney
Sara Parme
Alce Parme
Cristian Grene
John Caple
Elizabeth Caple
Ann Caple
William Smart
Anne Smart
Jone Smart
Elizabeth Franckelin
Dorothey Day
John Holloway
Jone Holloway
James Barfote
Gemina Barfote
Frances Barfote
Edward Buckeingham
Jane Buckeingham
Susanna Altofe
Edward Hopkings
Margreat Hopkins
Richard Chadwell
Ellian Chadwell
Edward Pencote
Mary Pencote
Mikell Pencot
Margreat Large
Elizebeth Large
William Pencote

Mary Pencote
Edward Day
Anthony Day
Ussila Day
William Walter
Margery Walter
Richard Bedwell
Jone Bedwell
Jone Bedwell *[sic]*
Elizabeth Yeatman
[f.145r, col. 3]
Steven Croftes
Elizabeth Croftes
Richard Sivers
Ellian Sivers
William Hopkings
Ann Hopkings
John Belgrove
Dorathey Belgrove
George Clemance
Alce Clemence
Richard Simons
Erne Simes
Jone Shirte
Edmund Shirte
Margreat Shirt
Gorge Edward
Darcos Cora
Richard Aplebe
John Flexney
Elizabeth Flexney
James Waste
John Worly
Margreat Winter
Henry Roulerite
Cristian Roulerite
William Haris
Edward Ewen
Thomas Ewen
Edward Ewen
Alce Ewen
Margreat Ewen
Charls Bowel
Margreat Clandfild
William Clanfild
Joyce Clanfild
Henry Clanfild
William Clarke
Jone Hill
Richard Sky
Agnis Sky
Shusana Sky
Ralph Flexney
Ellian Flexney
Henry Duncom
Fallantine Horne
Mary Euens
Frisos Hopkings
Steven Hopkings
Katherne Hopkings
Henry Badcocke
Jane Badcocke
John Scriven
Robert Enstone
Judeth Enstone
John Enstone
Owen Flude
Anthoney Bayly
Katherne Bayly
John Ellis
Margreat Ellis
Thomas Longe
Thomas Longe *[sic]*
Ann Longe
Susanna Longe
Henry Enstone
Alce Enstone
John Enston
Thomas Folly
Elian Folly
John Haseley
Ann Haseley
William Smith
Mary Smith
William Gadfild
Jone Gadfild
[f.145r, col. 4]
Richard Sky
William Secall
John Pickerill
Jane Pickerill
Thomas Wisdome
Isabell Wisdome
Margreat Brish
Jufery Walle
Ellian Walle
Jane Yeate
Fardinandoe Druet
Margery Druet
Roberte Yeate
William Huckes
Margreat Enstone
John Bachelar
Mary Bachelar
Thomas Dier
Jone Dier
Walter Towensend
Margaret Towensend
Thomas Clandfild
Ann Clandfild
Oliver Druet
Robert Haseley
Jone Hasely
Richard Boner
Ann Boner
Dorathey Dreuet
Jane Dreuet
Ann Kates
Susana Egila
Alce Ducke
Ellian Redborne
Judeth Folly
Richard Druet

We returne for not taking of the protestation
Mrs. Katherne Smith and
Mrs. Elizabeth Philipson

Edward Smith, *Minister*
Constables:
Thomas Flexney,
Edward Ewen
Churchwardens:
Thomas Franckelin,
Thomas Wood,
William Wast
Overseers of the poore
James Wasty
John Greene
Fardinando Dreuet

TACKLEY

[f.146r. Single column, with some signatures.]

Tackley Feb 23 1641

Those whose names are here subscribed have taken the protestation according to the direction of the speakers [62]

John Standarde
John Harborne
Edward Standard
John Craker
Michaell Shipperd
Edw: Smith
Thomas Filde
William Smyth
Robert Heath
Robear Moore
Edw: Tymmes
John Parker
Robarte Harthorne
Richard Tredwell
John Langley
Maredehed Flide
Wilame Colese
Edward Borman
Edward Grantham
William Grantham
Thomas Adkines
Robarde Hurluck
William Greninge
John Tailer
John Walker
[f.147r]
Thomas Smiteh
John Jones
John Swift
James Swift
Jaret Ailworth
Thomat Swarbrocke
Hue Minn
Thomas Coales
Willim Coales
Umphre Silver
Thomas Filde
John Coates
Robarte Dalle
Edward Smiteh
Thomas Treurner
John Archer
Williame Aris
Thomas Williames
Grifin Simes
Richard Parker
John Parker
Antoney Spiere
John Times
John Hipcase
John Grantham
Foucke Smieth
Richard Greene
Edward Flexen
Robart Cunstalel
Richard Heath
Thomas Berey
Gorge Times
Richeard Tayler
John Hanbrig[?]

George Smiteh and Francis Walker, *Churchwardens*
Thomas Coales, *Cunstabel*

GREAT TEW and LITTLE TEW

[f.148r, in four columns.]

Tew magna et parva
February the 20th 1641

The protestation According to the order of parliamnt, was taken by the parishioners & Inhabitants of the parish of great Tew in the County of Oxon, whose names are here under written, in the presence of the minister, constables, Churchwardens, & overseers of the poore. [166]

[f.148r, col. 1]
Thomas Evans
William Francklyn Ju'
William Lowe
William Stowe sen'
John Spencer
Sampson Williamson
Gyles Linett
Thomas Bosely
Edward Gamage
William Stowe Ju'
John Francklyn
William Hedges
John Fletcher
Nicolas Raynolds Jun'
William Francklyn sen.
John Hyorne Ju'
Edward Dowson
John Stowe
Nicolas Crosse
Thomas Stowe
George Stowe
Henry Raynolds
Thomas Luckett
Thomas Snellson
John Lord
Robert Clifford
Simon Hyorne
William Worley
Sampson Kings
Walter Wattson
Edward Snelson
Edward Blicke
James Pridee
Hercules Flood
Richard Scarlett
John Hyorne sen'
Thomas Lowe
William Raynolds Ju'
Gyles Ashbee
Henry Linett
Mr. William Rainsford
Hugh Baylies
William Raynolds sen'

[f.148r, col. 2]
John Snellson
James Pholl
Hugh Rymill
John Jenings Ju'
John Hyorne tayler
John Greenwood
John Abergayney
William Baylies
William Maynerd
John Sly
John Robens Ju'
Abraham Worley
John Attkins
Robert Knight
Edward Rymill
Thomas Mason
Thomas Gylks
William Hester
Robert Rymill
Thomas Hedges
John Rymill
Thomas Castle
William Potter
Richard Moberly
John Hicks
William Calcott
Edward Marshall
Edward Lord
Thomas Rymill
Anthony Francklyn
Henry Drinkwater
John Jarrett
Thomas Gable
John Castle
Richard Hill
Richard Toms
William Hemming
William Hancocke
William Freeman
Richard Warner
Ralph Marshall sen'
Abraham Neale
Edward Busby Ju'
John Bysshopp

[f.148r, col. 3]
Mr. Thomas Loggin
John Robens sen'
William Simons
William Smith
Anthony Rymill
William Tasker
Richard Vickars
William Reeve
Humfrey Coates
Robert Willes
Richard Holloway
Mr. Thomas Hinton
Mr. John Garrard
Thomas Charman
Henry Davy
Robert Robens
Edward Wisedome
Thomas Hicks
John Pridee
William Coates Ju'
James Coates
William Coates sen'
Edward Harris
Thomas Fletcher
William Busby
Edward Richinson
John Evans
Richard Gray sen'
Thomas Hore
Thomas Reeve
Sampson Harris
Humfrey Snellson
Mr. Andrew Tempest
Richard Gray Ju'
Edmund Carter
Edward Haughten
Edward Jenings
Daniell Flood
Robert Jeffes
Daniell Carter
John Jenings sen'
Richard Jenings
Robert Sheerly

[f.148r, col. 4]
James Wattson
Richard Rymill
Henry Boutcher
William Ankorne sen'
William Brotherton
John Wattson
John Collect
John Barnes
James Snellson
William Crosse
Edward Tolly
John Alexander
John Willson
Robert Payne
Richard Bickerstaffe
John Scarlett
John Wimmidge
John Horsman
John Blunt
John Sadler
Nicholas Raynolds sen'
Edward Swift
Humfrey Kings
Edward Busby
Henry Raynolds
John Davy

The Protestation was taken in the presence of us by those whose names are here above written
Henry Prawde, *vic de Tew Magna*
Constables:
Robert Colesborne
William Hyorne
Ralfe Marshall
Churchwardens:
William Hyorne
William Lord
John Hiorne
Overseers:
Anthony Crosse
William Smith
Edward Coates

[For Westcott Barton, see page 122.]

WOLVERCOTE

[f.149r, in two columns.]

The names of the Parishioners of Wolvercott in the County of Oxford, beinge above the Age of Eighteene [53]

[f.149r, col. 1]

Mr. Richard Collins
Ethelbert Weller
Richard Butcher
William Caterman
John Jackman
John Giles
Robert Edwards
William Dubber
William Fletcher
John Edwards
Richard Dewe
William Lydiatte
Stephen Horne
William White
Hugh Dubber
Hugh Day
Henry Prickett
Jeffery Webbe
Mr. John Smith
Thomas Hopkins Jun'
Edmunde Prince
Richard Dubber
William Herne
Gregory Sheires
William Nix
Thomas Hopkins sen:
John Howell
James Pickeringe
Jeffery Polly
Thomas Clayton

[f.149r, col. 2]

John Lander
William Ball
John Howell
Hugh Weller
Hercules Caterman
Jeffery Morton
Valentine Prior
Robert Canes
Michael Kenser
Richard Giles
William Hibberd
Richard Palmer
Thomas Loe
Richard Dubber
William Polly
Ralph Smith
Maurice Crofts

Mr. Mathewe Cheriton refuseth to take the protestation.

These of the Parishioners of Wolvercott whose names are crossed tooke the Protestation.

Alen: Fisher. *Vicar of St. Peters in the East - Oxon'*
William Fletcher, *Counstable*
Ethelbert Weller,
Thomas Hopkins, *Church Wardens of Woolvercott*
Jeffery Webb,
William White, *Overseers of the Poore*

WOOTTON

[f.150r, in two columns.]

Wooton

The names of all those that tooke the Protestation on the parish of Wotton in the County of Oxford. Febr. 20th 1641. [97]

[f.150r, col. 1]
John Hoffman, *Rector*
Jonas Weare
George Collins
Henry Field
George Brent
Arthur Claver
Henry Maud
Thomas Gregory
John Whitton
Thomas Blagrave
[The names of the constable, churchwardens and overseers appear here.]
Simon Rash
Jonas Templar
William Archer
Francis Gregory
Richard Horne
Henry Archer
William Keene
Richard Simons
John Scarcebrook
Edward Leister
William Hiat
William Durran
Fortune James
William Watts
Bartholomew Perry
Robert Kent
Thomas Hoare
Sylvester Cave
John Ferrew
Richard Ascholr [?]
John Carter
William Greene
John Butcher

[f.150r, col. 2]
Richard Templar
Augustine Freeman
John Blay
Thomas Mosse
Robert Boudon
Robert Bew
William Boswell
William Mager
Richard Kilby
John Bew
William Westhood
Richard Watts
Francis Hawse
Edward Kilby
John Howse
Henry Perry
John Perry
Thomas Widdowes
William Blake
William Boulton
Thomas Turner
William Todman
Nicholas Cleeves
William Lucas
Simon Justice
John Gun
Gerrard Whitton
Richard Adderton
John Templar
Antony Hankes
Edward Broadwaton
William Redhead Junior
John Brawly
Thomas Bayly
John Page
John Civers
Stephen Kent
John Ferring
Nicholas Cowly
John Redhead

[f.150v]
Richard Phips
Antony Manning
Thomas Smith
Timothy Horne
Francis Richardson
Richard Boltner
Thomas Mosse Jun:
Thomas Templar
William Stockely
John Atkins
John Turner
William Judge
Richard Tybbs
Thomas Parcye
Robart Brodwarton
Richard James
John Jeffry Jun:
John Clarke
Simon Wilkinson
Thomas Stone

Thomas Willgoose,
Constable
Richard Freeman,
Richard Grantham,
Churchwardens
John Jeffry,
William Redhead,
Overseers of the poore

[f.151r]
Mr. Nappier a papist resideth at Oxford all the Winter and spendeth part of the Sommer at Ludwell his farme, in the parish of Wotton, neither he nor any of his servants have taken the protestation at Wotton. All the rest of the Inhabitants of the foresaid parish of Wotton have taken it.
Ita testor
John Hoffman, *Rector*.

NETHER WORTON

[f.152r, in two columns.]

February the 20th 1641

The protestation was taken by the inhabitants of Nether Woorton in the presence of minister Constable Church-wardens & Collector the day above written whose names are here underwritten. [18]

[f.152r, col. 1]
Mathew Weston Sen,
Mathew Weston Ju'
Thomas Hawten
Simon Corner
John Worcester
Simon Rymill
Thomas Whittley
Thomas Baylies
William Leister
[f.152r, col. 2]
Robert Bennett
Richard Belcher
Thomas Browne
William Attkins

Henry Prawde, *minist'*
Richard Parsons,
Collector
Francis Granthames,
Thomas Wells,
Churchwardens
John Buckingham,
Constable

OVER WORTON

[f.153r, in two columns.]

February: 20: 1641

The Protestation was taken the day & yeare above written by the Inhabitants of Over-Worton in the County of Oxon', whose names are underwritten. [15]

[f.153r, col. 1]
Richard Carter
Thomas Hartwell
John Allabones
Jeffery Baker
John Pittum
Edmund Heynes
[f.153r, col. 2]
John Kinch
Thomas Morier
James Baylie
John Burroughs
William Morley

Mr. Robert Mees Esquire
Mr. John Mees his sonne
were at London these men hath not taken the protest-ation with us

In the presence of
William Stevenage,
Curate
John Mosely, *Constable*
William Baylie,
Edmund Pittum,
Churchwardens

[For Worton in Cassington, see page 123.]

YARNTON (Eardington)

[f.154r]

Yarnton returne, to the business concerning our neighbours taking the protestacion, delivered unto the high constable of our division of the hundred of Wotton. Feb: 28. 1641.

Wee whose names are hereunder written the Minister, Churchwardens, and overseers of the parish of Yarnton, doe certifye those whom this may concerne; that uppon Wednesday last the 23th day of this instant Februarye, in obedience to a recommendacion wch we reseaved from his Ma'ties iustices, mett together for this busines, wch was also recommended to them by the high Court of Parlaiment, did call together all the Males of our said parish, and tendered to them the Protestacion, and every man willingly, and freely tooke it, without any kind of opposition, deniall, or refusall. In witnesse hereof we have sett our hands the day and yeare above written.

Nathanaell Harris, *Minister*.
Nicholas Myn, Steven Forti, *Churchwardens*.
Henry Phipps, *Constable*.
Edwarde Sharpe, John Phippes, *Overseers*.

[No return of names was attached, and the above preamble is all that appears in the first edition. However, since that transcription, the nominal return has been discovered by Mr M.A. Faraday under the name 'Erdington' (an early name for Yarnton) and filed under 'Shropshire', at folio 178 of the same volume as the Oxfordshire returns.]

The names of the inhabitants of Eardington which have taken the p'testation, as followeth:

Thomas Leigh, gent.
Thomas Stone
John Sanders
Anthonie Crosse
William Hedges
William Handcocke
Walter Sparks
Miles Leigh
William Parrante
William Parrante *[sic]*
William Shillingworthe
Richarde Russell
Nathaniell Slemaker
Vincente Hurlocke
John Eedes
Frances Mall
Richarde Dorebridge
Richard Franckline
Edwarde Cooke
George Townesende
Thomas Hauckes
Frances Dewe
John Hutt
Arthur Dewe
Richard Morris
Stephen Hutt
William Smith
John Browne
William Hutson
Richard Cox
Frances Hurlocke

Mr Nathaniell Harris, *Minister*
Nicholas Mynne, Stephen Fortie, *Churchwardens*
Henrie Phipps, *Constable*
John Phipps, Edwarde Sharpe, *Overseers*.

LIST OF RECUSANTS

[See Introduction, pages xiv-xvi. Names as they appear in the parish returns, where they differ, are shown in square brackets.]

[f.155r]

A catalogue of the names of those who in the County of Oxon' refuse to take the Protestation.

Hundreth de Chadlington

Chorlebury *[actually in Banbury Hundred]*

Anthony Tenant refuseth.

John Phippes simplie refuseth not, but demurs upon it, as pretending not to understand what is ment by the true reformed Protestant Religion.

Chipping-Norton

Richard Fryers
Wm. Yarnall
Wm. Grainger
Thom: Eddkins
These being warned came not to take the Protestation

Salford

Edward Huckings

Minster-Lovell

Francis Ewre, Esq.
Richard Ewre
Shellie Morgan
Margret Ewre
Prudence Hubert
Ellen Ewre
Bridget Hatten
Bridget, Mrs Huberts made
Paulina Hooper
Anne Palmer

Hundr: de Bampton

Witney

Leonard Pitt, who is sicke
Ed: Pitt, sicke
Rich: Martin, sicke
Will: Foster, sicke
Rich: Galloway, lame
Alexander Gardner, lame
Edw. Stepto
Joh: Smith, old and lame
Jos: Peirce
Adam Butler, lame
Roger Lane, old & lame
Peter Rider
Joh: Babs, sicke
Edw. Hames
Tho: Gold, old & blinde
Rob Binkes, old & lame
Joh: Cotton, blinde
Phil: Norton, sicke
Henry Fitchet, old & lame
Mr. Walter Yate, lame
Mr. Jos. Pridie, sicke
Mr. Francis Rathborne, recusant

Astall

Edward Saunders
Mary Saunders uxor ejus
Eliz. Cooke wid
being all recusants

Brize-Norton

Mr. Thom: Greenwood sen
Mr. Thom: Greenwood jun
Mr. Rich Todkill
Willm Lince
all these are recisants

Hundreth de Wooton

Cassington

Willm Reynolds & Edmunde Reynolds being recusants

Sandford [St. Martin]

Antony Appleton [Appletree]
John Ludyeate
Alce Ludyeate
all recusants

Steeple-Barton

Mr. Ralph Sheldon wth his family being recusants
Joh Yorke
Anne Jadnam [Tadnum]
Elizabeth Baker
Katherine Baker

Dedington

Edward Smith
Richard Cooke
James Cooke
John Aris alias Derny [Derry]

Wolvercott

Mr. Mathew Cheriton

North-leigh

Mounser Dibinion
Willm Pitman

Cuddington [Kiddington]

Mr. Peter Browne Esqr.
Fran. Winter
Thom. Batmason
Willm Flint
Willm Nichols
Thom. West

Stanton-Harcourt

Mrs. Katherine Smith
Mrs. Eliz. Philipson

Wotton

Mr. Nappier a Papist & all his familie refuseth.

UNIVERSITY OF OXFORD

[f.157r]

The Protestation by the House of Commons commended to the Universitie of Oxford was upon the 18th of Februarie 1641 taken with such Marginall Notes and Interpretations as are underwritten by the Heads of Houses or their Deputies whose names are subscribed.

I A B doe in the presence of Almightie God promise vow and protest A to mainetaine and defend so farre as lawfullie I may B with my life power and estate the true reformed Protestant Religion expressed in the Doctrine of the Church of England against all Poperie and Popish Innovations within this Realme contrarie to the same doctrine and according to the dutie of my Allegiance his Ma'ties Royall person honour and estate C As also the Power and Privileges of Parliament: The Lawfull D rights and Liberties of the Subject, E and every person that in the lawfull pursueance of the same. And to my power and as farre as lawfullie I may F I will oppose and by all good waies and meanes indeavour to bring condigne punishment all such as G as shall either by force, Practise, Counsells, Plotts, Conspiracies, or otherwise do anie thing to the contrarie of anie thing in this present Protestation contained. And further that I shall in all Just and honourable waies endeavour to preserve the Union and Peace between the three Kingdomes of England Scotland and Ireland. And neither for hope feare nor other respect reliquish this promise vow and Protestation.

A So farre as warrantablie I may and with subordination to the Oaths of Supremacie and Allegiance.
B And shall bee called thereunto by lawfull Authoritie
C Against whom I verilie believe no Subject of this Kingdome may with safe conscience take up Armes either offensive or defensive
D And common
E So farre as the said Privileges Rights and Liberties shall bee made knowne and evidenced unto Mee to bee such
F And shall be called thereunto by lawfull authority.
G His Mties Subiects.

Dr. Tolson Pro vice chancellor and Provost of Oriell Col:
Dr Fell Deane of Christ Church
Dr Pinke Warden of New College
Dr Mansell Principall of Jesus College
Dr Baily President of St Johns College
Dr Sheldon Warden of All Soules College
Dr Potter Provost of Queenes College
Mr Richardson Vice-Principall of Brazen-nose College

The Protestation by the House of Commons commended to the Universitie was upon the same day taken according to the printed Coppie without the above mentioned notes by such Heads of houses or their deputies whose Names are underwritten. vizt:

Dr Wilkinson Principall of Magdalen Hall
Dr Hood Rector of Lincolne College
Mr Rogers Principall of New Inne hall
Mr Trimnell Vicegerent of Bailioll College
Mr Boles Vicegerent of Pembrokke College
Mr. Corbett Subwarden of Merton College
Mr Chapman Vice-Principall of Alban Hall
Dr Airey Principall of Edmund hall
Mr Proctor Sub-Rector of Exeter College

In presentia mei Johannis French notarii publici et Registrarii Universitatis Oxon'.

CHRIST CHURCH [196]

[f.158r, in four columns.]

Vicesimo primo die Februarii 1641 Protestati sunt secundum formam a Dom: Com: missam. Ex Aede Christi.

[f.158r, col. 1]
Dr Stroud, Subdeane
Hen: Ld Bp of Chichester. *ab*
Dr Gardener
Dr Wall
Dr Morris
Dr Isles
Mr Paine *ab*
Mr Auditor *ab*
Mr Morley
Mr Heylin *ab*
Mr Hill
Mr Clutterbuck
Mr Bennett
Mr Barkley *ab*
Mr Wild
Mr Seise
Mr Fulham
Mr Busbie *ab*
Mr Aubrie
Mr Maine *ab*
Mr Terrant [?] *aegrotat*
Mr Rise *ab*
Mr Beare
Mr Stutwill *ab*
Mr Darell
Mr Cartwright
Mr Glisson
Mr Mills
Mr Hipslie *ab*
Mr Edwards
Mr Wood *ab*
Mr Tyos
Mr Killigrew
Mr Randell *ab*
Mr Waring
Mr Maplett
Mr Holway *ab*
Mr Gargrave *ab*
Mr Burlace *ab*
Mr Gray
Mr Cotton *ab*
Mr Powell
Mr Ireland *ab*
Mr West
Mr Master
Mr Lowen
Mr Washburne
Mr Jones
Mr Gregorie
Mr Chilmead
Mr Zouch
Mr Babington *ab*
Mr Castilion
Mr Weaver
Mr Lowe

[f.158r, col. 2]
Mr Howe
Norgate *ab*
Thornbrough
Townson
Croyden *ab*
Meade
Greslie *ab*
Towers *aegrotat*
Day *ab*
Smith
Goodridge

Ramsay *ab*
Isham
Jackson
Gyar *ab*
Bennet
Tray *ab*
Llewellin
Morecroft
Lute
Leigh
Allestree
Chandler
Plumtree *ab*
Fettiplace
Everard
Sharpe
Benson *ab*
Godfrie
Palmer
Isles
Whalie
Hillman
Biam

Wood *ab*
Snow
Geale *ab*
Godfrie *ab*
Severne
Ditchfeild
Richardson
Quin
Underwood
Nicolls
Nicolls
Chuce
Hunt *ab*
Crone
Hill
Alford
Dugdale
Wilcox *ab*
Higgins *ab*
Colman *ab*
Wilde *ab*
D's Johnson *ab*
Weaver *ab*
Gough

[f.158r, col. 3]
Lowe *ab*
Acres *ab*
Feges *ab*
Pickhaver *ab*
Bolton *ab*

Mr Draper *ab*
Owen
Kersley
King *ab*
Newport
Mallington
Fowler
Huntlie
Clarke *ab*
Harvey *ab*
Stile *ab*
Stroad *ab*
Thorburgh
D's Stanilie *ab*
Ernlie

Bradbridge
Read

Walton
Godfrie *ab*
Reading
Skinner
Gale *ab*
Sanders *ab*
Littleton *ab*

Vanling
Hill
Munday *ab*
Dixon
Locksmith *aegrotat*
Bley
Fyfeild *ab*
West
Hawkes *ab*
Wilkins
Jay
Lee
Browne
Money *ab*

Sansburie
Miles
Shreife
Edward
Mr Pinhorne
D'us Gove *ab*
D'us Willis
D'us Scriven *ab*
D'us Brame
D'us Frampton
D'us Cupper
D'us Bettison *ab*
Vincent *ab*
Smith *ab*

[f.158r, col. 4]

Connor
Frohoch
Kenrick *ab*
Barrett
May
Lewis
Westron
Pepper

Jarvis
Hall
Hutch
Jacob
Fox
Pachton
Roderick
Vaughan *ab*
Morris *ab*
Gwin
Hilton *ab*
Tipton *ab*
Hall

D's Jones
Upton *ab*
Rixon
Jarvis
Collins *ab*

In presentia mei John French notarii publici et Registrarii Universitatis Oxon'

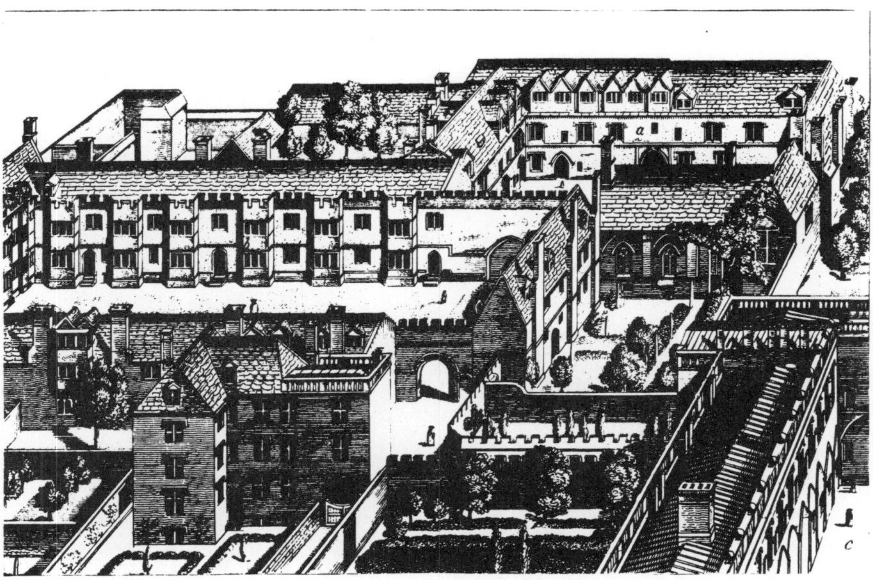

MERTON COLLEGE [69]

[f.159r, in two columns.]

Vicesimo primo die Feb: Protestati sunt

[f.159r, col. 1]

Sr Nath. Brent, *ab e Col. Merton*
Sr Charles Shirlie
Dr Turner *ab:*
Mr French
Mr Fisher
Mr Greaves
Mr Nevill *ab*
Mr Howson
Mr Wright
Mr Jacob
Mr Brent
Mr Owen
Mr Broad
Mr Clarke
Mr Coplie
Mr Button
Mr Priaulx
Mr Sayer *aegrotat*
Mr Fowle
Mr Lovejoy

D'us Lee
Whistler
Jones
Mr Gurganie
Crofts *aegrotat*
Dr Bainbridge
Mr Burton *ab*
Mr Allen
D's Woods
Kettlewell

Flower *ab*
Barnard
Janes
Boxley
Moore *ab*
Griffin
Thomas
Applebee
Blackham *ab*
Hawkins
Chittenden *ab*

[f.159r, col. 2]

D'us Coles
Benson
Kent *ab*
Martin *ab*
Towgood *ab*
Fawkner *ab*
Shortgrave
Loader
Nethersoll
Caldicott
Duncombe
Woods
Smith
Stokes
Miles *ab*
Pocock
Clarke *se ab*
Peirse
Carre *ab*
Ware *ab*
Cooper

Parrott
Plant
Wheatley
Buckner *ab*
Tarrant *ab*
Adams
Mr Blagrove *olim Mertonensis*

In presentia mei John French notarii publici Registrarii Universitatis Oxon'

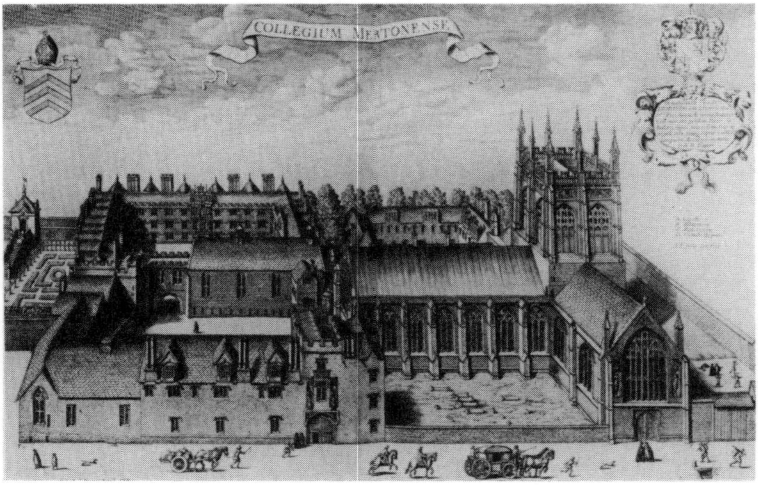

MAGDALEN COLLEGE [106]

[f.160r, in three columns]

Vicesimo primo die Februarii Protestati e Col: Magdalen:

[f.160r, col. 1]
Dr Frewin, Presidenses *ab*
Mr Chibnall, Vice Presidenses
Dr Nourse *ab*
Mr Fleming
Forman
Williamson
Walworth
Law. *ab*
Drope
Langton
Holden
Clay *ab*
Parkhurst *ab*
Diggle
Harris *ab*
Wake *ab*
Potman
Yorke
Yalden. *ab*
Jennings. *ab*
Flood
Barrell
Westlie
Pelham *ab*
Bravell
Bigge
Haughtin
Hunt
Tailor
Rogers *ab*
Dale *ab*

D'us Riland *ab*
Mr Hobbs
Mr Dingley
D'us Stroud
Langton
Dale

Mr Smith
Nicolls
Moory
Stanlie *ab*
Mr Boughton
Sayer
Ludd
Quarterman
[f.160r, col. 2]
D'us Smith
Durston
Holland
Steevens

Mr White
Hide
Cheeke
Phillips *ab*

Langton
Clinkard
Slade
Prickett
Cooper *ab*
Lovell *ab*
Heath *ab*
Tomlins

Mr Litcott *ab*
Cox
D'us Otis
Webbe
Worthington
Hooper
Browne
Joyner
Jackson *ab*
Baskett
Palmer
Morgan
Clitherow
Clarke *ab*
Peirs
Acton

Mr Harrison
Puleston
D'us Fitzherbert
[f.160r, col. 3]
Penson *ab*
Denham *ab*
Newarke *ab*
Hill
Hillard
Swinson *ab*
Hall
Upton
Egan
Turrin
Neale
Izaax
Purfrey *ab*
Turner
Coningsby
Scott
Clarke
Kings
Toachin [*or* Touchin]
Arnoll *ab*
Harriatt *ab*
Lewes *ab*
Wyatt
Norman
Bartlett *ab*
Wilson

In presentia mei John French notarii publici et Registrarii Universitis Oxon'

[f.160a]
[Attached to the sheet containing the names from Magdalen College is a separate piece of paper bearing the following statement of Protestation as made by Robert Barrell, the first words of which were written upon the folio sheet :-]

"I Ro. Barrell take this Protestation so farr forth as it is not contrary to the mayntinance of the Kings Royal Prerogative, the Doctrine & Discipline of the Church of England by law established since the Reformation, The Present statutes of the University of Oxon confirm'd under the Kings broade seale of England, to all wch I have been formerly sworne"

Teste me Robert Barrell
Will: Hobbs

NEW COLLEGE [106]

[f.161r, in three columns]

Vicesimo primo die Februarii in eandem formam in quam Protestatus est Dr Pinke Custos Collegii Protestati sunt e Collegio Novo

Mr. Good vice custos did protest referring himself to the paper annexed.

[f.161r, col. 1]
Dr Read *ab*
Dr Masters
Mr Stringer
Gardner *ab*
Hungerford
Pottinger
Parsons
Barker
Masters
Phillips
Young *ab*
Lucas *ab*
Grove
Zouch
Maylard
Gulson
Oglander *ab*
Gulson *ab*
Marrow
May
Hampson *ab*

Mr Marrow *ab*
Bailie *ab*
Terrie
Eldred
Williams *ab*
Vivian *ab*
Tichborne
Morecroft
Twisse
Mr Beelie *ab*
Lamphire
Windebanke

Dr Coles sen'
Coles iun'
Appleford
Bew
Wickham
Harris sen'
Sachevrell
Feilder *ab*
Rives
Harris iu. *ab*
[f.161r, col. 2]
Love
Tichborne *ab*
Love
Blincowe *ab*
Smith *ab*
Williams
Ailiffe
Jones
Geeres
Blake
Hobbs
Price
Alanson *ab*
Lydiatt
Ailworth
Richards
Withers
Rivers
Rowlanson
Hussy
Beard
Complin
Alexander

Mr Haskett *ab*.
Grebbie
Holland
Pinke
Terry *ab*
Longman *ab*
Hodges
Warrener
Unett
D's Lydiatt
Mr Read
D's Betham
Dawson
Coleman
Jones
Teddar *ab*
Cooke *ab*
Mason
[f.161r, col. 3]
Finch
Leech
Parne
Nobes
Finch
Flexnie
Toms
House
Stubbs
Stubbs
Farre
Knight
Wickham *ab*
Crosse
Walbanke
Higgs
Master *ab*
Aire *ab*
Iremonger
Eedes
Holloway

In presentia mei Johannis French Notarii publici et Registrarii Universitatis Oxon'

[f.161a]
Mr Good Vice custos Protestatus secundum hanc formam annexam
A I understand the Doctrine allready established in the 39 Articles.
B I understand all Popery Doctrinall, and Innovations Practicall, contrary to the Doctrine allready established.

C I understand this so far, as they shall be evidenced to me, by the Standing Lawes of this Kingdome, Not repugnant to the Lawes of God, to be undoubted, Privileges and Rights. And further, the Maintenance of these Rights of Subjects; I understand not wth reference to one another, to be hereby bound, to imbroyle myself in every private Man's quarrell though I conceive right, but wth Reference to the Publike State .

D I will maintain every person etc. This maintenance I understand not to bind me to maintain them by myself alone but together wth others, consenting and Lawfully authorized. The same, I understand of Opposing in the next clause.

E In all the severall Clauses, I expressly except His Sacred Majestie, and His Lawfull Successors, according to my Oath of Allegiance, not daring to think a disloyal thought, much lesse to lift up my hand against the Lord's Annointed.

F Unlese the States shall think it expedient to Alter, or Revoke it, in wch case I reserve my Freedom.

I A B. doe in the presence of Almighty God, promise, vow and Protest to Maintain and Defend, as far as lawfully I may, wth my Life, Power and Estate, the True reformed Protestant Religion, expressed in the Doctrine A of the Church of England, against all Popery B and Popish Innovations, within this Realme, contrary to the same Doctrine; and according to the Duty of my Allegiance, His Majesty's Royall Person, Honour and Estate; As also the C Power and Privileges of Parliament; The Lawfull Rights and Liberties of the Subject, and every D person that maketh this Protestation, in whatsoever He shall do, in the Lawfull Pursuance of the same. And, to my power, and as far as Lawfully I may, I will E oppose, and by all good wayes and means, indeavour to bring to condigne punishment, all such as shall either by Force, Practise, Councils, Plotts, Conspiracies, or otherwise do anything to the contrary of anything in this Protestation contained. And further that I shall, in all just and honourable wayes, indeavour to preserve the Union and Peace between the Three Kingdomes of England, Scotland and Ireland. And neither for Hope, Feare, nor other F* Respect shall relinquish this Promise, Vow and Protestation.

** This intial 'F' inserted between lines.*

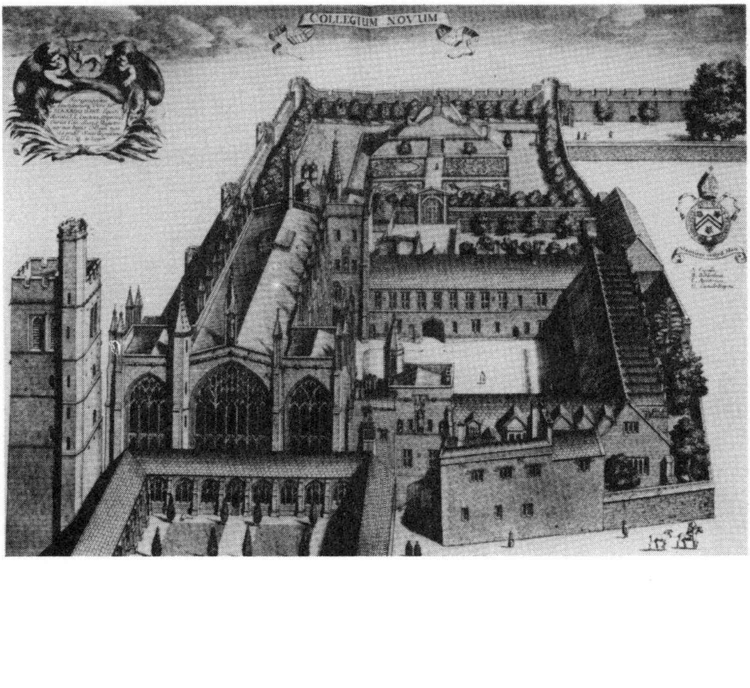

BRASENOSE COLLEGE [121]

[f.162r, in three columns]

Februarii 21: Aenei-nas' Protestati sunt.

[f.162r, col. 1]
Dr Radcliffe, Principalis
Mr. Sixsmith, Viceprinc:
Mr Richardson
Hutchens *ab.*
Newton
Houghton
Byron
Eaton
Hyfeild
Roberts
Church
Dr Scudamore
Mr Holland
Holland
Blundell
Leigh
Radcliffe
Ward
Dicus [?]
Barrow
Walton
Ormerod
Douglas
Warton
Sharples
Crompton
Cadwick *ab.*
Porter
Pipard
Bindon
Bates
Merideth
Yates
Eaude
Ashbrooke
Wild
Young
Gaskell
Hamilton
Marton
Coke
Birch
Woodison
Lowe
Forth
Taylor
Gammon
Beddow
Holbrooke *aegrotat*

[f.162r, col. 2]
Parker
Ogle
Dawley
Blackborne
Blackborne
Widdowes
Dicus
Shettiworth
Broxop *ab*
Parsons *ab*
Holman *ab*
Croxton *ab*
Jones ab
Aspinall
Bonnett *ab*

Richardson
Davis
Peisly
Peirs
Shelton
Radcliffe
Bavin
Prickett
Willoughby

Hi non sunt domi:
Mr. Ralph Richardson
Mr Bostock
Yates
Heywood
King
Leigh
Aldersey
Scudamore
Smith
Jennings
Griffith
Marburie
Radcliffe
Drake
Clement
Morris
Fogge
Morsdein
Gatley
Clarkson
Browne
Jackson

[f.162r, col. 3]
Greene
Halloway
Smith
Carter
Riland
Leicester
Worsley
Gilbert
Harpur
Elcock
Barlow
Hall
Williamson
Gerard
Wright
Penros
Fisher
Jackson
Blease
Wilkes
Duckworth
Cowley
Bold
Norton
Elton

In presentia mei Johannis French notarii publici et Registrarii universitatis Oxon'

THE QUEEN'S COLLEGE [64]

[f.163r, in three columns]

Vicesimo primo Februarii in eandem formam in quam protestatus est Dr Potter Praepositus Protestati sunt e Col: Reginae

[f.163r, col. 1]

Mr Lowgh
Airey
Head
Haughton
Stanwix
Yare
Barlow *ab*
Langbane *ab*
Archer
Stanly
Carus
Dobson
Sanderson *ab*
Robinson
Aglionby *ab*
Smith

Mr Sanders
Mawson
Wetherell
Owen
Smith
Sagittarie

[f.163r, col. 2]

Dr Smith
Lamplugh
Tullie
Rallinson
Nicholson
Barlow
Curray
Fisher
Addison
Airey
Fisher
Rogers
Jesson
Smith

Browne *ab*
Clavering *ab*
Bellingham
Hinton
Parrott
Scott

[f.163r, col. 3]

Wilkinson
Ainge
Gascoigne
Han

Richardson
Garnet
Wilkinson se
Nicolson
Fairer
Addison
Martin
Read *ab*
Eglesfeild
Brathwait
Airey
Burges
Dobson *ab*

Fisher
Gregorie
Hill
Boreton *ab*

Mr Deane Collect: Redit - Col. Regia'

In presentia mei Johannis French notarii publici et Registrarii Universitatis Oxon'

UNIVERSITY COLLEGE [36]

[f.163r, in two columns.]

Vicesimo primo Februarii protestati sunt e Col: Universitatis.

[f.163r, col. 1]

Dr Walker, Magister *ab*
Mr Woodhead, Procurator Universitatis
Dighton
Watkins
Walker
Rockly
Santy ab
Bilson
Ernshaw
Bankes
Bostock
Richardson
Ds Horsmanden
Walker
Copley
Gilder
Brooke

Brickenden
Tinte
Walters
Hutford
Morgan

[f.163r, col. 2]

Holloway
Evans
Tounge
Norton
Hanson *ab*
Blackcollar
Wilson
Evans
Willis
Cole
Robotham
Jackson
Selwood
George

In presentia mei Johannis French notarii publici et Registrarii universitatis Oxon'

CORPUS CHRISTI COLLEGE [57]

[f.164r, in three columns]

Februarii 21 e Col: Corpus Christi Protestati sunt

[f.164r, col. 1]
Dr Newlin, presidenses
Mr Pocock
Twine
Gorsteloe
Kerswell
Wrench
Simpson
Stratford
Sparke
Lake *ab*
Newell
Greaves
Hillarsden
Samwaies
Franklin
Welford
Powell *aegrotat*
Heywood
Hide
Carow *ab*
Hackwell
Kind
Chidley
Birch
[f.164r, col. 2]
Clayton *ab*
Lambe *ab*
Smith *ab*
Tooke
Drurie
Sparke
Sutton
Jackson *ab*
Barker
Benson
Gale *ab*
Speeding
Swete *ab*
Carter *ab*
Seymour *ab*
Downes
Seymour
Parne
Harrison
Hill
Price *ab*
Bowden
Parkhurst *ab*
[f.164r, col. 3]
Morton
Sclatter
Elliott
Webbe
Crumlum
Trosse
Powell *ab*
Vaughan
Shirlock
Wall

In presentia mei Johannis French notarri publicii et Registrarii universitatis Oxon'

ST. EDMUND HALL [23]

[f.164, continued, in three columns.]

Februarii vicesimo primo ex Aul: Edmundi Protestati sunt

[f.164r, col. 1]
Mr Ailworth *ab*
Cleaver
Leigh
Peirse
Chamberlaine *ab*
Bate
Hull
Colebrand
[f.164r, col. 2]
D's Haviland
Newton *ab*
Butler
Sculthorp
Bourne *ab*
Browne
Leeves
[f.164r, col. 3]
Cleeve
Hite
Haydon
Gowen
Harris
Tubb
King
Golding

In presentia mei Johannis French notarii publici Registrarii Universitatis Oxon'

MAGDALEN HALL [145]

[f.165r, in three columns]

Vicesimo primo Februarii protestati sunt ex Aul Magdalen':

[f.165r, col. 1]
Dr Lenton
Mr Wilkinson *ab*
Lambert *ab*
Tredcroft
Warner *ab*
Long
Perkins
Crosse
Harward *ab*

Twist *ab*
Skinner
Alnut *ab*
Wilkinson
Hodges *ab*
Barksdale *ab*
Morgan *ab*
Dewell *ab*
Million *ab*
Wharton *ab*
Collins *ab*
Wooldridge *ab*
Eyre
Tomlinson *ab*

D's Smith *ab*
Brunsell *ab*
Ireton *ab*
Thackham
Nelme
Kempe
Darlie *ab*
Morton
Barksdale *ab*
Cox *ab*
Oxton [Orton?] *ab*
South
Spicer *ab*
Pele
Hardie
Broughton *ab*
Foorde
Bailie
Goodrick *ab*
Trueman *ab*
Adams
Weaver *ab*
Strange *ab*
Carte *ab*
Moore
Pinckney
[f.165r, col. 2]
D's Streete *ab*
Hiller *ab*
Hutchinson
Woodman *ab*
Wallis *ab*
Burnhill *ab*
Blundeston

Purse *ab*
Berker
Love
Madgwick
Barton
Martin
Brooke *ab*
Woodman
Norwood
Montague
Morris
Barber
Hooke
Jackson *ab*
Seymour
Walbanke *ab*
Jaques *ab*
Toup *ab*
Gilbie *ab*
Hull
Easton *ab*
Pilsworth *ab*
Cox *ab*
Smoake
Poore
Dougan *ab*
Stopes
Reyner
Wise *ab*
Dunch
Francklin
Farroll *ab*
Watersfeild
Donne
Charnock *ab*
Ridge *ab*
Deene *ab*
Coxwell
Clements
Baker
[f.165r, col. 2]
Wilson
Fleetwood
Pie
Eversfeild
Sawkin
Hulwood *ab*
Wittam
Cummins

Bridger
Browne
Martin *ab*
Corbin
Baker
Jones *ab*
Turbervill *ab*
Hooke *ab*
Middleton
Middleton
Cooke *ab*
Vaughan
Jones *ab*
Griffiths
Hooper *ab*
Wordman
Broughton *ab*
Parkhurst
Winston
Winston
Bexhill
Steward *ab*
Brunsill *ab*
Twist *ab*

Crosse
Wells
Robinson
Olive *ab*

Jacombe
Dyer *ab*
Evans
Segery
Palmer *ab*
Dyer *ab*
Perkins
Pegler
Gowers

Crosse
Badcock
Pyke
Edward

In presentia mei Johannis French notarii publici et Registrarii universitatis Oxon'

PEMBROKE COLLEGE [90]

[f.166r, in four columns.]

Februarii 22 Protestati sunt a Col Pembrochiensi

[f.166r, col. 1]

Dr Clayton, Magister Collegii
Mr Whitwick *ab*
Whitwick *ab*
Tisdale
Darbie *ab*
Joyner *ab*
Haw *ab*

D's Cary
Steed
Brickenden

Mr Langlie
Whitwick
Little
Daffie
D's Whitwick
Wyat *ab*
Dew
Brickenden
Paine *ab*

Mr Pargiter *ab*
Duke *ab*
Bushnell
Bowre
Steevenson
Staply *ab*
Chamberlaine

[f.166r, col. 2]
Mr Peacock
Bolt
Tipping
Greenfeild *ab*
Washington *ab*
Master
Aronsham
Rogers
Boscawen

D's Bedhall *ab*
Tomlins *ab*
Blandy *ab*
Scruggs
Whithorne
Norris
Price
Jolliffe
Steevens
Combe
Mayo
Feild *ab*
Smith *ab*
Humfry
Barney
Sander
[f.166r, col. 3]
D's Withins
Dolling

Mr Rumsy *ab*
Jones
Hill *ab*
Herne
Tompson *ab*
Arnold *ab*
Wightwick *ab*
Gregorie *ab*
Dayrell
Stanly *ab*
Alflatt
Crichlow
Stephens
Dike
Terrie
Whittington
Taylor
Drope *ab*
Hathcott
Waythen
Bonner *ab*
Day
[f.166r, col. 4]
Linn
Taylor
Sanders
Turner
Sewell
Durant *ab*
Durman
Malden
Dolphen
Barfoot
White *ab*
Dutton
Sargent
Lane *ab*
Canner

In presentia mei Johannis French notarii publici et Registrarii Universitatis Oxon'

GLOUCESTER HALL [29]

[f.166r continued, in two columns.]

Feb: 22do Protestati sunt ex Aul: Glocest:

[f.166r, col. 1]

Mr. Wheare, Principalis
Mr Dixon *ab*
Dunch *ab*
Sharsell protested wth the limitations annexed
Wheare *ab*
Wheare *ab*
Hankes
D's Rolle
Aston
Sanderson
Lewis
Dikes
Collins
Dell
Torre
Deeble
Jeffreis
Gibbon
Haris

[f.166r, col. 2]

Tailor
Norton
Greivill
Crofts
Rose
Grant
Hipslie *ab*
Sambach *ab*
Moses
Martin

In presentia mei Johannis French notarii publici et Registrarii Universitatis Oxon'

[f.166a: attached to the sheet by a silk thread is the following alternative form of protestation as taken by Sharsell:-]

Whether this interpretation or such like might be accepted :-

1 I sweare to maintaine the doctrine expressed in the Church of England etc: I understand the doctrine already established in the 39 articles

2 I will maintaine this doctrine against all Popery & Popish innovations etc: I understand all Popery doctrinall & innovations Practicall contrary to the doctrine already established.

3 I sweare to maintaine the power and priviledges of Parliament & the rights of Subjects etc: I understand this as farre as they be evidenced to me by the standing lawes of this kingdome not repugnant to the lawes of God to be undoubted priviledges & rights & further the maintenance of those rights of subjects: I understand not to embroille my self in every private mans quarrell, though I conceave right, but wth reference to the publicke state.

4 I will maintaine every person that maketh this Protestation in wtsoever he shall doe in the Lawfull pursuance of the same etc: This maintenance I understand not to bind me to maintaine them by my selfe alone, but together wth others consenting & lawfully authorized, the same I understand of opposing in the next clause.

5 I will oppose & bring to condigne punishment etc: in all the severall Clauses I expressly except his Sacred Majesty & his Lawfull successors according to my oath of Allegiance, not daring to thinken a disloyal thought, much less to lift up my hand against the Lords annointed.

6 I will never relinquish this protestation etc: unless shall thinke it expedient to alter or revoke it, in wch case I reserve my freedom.

BALLIOL COLLEGE [68]

[f.167r, in three columns]

Februarii 22 Protestati sunt e Col: Balioll

[f.167r, col. 1]

Dr Laurence, *Mr Collegii ab*
Mr Savage
Merest
Good
Harris
Bradshaw *ab*
Michell
Palmer
Crouch
D's Thrikin

D's Chibnall
Davies
Nashion
Feilding *deliberabit*
Hickman *ab*
Pitt
Martin

Good
Anstey *ab*
Best
Kersley

Godfrie
Wildie
D's Ballard

[f.167r, col. 2]

Mr Silvester
Capper ab
Lancashire *ab*
Hill *ab*
Barwick *ab*
Trotman

D's Moore
Nanfan
D's Oldisworth
Lister
D's Doverdale
Abrahall
Levett
Edwards
Underhill
Haslock
Bruer *aegrotat*

White
Ady
Norris
Palmer *ab*
Pemberton *ab*
Smith
Birch ab
Cooper
Cartwright *ab*

[f.167r, col. 3]

Kinnersly *aegrotat*
Morris

D's Mosse
Reeve
Moushall

Jackman
Pope *ab*
Poore
Buzzard
Wind
Johnson *aegrotat*
Eburne
Parkes *ab*

Lowday *ab*
Smith
Watson
Winter *ab*
Steevens *ab*

In presentia mei Johannis French notarii publici et Registrarii Universitatis Oxon'

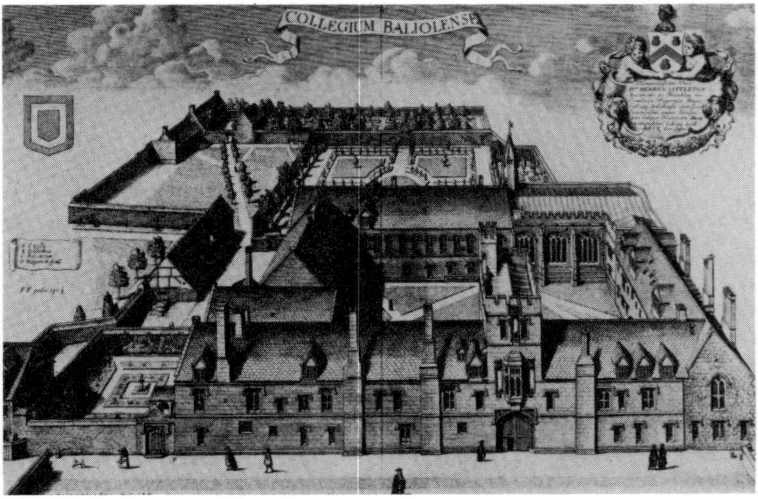

NEW INN HALL [114]

[f.167r continued, in five columns.]

Februarii 22 Protestati sunt ex Aul: Novi Hospitii

[f.167r, col. 1]
Mr Rogers, Principalis
Rogers
Cooper
Garbrands *ab*
Steevens *ab*
Luffe *ab*
Benion *ab*
Yeo
Osborne
Gay
Dolman *ab*
Balam *ab*
Meux
Temple
Ireland *ab*

D's Love *ab*
Allen *ab*
Lodge
Allen *ab*
Richards *ab*
Jordan *ab*
Paston
Wright *ab*
Baxter *ab*
Richards *ab*
Byfield
Phillip
Sneade
[f.167r, col. 2]
D's Wyatt
Hall
Lewis *ab*
Hart
Milward
Ware *ab*
Andrewes
Roode
Addington
Newell
Bennett
Safford
Hopkins
Drake
Collier
[Withorne - *deleted*]
Henshaw
Balbe

Withorne
Wilson
Wheatlie
Raleigh
Holled
Browne
Jones
Steevens
Doderidge
[f.167r, col. 3]
Maniford *ab*
Votier
Sterrie *ab*
Strother
Wakelie
Wilkins
Russell
Johnson
Widmer *ab*
Flower
Ible ab
Sprigg
Banister
Selwin *ab*
Parsons
Phillip
Buckingham *ab*
Gillpin
Nash
Hodges
Clarke
Wilcox
Clarke
Bradford
Bates *ab*
Gilder
Painter *ab*
[f.167r, col. 4]
Howell
Makin
Leagh
Pine

Rockett
Langley
Huddy
Richards *ab*
Eares *ab*
Fisher
North
Molineaux
Tailor
Bazelie *ab*
Thorougood
Avery *ab*
Bachelor *ab*

Gwin
Jennings
French
Haine
Shaxton
Hathway
Hounsell
[f.167r, col. 5]
London
Hoy
Williamson *ab*
Smith
Cope *[altered to* Coke*?]*

Gollidge
Jones
Bolt
Jellyman

In presentia mei Johannis French notarii publici et Registrarii universitatis Oxon'

ST. JOHN'S COLLEGE [85]

[f.168r, in two columns.]

Feb: 22 Protestati sunt e Col: D.Johannis Baptistae

[f.168r, col. 1]

Mr Croocher, Vice presidenses
Dr Edwards
Mr Warner
Vilett *ab*
Cuffe
Inkersell
Pixley
Crouther *[see below]*
Bankes *ab*
Gisbie
Brackston
Tuer *ab*
Goddard
Wright
Buckeridge *ab*
Greene *ab*
Webbe
Creede
Farmer *ab*
Snelling
Goad
Painter
Walwin *ab*
Elliott *ab*
Westly *ab*
Ward *recusat*
Miller
Amherst *ab*
Wright
Ellis

D's Steevenson *ab*
Kinglake
Tilsley
Pulley
Osbaston
Mewes
Tooker *ab*
King *ab*
Jennings
Smith
Lownes
Conniers
Aston
Buckeridge
[f.168r, co. 2]
Osburne
Jenkins
Wells

Heycock *ab*
Pen
North
Walker
Meridith
Frime
Selwood
Clarke *ab*
Wood

Mr Branthwait *ab*
Turner *ab*
Ballard
Gayton
Baily *ab*
Hammerslie
Wallis *ab*
Savage *ab*
Gwin
Duckett *ab*
Dr Meese *ab*
Hodges
Webbe
Johnson
Amherst
How
Rolles
Shipman
Tucker *ab*
Tailor
Wyatt
Stichall
Wilson

Ray
Flexney *ab*
Batts
Curtis
Holloway
Parsons
Jackson

In presentia mei Johannis French notarii publici et registrarii Universitatis Oxon'

[f.168a: attached to the sheet bearing the names of St. John's College is the following statement by Crowther, written on a small slip of paper:-]

"I Joseph Crowther being doubtful in some passages of proposing the Protestation, and not presuming to limit the sense of it, till I understand how the Honourable House will admitt any to do so, do humbly and thankfully accept the indulged licence of Deliberating".

EXETER COLLEGE [136]

[f.169r, in six columns.]

Februarii 24 Protestati sunt e Col: Exon

Reverendus in Christo Pater ac D'nus Dominus Johannes [John Prideaux] Episcopus Wigornensis Rector Collegii Vicecan: Universitatis Oxoniensis

[f.169, col. 1]

Mr Tozer
Maynard
Dennis
Kendall

Ackland Proc: sen: Universitatis
Conant
Fortescue *ab*
Prideaux *ab*
Polwheele
Hall
Jesse
Clifford
Porter *ab*
Captaine William Prideaux
Mr Short *ab*
D's Vilvaine
Crymes
Haydon
Erissey
Fortescue
Lutterell
Warren
[Fortescue *deleted*]
Chetwind
[f.169r, col. 2]
Nicolls
Berrie
Mallock
Short *ab*
Levelis
Prouze
Rowcliff *ab*
[Carter *deleted*]
Rainell
Bainfeild
Gater *ab*
Trevill *ab*
Ham
Thruston
Coleman
Chetle *ab*
Dixon *ab*
Turner *ab*
Fortescue
Buller
Cudmore
Eastman
Robins *ab*
Hardy
Marwood
Ousley *ab*
Lide

[f.169r, col. 3]
Tremaine

Mr Vernevill
Voisey
Burrington
Barron
Serle
Hammon

D's Veale
Owen
Tinconbe
Dyer
Ball *ab*
Williams
Newman
Pope
Parre
Croote
Soreton
Hussy
Lock
Norman
Birdall

Herneman *ab*
Sanford
Berry
Lawrence *ab*
Belfeild
Martin
[f.169r, col. 4]
Smith *ab*
Veale
Bettie
Searle
Rolle
Edgcombe
Sheares *ab*
Speed
Hancock
Keckwich
Turner *ab*
Baker *ab*
Shortrudge *ab*
Ashwood
Ward [?]
Rumbellow
Bowden
Standard *ab*

Andrewes
Nixon *ab*
Higham *ab*
D's Hopkins
Harding
Smith
Small
Edgcombe
Lovis
[f.169r, col. 5]
Graves
Spinnedge
Prideaux

D's Horne
Mauditt

Helme
Haslam
Stevens *ab*
Baily
Pendarvis
Cary
Raw
Moone
Arundell
D's Bankes
D's Haydon
Short
Barbon *ab*
Long
Steevens
Durant
Hawkey
Cobley
Browse
Phillips *ab*
[f.169r, col. 6]
Channon
Conant
Kempthorpe
D's Binmore
Gilliard
Vesper
Sheppard *ab*

In presentia mei Johannis French notarii publici Registrarii Universitatis Oxon'

ORIEL COLLEGE [75]

[f.169 continued in four columns.]

Februarii 24 Protestati sunt e Col: Oriel

[f.169r, col. 1]
Mr Rouse
Brookes
Horne
Duncombe
Eccleston
Lloyd
Winch *ab*
Wyatt
Smalbone *ab*
Farren *ab*
Say
Sanders
Washburne
Chamberlaine
D's Shepeard
Knightley
Sheldon
Acland

Mr Warren *ab*
Whittingham
Ballow *ab*
Wyatt *ab*
Lloyd *ab*

[f.169r, col. 2]
D's Sutton
Hughs *ab*
Mr Standard
Middleton *ab*
Owen *ab*
Lewis *ab*

Rous
Gammon
Broadwater
Jennings
Yates
Blackman
Mould

Mr Steevenson *ab*
Cresset *ab*
Freeman *ab*
Parkes
D's Smith *ab*
Warren *ab*
Howard *ab*
Harwell
Albin *ab*
Win
Porter
Lydall
[f.169r, col. 3]
D's Hooke *ab*
Lee

White
Sanchie
Bellew *ab*
Clynton *ab*
Heron
Rose
Tanner *ab*
Izod *ab*
Whitney

D's Sanders *ab*
Lloyd *ab*
Pritchard *ab*

Thomas
Berriman
Price
Jones
Froggs
Scaundrett
Evans *ab*
Davich *ab*
Bouch
Hicks
[f.169r, col. 4]
Milward *ab*
Jenkes
Rouse *ab*

In presentia mei Johannis French notarii publici et registrarii Universitatis Oxon'

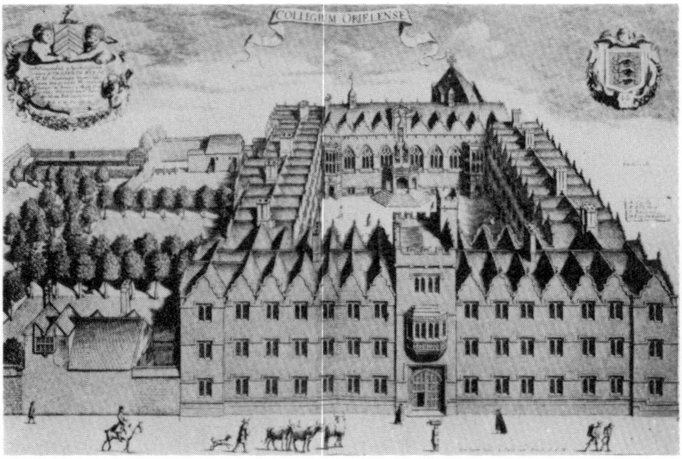

ALL SOULS COLLEGE [74]

[f.170r, in four columns.]

Februarii 24 Protestati sunt e Col Omnium Aucinarums

[f.170r, col. 1]

Mr Dayrell, Vice Custos
Dr Page
Dr Ailworth
Dr Gerard
Dr Lloid
Dr Bassett *ab*
Dr Greaves *ab*
Dr J'Anson *ab*
Mr Watkins
Greaves *ab*
Gorge
Barker
Prestwitch
Diggs *ab*
Baglie
Lloid
Coventry *ab*
Crofts
Wainwright
Hungerford
Newton
Birkhead
Lloid Ju:
Napper *ab*

[f.170r, col. 2]

Mr Newman
Thickens *ab*
Wells
Birkenhead
St. Johns
Whitlock
Norton
Baldwin *ab*
Boham *ab*
Bowman

[f.170r, col. 3]

D's Darell
Fisher
Smith *ab*
Harington
James
Stradling
Jepson

Hollingworth
Carleile
Martin
Williams
Wood

[f.170r, col. 4]

Harding
Snow *ab*
Sambach *ab*
Bolton *ab*
Gilkes
Poyner *ab*
Brookesby
Butler *ab*
Pritchard
Barksdale *ab*
Rawlen *ab*
Vicary
Bull
Ellow *ab*
Bolton *ab*
Baxter *ab*
Jenkes *ab*
Griffin *ab*
Gibbs *ab*
Davis *ab*
Powell
Paine *ab*

[f.170r, col. 5]

[Gillingham *deleted*]
Lister *ab*
Carter
Caunt *ab*
Skinner
St Hill [*or* St. hill?]
Price

In presentia mei Johannis French notarii publici et Registrarii universitatis Oxon'

WADHAM COLLEGE [94]

[f.170r continued, in four columns.]

Februarii 24 protestati sunt e Col: Wadham

[f.170r, col. 1]
Dr Eastcott, Guardianus
Mr Warren, Vice-Guardianus
Dr Blake *ab*
Mr Abraham *ab*
Mr Sugg
Simons
Chaplin *ab*
Knightbridge
Goodridge
Ashwell
Atkins
Parsons
Nourse
Shaw

Mr Stokes
Arnold

Dr Boswell
Mr Jordaine
Crofts *ab*
Doily *ab*
Monke *ab*
Bartlett
Matthewes
Masy
[f.170r, col. 2]
Ds Stucley
Warre *ab*
Leigh
Blanford
Dingley
Knightbridge
Grimes
Pine
Crabbe *ab*
Phillips *ab*
Rouse
Rouse
Heart *ab*
Turbervill *ab*
Stringer *ab*
Sanders
Golsey
Joyce *ab*
Hill *ab*

Williams
Axe
Malam
Billingsley
Billingsley
[f.170r, col. 3]
Sergeant
Maior
Prickett
Healthfeild

Strangwaies
Gifford
Thomas
Tucker
Hopkins
Okeover *ab*
Waller
Newman
Westcombe *ab*
Forrester
Wills *ab*
Leigh
Maskall *ab*
Hilliry
Melksusk
Gray
St Albons *ab*
Huish *ab*
Woolcott
[f.170r, col. 4]
Newbery
Markes
Browne
Adams
Sheppard
Leive
Page
Ford
Michelson
Wallwin *ab*
Burt
Hoder

Mander
Pettie
Phillips
Nicoll
Coward
Butt
Pitt *ab*
Drake
Way
Smith
Hall

In presentia mei Johannis French notarii publici et registrarii Universitatis Oxon'

JESUS COLLEGE [52]

[f.171r, in three columns]

Feb 24 : Protestati sunt secundum eandem formam in quam protestatus est Principalis e Col: Jesu

[f.171r, col. 1]

Mr Evans, Vice-principall
Mr Birch *ab*
Flower
Jones sen
Brevint *ab*
Rolles
Edwards
Jones *ab*
Adams *ab*
Vaughan se. *ab*
Vaughan
Lewis
D's Lewis *ab*
Winne

Mr Lloid

Vaughan *ab*
Feild
Brabourne

D's Boulton
Collins *ab*
Butler
Vaughan

[f.171r, col. 2]

Fletcher *ab*
Gwin *ab*
Evans *ab*

Tudder *ab*
Garnett *ab*
Gourton *ab*

Lewis *ab*
D's Mansell *ab*

Bloome *ab*
Edwards *ab*
Jenkins *ab*
Owens *ab*
Williams *ab*

Phillips *ab*
Watkins *ab*

Phillips *ab*
Jones *ab*
Win *ab*
Herbert *ab*
Herbert *ab [sic]*

[f.171r, col. 3]

Thomas *ab*
Wilkins *ab*
Jones *ab*
Evans *ab*
Davies sen. : *ab*
Weston
Lewis
Jones *ab*
Thomas *ab*
Rice

In presentia mei Johannis French notarii publici et Registrarii Universitatis Oxon'

ST. MARY'S HALL [56]

[f.171r continued, in three columns.]

Feb: 24 ex Anla Sanctae Mariae protestati sunt

[f.171r, col. 1]

Dr Sanders, Principalis
Mr Middleton
Sanders *ab*
Dyke *ab*
Westcombe *ab*
Benson
Clarke sen: *ab*
Clarke iu
Mallory *ab*
Godly *ab*
Thistlethwaite *ab*
Fowler *ab*
Rishton *ab*
Lockett ab
Jacob *ab*

Mr Minniett
D's Wills *ab*

Walsh *ab*
Gollop *ab*
Clayton *ab*
Smith
Martin *ab*
Harwar *ab*

[f.171r, col. 2]

D's Baily *ab*
Penruddock
Upton *ab*
Abbot *ab*
Whittingham

Garrett
Gibbes
Sanderson *ab*
Clarke *ab*
Slatyer *ab*
Eyton
Smith *ab*
Dike *ab*
Tynt *ab*
Harris *ab*
Goldston *ab*

Sheldon *ab*
Gey
Harrison
Wilkenson
Whitmore

[f.171r, col. 3]

Spencer
Fry
Franclen
Misson

Davies *ab*
Warbrake
Dibble *ab*
White
Powell *ab*
Dilworth
Hart
Osborne

In presentia mei Johannis French Notarii publici et Registrarii Universitatis Oxon'

TRINITY COLLEGE [65]

[f.172r, in three columns]

Februarii 24 e Col: Trinitatis

[f.172r, col. 1]
Dr Kettle, Presidenses
Dr Potter *ab*
Dr Marsh *ab*
Dr Read
Dr Hobbs
Mr Simpson
Bathurst
Blithman *ab*
Richards *ab*
How
Cranford
Bathurst

Dr Glenham
Mr Whistler *ab*
Roberts
Lardie *ab*
Clarkson *ab*
Roles *ab*
Bull *ab*
Weston
Brace
Pike

Yates
Lambert *ab*
Denham *ab*
Thomas
Paviott
[f.172r, col. 2]
Dr Halse *ab*
Breedon

Smith *ab*
Carter
Charlett
Gunter *ab*
Gascoigne *ab*
James *ab*
Egerton *ab*
Tooker *ab*
Morgan *ab*
Barrett

D's Browne
Walker
Hawes
Woolly *ab*

Heymer
Wright
Douch Sen.

Lydall
Ratford
Douch iu
French

D's Feild
Martin

Waddon
[f.172r, col. 3]
Banger

D's Okey
Barnard
Sacheverell
Buccock *ab*

Wales
Cobb
Corderoy

Oldcroft
Hawes
Spencer
Lane

In presentia mei Johannis French notarii publici et Registrarii Universitatis Oxon'

[f.172a: attached to the sheet bearing the names of Trinity College is a small slip of paper on which the President of the College has written:-]

I Raffe Kettell president of Trinitie College Oxon having beene broughte up about sixtie & three years in this Universitie doe protest syncerely this protestation tendred unto us as Consonant unto the oaths of supremacie & allegiance wch I have often taken, that subscription which I have often subscribed & the dutiful Prayer which this Parliament time is published for the holy safetie of this Church & realm in England.

Ita protestor R Kettell

LINCOLN COLLEGE [92]

[f.172r continued, in four columns.]

Feb 24 e Col : Lincoln' protestati sunt

[f.172r, col. 1]
Mr Chalfont
Hoough
Kilbie *ab*
Watts *ab*
Tireman *ab*
Crosse
Webberlie
Houghton
Kelham
South
D's Gilbert

Mr Cornish *ab*
Wright

D's Jones *ab*
Chilton *ab*
Marshall

Mr Rith
Bury
St John
Austen
Burrowes
Weldon
Eustace
[f.172r, col. 2]
Mr Smith *ab*
Levinz *ab*
Bolton
Manship
Blackmore
Rogers

D's Adams
Harrison *ab*
Hollings
Hill
Pearce *ab*
Gardner
Lockett
Bachelor
Thorpe
Robinson
Adams
Darell *ab*
Hathwett
Hardie
Archdale
Matthew
Harpur
Thornton
Pope
[f.172r, col. 3]
Ramsden
Tracie *ab*
Morley
Vernon
Trist
Badger
Reade
Cade
Smith
Blower
Steevens
Sanderson
Rich
Tracy *ab*
Smith
Bourchier
Alford
Burrowes
Peck
Browneing *ab*
Southby
Vasie

Ewen
Robinson
Sergeant *ab*
Edwards
[f.172r, col. 4]
Abdie
Pearse
Robinson *ab*
Bonell
Musson *ab*
Gibbs
Moore
Heskins
Tailor
Birton
Byfeild
Segle
Harford

Shelton
Sergeant
Neale *vacie*
Sarney *vacie*
Mr Farmer

In presentia mei Johannis French notarii publici et Registrarii Universitatis Oxon'

ALBAN HALL [32]

[f.173r, in two columns.]

Feb: 24 Aul: Albana protestati sunt

[f.173r, col. 1]
Dr Zouch, Principalis
Mr Powell
Bethell
Stapylton *ab*
Abbotts
Elliott

D's Lewis
Ainscombe
Wall

Mr Coker
Forrester
Bourchier
Mason *ab*

Higgens
Birkened
Masters *ab*
Stile
Lewknor
Sabin
Norborne
Mortimer
Towgood
[f.173r, col. 2]
D's Dandie *aegrotat*

Glynne *ab*
James

Creese
Clarkes
Phillips
Lampeer

Kerry *ab*
Paine
Addams

In presentia mei Johannis French notarii publici et Registrarii Universitatis Oxon'

HART HALL [35]

[f.173r continued, in two columns.]

Feb 24 ex Aul: Cervina protestati sunt

[f.173r, col. 1]
Dr Parsons, Principalis
Mr Haysome
Lewis
Andrewes *ab*

Cooper
Kempe

Pitt
Knitht
Fletcher

D's Estmond
Rainstorpe
Morris
Frampton
Johnson

Mallett
Pawly
Everet

Davis
Edwards

Tomson
Harpur
Owen
Hart
Gosling
Harding *ab*
Webbe

In presentia mei Johannis French notarii publici et Registrarii Universitatis Oxon'

[f.173r, col. 2]

Protestati sunt
Mr Crosse Bedellus in Jure superior
Lichfeild Bedellus in Jure inferior
Ball Bed: in Art: inferior
Davis Virgifer
Rogers Chirurgus
Hirst Scriba
Gilliver Aedituus
Roper Subserviens
Pomfrey Serviens Procurat Sen:

In presentia mei Johannis French notarii publici et Registrarii Universitatis Oxon'

BERKSHIRE: ABINGDON DIVISION

MORETON, OCK and HORMER HUNDREDS

[f.2r, single column. This list, like that for Bampton (Oxon.) Hundred, is of the Ministers, Churchwardens, Constables and Overseers of the Poor who took the Protestation Oath, probably at Abingdon, on 28th February (a fortnight after that at Woodstock), see Introduction, page xiii. The list is much more accurate than that for Bampton; the usually minor differences in the names as they appear in the parish returns are shown in square brackets.]

The Names of the Ministers, Constables, Churchwardens & Overseers of every severall p'ish within the Hundreds of Morton, Ocke & Hormeare within the division of Abingdon in the County of Berks who have taken the Protestation made by the Hono'ble howse of Commons assembled in Parliam't the Third day of May in An'o d'ni 1641 before Charles Tooker d'cor of Lawes one of his Ma'ties Justices of the peace for the County of Berks the 28th day of Feb'ry 1641.

Hundred de Morton

The p'ish of **Brightwell** *[no return]*
Thomas Godwyn, d'cor of divinity, *R'cor* there
John Narroway, *Constable*
Willm. Leaver, John Winge, *Churchwardens*
James Kerby, Richard Eldridge, *Overseeres*

The Township of **Sotwell** within the p'ish of St. Leonards in Wallingford *[no return]*
John Astell, *Minister*
John Rowland, *Constable*
Richard Maborrough, John Matson, *Churchwarden & Overseeres*

The Township of **Upton** within the p'ish of Blewbery
Thomas Buckle, *Constable & Churchwarden*
Phillipp Allen [Allin], *Churchwarden*
Thomas Harwood [Harword], Thomas Higges [Higgs], *Overseeres*

The p'ish of **Streatly**
Gilbert Hinde, *Vicar*
Willm. Woodington [Wooddenton], *Constable*
Willm. Higges [Higgs], *Churchwarden*
Willm. Whistlar, Robert Skirmore [Skirmer], *Overseeres*

The Tythinge of **Aston Upp Thrupp** [Aston Upthorpe, in Blewbury parish]
Leonard Slade, *Constable*
Henry Slade, Nicholas Cox, *Churchwardens*
Thomas Parsons, John Cox, *Overseeres*

The p'ish of **East & West Hagburne**
Richard Bristowe [Bristow], *Vicar*
Richard Simmes, *Constable*
John Dandridge [Dandredge], John Stacey [Stacy], *Churchwardens*
Richard Cersell [Cressell], *Churchwarden of West Hagbrn.*
Thomas Humphrey, Henry Bunce, *Overseers*
Henry Floodyard, *Constable of West Hagburne*

The p'ish of **Didcott**
Richard Bristow, *Vic'r*
Israel Sayer [Sawyer], *Constable*
Richard Blake, Richard Horsley, *Churchwardens*
Willm. Hall, Willm. Smith, *Overseeres*

[f.2v]

The p'ish of **Basseldon**
John Singleton, *Vicar*
John Goslinge, *Constable*
Thomas Buckeridge, Thomas Hiscoke [Hichcocke], *Churchwardens*
Willm. Mathew, Willm. Beckford, *Overseers*

The Townshipp of **Moulsford**
John Kinge [King], *Constable*
Frauncis Cox, *Churchwarden*
Henry Carter, Richard Quelch, *Overseers*

The p'ish of **Ashampsteed**
John Singleton, *Vicar*
John Greene [Green], *Constable*

Ashampstead *continued*
Abraham Yeat [Yates], Thomas Cripps [Crips], *Churchwardens*
John Sharp [Sharpe], Willm. Pococke, *Overseers*

The p'ish of **South Morton**
Edmund Leigh, *R'cor*
Edward Due [Dewe], *Constable*
John Styles [Stiles], Lawrence Luendon, *Churchwardens*
Franncis Styles, Clement Styles, *Overseers*

The p'ish of **North Morton**
John Comyn, *Vicar*
Nicholas Feild, *Constable & Churchwarden*
John Gregry, *Churchwarden*
Ralph Feild [Feeld], John Spooner, *Overseers*

The p'ish of **Aston Tirrold**
Edward Bellenger [Bellinger], *Curat*
Willm. Butler, *Constable*
Thomas Rigby, Richard Tirrold [Terroll], *Churchwarden*
John Sadler, Overseer

The p'ish of **Harwell**
Hugh Lloyde [LLoide], *Vicar*
John Woodley, John Loader [Loder], *Constable*
Stephen Keat [Keate], Robert Rowland, *Churchwardens*
Salomon Aldworth, Richard Elderfeild, *Overseers*

[f.3r]

Hundred de Ocke

The p'ish of **Kingston Bagpuze**
John Sone, *Minister*
Frauncis Yeat, *Constable*
John Wheeler, John Stevenson [Stevinson], *Churchwardens*
John Sone, John May, *Overseers*

The p'ish of **Appleton**
Willm. Snowe [Snow], *Curat*
Richard Selwood [Sellwood], *Constable*
Edward Dudson, John Morris, *Churchwardens*
John Lane, Thomas Selwood [Sellwood], *Overseers*

The p'ish of **Milton**
John Keate, *Minister*

Milton *continued*
Richard Weekes [Wickes], *Constable*
John Bewdon [Bewden], Robert Keate, *Churchwardens*
Richard Weekes [Wickes], Richard Joyner, *Overseers*

The p'ish of **Sutton Courtney**
Nicholas Sheppard, *Vicar*
John Wattes [Wats], *Constable*
Nicholas Rayer [Raier], John White, *Churchwardens*
Richard Curtis, George Hagar, *Overseers*

The p'ish of **Fifeild**
John Pearce [Pierce], *Minister*
Edward Smalbone, *Constable*
Edward Carter, Willm. Bartholomew [Bartholim'], *Churchwardens*
Humphrey Greenway, John Gallant [Gayland], *Overseers*

The p'ish of **Longe Witnam**
Willm. Prowse, *Vicar*
Thomas Lovegrove [Laggrove], *Constable*
Willm. French [Fence], David Child [Childs], *Churchwardens*
Willm. Strange, John Sadler, *Overseers*

The Townshipp of **Lyford** within the p'ish of Hanney
Thomas Jauncy, *Vicar*
Thomas Cox, *Constable*
Richard Cox, Edward Dastin [Dawstyne], *Churchwardens & Overseers*

The Townshipp of **Goosey** in the p'ish of Stanford in vale *[no return]*
John Stevens, *Constable & Churchwarden*
Richard Woodley, *Overseer*

[f.3v] The p'ish of **Steventon**
Gabriel Harrison, *Curat*
Richard Westton [Weston], *Constable*
James Stone, Willm. Smalbone, *Churchwardens*
Francis Hopkins, John Wells [Welles], *Overseers*

The Townshipp of **Garford** in the p'ish of Marsham
John Peirce [Pierce], *Curat*
James Stone, *Constable & Churchwarden*
Nicholas Badcocke, *Churchwarden*
William Younge, Richard Doe, *Overseers*

The p'ish of **Drayton**
John Stone, *Minister*
Thomas Tirrold, *cheif Constable*
Bartholomew Weston, *petty Constable*
Edward Tirrold [Terrald], John Bartlott [Bartlett], *Churchwardens*
Walter Tirrold [Terrald], Robert Hobbs, *Overseers*

The Townshipp of **Frilford** in the p'ish of Marcham
Richard Knapp [Knape], *Constable*
Richard Aldworth, *Churchwarden*
Edward Shiprey [Sheppery], Henry Pead [Peade]

The p'ish of **Marcham**
Thomas Hall, *Vicar*
Edmond Wriglysworth [Wrigglesworth], *cheife Constable*
Phillipp Prince, *petty Constable*
Richard Hawkins, Richard Hopkins, *Churchwardens*
Henry Newman, Richard Couzens [Cossens], *Overseers*

The p'ish of **Little Wittnam**
Ralph Adams, *Curat*
Willm. Millman, *Constable*
Thomas Harford, Nathaniell Sheene, *Churchwardens*
Edmond Pisley [Pisly], Thomas Lawrence [Lawrenc], *Overseers*

The Townshipp of **Appleford** in the p'ish of Sutton Courtney
Edmond Bradstocke [Bradstock], *Constable*
Thomas Whichelowe, Thomas Justice, *Churchwardens*
Thomas Nevill [Nevell], John Blake, *Overseers*

[f.4r]
Hundred de Hormeare *[Hormer]*

The p'ish of **Comner** [Cumnor]
Thomas Drope, *Vicar*
Thomas Dalby [Dalbie], *cheife Constable*
Richard Perry, *petty Constable*
Richard Stibbs, Richard Crowder, *Churchwardens*
Thomas Godfrey, Willm. Nurth, Thomas Wordnam [Wernham], *Overseers*

The p'ish of **Radley**
John Herbert, *Donotary*
Henry Avery, John White, *Churchwardens*
Thomas Eyres [Ayres], *Overseer*

Thrupp in the p'ish of Radly
Richard Dorter, *cheife Constable*

The p'ish of **Sunningwell**
Ralph Bazely [Bassly], *Constable*
Thomas Stevenson, Edward Webb Junr, *Churchwardens*
Thomas Bazely junr., Edward West senr, *Overseers*

The Townshipp of **Shipton** [Shippon] within the p'ish of St. Hellens in Abingdon
Thomas North, *Constable & Churchwarden*
John Hawkins, *Churchwarden*

The p'ish of **Besselsly** [Besselsleigh]
George Carter, *Churchwarden*
Richard Bazely, *Churchwarden & Overseer*

The p'ish of **Wytham**
Anthony Hodges, *Curat*
John Lucas, *Constable*
Jasper Weller, *Churchwarden*
John Wildgoose, *Overseer*

Charles Tooker

The names of those w'ch appeared not to take the Protestation.

Henry Warner, R'cor of Kingston Bagpuze beinge Resident in Oxon, appeared not.
John Weston, Vicar of Cholsey & Moulsford being at London appeared not.
John Curtis, Constable of Besselsly appeared not.
[Thomas Harper one of the Overseers of the p'ish of Radly appeared not - *deleted*]
Thomas Hicks one of Churchwardens of Wytham appeared not.

Charles Tooker

[f.4v]
The names of those p'ishes & Hamletts w'ch have not made their Returnes.

The p'ish of Brightwell; The Hamlett of Sotwell; The Hamlett of Goosey.

Charles Tooker

ABINGDON

[The Protestation Return for the Borough of Abingdon and its constituent parishes does not survive, except for the township of Shippon, page 197. The Borough forms part of the Hundred Hormer, for which the Assessment, PRO E179/238/146, is virtually certainly that of May/June 1642. Unfortunately the first membrane, which contained not only the preamble and date but also presumably the major part of Abingdon, is lost. The opening membrane (here numbered 2) has no heading but the first forty entries conclude with a sum of £68.5s. The comparably sized borough and parish of Banbury (with Neithrop) totalled £64.5s.1d. Barton and Northcourt, Dry Sandford, and Shippon, all parts of Abingdon St. Helen, were separately assessed.]

*[**Assessment.** Membrane 2]*

S'r Ralphe, £1.10s.
Henry Jevon & his Mother, 12s.
Mr Dorell and his Mother, £1
Edmond Bastocke, gen. and William Bastocke, gent, £2.8s.
Mrs Bostocke, vid., £2
Ralphe Sherwood, 4s.
Widdow North, 4s.
John Ashwell, 4s.
John Lenne, 3s.
John Branch, 1s.
Richard Thatcher, 1s.
James Hawkes, 2s.
James Towensend, 2s.
Nicholas Atherton, 2s.
George Lee, 2s.
Willm. Davyes, 2s.
Tho: Egge, 1s.
Henry Bell, 1s.
Abraham Cozens, 1s.
Henry Collens, 1s.
Willia' Pound [*or* Ponnd], 1s.
William Coxeter, 1s.
Willia' Warner, 1s.
Richard Corderey, 1s.
Arthur Robbinson, 1s.
John Harris, 1s.
John Rutter, 1s.
Anthony Archer, 6s.
John Clarson, 2s.
Willia' Barnes, 2s.
John Barnes, 1s.
Robt. Stafford, 2s.
The Feofees of Sunningwell, 3s.
John Shaw, 6s.
Francis Payne, 2s.
Nicholas Butler, 2s.
Giles Pawlett, gent., 6s.
Edward Absoleme, 2s.
Alexander Bassett, 2s.8d.

The Sume is £68.5s.

Barton and Norcott *[Northcourt]*

*[**Assessment.** Membrane 3, following Thrupp.]*

S'r Thomas Read, kn't , for Barton, £2.13s.2d.
S'r Thos. Reade, kn't, for Norcott, 5s.6d.
Humfry Hyde, Esq., 5s.6d.
Willia' Porter, gent., 8s.4d
Richard Overton, gent., 8s.8d[?]
Edward Loader, 5s.6d.
Willia' Bouckland, 13s.8d.
William Weston, 4s.6d.
John Maulter [*or* Walulter?], 2s.8d.
Tho: Barrett, 2s.8d.
Richard Haynes, 1s.4d.

Sume £5.11s.4d.

Sanford *[Dry Sandford]*

*[**Assessment.** Membrane 3, following Besselsleigh.]*

William Jennens, 10s.9d.
William Lane, gent, 3s.5d.
Richard Orpwood, 6s.10d.
Jane Bond, widoow, 16s.2¾d.
Goodman Powell, 1s.8½d.
Richard Bowles, 1s.8½d.
Widdow Burnett, 2s.6¾d.
Marrian Francklen, vid., 13s.6d.
Richard Lamboll, 2s.10d.
Edward Hall, 6s.10d.
John Hawkins, 1s.8½d.
Widdow Hutt, 6s.10d.
John Mitchell, 3s.5d.

Sume is £4.2s.6d.

[For Shippon, see pages 197-98.]

APPLEFORD

[f.7, in two columns]

A note of all the names of the inhabitants of *[deletion]* Appleford in the County of Berks of the age of eighteene yeares and upwards who have taken the protestation and subscribed thereunto according to the order of Parliament [32]

[f.7r, col. 1]
Householders
Thomas Whiceloe
Francis Trulock
John Coates
David Allum
John Godfrey
Anthony Aires
John Whiceloe sen.
Richard Tuckwell
Thomas Quelch
John Cox
John Church

[f.7r, col. 2]
Children and servants
Thomas Nevill jun.
John Roise
Griffeth Smart
Thomas Church
Robert Hoare
Thomas Bedford
Richard Church
Andrew Allum
John Whiceloe Jun.
Edmond Whiceloe
Anthony Wilkins
Andrew Cowley
John Allum
John Smith
John Dod
Thomas Chainey
Richard Allum

In Witness where of wee the Minister, Constable, Churchwardens and overseers of the poore have here unto subscribed our names.

Nico. Shepard, *Vicar*
Edm. Bradstock, *Const.*
Tho. Justice
Thomas Nevell

APPLETON

[f.8r, in two columns, with signatures and marks (asterisked).]

***Appleton** in Com. Berks.*

The names of such as have made the protestation enioyned by an order of Parliament. [73]

[f.8r, col. 1]
Robert Southby
Ed. Risetrens[?]
Walter Wightwick
Robert Morice
Edward Stevens *
Tho. Shreive
Richard Champion *
John Stevens
Thomas Sellwod
Robert Baker *
Simon Shreeve *
Thomas Shreiv
Simon Battin
Willm. Kible *
Simon Hawkins *
Jerime Sims *
John Palmer *
Thomas Wastell
Richard Burden *
Simon Battin *
Robert Kempster
John Hawkins *

[f.8r, col. 2]
Willm. Higgins *
John Cooke *
John Cotmore *
John French *
William Miles *
John Collingwood *
Richard Campion the younger *
Edward Shreeve *
Oliver Unnion *
John Phillips *
John Bucher [*or* Burger?]
James Walter *
John Yeomans *
Henry Couldry
William Bond
Robert Butler
Henry Michell *
Thomas Leaver *
Robert West *

[f.9r, col. 1]
Jn. Steiens *[sic]*
Isaack Yate
Christopher Wedge *
Robert Hasely *
Thommas West *

Andrew Johnsonn
Thommas Leach *
Simon Hawkins
Martin Bouthe
John Gari *
William Keol[?]
Sampson Kinge *
Thomas Rayman *
Willm. Wiblin *
Richard Oakly *
John Sellwood *
Thomas Betts *

[f.9r, col. 2]
William Tub *
John Steevens
Francis Hames *
Henry Roberts *
Richard Kempster
Richard Walter *
Richard Barnes *
Robert Franklin *
Thomas Baseley *
John Baseley *
John Standbrooke *

They whose names are afore written have taken the protestation in the p'sence of us

Willm. Snow, *Curate*
Richard Sellwood, *Constable*
Edw. Dudson, *Churchwarden*
Thomas Sellwood *, *Ov'seer*

ASHAMPSTEAD

[f.10, in two columns, with signatures and marks (asterisked).]

***Ashamsted** Parish.*

The names of the men of Ashamsted from 18 yee[rs] old and upwards w'ch have taken the Protestation and subscribed therto: March 6th 1641. [58]

[f.10r, col. 1]
Edward Pocock
Thomas Parsons
William Franckham *
John Whiller
John Wheeler *
Edward Wise
John Justice *
Thomas Gray *
Thomas Wheeler *
Richard Bickerdicke *
William Stampe *
Antony Sadgrove
William Chamberlaine *
Ralph Strike *
John Green *
William Higgs
Hugh Gotheridge *
Francis Cooper *
Thomas Quelch *
Thomas Strike *
John Meriot *
John Welman *
William Stevens *
William Quelch *
John Mathew *
Thomas Wise *
William Stamp *
John Knappe *
John Pococke
Robert Smith

[f.10r, col. 2]
John Strike *
John Picke [*or* Pitte]
William Purtlocke *
John Welman *
Robert Meriot *
Ralph Strike *
John Barnard *
Ralph Knappe *
William Pococke *
Humfrey Welman *
Edward Macey *
Henry Newbery *
John Pococke *
Robert Deane *
John Pratt *
Jeremy Torraller
John Ford
George Grantham *
John Witt *
Tobie Ilsley *
Edward Martin *
James Mathew

These have taken the Protestation & subscribed thereunto in ye p'sence of us

John Green*. *Constable*
Abraham Yates *,
Thomas Crips *,
Churchwardens
William Pococke *,
John Sharpe *,
Overseers for the poore
John Singleton, *Vicar*

And none have refused as they returned.

ASTON TIRROLD

[f.11, in two columns]

Berks.

March 7th Anno 1641

The names of the inhabitants of the parrish of Aston Terroll in the County of Berks who have taken ye Protestation made by the hono'ble Howse of Commons the 3d of May last in the presence of us whose names are subscribed, the day and yeare first above written. [59]

[f.11r, col. 1]
Henery Lewindon
Christopher Alnewick
John Cox
Henery Sadler
John Absolon
William Neale
Richard Rothell
John Sadler
Thomas Sadler
Richard Pope
John Tirroll
Henery Lewindon
Thomas Neale
John Burdon
Henery White
Humphery Learner [*or* Leamer]
Richard Pauling
Mathew Parsons
Thomas Fillmore
John Cripps
John Pauling
Thomas Rothell
Jeames Kimber
Christopher Neale
Richard Gooddale
Thomas Pope
Thomas Lewis
Henery Maskall
John Felp
Thomas Neale
Thomas Cox
John Keate
John Sadler
Henery Watford
Thomas Sadler
John Weadon
William Leaver
Richard Cox
John Cooper

[f.11r, col. 2]
Richard Hayward
John Gooddale
Ralph Gooddale
Robert Howse
John Keate
Richard Lewindon
John Weadon
Richard Willmott
Thomas Sader *[sic]*
Richard Androws
John Hayward
Edward Butler
Richard Absolon
William Leaver

All the inhabitants of the parrish above sayde have taken the protestation, none refused.

Edward Bellinger, *Curat.*

William Butler, *Counstable*, by his marke.
Richard Terroll, Thomas Rigby, by their marks, *Church wardens.*
John Sadler, by his mark, Richard Tirroll, by his mark, *overseers*

ASTON UPTHORPE (in Blewbury) [37]

[f.12, in two columns]

Berks: ***Aston Upthrupp***:
March the 6th Anno : Dom: 1641/2

[f.12r, col. 1]
John Cagburd
Thomas Cagburd
Richard Buckeridg
William Loader
Henery Absolon
John White
Henery Baseley
Edward Neale
Euans Blewitt
John Pope
Ambrose Pope
John Wiggenton
William Pope
Henry Simms
John Slade
John Slade *[sic]*
Henery Cox
Thomas Cox
Charles Burges
Bartholomew Slade

[f.12r, col. 2]
John Allin
Richard White sen.
Richard White junior
Richard Holder
Richard Slade
John Hill
William Pope
William Whitherole
William Howse
John Paulinge
Richard Ellyott

The P'testation was generally taken according to the ordre by the Inhabitance of Aston Upthrupp in the parrish of Blewberry, none refused, in the presence of

John Sampson, *Vicar*
Leonard Slade, *Constable*
The marke of Henry Slade
The marke of Nicholas Cox, *Church wardens*
Thomas Parsons, John Cox, *overseers.*

BASILDON

[f.13, in three columns. The first ten appear to be signatures, and those asterisked have marks.]

Com. Berks.
***Basledon** Parish*

The names of ye men of Basledon from 18 yeeres old and upwarde w'ch have taken the Protestation and subscribed thereunto. March 6th 1641. [107]

[f.13r, col. 1]
Griffin Ward, *Clerke*
Robt. Clark
Richard Allin
Henry Allen
John Allin
Ric. Potinger
Richard Allin
Richus Buckeridge
Richard Woodley
John Curtyce
Griffth Lundon
Richard Maskall
John Whighting
Griffth Lundon
Thomas Hannington
Thomas James
Richard Lanne
Thomas Castell
John Lill
John Note
Roger Stevens
Frances Godet
John Briant
Robert Chiles
Larance Amberes
Edward Pinke
Thomas Frye
Richard Wooten
Steven Swayne
John Hull
Hughe Frost
Richard Skinner
Thomas Broune

[f.13, col. 2]
Richard Wilder
William Wilder *
William Skinner
Thomas Long
Thobyas*[sic]* Chake *
Aurther Frye *
John Gidron *
Thomas Woodly *
William Butler
Edmond Lovgrov *
Thomas Cordry *
Thomas Wells
Richard Cratur
John Frye *
Robart Fay
Steven Whiller *
John Note *
Richard Frye *
Frans Fillmer *
Thomas Tether *
Symon Aris[?]
Joseph Singleton
Nicolas Simons
Frances Godet
Edward Castell
Robert Giles
John Higs
[f.13r, col. 3]
Thomas Higs *
John Compton *
Adam Broodrik *
Richard Millerd *
Thomas Craye *
John Loder *
John Keate *
William Allbery *
Micll Evens
Astin Mayne
John Bolt *
John Young *
William Higgs
Thomas Hadnam
William Dyer
John Fisher
Jeames Higs
Phillip Gillett

Thomas Hieron
Gaberell Gibs
Richard Wilder
John Abere
Abraham Hiron
William Fiterer[?]
Simeon Wells
John Hieron
[f.14r, col. 1]
John Allen
John Edin
John Pockcoke *
Richard Bushnell
Edward Potshard
William Bediant
William Higges
John Stamp
[f.14r, col. 2]
Frances Evens
Thomas Billemer
John Wooldridges *
William Higges * of Woodgreens
John Astall
Edward Higgs
Roger Young

Theise are to Certifie that all parishioners of Basledon in the count' of Berks above the age of 18 yeares have taken the protestation and not any one in the said parish that refused.

In Witnesses whereof wee have subscribed our names the six day of March 1641.

John Singleton, *Vicar*
Thos Buckeridg,
Thomas Hichcocke,
Church-Wardens
John Goslinge, *Const.*
Willim. Mathew,
Will. Beckford,
Overseers

BESSELSLEIGH

[f.15, single column, signatures and marks (asterisked).]

A Returne of the names of the Inhabitants of **Baselsleigh** that have subscribed to this pr'sent Protestation made by John Curtis, Constable, & George Carter & Richarde Baselye, the Churchwardens and overseers. [18]

Robert Lambordine *
William Shawe *
Anthonie Stratton *
Richard Feeld
Edward Nobes
Thomas Dungate
Henry Straton
Gerswn Strotton *
Thomas Weston *
John Watkins *
Richarde Badnall *
Zachary Dubber *
William Davis *
John Wilkes *
William Weston *

Savinge all my former subscriptions *[i.e., when he took his degrees (if any) and when he was ordained]*, & what I doe not knowe nor under-stande, I subscribe in the Protestation proposed
William Dickinson, *Rect:*

Richard Greene *
John Curtis

All these subscribed to the peticon & no man of o'r Parish refused, only John Nobes was absent being at Sarum.

George Carter

*[**Assessment.** Membrane 2, following on Swinford.]*

Besselsley

Willia' Lenthall, Esq., 18s.
Willia' Dickenson, 8s.
Richard Baseley, 3s.3d.
Richard Orpwood, 3s.9d.
Widdow Francklen, 5s.2d.
William Lane, 6s.10d.
John Nobs, 1s.6d.
Willia' Shaw, 3s.
Tho: Brickland, 2s.
Edward Dudson, 1s.4d.
Robt. Kempster, 2s.
Richard Badcock, 3s.9d.
John Stephens, 1s.
Willia' Davis, 3s.
Jacon Stephens, 6d.
John Hansaker, 1s.4d.
George Carter, 1s.
Robt. Lamberdine, 10d.
Tho: Weston, 9d.
Widdow Bond, 1s.
Anthopny Strotton, 10s.
Willia' Daves, 2s.
George Carter, 4s.
Richard Field, 1s.

Summ is £4.5s.

CUMNOR

[ff.16-16a (three long pages), in two columns. Most names on f.16r and the first column of 16v have an 'x' preceding them, and some a further 'x' following them. There are no signatures (apart from the Vicar's at the end), so these cannot mean the person's mark.]

***Comner** Parish :*
Com : Berkes.

Their names who have Protested. 1641. [252]

[f.16r, col. 1]
Mr Willm. Lanes se:
Willm. Lane iun:
Anthony Read
Henry Taylor
Jeffery Barnes
Richard Perry
John Perry sen:
John Perry iun:
James Perry iun:
Thomas Smith
Richard Gasey
Willm. Denman
Thos. Hart
Richard Slow
Robert Collis
Willm. Perry sen:
Willm. Perry iun:
Samuel Denny
John Ruffin sen:
Willm. Ruffin
Tho: Ruffin
John Ruffin iun:
Willm. Nevel sen:
Willm. Nevell iun:
John Blackman
Rich Blackman
Tho: Howell
Rich: Fowler
Humfrey Quainton
Mr Robert Phillipson
Mr Willm. Philipson *[sic]*
James Greening
Robt. Sivers
Rice Carpenter
Thomas Flowre
John Smith
Henry Storry
Francis White
Edward Bachelour
Bryan Bowghen
John Eldridge
Henry Hutt
John Pead
John Holding
Anthony Tame
Thomas Wernham
Toby Wernham
Henry Southrick
Willm. Bond sen:
Willm. Bond iun:
James Perry se:
Willm. Gyles sen:
Willm. Gyles iun:
Richard Stibb
Nicolas Feild
Henry Adams
John Neale
Richard Sadler
Stephen Francklin
John White
John Martin
James Davis
John Glover
John Hedges
Francis Tanner
Arthur Castle
Edward Cox
[f.16r, col. 2]
Robert Francklin
Thomas Pettipher
Thomas Drope
George Ives
Henry Ives
Thomas Ivy
Thomas Tomlins
[*name deleted:* John B--ks]
John Beechy
John Higs
Nicolas Quainton
Rich: Hall
Willm. Langley
Martin Langley
Willyam Spooner *[added later]*

*[**Assessment**. Membrane 2, following on Abingdon.]*

***Cumner** in Membris:*
Cumner, Hinwood [Henwood] and Bradly

William Lane, £1.5d.
William Lane *[sic]*, 18s.
Richard Carpender, 2s.5d.
William Bond, 18s.4½d.
Joseph Fletcher, 9s.
William Perry, 1s.3½d.
Richard Stibbs, 10s.2½d.
John Belcher, 4s.1d.
Tho: Ivy, 4s.1d.
Henry Hutt, 4s.1d.
George Nicholes, 8s.2d.
Willia' Perry, 8s.2d.
Richard Perry, 8s.2d.
John Perry, 4s.1d.
Anthony Buckner, 4s.1d.
Humfry Quenton, 1s.
Tho: Drope, Clerke, 7s.½d.
Tho. Hauell [*or* Havell], 1s.¼d.
Tho: Wirdnam, 11s.2¾d.
John Hodges, 1s.¼d.
Richard Badcocke, 12s.3d.
Edward Stevens, 4s.1d.
Edward Wray Esqr., 8s.2d.
Elizabeth Ivie, 2s.½d.
Robert Phillipson, 6d.
John Peade, 1s.6d.
John Martin, 1s.6d.
John Glover, 1s.6d.
Widdow Childe, 6d.
Stephen Francklen, 6d.
Richard Gasey, 6d.
John Eldridge, 2s.
John Ruffen, 8s.2d.

Sume is £9.5s.

Chauley *[Chawley] tithing*
[f.16r. col. 2]
Mr John Peacocke
Mr Thomas Holt
Richard Bowell
Francis Cotmore
John Hopkins
Thomas Leech
Henry Godfrey sen.
Willm. Godfrey
Willm. Bruce
Anthony Buckner
John Buckner
Thomas Moulden
Martin Langley

*[**Assessment.** Membrane 2, following on Cumnor.]*

Chawley
John Tudball, gent., £1.1s.
John Peacocke, gent., 12s.
John Hopkins, 8s.
Henry Godfrey, 8s.
John Coxe, 4s.
John Sambach, 3s.
Tho: Moulder, 1s.
Anthony Clapton, docter, 2s.

Sum is £2.19s.

Botley *tithing*
[f.16r. col. 2]
Thomas Dalbie
Richard Walter
Richard Corbet
Thomas George
Joseph Cantwell
Thomas Write
John Sambach
Philip Sambach
Simon Colgrove
Thomas Prior
John Collingborne se:
John Collingborne iu:
Thomas Broughton
Henry Broughton
Thomas Godfrey
James Rippingale
[*deleted:* Robert C----gwell(?)]
Willm. Cantwell

*[**Assessment.** Membrane 2, following on Hill End.]*

Botley
John Peacock, gent., 5s.6d.
John Sambach, 5s.6d.
Anthony Clapto:, doctor, 5s.6d.
Robt. Cantwell, 5s.6d.
John Tudball, gent., 1s.10d.
Alice Browton, widdow, 3s.8d.
Tho: Davis, 1s.10d.
Robt: Andrews, 1s.10d.
Tho: Wright, 1s.10d.
Willia' Leavine, gent., 7s.

Sume is £2.

Hillend *[Hill End] Tyth:*
[f.16r. col. 2]
Thomas Davis
Willm. Davis
Willm. Twinch
Richard Elliman
Daniell Hawkes
Richard Stiles
John Noble
Thomas Rodes
Rich: Pinnock
[f.16v, col. 1]
Mr Francis Peacocke
Robt. Feild
Besels Geering
John Speene se:
John Speene iu:
Willm. Stiles
Anthony Feild

*[**Assessment.** Membrane 2, following on Chawley.]*

Hillend
John Peacock, gent., 5s.
Robt., Bowle, 2s.6d., *Affid.*
Francis Peacock, gent., 7s.6d.
Tho. Davis, 7s.6d.
Henry Godfrey, 5s.
Edmond Riggins, 6s.
John Cox, 6s.6d.
John Speene, 10s.
William Cheyney, 10s.
John Noble, 2s.6d.

Sum is £3.2s.6d.

Whitley *[Tything]*

*[**Assessment.** Membrane 2, following on Botley.]*

Robt. Philipson, £1.2s.
Edward Dudson, 1s.
Joane Langley, 6s.
Richard Hall, 1s.6d.
John Hedges, 9d.
Robt Franckley, 9d., *Affid.*

Sume is £2.3s.

Stroud *Tything*

[f.16v. col. 1]
Tho: Ring
Rich: Sadler
Henry Taylor
Richard Broughton
Mathew Dod
Rich: Dod
Tho: Speakman
Deodatus Collis
Tho: Moulder
Simon Mannings
Martin Langley
James Collingborne
John Smith
Richard Townsend
Tho: Dod
Thomas Heywood
Alexander Heywood
John Neat
Thomas Orchard
John Foord
Henry Herbert

*[**Assessment.** Membrane 2, following on Whitley.]*

Stroude
John Whisler, Esq., 12s.6d.
Richard Barton, 12s.6d.
Jacob Stevens, 8s.4d.
Deodatus Collins, 8s.5d.
Tho: Ringe, 8s.5d.
Stephen Fayrebeard, 4s.2d.
Henry Tayler, 4s.2d.

Sume is £2.18s.6d.

***Swinford** [Tithing]*

*[**Assessment**. Membrane 2, following on Stroud.]*

Edmond Dunche, Esqr., £3.5s.
Thomas Hagword, 4s.

South Hinksey

[f.16v, col. 2]
Willm. Mason
John Gardiner
Thomas Baseley
Francis Baseley
Robt. Webb
Robert Prince
Rich: Wiggins
Tho: Jacob
Tho: Eldridge
Daniel Peirse
Thomas Peirse
John Smith
John Kempe
John Thrift
John Edmunds
Willm. Anscoe
John Williams
Tho. Taylor
John Ellis
John Hillocke
Tho. Fawkner sen:
Tho. Faukner iun:
Joseph Fawkner
Rich: Carwood
Bennet Baseley
Christopher Foord
Hugh Collins
Rich: Awman
Tho: Gardiner
Michael Gardiner
Anthony Gardiner
Robert Parker
Richard Fawkner
John Coleman
Thomas Ford
William Whitfeild
John Willis

*[**Assessment**. Membrane 4, following on Sunningwell.]*

Southinksey
S'r Francis Norris, 17s.10½d.
Daniell Bateman, gent., 10s.
Mrs Cristian Smith, £1.0s.6d.
Olliver Smith, gent., 1s.6d.
Mr Stevens, 3s.3d.
Margret Pearce, vid., 8s.1d.
Margret Jacobe, vid., 6s.6d.
Alfred Raunce, 4s.2d.
Robt. Prince, 6s.6d.
Tho: Pearce,, 1s.
Richard Wiggens, 3s.3d.
John Gardiner, 2s.
Alice Eldridge, vid., 3s.3d.
[Membrane 5]
William Whitfield, 3s.3d.
John Willis, 9s.8d.
Peter Johnson, 8d.
Tho: Jacobe, 1s.8d.
Tho: Gardner, 10d.
Cristofer Foord, 1s.7½d
Tho: Beasley, 1s.6d.
Richard Pearce, *Recu.*, 6s.6d.
Richard Goodyard, *Recu.*, 6s.6d.
Avis Pearce, *Recu. & p'old*, 1s.4d.
Elizabeth Anscoe[?], *Recu. & p'old*, 1s.4d.

Sum is £6.2s.9d.

***Wotton** [Wootton] tything*

[f.16a-r, col. 1]
Rich: Badcocke
Edward Badcock
Willm. Badcock
Willm. Woodley
John Cornish
Thomas Richards
John Buckingham
John Tubb
Leonard Haukins
Edward Hilliard
John Badcock
Jacob Heys
John Adkins
Willm. Stiles
Willm. Badcock
Willm. Bond
Willm. Griffin
John Rose
John Battin
John Bond
Rich: Parker
George Parsons
Fran: Stiles
Peter Barfoote
Willm. Atkins
Rich: Vicars
Tho: Brickland
Phillip Davis
John Paty
John Stockbridge
Nicholas Mayoh
Richard Broughton
Willm. Bowell
Edward Orpood
John Faukner
Tho: Warner
Rich: Hore
Rich: Rose

*[**Assessment**. Membrane 3, following Dry Sandford.]*

Wootton
George Hade Esq., £2.18s.6d.
William Stevens, 3s.1d.
Richard Badcocke, 9s.
Avis Mayowe, vid., 6s.
Richard Broughton, 1s.6d.
Thomas Coxe, 1s.
Mr Barton, 6s.2d.
Widdow Bowell, 7s.8d.
William Badcocke, 12s.4d.
William Woodley, 9s.
Widdow Badcocke, 7s.3d.
Widdow Bond, 9s.
Thomas Richards, 4s.5d.
Widdow Trewlocke, 7s.3d.
Nicholas Mayowe, 4s.7d.
Widdow Mayowe, 3s.1d.

Sume is £7.10s.

North Hincksey

[f.16a-r, col. 2]
Richard Stone
Roger Stone
Richard Smith
Tho: Baker
Robt: Archer
John Halloway
Henry Hall
Edward Greene
George Nicols
Christopher Andrews
Thomas Nicols
Henry Costard
Robt. Boordman
Tho: Horne
Tho: Billinsley
Willm. Street
Thomas Cox
John White
Walter Gerry
Willm. Macham
John Nicols
George Howell
Mr Finmores
Andrew Wilkins
Daniel White
Thos: Willis
Edward Wills
John Chapman

Richard Pearse, Richard Goodyeare, both Recusants, stout ones [2]

All the Rest have protested & have nott refused for ought that I doe know, nither will they when they know of it as I presume beeing sick some or some not summoned for when I can not stay, beeing called uppon for my returne.
Thomas Drope, *Vicar ibidem.*

*[**Assessment.** Membrane 4, following Wytham.]*

North Hincksey
Olliver Smith, gent., 5s.
Mr Hilliard, 5s.
Tho: Dalbie, 5s.
Mr Wallis, 3s.7d.
Mr Leavens, 7s.2d.
Mr Best, 14s.4d.
Willia' Finmore sen., 17s.11d.
William Finmoore ju', 7s.2d.
Edward Willis, 7s.2d.
Tho: Nicholes, 7s.2d.
Tho: Willis, £1.1s.6d.
John Nicholes, 3s.7d.
Daniell White, 3s.7d.
George Howell, 2s.6d.
John Davis, 3s.
Edward Greene, 1s.
Willia' Streete, 1s.
Roger Stone, 1s.
John Chapman, 6d.
Robt. Androws [*or* Andrews], 1s.

Sume £5.18s.2d.

DRAYTON [97]

[f.16b. In three columns. The heading is in very handsome calligraphy.]

***Drayton**, Ock Hundred. March 2, 1641.*

The names of the Inhabitants of Drayton which have taken the protestation in the p'sence of John Stone, minister, Bartholomew Weston, constable, Edward Terrald, John Bartlett, Church wardens, Watler*[sic]* Terrald, Robert Hobbs, overseers of Drayton, by virtue of an order sent from ye p'laiment*[sic] [Terrald appears to have been altered from Turrald]*.

[f.16b-r, col. 1]
John Peerce
Thomas Knapp
John Hunt
Wm. Willmott
Avery Terrald
Edward Wicks
Richard Haukins
Fancis*[sic]* Smithe
John Hobbs senr.
John Hobb ju.
Richard Hobbs
Thomas Wicks
Joseph Aldworth
Richard Aldworth
Marke Hatt
John Robens
Richard Billingley
Frncis*[sic]* Smith ju.
Robert Ley
William Harris
Robert Terrald
Walter Thurch
Robert Pounnd

Thomas Smith
Nicholas Chare
Avery Simpson
Peeter Chare
Richard Pembroke
Cutbert Tubb
Robt. Harris
Richard Nevill
Henrie Bernard
Thomas Hunt
William Terrald jun.
Avery Bilson
Richard Hobbs
William Greene
Avery Hobbs
[f.16b-r, col. 2]
William Aldworh*[sic]*
Robert Robens Ju.
Robert Nicholls
John Hobbs
John Walker
Thomas Aldworth
John Smith
Wm. Clarke
John Bilson
Edmund Morse
Wm. Hunt se.
Richard Bilson
Robt. Hunt
Wm. Terrald se.
Francis Hatt
Wm. Champion
Wm. Simpson
Thomas Chare
Robert Wilmott
Richard West
Robert Roberes
Edward Weston
Willm. Bilson
John Jeffery
Thomas Pemerton
Robert Bernard
Wm. Bilson ju.
Richard Higgins
William Thatcher
Robert White
Wm. Terrald senr.
Thomas Wilmott
Avery Hobb ju.
William LLoyd*[sic]*
Robert Brooks
William Hunt Ju.
Robert Terrald ju.
Richard Digweed
Thomas Hatt
[f.16b-r, col 3]
Thomas Terrald ju.
Avery Terrald ju.
Simon Watts
Wm. Hunt ju.
Anthoney Arden
William Feild
John Gibbs
John Hobbs
Richard Slatter
Thomas Robenson
Anthoney Bilson se.
Anthoney Bilson ju.
John Weston
Robert Hobbs

John Stone, *minister*
Edward Terrald his marke,
John Bartlett,
Church wardens
Walter Terrald his marke,
Robert Hobbs his marke,
overseers

DIDCOT

[f.17, in one column.]

A note [of all - *deleted*] of ye Inhabitants of Dudcott in ye Countie Berks, who have taken the Protestation, whose names are here subscribed. [36]

Richard Bolter
William Smith senier
William Smith junier
Edward Lasley
Edward Tirrole senier
Edward Tirrole junier
Robert Smith
John Tayler
Robert Torrole
Richard Smith senier
Nicolas Fuller
James Lee
Thomas Moulden
Richard Parsones
Edward Sayer senier
Edward Sayer junier
John Curtis
Thomas Godfrey
William Harris
Joseph Sayer
Edward Sayer
John Bond
John Fleare [*or* Floore]
John Wates
Robert Smith
John Fox
Richard Smith
John Parkins
Richard Blake senior
Robert Rowland

None within our parish that refusseth it
Richard Bristow.

Israell Sawyer, *Const.*
Richard Blake, The marke
of Richard Horsley,
Church Wardens
William Hall, Willia' Smith,
Overseers

FRILFORD [31]

[f.18, in one column. This has an unusual layout, most lines preceded by 'Item' and consisting of three names, except for the last two.]

Imprimis, John Pead, Robert [William *deleted*] Pead, Thomas Tomkines
Item, Grigory Keatte, Thomas Keatte, William Harris
Item, Hendry Bunce, John Boulles, Thomas Manns
Item, John Norkett, Andrue Welles, Richard Welles
Item, John Smith, Hendry Haines, John Facknerr
Item, John Dickenson, Thomas Dod, Richard Coxe
Item, John Childry, Thomas Welles, Thomas Dooe
Item, Hendry Shiprey, John Pusie, Richard Kinere[?]
Item, Richard Finpee [*or* Kinene?], Robert Knape, William Ayeres
Item, William Burnett
Joh Fawkner

All those whose names are above written have taken the p'testacon & none have refused.

Ita testor

Tho: Hall, *vic de Marcham*
Richard Aldworth, *Churchwarden*
Henry Peade
Edward Sheppery
Richard Knape *[Constable]*

FYFIELD

[f.19, in two columns.]

***Fifield**, Berks.*

The Names of the Inhabitants of Fifield in the County of Berks in Ocke Hundred who have taken the Late Protestacon: [81]

[f.19r, col. 1]
John Pierce, *Minist'r*
Edward Smalbone, *Constable*
Edward Carter, Willya' Bartholomew, *Church wardens*
Humphry Greenwaye, John Gayland, *Over-seers*

John Bullock sen.
Henry Hodghson*[sic]*
Richard Keene
Willyam Peade
Willyam Stone sen.
Ralph Whiseler
Richard Bullock
Benedict Bullock sen.
Nicholas Batt
Simon Ferriman
Edward White
Richard Couldry
Walter Preston
John Jones
Ralph Preston
Willyam Norman
Thomas Fisher
John Lay
John Stone
Thomas Carter
Thomas Haines
Henry Haines
Thomas Cock
George Twinch
Richard Coxe
Christopher Munden
Willyam Stone junr.
John Bullock junr.
Thomas Miles
Isaac Walter
Edmund Smalbone
John Beecham
Christopher Newman
Roger Newman
Willyam Walter
Oliver Townesend
Hugh Ellis
James Stone
Richard Ellis
Benedict Bullock ju.
Richard Dawson
Humphry Collins
Willyam Greenway
Humphry Greenway
Francis Sheene
Martin Leonard
Richard Surman
Richard Guydon
[f.19r, col. 2]
Henry Greene
Francis Norman
Fettiplace Young
John Greene
Richard Leonard
James Mascoll
Thomas Walter
Thomas Wyatt
James Archer
Henry Cocke
James Preston
Willyam Lay
Edmund Surman
Simon Couldry
Richard Keene ju.
Steeven Kember
Edward Greene
Robert Kember junr.
John Church
Robert Kember sen.
Willyam Greene
Richard Reade
Francis Coxe
John Waters
Isaac Batt
Thomas Crippes
John Young

All these whose Names are here described beinge the whole number of the Inhabitants of Fifield from Eighteene yeeres of age & upwards, Have taken the Late Protestation in the p'sence of us, there being none in o'r parish that have refused.

John Pierce, *Minist'r*
the marke of Edward Smalbone, *Constable*
The marke of Edward Carter, William Bartholim, *Church-wardens*
the marke of Humphry Greenway, the marke of John Gayland, *Overseers*

GARFORD (in Marcham)

[f.20, in one column.]

The Names of the Inhabitants of Garford in the p'ish of Marcham who have taken the protestation. [33]

James Stone, *Constable*, &
Nicholas Badcocke, *Church wardens*
Willya' Young,
Richard Doe, *Overseers*

John Bunce
Simon Badcocke
Thomas Badcocke
Henry Badcocke
Joseph Badcocke
Francis Badcocke
Henry Wilkins
John Stone
Thomas Rowland
Richard Louch
James Bagnoll
Willyam Heyward
Thomas Heyward
Robert Doe
Willyam Atkins
Thomas Pecke
Benjamin Browne
John Hansaker
Peter Howlett
Gregory Wilder
Robert Compton
John Rogers
Richard Impe
Thomas Ferriman
Austen Varney
John Pendegrace
Robert Gidding
Giles Fowler

All those whose Names are here described beinge the whole number of the Inhabitants have taken the protestation in the p'sence of me, none refused.

John Pierce, *Curatt*
Nicho: Badcocke, *Churchwarden*
James Stone, *Cunstable and Churchwarden*
William Younge, the m'k of Richard Doe, *Overseers*

GRANDPONT (Cumnor)

[f.21, in one column.]

The names of the Inhabitants of Grandpold *[Grandpont]* within the p'ish of Comner in the County of Berks w'ch have taken the Protestation accordinge to the order of Parliam't. [13]

Alfred Raunce
Robert Panton
Willm. Edgly
John Richason senr.
John Richason Junr.
George Treadwell
Lawrence Willyer
Thomas Jerome
Edward Fipps
Thomas Slatter
Sacharias Wallington
Richard Gardiner
Mathew Richardson

Those whose names are above written tooke the p'testacon before me voluntarilye, havieng no Officers w'thin that Tything to certifye
Ch. Tooker.

*[**Assessment.** Membrane 3, following Barton and Northcourt.]*

Grenpoole

Mathew Langleigh, 4s.
Richard Farmer, 8s.4d.
William Freeman, 8s.
Tho: Edgerlie, 8s.
George Hilliard, 4s.
Corpus Cristi Colledge land 4s.
Alphred Raunce, 4s.3d.
John Mander, 8s.
Mary Deane[?], vid., 4s.
Edmond Cozens, 4s.
Robt. Pantinge, 2s.

Sum £2.18s.7d.

EAST and WEST HAGBOURNE

[f.22, in four columns.]

A Bill of all the names and surnames of those p'sons in East & West Hagborne w'ch have taken their protestacon. [158]

[f.22r, col. 1]

Hugh Keate senior, gent.,
and his fower sonnes
Hugh Keate
John Keate
William Keate iun'r
Paul Keate iun'r
and also his five servants:
William Bowles
William Armstrong
Thomas Kent
James Davis and
William Sadler
Thomas Burden and
John Michell his servant
Gregory Bushnell
John Kirfoot
John Dixon
William Bushnell
William Smith
Robert Smith
William Bold
Richard Simmons
Richard Child
Thomas Humfrey
Thomas Griffith
Henry Armstrong
Thomas Smith
Richard Harwood &
John Blandy his man
Robert Hide
Nicholas Wicke
Arthur Rowe
William Hide
John Annger
Thomas Holloway
Laurence Acres senior
Laurence Acres his sonne
John Fluddier
Richard Pumfrey
William Heath
Henry Harrington

[f.22r, col. 2]

Edmund Bosley
Henry Bosley
John Bosley
William Armstrong
Edward Burnham
William Wise
William Stacie
Thomas Wright
Thomas Annger junr.
Gregory Acres
William Acres
Henry Steevens
Alexander Farmer
Thomas Kente &
Edward Stiles his man,
John Stacie &
John Bird his servants
Roger Lewendon
Thomas Poole
Samuel Fulbrookes
Robert Hore
William Hore
Thomas Hooker
Thomas Annger senr.
Richard Thatcher
John Dandridge
Thomas Wicks
John Harwood
Hugh Childe
John Carter
Henry Baggs
William Bunce &
Richard Nevell his man
Ralph Keate
Fraunces Keate
Richard Sayer &
Thomas *[blank]* his
servant
Brooke Tirrold
Henry Bunce

[f.22r, col. 3]

Henry Pinck
Thomas Bushnell
William Bushnell
Andrew Apsbon &
John Beache his man
Richard Armstrong
Ralph Sayer &
Robert Sayer his sonne
John Whistler
Ralph Whistler
William Platt
Ralph Platt
William Slade senior
John Slade
William Slade junr.
John Lawrence his man
William Sayer senior
Robert Sayer senior of
Coscott and Robert Sayer
junr.
Richard Sayer
William Ward
John Read
John Kember and
John Willicutt(?)
Richard Simmes
John Simmes
Thomas Prior
William Hughes
John Basley
Thomas Richesson
Gregory Dearlove
Andrew Blake
William Sayer junr.
Ralphe Simmes
Hugh Harwood
Robert Roumsey,
servant to Brook Tirrold
Thomas Wilder
Thomas Gammon

[f.22r, col. 4]

West Hagborne

Henry Cressell
Robert Walter
Robert Townesend
Stephen Silence
James Perker
William Tirold senior
William Burrough
Thomas Field
Gyles Hasley
William Ling
Avery Dearlove
Robert Tirold

William Tirrold junr.
Richard Thatcher
Gregory Coxhead
William Wellman senior
William Welman jun.
Richard Sayer
Robert Winter
William Louch
Thomas Goode
Thomas Asheridge
Mathew Dearlove
William Dearlove

Peter Buttler
John Rose
Thomas Hutchens
John Fray
Thomas Bosley
Stephen Clift
Richard Coxhead
Fraunces Coxhead
John Stacy
Avery Reinolds
Richard Cressell
Henry Fluddier

All these sev'all p'sons above written respectively have taken their p'testacon accordingly

Richard Bristow, *Vicar*
Richard Simmes,
Henry Fludier his mark, *Constables*
John Dandredge, John Stacy, *Churchwardens*
Henry Bunce by his mark, *Overseers [sic]*

HARWELL

[ff.23-26, single columns.]

Apud ***Harwell*** *Septimo die mensis Martii Anno Dni 1641.*

The names and surnames of the p'ishon'rs and inhabitants of Harwell aforesaid in the countie of Berks, that have taken the p'testation before Hugh LLoide, vicar of Harwell aforesaid, John Woodley and Steven Keate, Constables, John Loder and Robert Rowland, Churchwardens, Sallomon Aldworth and Richard Elderfeild, Overseers of the poore there, are here under named as followeth. [128]

[f.23r]
Robert Loder senr.
Robert Loder junr.
John Loder senr.
Richard Wise
John Jennens
John Rowland
John Burgman
John Wise senr.
John Keate senr.
Robert Poope senr.
Nicholas Keate junr.
Robert Lydale

Fraunçis Elderfeild
John Knapp
Nicholas Keate senr.
John Wise junr.
John Poope
Robert Keate
Lewes Hansonne
Steven Arnold
Hugh Aldworth
John Mose
John Loder als Austen
Richard Weston senr.
Thomas Morton
Mathew Talbutt
John Kinge senr.
John Kinge junr.
Robert Wise senr.
John Nutt
William Burges
[f.24r]
John Wright
John Hearne
Phillipp Loder
John Woodley Senr.
William Woodley *[*senr., *deleted]*
Robert Waterman
Edward Waterman
Edward Symons senr.
Edward Symons junr.
Richard Keate senr.
Adam Weston
Leonard Alline
George Keate

Thomas Keate
John Rose senr.
David Rose
John Rose junr.
Lewes Hasley
Anthony Weston
Edward Weston
William Weston junr.
John Coule
William Chaunclor
Robert Wise junr.
Edward Burgman
William Androse
Thomas James
William White
Edward Yeates
William Dunsdon
John Dunsdon
John Keate junr.
Robert Bullocke
John Yeates
Richard Weston junr.
Adam Jennens
William Weston senr.
John Weston
John Bosley
Richard Symons
Thomas Spindler
John Bond
[f.25r]
Thomas Flexman
John Bewton
Richard Baylie
Henry Eve

Steven Keate junr.
William Weston
John Loder als Austen junr.
John Aldworth
Henry Bagge
William Coate
Frauncis Symons
Thomas Wilkins
William Wise
James Hasley
John Symons
Robert Pearce
Marke Keate
Ambrose Keate
John Lundon
Richard Warricke
Robert Fortie
Robert Knige *[sic]*
John Fortie
Thomas Fortie
Thomas Loder
William Absolon
Robert Dunsdon
John Casborne
Thomas Newporte
Frauncis Poynter
Andrew Rumble
Richard Staite
John Wise
Bartholomew Brumingem
Adam Loder
Frauncis Warricke
Richard Symons
Thomas Goddine
John Frauncis
Robert Symons
[f.26r]
John Porter
William Yeates
John Skeate
John Warricke
William Pearse
Henry Greene
Robert Poope
Richard Keate junr.

Richard Keate the sonne of Frauncis Keate and Thomas Tanner als Coopper beinge warned by the Officers to come to the place of mettinge to take the p'testacon refussed to come.

Three old, poore, impotent and feeble men *(vidlt.)* John Waterman, Edward Keate and John Giles, beinge warned by the Officers, were not able to Come to the place of mettinge, have not taken the p'testacon, But as longe as they were able they Constantlie came to Church.

All the rest of taken the p'testacon.

To the trueth hereof wee have hereunto sett our names *(vidlt)*

Hugh LLoide, *vic. of Harwell*
John Woodley,
Steven Keate, *Constables*
John Loder, Robert Rowland, *Churchwardens*
Salomon Aldworth,
Richard Elderfield,
Ov'seers of the poore.

KENNINGTON (in Radley and Sunningwell)

*[**Assessment.** Membrane 4, following on North Hinksey]*

Berry Meads, £1. *Affid.*
Egrones *[blank]*, 5s.
Anthony Hurlock, gent., £1.
John Smith, 10s.
Joane Swadlinge ju', vid., 10s.
Joane Swadlinge sen., vid., 5s.
Widdow Ayres, 5s., *Affid.*
William Curten, 5s.
John Chilton, 5s.
Willia' Hall, 3s.
Tho: Swadlinge, 2s.
Edward Swadlinge, 1s.
Widdow Prince, *Recu.*, 2s.6d.

Sume is £4.19s.

KINGSTON BAGPUIZE [39]

[f.27r, in two columns.]

Kingstone Bagpuze,
Comite. Barks.
1641, March 6th

[f.27r, col. 1]
Richard Castell
Robert Stevinsonn
John Gould
Arthur Stevinsonn
Andrew Stevinsonn
Hughe Ceely
William Lovesley
Thomas Draper
William Heycraft
Mathew Roberts
Richard Morris
William Ingram
John Drew
Cutbeard Drew
William Walter
William Tomkins
William Buckley
John Tubb

Thomas Woodbridge
Richard Stone
James Stevinsonn
Facke Sexton
Thomas Haynes
William Day
John Rhoades
Daniell Eustus
Andrew Stone
Christopher Keene
Edward Broman
James Burgis
Andrew Stevens
[f.27r, col. 2]
William Downe
Thomas Tame
John Wiblin
John Clarke

All these have taken the protes-tation made by the Honourable house of Commons Assembled in Parliament on Sunday the 6th of March.

John Sone, *Curate ibid.*
The marke of John Wheeler,
John Stevinson, *guard.*
the marke of Francis Yeat, *Constable*

[Little and Long Wittenham - see pages 203-204]

LYFORD

[f.29, in two columns; f.29 logically precedes f.28. A difficult hand marred by blots; some apparent signatures.]

***Lyford** in com. Berks.*

A Returne of the names of those persones that have taken the vowe and Protestacon. [45]

[f.29r, col. 1]
Jo: Ayshcombe
Willia' Ayshcombe
Rich: Ayshcombe
Rychard Wild
Fra: Derbey Esq.[?]
Tho: Chesterman Esq.[?]
Edmond Pip[er] [?]
Will: Lay senr.
Henry Stone
John Elliott
John Stil[e-] [? or Stille]]
Thomas Wild
Walter Spenser
Robert Tame
John Hobbs
Anthony Narroway
Richard Keepe
Thomas Grunere [?Gunnere]
John Kinge
Richard Surd
William Fullway
William Swaine
Edward Sayre
Richard Belcher
Thomas Strange
William Banks
Edward Badnoll
Richard Drew
William Cox
Peter Foster
Oliver Wild
John Gibbs
Richard Shingleton
[f.29r, col. 2]
William Tubbe
John Parker
William Ley Junr.
Izacke Wild
Edwarde Ellis
William Chunne
Richarde Newman
Robert Rate

Thomas Jauncy, *Vicar*
Thomas Cox, *Constable*
Richard Cox,
Edwarde Dawstyne, *Church Wardens*

[f.28]
The Returne of the Minister and Church-wardens & Constable of Lyford concerninge the Protestation.

Right Worshipfull These are to certify that all Men w'th us at Lyford above the adge of Eighteene yeares have taken the Protestation except certen persons mentioned and subscribed In this returne.

The Returne of the Names of such Persons that have not taken the Protestation at Lyford Chappell w'hin the Parish of Hannye, being tendered unto them.

Thomas Yates Esquier
William Yates sonne of Thomas Yates
William Cullam, husbandman

Witnesses
Thomas Jauncye, *Vicar at Lyford*
Thomas Cox, *Constable*
Richard Cox, Edward Dusten, *Churchwardens*

MARCHAM

[ff.30-31, in three columns; virtually all names are preceded by a cross, except for Symon Hawkins and Thomas Hawkins senr.]

***Marcham** this 4th of March Anno. Dom. 1641.*

A note of all the names and sirnames of all men that are above the age of Eighteene yeares that have taken <there Othes of> the Protestacion that is now <..rantted> commended by the <acte of> Parlement Whosse Names are here under Written. [113]

Imprimis, Thomas Hall, *Vicker*

[f.30r, col. 1]

Alban Piggott Esqr.
Frances Piggott, gent.
Thomas Shury
Drury Shury
William Wriggylsworth
Edmond Wrigelsworth
Edmond Riggins
William Tirrall
Richard Hawkins
John Shury
John Swayne
John Prince
John Bunce
Richard Whitt
Phillip Prince
John Hawkins
John Watts
William Bunce
Frances Shury
John Bowles
Thomas Pusi
Richard Hopkins
Henery Newman
Richard Cozens
Edmond Jinnon
Alvery Bingly
Frances Belcher
William Tame
Marke Loder
Faithfull Prince
William Higgins

[f.30r, col. 2]

Patrick Boyze
Thomas Daniell
Richard Castell
Robert Tame
John Chapman
Richard Stacie
Thomas Hopkins
Barton Keatt
Thomas Hawkins junr.
John Hopkins
Frances Tame
Daniell Chapman
Frances Chapman
Thomas Prince
Richard Johnson
Richard Bond
John Cozens
Hugh Leeke
Symon Hawkins senr
Thomas Chapman
Thomas Horsly
William Higgins junr.
Thomas Hawkins senr.
John Higgins senr.
John Higgins junr.
William Cox
William Chapman
Henry Spendler
John Shury senr.
Richard Colls
William Lawrance
Richard Curtis
Thomas Ellioat

[f.30r, col. 3]

Thomas Browne
William Hinninge
Richard Halle
John Hale
Richard Sansome
John Blunte
Abraham Marshall
Tymothy Jarman junr.
John Elliman
Timothy Jarman senr.
Richard Tame
Robert Hawkins
Edward Busbey
John Hobbs
Symion Colls
Nickolis Smith
Symon Bond
Thomas Coldrey
Edward Castell
William Bowles
Richard Hawkins senr.
Richard Hawkins junr.
William Crofts junr.
Robert Hopkins
John Bedford
Henry Pryer
Phillip Prince senr.
Phillip Prince junr.
Richard Watts
Thomas Sanders
William Hawkins

[f.31r]

Richard Chapman
Symon Dean
Richard Clement
Henry Lougie
John Sandford
Richard Hobbs
William Pinell
John Newman
William Crofts
John Crofts
Thomas Hatton
Owen Aylworth
Peeter Kent
Frances Shury
Tho. Johnson
John Custen
Richard Shury

All those whose names are above written have taken the Pro-testacon & none have refused.

Ita est

Tho: Hall, *Vic. de Marcham*
Edmond Wrigglesworth, *High Constable*
Richard Hopkins, Richard Hawkins *[Churchwardens]*
Richard Cossene, Henry Newman *[Overseers]*

MILTON

[ff.32-33, in two columns, with signatures and marks (asterisked).]

***Milton**, Hundred de Ocke in Com. Berk.*

The names of those that have taken the P'testacon and subscribed their hands the fifte day of March Anno Dom. 1641 as followeth. [38]

[f.33r, col. 1]
Richard Mylles
William Weeks
Henry Smith
John Platt *
William Hickes *
Thomas Thomas *
John Neebes
John Jones *
Thomas Mott *
Henry Shray[?] *
John Keate *
Edmund Stevens
John Kent *
Thomas Platt *
William Greene *
Richard Ryme *
[f.33r, col. 2]
William Yateman
Lawrence Bestlye *
Thomas Cotes *
John Weston *
John Scarlett *
Thomas Cox *
Richard Bradfeilde *
Thomas Hore
Fran: Yateman
James Hore
Thomas Combe *
Stephen Kinge *
Edward Ludlowe *
William Weeks *
Francis Bentlye *
Nicholas Carpenter *

These abovewritten have taken the p'otestacon and subscribed their names in the p'sence of
John Keate, *Minister*
Richard Wickes, *Constable*
John Bewden *, Robarte Keate, *Churchwardens*
Richard Joyner, Richard Wickes, *ov'seers*

[f.32r]
Wee returne one John Yate who did not com in to take his protestacon and doeth refuse neither will he take itt. Hee is a servant to Mr William Yateman of Milton aforesaid.

This returne was made thus by the Parish.
C.T. [Charles Tooker]

NORTH MORETON

[ff.34-35, single columns.]

***North Mourton**, Berks.*

Die sexto Martii Anno Domini 1641.

A returne of the names of all those that have freely consented unto and willingly taken the vow or p'testaco' set forth by the honourable assembly of the house of p'liament. [65]

Before us
John Comyn, *Vic.*
John Gregory his marke, Nicholas Feild, *Churchwardens*
Ralph Feeld his marke, John Spooner his marke, *Ov'seers*

Mr Richard Bagnall
William Baker
John Mayne
Frances Plotte jun.
Frances Leaver senr.
Richard Grigory
Henry May
Henry Slade
Thomas Goldwine
Robert Grigory
Peter Wing
John Eyers
Clement Norcotte
Richard Feild
John Grigory senr.
Richard Colles
John Munt
Robert Mouldue[?]
Frances Plotte sen.
Andrew Grigory
Richard Hobgood
Richard White
Richard Slade
Edward Grigory
Henry Coxe
Thomas Low senr.
Richard Baker
Richard White jun.
William Poole senr.
Thomas Baker
Bartholomew Slade
Hugh Nicholas
Frances Leaver ju.
Willia. Leaver ju.
Willia. Baker
James Boseley
Thomas Leaver
[f.35]
Ralph Plotte
Willia, White
John Kerfoote
John Tadmartine

Richard Tayler
Richard Spooner
Richard Feeld senr.
Nicholas Wise
James Grigory
Richard Goldwine
Richard Feild ju.
Samuell Feild sen.
Samuell Feild junr.
Robert Huesley [*or* Hoesley]
Richard Poole
Willia' Norcotte
Richard Feild
Willia' Poole ju.
Thomas Low ju.
Robert Bond
Willia' Nicholas
Willia' Munt
James Munt

None in this p'ish refused the said p'testacon.
Nicholas Feild.

SOUTH MORETON

[f.36, in two columns.]

Martii 3 A'o. 1641.

The names of ye Inhabitants of ye parish of South Moreton in ye County of Berks who have taken ye Protestation (made by the Hon'ble House of Comons ye 3d of Maij last) in the presence of us whose names are subscribed ye day & yeare first above written. [66]

[f.36r, col. 1]
John Curtis
William Elmes
John Hambleton
John Arnold
Thomas Corderey th'elder
Francis Gregorie
John Corderey
Nicholas Harley
Edward Daniel
Mathewe Denley
Thomas Beach
Thomas Corderey ye yonger
John Norcott
William Wigginton
Nicholas Kirfoote
John Burges
Henry Graye
Henry Mathewe
John Sadler
William Ayres
William Whichlowe
Richard Dewe
Richard Fullbrooke
Thomas Knapp
Thomas Horsley
George Benham ye elder
Augustine Gardiner
John Boswell
Thomas Feild
Jacob Bennett
Giles Tillen
[f.36r, col. 2]
William Whistler
Bartholomewe Tarver [*or* Tawes?]
Clement Leaver
Bartholomewe Sims
Thomas Shadd
Richard Whichlowe
Woollstan Corderey
Nicholas Sims
Clement Sims
John Pratt
Charles Pratt
Michael Belchard
William Adkins
Nicholas Leaver
Edward Dewe ye yonger
George Benham ye yonger
William Norcott
Samuel Hore se.
Richard Norcott
Thomas Fullbrooke
Thomas Cordery minor
John Wigley
John Whichlowe
John Dewe
John Hareborne
Edward Leaver
Joseph Leaver
Charles Bowne
Antonie Gregorie
Thomas English ye elder
Thomas English ye yonger

All ye parishioners of South Moreton abovesaid who were att home att ye warninge being of ye age of 18 yeares & upwards, have taken ye foresaid protestation *[followed be several deleted words]*.

Edmund Leigh: *Rector ibid:*
The marke of Edward Dewe, *Constable*
Francis Styles, *Overseere*
John Stiles, *Churchwarden*

MOULSFORD [50]

[f.37, in two columns.]

***Moulsford**, Berks.*
1641, March: ye 6th

[f.37r, col.1]
Sr. Hen: Samborne. knt.
Hen: Samborne Esq.
Mr Will: Samborne, gen.
Mr John Whistler, gen.
John Leaver
Tho: Wright
Edm: Lovegrove
Luke Havill sen.
John Baker
Ed: Quelch
Rich: Collins
Luke White
John Sone
Tho: Havill
Rob: Baker
Ed: Lovegrove
Rich: Chalke
John Burrer
Rich: Cummin
John Breach
Tho: Cummin
Will: Singleton
Rich: Norman
Laurence Pecka[m]
[f.37r, col. 2]
Hugh Havill
Christ: Larner
Rich: Cummin
John Wilmott
Rob: Cokly
John Grey
George Moore
James Breach
Tho: Cummin
John Cox
John Purden
John Fuce
Rich: Bennet
Rob: Hoare
Will: Lovegrove
Andrew Singleton
Tho: Wilmot
Ed: Thorpe
John Bennett
Will: Bennett
Luke Havill iun.

All these protested on Sunday in ye afternoone being the sixt day of March, & there is none refuses, in regard, we have noe popish recusants.

Dan: Singleton, *Curat ibid.*
Fran. Cox *[mark], Church warden*
John King *[mark], Constable*
Hen. Carter *[mark]*, Rich. Quelch *[mark], over-seers*

RADLEY

[ff.38-39, in two columns, with signatures and marks (asterisked).]

The names of those that have taken the protestation in the parish of Radley, March 4, 1641. [81]

[f.38r, col. 1]
Jo. Curten
William White *
Henrie Crouch *
William Brookes *
Martin Crouch *
Robert Harwood *
Walter Coxe *
Walter Crouch *
Edward Coxe *
Thomas Cunstable *
Thomas Walker *[or* Walter *- name blotted]* *
[f.38r, col. 2]
John Willis *
Nicholas Willis *
John Willes
Edward Eling *
John Sawier sen. *
John Sawier jun. *
Henrie Avery sen. *
John Willis sen. *
James Bond *
Raphe Sawier *
Willm. Cheere *
Thomas Robinson *
John Gering *
Thomas Eling *
[f.38v, col. 1]
Tho. Halsey
Henry Stevenson *
Simon Badcocke *
John Stasie *
Edward Palmer *
Richard Eling *
Edward Ilsberrough *
Richard Dorset *
Andrewe Yonge *
John Twinch *
Charles Tayler
Walter Grove *
Henry Steere
John Cheiney *
Richard Haines *
John Timberly *
John Impe *
John Piggin *
William Carpenter *
[f.38v, col. 2]
Richard Porter *
William Cheiney *
Robert Impes *
William Crouch *
John Truelocke *
Thom' Harpar *

Thomas Trulocke *
Antony Grove *
Henrie Nicols *
John Avery *
Richard Arpud *
Francis Mault *
Edward Hunny *
John Trulocke *
Thomas White *
William Barnes *
[f.39r, col. 1]
Richard Wise *
William Crouch *
John Crouch *
Richard Cheiney *
William Curtyn
William Butler *
Edward Tomkins *
Benjamin Fisher *
John Swadling *
Edward Swadling *
Francis Gre[a]nway *
William Dorser [Dorset]
Thomas Niccolese
Martin Barnes *
Matthew Crouch *
[f.39r, col. 2]
Thomas Nicholls senior *
John Taylar

All these have taken this protestation and none of our parish have refused to take it.

John Herbert, *minister*
Henry Avery, *Churchwarden*
Thomas Harpar *, *Overseer of the poore*
Thomas Ayres *, *Overseer of the poore*

*[**Assessment.** Membrane 3, following Wootton.]*

Radly

S'r George Stonehowse, Bart., £4.1s.6d.
John Willis jun., 15s.
John Trewlocke, 9s.
John Gerrey, 6s.
William Crowch, 6s.6d.
Henry Nicholes, 9s.6d.
John Tayer, 4s.
Willia' White, 43s.
John Willis sen., 3s.
Martin Crouch, 7s.
John Curten, 3s.
Widdowe Shinne, 3s.
Mr Harbert, 3s.
Henry Avery sen., 6s,
Thomas Ayers, 3s.6d.
Thomas Harper, 3s.
Walter Crowch, 3s.
Walter Coxe, 4s.
Henry Avery jun., 3s.
Mrs Hyde, 9s.
S'r Thomas Reade, 9s.
The Widdow Barnes, 3s.
Thos. White, 1s.
Richard Wise, 1s.
James Bond, 1s.
Tho: Trewlocke, 1s.
Robt. Thorwood, 1s.
Tho: Robinson, 1s.
Widdow Porter, 1s.
Richard Porter, 1s.

Sum is £10.5s.

Thruppe

*[**Assessment.** Membrane 3, following Radley.]*

S'r Tho: Read, kn't, 6s.
John Gerrey, 12s.10d.
Richard Haynes, 3s.6d.
Richard Porter, 2s.4d.
Henry Avery, 2s.4d.
John Sawyer, 2s.4d.
Robt. Emps, 2d.
Mr Hyde, 2s.2d.

Sum is £1.12s.

SHIPPON

(township in Abingdon St. Helen)

[f.40, in one column.]

Shippon,
Hormore Hundred.

The names of the Inhabitants of Shippon w'ch have taken the p'testation according to an order of Parliament: March 7 1641. [18]

Raph Sherwood
John Theacher
Edward Sherwood
Robert Sim[?]
John Wyet
Thomas Corhelles [*or* Coxhelles?]
Willyam Robbensonn
John Thatcher
William Hute[?]
Jhon Boddington
Jhon Ednee
Jhon Henton
Hary Welles
Richard Overberye
Humfree Wisse
Raphe Nevell

None refused

A True p'testation Taking by The Church wardens and Tithing man of Shippon

Thomas North *[Constable and Churchwarden]*
Jhon Hawkines, *Church wardenes and Tithingman*

[Assessment - see page 198]

*[**Assessment.** membrane 4, following on Kennington.]*

Shippon

Doctor Walker, 19s.10d.
Raphe Sherwood, 15s.5d.
Wm. Weston, 18s.
Tho: North, 14s.1d.
John Wyett, 4s.2½d.
John Thatcher, 10s.
John Boddingdon, 8s.6d.
Bedford Stacie, 1s.5d.
Widdow Hawkins, 1s.6d.
Richard Badcock, parson, 9s.
William Bostock, parson, 4s.
Widdow Buffen, 4s.4d.
John Mitchell, 11s.4d.
John Wise, 1s.5d.
John Hawkins, 1s.5d.
William Hutt, 1s.5d.
Robt. Boddingdon, 2s.2½d.
Humfrey Wise, 2s.

Sume is £6.10s.1d.

STEVENTON [111+3]

[ff.41-42, in two columns, with signatures and marks (asterisked).]

March 6th: 1641.

The names of the Inhabitants of Steventon which have taken the protestation in the presence of Gabriell Harrison, Curate, Richard Weston, Constable, Willia' Smalebone & James Stone, churchwardens, Francis Hopkins & John Welles, Overseers, by virtue of an order sent from Parliament.

[f.41r, col. 1]
Richard Sayer
Walt. Doe
Tho. Doe
James Smalbon
Robert Weston
Henry Weston *
Nicholas Workes
Thomas Brickett *
John Barnes
Bryan Barr *
Willia' Smith *
Francis Bath *
Edward Humphrey *
Thomas Perse *
Bartholomew Spiser *
William Bennett *
William Edmunds *
Willia' Smith *
Thomas Hollowway *
William Johnson
Richard Barnes
Henry Stevens *
John Robinson
John Middleton *
John Garner *
Henry Ludler *
Willia' Rose *
Richard Robinson *
Thomas Powell *
Edmund Robins
Robert Harris *
[f.41r, col. 2]
Edward Stevens
William Stevens
Joshua Grove
Thomas Sympson *
Thomas Stevens
Robert Rhys [?]
William Doe
William Stampe
John White
Richard Smalebone *
Richard Trewlock
James Stone
Robert Weston
John Liner *
Francis White *
William Weston
Edward Gammon *
John Hunt *
John Lees *
Francis Steevens
Richard Hopkins *
Henry Smalebone *
Thomas Mansell *
Thomas Cooke *
Thomas Jefferey *
Richard Smalebone *
William Hamon
Edmond Pokinns
William Midelton
Thomas Middleton *
William Ludler *
Richard White *
Robert Welles *
Willia' Jeames *
[f.42r, col. 1]
Robert Lyford
John Edwards *
Willia' Clarke
Willia' Mosse *
Richard Cowdrey *
Willia' Whistler *
Richard White
Richard Arnoull
Willia' Gidding *
Jhon*[sic]* Hopkins
Richard Ludler *
Thomas Deyer *
Thomas Ellenger
Henry Hemming *
Willia' Birding *
Willia' Gidding *
Edward Dawson *
Thomas Hopkins
Willia' Stevens *
Robert Stevens
Richard Prittey *
Alexander Miles *
David Weston
Robert Welles *
Willia' Stevens *
Willia' Burrey *
John Brookes *
John Owen *
Henry Daniell *
Ambrose Adams *

Willia' Milles *
John Yeates *
John Milles *
Willia' Daniell*
John Westbrooke *
[f.42r, col. 2]
Richard Stevens *
Thomas Rose *
Willia' Symson *
Thomas Higgins *
John Goodenough *

This was performed in ye presence of us whose names are underwritten:

Gabriell Harriso', *Curate*
Richard Weston, *Constable*
Willia' Smalebone *. James Stone, *churchwardens*
Francis Hopkins, John Welles, *overseers*

None of ye parish refused, onely two upon necessary occasions were absent being Barge men & imployed in y'r vocations.

Gab: Harrison
James Stone
Richard Weston

STREATLEY [84]

[f.43, in three columns, with signatures and marks (asterisked).]

***Streatley**, Com. Berks.*
6 Martii 1641.

We the Inhabitants of Streatley whose names are here subscribed have taken the Protestation made by the house of Commons the third of May last past, upon the day & yeare above written.

[f.43r, col. 1]
John Harrison
Wm. Fruyn *
Robert Fruin [*or* Frain]
John Fruin [*or* Frain]
William Willson *
John Pocock *
John Higgs
Robert Higgs
Richard Butler *
Robert Chamberlin *
William Kirsell *
John Full
Richard Pawling *
Richard Skirmer *
Wm. Kinge *
John Michell *
Wm. Pinnock *
Thomas Marks *
Thomas Marks iun. *
Wm. Marks *
Salomon Endall *
Richard Clarke *
John Clarke *
John Denley
Thomas Denley *
Robert Davis *
Richard Sulham *
John Frizar *
Robert Ellyott
[f.43r, col. 2]
Alex. Ansland *
Daniell Laurence *
Daniell Laurence junr. *
John Ansland *
John South *
Wm. French *
John French *
John Wooddenton
William Wooddenton
Edward Stacy *
Henry Smith *
Henry Money *
John Money *
Richard Money *
Wm. Woodley *
Wm. Woodley junr. *
Robert Barnes *
Wm. Butler *
John Whicheiloe
Francis Ambrose *
Thomas Keene *
Tho. Hill *
John Pound *
John Butler *
John Butler junr. *
Hugh Winterburne *
Hugh Frizar *
Tho. Cox *
John Allin *
Hen. Acres *
John Beckford
Robert Beckford
[f.43r, col. 3]
John Baily
Rich. Morecock *
Tho. Butler *
Tho. Astell *
Rich. Shaw *
William Cox
Tho. Garter *
Nicholas Cox
Edward Butler *
Wm. Bowdry *
Hum. Bayly *
Nathaniell Bailie
John Bayly *
Rich. Griffith *
Tho. Burden *
Wm. Stone *
Wm. Knight *

The protestation was taken by the before written parties in the presence of
Gilbert Hinde, *vicar*
William Wooddenton *, *constable*
Willia' Higgs *,
George Stacy *, *Church wardens*
William Whistlar, Robert Skirmer *, *Overseers*

And none refused as they above.

SUNNINGWELL [60]

[ff.44-45, single columns, with signatures and marks (asterisked); a difficult hand marred by blots.]

[f.44r.]
The Parish of ***Suningwell.***

Anthony H....... [*or* L.......?]
William Sheref *
John Bradstock *
John Stevenson
John Harper *
Thomas Gerrye[?]
Thomas Adkins *
John Basele *
Edward Basselye *
Edward Hunye *
John Hall
Edward Hall junr.
Richard Hichman *
Richard Banckland *
William Kinge[?] *
John Michell *
Johne Bradley[?]
John Sherefe *
John Banckland
John Stevenson
John Hore *
Ambrose Stevinson
Cristofer Vinor *
Richard Pamer [Palmer] *
Robrt*[sic]* West
Francis[?] Plat
John West
Edward Hore
Thomas West *
John West *
William Cockse

[f.44v]
Gorg Stevenson *
William Sheppard *
John West *
Richard Bisley
Thomas Hore *
Gorge Alline *
Vallintine Turner *
Olliver Chaine *
John Hore *
William Holliy[?]
John Hollowell *
John Chanye *
Robert Cox *
Humfrey Gardner *
William Bew
John Chilton
Thomas West *
[Robert ..dins[?] *deleted*]
Peter Willis *
Thomas Weller(?)
Antony Adams *
Christover Blakman
Francis Grinafe [*or* Grinase?] *
Edward Willis *
William Simons *
Thomas Sandhill *
John Adams *

All thes parsons have taken this protestation and none refused.

Thomas Stevenson, *Church warden*
Thomas Stevenson, Raphe Bassly *, *Cunstabls*

William Ariese have not taken it, he concealeth himselfe being in debt as they alledge.

***[Assessment.** Membrane 4, following on Shippon.]*

Suningwell

Haniball Baskerfield, Esq., £1.13s.
Docter Fell, Rector, £1.5s[?], 6d.
Charles Holloway, gent., 8s.
Richard Stevenson, gent., 6s.
John Tidball, gent., 5s.
Frances Besley, vid., 7s.
Edward West, 8s.6d.
Tho: Stevenson, 2s.
Mr Roode, 2s.
Mary Besley, vid., 11s.
Ann Stevenson, vid., 9s.
John Brookland, 4s.6d.
Ann Hall, vid., 3s.6d.
Tho: Beasley, 6s.
John Stevenson, 4s.6d., *Affid.*
John Bradstocke, 1s.3d.
John Hall, 2s.
Ralphe Beasley, 3s.6d.
Willia' Shread*[sic]*, 1s.6d.
Joane West, 4s.6d.
Tho: Besley, 1s.3d.
Ann Beasley, vid., 1s.3d [?]
Richard Palmer, 1s.6d.
John Harper, 1s.6d.
Cristofer Vine, 2s.3d.
John Hoare, 1s.
Valentine Turner, 1s.
Edward Hall, 2s.3d.
John West, 2s.3d.
Henry Huggens, 1s.
Nicholas Aderton, 1s.
Jane Clydon, 1s.

SUTTON COURTENAY [150+6]

[ff.45-46. Each page is in two columns, the left hand headed 'Housholders' and the right 'Children & servants'. There are occasional short horizontal lines in each column, shown here by breaks in the column. These do not appear to correspond with the parallel column. In this edition the list of householders, over three pages, is presented first, followed by the 'children and servants', which extends just over one page.]

March the third, A'o 1641.

A note of all the names of the inhabitants of Sutton Courtney and Werke [Wick] in the County of Berks of the age of eighteen yeares and upward who have taken the protestation and subscribed thereunto according to the order of Parliament.

[f.45r, col. 1]
Housholders

Richard Turner senr.
Timothy Watts senr.
Andrew West
Richard Bartlett
Richard Jennings
William Curtis senr.
Andrew White junr.
Richard White senr.
Edmond Glover
Gregory Street

Nicholas Pembrooke
John Smith senr.
George Whiteloe
Richard Bould
Henery Burges
Richard White junr.
Henery Weston
John Hill
Thomas Smale
John Grove

William Jennings
Edmond Hall
John Wallis senr.
Raph Addams
John Rawlins
John Martin
Robert Brooks
Thomas Cary

Xpofer Hoare
John White fil: Rici. White

Richard Bonwell
Edward Streete
John Smith fil: Petri Smith
Thomas Quelch
Jeames Leatchaside[?]
Richard Small
Luke Bonwell
Thomas Bolloke
Richard Billington
Richard Bennet

John Blake

[f.45v, col. 1]
Richard Grove
Nicolas Smith
John Rayer
Richard Perott
William Curtis junr.
Thomas White
Thomas Smith <Prince>
Raph Basley
John Sumpter

Christopher Bartlett
William Maddox
Daniell West
John Smith jun.
Andrew White fil: Rici. White
Richard Pitman
John Barnes
Thomas Trulocke senr.
William Montague
[? break or crease]
Richard Turner junr.
Toby Sawyer
Thomas Bonwell
Thomas Lann
William Maine
Richard Rayer
Richard Sanders
Edward Smith

Richard West

Thomas Sherwood senr.
Thomas Sherwood junr.
Richard Vokins
Frances Tirrald
John Cornish
Richard Sherwood
Henery Weale
Edward Nobes
Rouland Michell
Adam Tirrald
Thomas Hobbs
Richard West de Gilbons

Thomas Packstaff
Richard Burry
Thomas Duffin

Richard Middleton
John Dearne
Xpofer Lann
Timothy Sumpter
[f.46r., col. 1]
John Sansom
John Porter
Richard Simpson
Robert Barnes
Richard Woodley
Robert Church

[f.45r, col. 2]
Children & servants
Hugh Day
Thomas Bilson
William Daniel
John Curtis
Tobias Herne
William Jennings junr.
Robert Duffin
Thomas Maine
John Wallis
John Boulter

Richard Leonard

William Bartlett
Timothy Harvey

Francis Perett
John Tappin

Richard White junr.
Richard Homes
Tymothy Watts
Robert Coxiter
William Bilson
John Sansom

John Allin
John Wallis
John Turner

Theophilis Cornish
Walter Weale
Mathew Tirrald
William Sherwood
George Elketon
Robert Harris
Michaell Burry
Thomas Stacy
Samuell Woodes
Francis West

John Bridgman
Thomas Trulock junr.
John Nevill
John Davis
John Middleton
William Cornish
Thomas Curtein

[f.46v, col. 2]

Samuel Peirce
John Bartlett
John Gardner
Edward Quelch
Walter Fourest
Peter Church
Jeames George
John Martin
John Wilks
William Harris
Andrew Bint

[f.46r]

In witness whereof wee the Minister, Constable, Churchwardens and overseers of the poore have here unto set our hands.

Nico: Sheppard, *Vicar*
John Wats, *Constable*
Nicolas Raire his marke,
The marke of John White senr. *[Churchwardens]*
Richard Curtis *[Overseer]*

Thomas Carpinter
Thomas Napper
Henery Street
Jeames White
Gabriell Towse
George Pembrooke

These parties last above named are not in the towne nor have bine since this protestation was in agitation in our parish and wee doubt not but when they returne they will protest it and subscribe unto it.

Nico: Sheppard, *Vicar*
John Wats, *Constable*
Nicolas Raier, *Churchwarden*

UPTON in Blewbury [47]

[f.47, in two columns.]

The Protestation according to the Order was generally taken by the Inhabitants of Upton in the Parish of Blewbury the 6th day of this p'sent March. In the presence of

John Sampson, *Vicar*
The marke of Thomas Buckle, Phillp*[sic]* Allin, *Church-wardens*
Thomas Buckle, *Constable*
Thomas Harword and Thomas Higgs, *Ov'seers of the poore.*

[f.47r, col. 1]

Richard Allin
Symeon Stanton
Phillip Allin
William Ely
Thomas Plott
Thomas Emes
Richard Bodye
Thomas Barnes
Anthony Beckingame
Christopher Barnes
Thomas Stanton
Thomas Higgs
Robert Erwell
Christopher Hadnam
Roger Bacon
William Stanton
Richard Fluddyer
Richard Barnes
Edward Tayler
Thomas Tayler
William Adams
John Sayer
Henry Sayer
Thomas Harwood
Robert Childe
Henry March

[f.47r, col. 2]

Thomas Buckle
Henry Buckle
Richard Harword senior
Richard Keatt
John Craye
Richard Buckle
Sacre Leatch
Richard Harword junior
Richard Daye
Mychaell Weyett
William Duckett
Robert Deckett *[sic]*
John Duckett
Richard Bonde
John Burden

Non with us have refused to the order of the p'testacion.

LITTLE WITTENHAM

[f.48, single columns, with signatures and marks (asterisked).]

Little Wittenham,
Comit. Berks.

THE Protestation of the high & honourable Court of Parliament made & taken in the howse of Commons Maij 3 anno d'oi 1641 in the 17th yeare of our soveraigne King Charles and taken by the Lords house 4 Maij, and by order 5 Maij commended to us. [38]

[f.48r]
Joseph Pislye senior
Bartholomew Moulden *
William Blandy
William Frinche
Ar. Wilson
John Milman *
John Pisly
Joseph Pysly junior *
James Stevens *
Thomas Blandy
Briant*[sic]* Moulden *
Thomas French *
John Golde
John Allam
James Goodlake *
William Hardwell
Christopher Furscroft *
William Blandy junior *
Thomas Cox *
Thomas Henwood *
Henry Rogers *
[f.48v]
Barth. Moulden *
David Burges *
Andrew Dickar *
Thomas Hardwell *
Ambrose Blandy *
Thomas Watson
Thomas Laurence senior *
Bartholomew Guy *
John Sheene *
Edw: French *

[f.48r]
according to the full tenour in everie clause word & syllable, We the Inhabitants of Little Wittenham have personally made & taken upon us to doe the things therein required.
Hen: Whistler,
rector ibidem.

[f.48v]
Ralph : Adams : *Curat ibid:*
William Millman,
Cunstabel
Nathaniell Sheene, Thomas Harford, *Church-wardens*
Edmund Pisly, Thomas Lawrenc, *Overseers*

None refusing to take the Protestation.

LONG WITTENHAM [91+1]

[f.50, in two columns, with signatures and marks (asterisked).]

Berks. The returne of the Minister, Constable, Churchwardens and Overseers of the poore of ***Longwittnam****.*

[f.50r, col. 1]
William Bedford *
Robert Bedford *
Edmond Harford *
William Coldrell
[*or* Coldiell?] *
Thomas Cater *
Henry Finmore *
Thomas Higgs *
James Prowse
Thomas Watson *
Michael Blackwell
Edward Hosly
Tobias Harford *
John Dicker
Thomas Shelton
Edward Fennenoss[?]
John Harford *
John Redford
William Bawyer
Richard Keate jun. *
Richard Sadler
Henry Coldrell *
Thomas Harris
Richard Finmore *
John Wesson *
John Finmore *
William Finmore junr. *
Thomas Cheere
James Collins *
Robert Barnes *
John Blewet sen. *
Francis Barnes *
John Sadler jun. *
Richard Grove *
Francis Breakespeare
William Harford *
William Finmore sen. *
David Tirroll *
Richard Harford *
Ralph Becford *
James Stevens *
[f.50r, col. 2]
Michaell Warner *
John Luggrove *
Anthony Harford *
John Blackwell sen. *
William Marten
Thomas Carter *
John Blewet junr. *
Robert Andrewes *

Richard Barkly junr. *
John Barnes junr. *
Thomas Harden *
Bartholomew Slade *
Marke Loder *
Richard Sadler junr.
John Parker *
Aaron Chitts
John Symons *
Richard Steventon *
John Tame[?] *
Frances Wise *
Robert Blackwell *
Thomas Semor *
Arthur Young
John Barnes senr.
William West
Richard Keate sen. *
John Midleton *
Thomas Luggrove junr. *
Hugh Burges *
John Boult *
Thomas Butler *
Edward Watts *
Andrew Weston *
Paul Weston *
William Prowse *
Richard Barkley sen.
William Seymor *
John Giddings *
William Stevens *
[f.50v]
James Jennens
Richard Jennens
Gregory Slade *
Edward[?] Keate[?]
Roger Armestronge *
Thom. Rosle[?] *

William Prowse, *Vicar*
David Childs,
William Frence*[sic]*, *Churchwardens*
Thomas Laggrove, *Cunstable*
John Sadler, William Strange, *Overseers*

William Joyner only hath not taken this protestation, the reason is his absence before any notice was given him of it.

David Childs, William French, *Churchwardens*

WYTHAM

[f.52, single column.]

A note of all ye Parishioners names of the Parish of Wytham in Barkshire who are eighteene yeeres and uppwards and have taken the Protestation this present 6th of March anno D'ni 1641. [56]

Mr Stockdell Geering
Mr George Unett
John Collett
Ralphe Crowdy
Thomas Hixe
Edmund Greene
Thomas Wildgoose
Antony Sadler
Nicolas Saby
John Smith
Edward Paynton
John Cowldery
Edward Doe
Thomas Gadney
Nicolas Binly
Arthur Butler
Joseph Alexander
Richard Speene
Michaell Cantwell
Robert Webb
Matthew Bowse
Robert Bowle
John Lucas
John Williams
Richard Hixe
John Matthew
Richard Cleve
Richard Eagleston
John Cleark
Thomas Showell
Jerome Atkins
Antony Hastings
Richard White
Ralphe Ayres
John Ayers
Tobie Embry
John Carryer
Thomas Sextons
Martine Clifford
Robert Coxehead
Charles Whittaker
Ralphe Reade
Richard Sargeant
Thomas Rogers
Thomas Higges
Peregrine Jessett
William Dubber
Michaell Townes
Richard Cantwell
Richard Cowldrey
Mysake Cowldry
William Foster
William Laye

Our whole parish whereof this is a list tooke the protestation this present 6th of March without any limitations or exceptions, ita testamur

Antony Hodges, *Curat*
The marke of Jesper Wellar,
The marke of Thomas Hixe, *Churchwardens*

*[**Assessment.** Membrane 4, following on Grandpont.]*

Edward Wraye Esqr., £6
John Wildgoose, 3s.3d.
Tho: Wildgoose, 4s.10d.
Tho: Hicks, 6s.6d.
Edmond Greene, 6s.6d.
Widdow Phillipson, 8s.1d.
Tho: Crane, 4s.1d.
James Coles, 6s.6d.
John Smith, 3s.3d.
Tho: Carpender, 3s.3d.
Reanold Coldrey, 3s.3d.
Doctor Brigendine, 15s.
Jeffery Farmer, 3s.3d.
John Crouch, 3s.3d.
Richard Speene, 3s.3d.
Tho: Speene, 3s.3d.
John Grante, 3s.3d.
Raphe Smith, 3s.3d.
John Mathew, 1s.6d.
Tho: Basley, 1s.7½d.
Michaell Cantwell, 1s.
Walter Couldrey, 1s.
Martin Clifford, 1s.
Edmond Dooe, 1s.6d.
Mathew Boould, 1s.
Raphe Cantwell, 1s.
Nicholas Sabie, 1s.
Cristofer Sulford, 1s.
Tobias Embry, 1s.

Sume £10.17s.6d.

APPENDIX A

Preambles to and totals of the Assessments

E.179/164/493, membrane 1: Assessment (Lay Subsidy) Roll. 31st May 1642. Oxfordshire: Bloxham and Banbury Hundreds. An identical preamble is on membrane 6, at the start of Banbury Hundred.

Com. Oxon. Hundred de Bloxham and Banbury.

The Estreats of the first paymt. of the sumes of money assessed uppon the said Hundreds of Bloxham and Banbury by the Comes. hereafter named beings pte of the sume of Six Thousand Foure Hundred Eighteene pounds Foure shillings and Nyne pence to bee payd at Two severall payments Charged uppon the said County by Act of Parliamt. holden at Westms. Decimo septimo Caroli Regis intytuled an Act for the Rayseinge and Levyinge of mony for the necessary defence and great affayres of the Kingdoms of England and Ireland etc Taxed and assessed uppon any p'son specified in this Estreat indented accordinge to ye Rules p'scribed in the said Act at Banbury the last day of May in the Eighteenth yeare of the raigne of our said Soveraigne Lord Kinge Charles over England etc before Sr Thomas Pope Kt, Sr Willm. Cobb Kt, Thomas Chamblayne and John Griffith esqr., Coms. amongst others in the County aforesaid for the Taxation levyinge and gatheringe of the said sumes.

Humphry Wickham of Swalkliffe esqr. High Collector.

E.179/164/496A. Assessment (Lay Subsidy) Roll. 18th June 1642. Oxfordshire: Ploughley Hundred.

Hundred de Poughey*[sic]* in Com. Oxon.

This Certificate Indented made the Eighteenth day of June in the Eighteenth yeare of the Raigne of O'r Sovraigne Lord Charles by the grace of God Kinge of England Scotland Frannce & Ireland Defender of the Fayth etc *Witnesseth* that wee whose names are heere under Wrytten Commissioners amongst oth'rs authorized for the County of Oxon for and towards the raiseing & leavying of moneyes for the necessary defence & greate affayres of the Kingdomes of England & Ireland and for paym't of debts undertaken by the Parliam't by vertue of an Acte of Parliam't made in the Seaventeenth yeare of his Mat's raigne that nowe is Have accordinge to the Division assigned & allotted to the said Hundred assessed and taxed every p'son therein for the paym't of the first Moytie chardged upon them according to the tenor and grant of the said Act as hereafter in the Schedules hereunto annexed appeareth the grosse and total sum whereof togethe'r w'th Surplussage money chardged upon the Recusants by vertue of the said Acte amounteth unto the sum of Fower Hundred and Twelve pounds, Seaven shillings & nyne penece half penny, And have apointed Richard Clemens of Bursiter als Burcester in the said County gent. High Collector w'thin the said Hundred to demannd leavy and receave the said p'ticular sums conteyned in the said Schedules & to make payment thereof to such p'sons att such tyme and in such place as in the said Acte is p'scribed, And for the more sure p'formance thereof wee the said Commissioners have taken one Obligation of the said Richard Clemens according to the forme p'scribed in the Said Acte w'ch wee doe also certifie hereunto annexed, *In* Wittnes whereof to this o'r Certificate Wee hav sett our hande and seales the daye and yeare above wrytten.

Fra: Norreys
Edm. Chamberlayne

The preambles to the Assessments for Bampton Hundred (Oxon.) and Hormer Hundred (Berks.) are lost.

Totals for the Oxfordshire Hundreds and Hormer Hundred in Berkshire

E.179/238/146

Bampton Hundred [at membrane 13]	£401.02s.09½d.
Surplusage money	£ 17.00s. 4d.
	£418.03s. 1½d.

E.179/164/493

Bloxham Hundred [at membrane 5]:	£205. 3s. 6d.
adjusted to	£205. 5s. 9d.
Banbury Hundred [at membrane 9]:	£196. 7s. 3½d.
	£205. 5s. 9d.
	£401.13s. 0½d.

E.179/164/496A

Ploughley Hundred, North Division	
[at membrane 4v]	£203.
adjusted to	£202.01s.10½d.
Ploughley Hundred, South Division	
[at membrane 9v]	£198. 1s. 3½d
adjusted to	£200.
The totall	£401. 1s. 3½d.
adjusted to	£402.10s. 1½d.
Total with 'Surplusaige'	£412. 7s. 6½d.
adjusted to	£413.15s. 3½d.

Delibat' p'manas et servam Robti. Blower gener. 25 Oct. 18 Charles.
Will. Page.

E.179/75/376

Hormer Hundred [at membrane 5]	
Surplusage money	18s. 5d.
Total	£172.13s. 0d.

Geo. Purefey
Tho. Fettiplace
Sam. Durcke

APPENDIX B

Protestation Returns in neighbouring counties

The survival of protestation returns for Oxfordshire is by no means complete; most of the eastern and southern hundreds are missing. The same is the case in neighbouring counties. In Berkshire, hundreds were grouped into divisions. The Abingdon Division, comprising Moreton, Ock and Hormer Hundreds, is included in the volume. There are also returns for the Newbury and Reading Divisions. Eastern and western hundreds are missing. In Buckinghamshire, there are returns for two out of the eight hundreds, Buckingham and Cottesloe. There are no returns at the House of Lords Record Office for Gloucestershire or Northamptonshire, though for the latter there are lists in the parish registers (similar to those for Caversham in Oxfordshire) for Great Doddington and East Haddon. For Warwickshire there are returns for Coventry City and County, and Knightlow Hundred.

The places consitituting these divisions or hundreds are as follows. Places on the (pre-1974) Oxfordshire border are asterisked.

Berkshire, Newbury Division (Compton, Faircross and Kintbury Eagle Hundreds): Aldworth, Avington (this was wrongly identified as Abingdon, so was listed under the Abingdon Division and filed with those returns), Beedon, Boxford, Brightwalton (Brightwaltham), Chaddleworth, East and West Challow, Chieveley (including Courage Snelsmore and Oare), Chilton, Compton, Enborne, Farnborough, Fawley, Frilsham, Greenham, Hampstead Marshall and Norris, Hungerford, East and West Ilsley, Inkpen, Kintbury, Leckhampstead, Letcombe Bassett and Regis, Midgham, Newbury, Peasemore, Shalbourne, Shaw cum Donnington, Little and West Shefford, Speen Church, Speenhamland, Stanford Dingley, Wasing, Welford, Winterbourne Danvers, Woodspeen and Bagnor, Yattendon; and Newbury Division (the list of officials, similar to those for Abingdon and Bampton).

Berkshire, Reading Division (Reading and Theale Hundreds): Aldermaston, Beenham, Blewbury, Bradfield, Bucklebury, Burghfield, Cholsey, Englefield, Padworth, *Pangbourne, *Purley, *Reading (St. Giles, St. Lawrence, St. Mary), Shinfield, *Sonning, Stratfield Mortimer, Sulham, Sulhampstead Abbots and Banister, Thatcham, Tedmarsh, *Tilehurst, Ufton, Woolhampton.

Buckinghamshire, Buckingham Hundred: Addington, Adstock, Akeley, *Barton (Hartshorn), Beachampton, Biddlesden, Caversfield (enclave in Oxfordshire, see page 109), *Chetwode, Edgcott, Foxcott, Hillesden, Leckhampstead, Lillingston Dayrell, *Marsh Gibbon, (Maids) Moreton, Padbury, *Preston Bissett, Radclive cum Chackmore, *Shalstone, Steeple Claydon, Stowe, Thornborough, Thornton, *Tingewick, *Turweston, *Twyford, *Water Stratford, *Westbury.

Buckinghamshire, Cottesloe Hundred: Aston Abbots, Cheddington, Cholesbury, Cublington, Drayton Beauchamp and Parslow, Dunton, Edlesborough, Grove, Hardwick and Weedon, Hoggeston, Great and Little Horwood, Ivinghoe, Linslade, Marsworth cum Hawridge, Mentmore, Pitstone cum Nettleden, Slapton, Soulbury, Stewkley, Swanbourne, Whaddon cum Nash, Whitchurch, Wing, Wingrave, Winslow; Cottesloe Hundred (officials).

Warwickshire, Coventry City and County: Ansty, Coventry (city), Exhall, Foleshill, Sowe, Stivichall, Stoke, Wyken.

Warwickshire, Knightlow Hundred: Arley, Harbury, Leamington Hastings (and townships), Napton-on-the-Hill, Offchurch, Ryton on Dunsmore, Stoneleigh, Wappenbury, Weston under Wetherley, Wolfhamcote, Wolston.

APPENDIX C

The Collection in Aid of Distressed Protestants in Ireland

This 'voluntary' collection or quasi-tax was gathered at much the same time as the Protestation Oath was taken. Indeed in Buckinghamshire, and doubtless elsewhere, the lists are often headed in words such as 'The names of all those within our parish that are of the age of eighteen and upwards who have given to the contribution and have taken the Protestation' (*Buckinghamshire Contributions for Ireland 1642...*, John Wilson, Bucks. Record Society, **21**, 1983).

The returns are in the Public Record Office. None survive for Oxfordshire. For Berkshire the following are extant, in SP 28/191 (except for Lyford, E 179/272/44):

Beynhurst Hd.: Shottesbrook, White Waltham. **Bray Hd.:** Bray. **Charlton Hd.:** Barkham, Finchampstead, [Broad] Hinton, Shinfield, Sonning (incl. Earley), Swallowfield. **Faircross Hd.:** Newbury. **Faringdon Hd.:** *for* Faringdon *see* Shrivenham Hd. **Ganfield Hd.:** Buckland, Charney Bassett, Hatford, Longworth, Pusey, Shellingford. **Lambourn Hd.:** Lambourn. **Moreton Hd.:** East Garston. **Ock Hd.:** Appleton, Frilford, Fyfield, Goosey, Kingston Bagpuize, Lyford [E 179/272/44], Marcham, Stanford in the Vale. **Ripplesmere Hd.:** Easthampstead, Winkfield. **Shrivenham Hd.:** Ashbury, Baulking, Bourton, Buscot, Coleshill, Compton Beauchamp, Eaton Hastings, Great Faringdon (Wadley, Littleworth and Thrupp in), Fernham [Feaunhamforth] (in Shrivenham), Longcott, Shrivenham (parish) incl. Watchfield Liberty; Uffington. **Sonning Hd.:** Arborfield, Hurst; *for* Sonning, *see* Charlton Hd. **Theale Hd.:** *for* Shinfield *see* Charlton Hd. **Wantage Hd.:** Ardington, Fawler (in Sparsholt), East and West Hendred, Kingston Lisle (in Sparsholt), East Lockinge.

APPENDIX D

Sources of illustrations and textual additions

Illustrations

The three main sources for illustrations are:

Skelton's Engraved Illustrations of the Principal Antiquities of Oxfordshire, from original drawings by F. Mackenzie. 1823 *['Skelton'].*

A Guide to the Architectural Antiquities in the Neighbourhood of Oxford, ed. J.H. Parker and W. Grey. Oxford Society for Promoting the Study of Gothic Architecture, 1846 *['Parker'].*

Oxonia Illustrata, D. Loggan. 1675 *['Loggan'].*

Page

5 Asthall. *Highways and Byways in Oxford and the Cotswolds*, by Herbert A. Evans, illustrated by Frederick L. Griggs. Macmillan & Co., 1905, reprinted 1908, page 370.

28 Witney butter cross and church. *Skelton*, Bampton Hundred, page 1.

38 Banbury church. *The History of Banbury, including copious historical and antiquarian notices of the neighbourhood*, by Alfred Beesley. London, 1842. Plate XIV.

59 Rotherfield Greys: Greys Court. *Skelton*, Binfield Hundred, page 1.

62 Adderbury: the home of Sir William Cobb, south front, as it was in the eighteenth century. *Adderbury*, by Henry J. Gepp. Banbury, 1924, facing page 64.

64 Alkerton Rectory, built by Thomas Lydiat. Photograph by P.S. Spokes, 1943 (N.M.R.), reproduced in *Victoria County History: Oxfordshire*, vol. IX, *Bloxham Hundred*, ed. Mary D. Lobel and Alan Crossley, 1969, facing page 46.

65 Barford St. John church, 1823, by J.C. Buckler [MS Top. Oxon. a.65, 71, Bodleian Library], reproduced in *Cake & Cockhorse* (Banbury Historical Society), vol. 3, no. 8, 1967, page 152.

70 Broughton Castle, home of Lord Saye and Sele and the Fiennes family. Print by S. & N. Buck, 1729, reproduced in *V.C.H. Oxon* IX, facing page 114.

Page

73 Hanwell church and Hanwell Castle. *Skelton*, Bloxham Hundred, page 11.

82 Chastleton church and Chastleton House, home of Henry Jones. *Skelton*, Chadlington Hundred, page 7.

94 Northmoor: the Parsonage House. *Skelton*, Chadlington Hundred, page 13.

99 Swinbrook: Fettiplace tombs in the chancel of the church; Edward Fettiplace is commemorated elsewhere in the church. *Skelton*, detail of full page plate, Chadlington Hundred.

100 Taynton: font in the church. *Skelton*, Chadlington Hundred, page 21.

111 Bicester House (detail), home of Cadwallader Coker. *Parochial Antiquities*, by White Kennett, 1695, reproduced in *The History of Bicester: its town and priory*, by J.C. Blomfield, 1884, facing page 76, and *Victoria County History: Oxfordshire*, vol. VI, *Ploughley Hundred*, ed. Mary D. Lobel, 1959, facing page 20.

118 Steeple Aston church. *Parker*, page 79.

123 Cassington church. *Parker*, page 131.

124 Cogges church. *Skelton*, Wootton Hundred, page 7.

127 Deddington: the church and 'rectorial farmhouse', home of Thomas Apletree (see 'Thomas Apletree of Deddington; Royalist or Parliamentarian?', Reg. Apletree, *Cake & Cockhorse*, vol. 12, no. 5, 1993). *Skelton*, Wootton Hundred, page 17.

129 Heythrop church, 1822, by J.C. Buckler [MS Top. Oxon. a.67, 327-8, Bodleian Library], reproduced in *Victoria County History: Oxfordshire*, vol. XI, *Wootton Hundred (Northern Part)*, ed. Alan Crossley, 1983, facing page 48.

132 Water Eaton House, *c.*1610. From 1624 it was the home of the Lovelace family. John Lord Lovelace was a prominent royalist. The family do not appear in the Protestation. *Parker*, page 70* [the asterisk denotes that page 70 was duplicated in the original].

144 Wolvercote Church. *Parker*, page 98.

151 Oxford University: Christ Church, showing (top) the old quadrangle of Canterbury College and (left) Peckwater quadrangle in its old state. Drawn by Loggan in 1673 and engraved by J. Skelton, 1819 (Centre for Oxfordshire Studies).

152 Oxford University: Merton College, *Loggan* (reproduced in *Victoria County History: Oxfordshire*, vol. III, *The University of Oxford*, ed. H.E. Salter and Mary D. Lobel, 1954, facing page 77).

155 Oxford University: New College. *Loggan* (*V.C.H. Oxon* III, facing page 149).

162 Oxford University: Balliol College. *Loggan* (*V.C.H. Oxon* III, facing page 77).

166 Oxford University: Oriel College. *Loggan* (*V.C.H. Oxon* III, facing page 124).

167 Oxford University: All Souls College. *Loggan* (*V.C.H. Oxon* III, facing page 180).

205 Wytham. *Highways and Byways in Berkshire*, by James Edward Vincent, illustrated by Frederick L. Griggs. Macmillan & Co., 1906, page 54.

Textual additions

The Assessments frequently omit Christian names. Where these can fairly easily and with some certainty be ascertained, they have been shown in square brackets. Often they are taken from the Protestation Return. However, for Ploughley Hundred, where this is missing, they usually derive from Vol. VI of the *Victoria County History: Ploughley Hundred*, or from J.C. Blomfield's eight part *History* of the northern part of Ploughley Hundred: *1. Deanery of Bicester; 2. Bicester; 3. Cottisford, Hardwick and Tusmore; 4. Middleton and Somerton; 5. Fringford, Hethe, Mixbury, Newton Purcell, and Shelswell; 6. Lower and Upper Heyford; 7. Fritwell and Souldern; 8. Ardley, Bucknell, Caversfield and Stoke Lyne* (1882-94). The latter work is a mine of antiquarian notes, alas unindexed, but which well repays examination by those with interest in these places. The relevant volumes of the *V.C.H.* have also been consulted in cases of uncertainty for other Oxfordshire hundreds.

INDEX OF PERSONAL NAMES

See last page (296) for explanation of how to use this Index

Batmason *see* Battmason

Index of Places and their Abbreviations

Note. The parishes in which chapelries and hamlets lay are shown in round brackets. Alternative spellings are shown in square brackets. Places were in pre-1974 Oxfordshire unless otherwise stated. Places listed in the Appendices (neighbouring counties; pages 208-09) are not included in this index.

Outside Oxfordshire and Berkshire

Using the Index of Personal Names

In the Index of Personal Names (pages 211-290), names are followed by abbreviated place names rather than page numbers. The Index of Places (pages 291-295) provides the key to abbreviations and the necessary page numbers.

The abbreviated place name reference may be followed by one or more of the following:

-1, -2, -3	=	page number (shown in running headline) in a place occupying significantly more than one page.
+S	=	the name occurs in the Subsidy (Assessment) list as well as the Protestation Return.
:S	=	the name only occurs in the Subsidy (Assessment) list. In the case of places with Subsidy (Assessment) lists only, and no Protestation Return, no such indication is needed or provided.
(2), (3), (4)	=	more than one occurrence of the name in the Protestation or Subsidy (Assessment) list for that place.
-AD	=	Abingdon Division (Berks., covering the Hundreds of Hormer, Moreton and Ock), parish clergy and officials, listed on pages 173-175.
-BH	=	Bampton Hundred (Oxon.), parish clergy and officials, listed on pages 1-3.
PH-Rec	=	Ploughley Hundred - Recusants in Assessment - listed on page 117.
Rec	=	Recusants in Oxfordshire Protestation Returns - listed on page 148.